Lecture Notes in Computer Science

Edited by G. Goos and J. Hartmanis

276

J. Bézivin J.-M. Hullot
P. Cointe H. Lieberman (Eds.)

ECOOP '87
European Conference on
Object-Oriented Programming

Paris, France, June 15–17, 1987
Proceedings

Springer-Verlag

Berlin Heidelberg New York London Paris Tokyo

Editors

Jean Bézivin
Laboratoire d'Informatique, LIB
Université de Bretagne Occidentale
6, avenue V. le Gorgeu, F-29287 Brest Cédex, France

Jean-Marie Hullot
54, avenue des Gressets, F-92700 La Celle Saint-Cloud, France

Pierre Cointe
Rank Xerox France, DRBI
12, place de l'Iris, Cedex 38, F-92071 La Défense, France

Henry Lieberman
The Artificial Intelligence Laboratory
Massachusetts Institute of Technology
545, Technology Square, Cambridge, MA 02139, USA

CR Subject Classification (1987): D.1, D.2.2, D.2.6, D.2.10, D.3.2-3

ISBN 3-540-18353-1 Springer-Verlag Berlin Heidelberg New York
ISBN 0-387-18353-1 Springer-Verlag New York Berlin Heidelberg

Library of Congress Cataloging-in-Publication Data. European Conference on Object-Oriented
Programming (1987: Paris, France) Proceedings. (Lecture notes in computer science; 276) 1.
Electronic digital computers—Programming—Congresses. I. Bézivin, J. (Jean) II. Title. III. Series.
QA76.6.E973 1987 005.1 87-23483
ISBN 0-387-18353-1 (U.S.)

© Springer-Verlag Berlin Heidelberg 1987
Printed in Germany

Printing and binding: Druckhaus Beltz, Hemsbach/Bergstr.
2145/3140-543210

Preface

In October 1983 an informal meeting was organized in Le Cap d'Agde with the help of the BIGRE bulletin. Sixty people turned out to hear more than ten presentations on object-oriented programming. More important was their unanimous demand for other, more structured encounters. So, about one year later, the Object group was created by AFCET. A second workshop was organized in Brest, and again one year later in Paris, each time showing increased attendance and interest.

The success of these meetings and the fact that similar activities were taking place in other European countries, especially Great Britain and Germany, led to the idea of an annual European Conference, providing a forum for theorists and practitioners interested in the object-oriented programming paradigm.

It is impossible to acknowledge here all the people and organizations that welcomed with great enthusiasm the birth of the ECOOP conference and contributed to its organization. More than a hundred submissions were received and the program committee had the unpleasant task of turning down many valuable contributions. We hope, however, that the selection of papers for ECOOP'87 emphasizes the fundamental issues and problems of object-oriented programming and will point toward interesting future research directions.

We hope also that ECOOP'87 will provide a pleasant meeting place for all working to exchange ideas about new tools, techniques and concepts that will be presented at subsequent ECOOP meetings or other related forums. We are particularly pleased to invite you to the ECOOP'88 conference that will take place on 15th - 17th August 1988 in OSLO, Norway.

Jean Bézivin, Jean-Marie Hullot (Conference Co-Chairmen)
Pierre Cointe, Henry Lieberman (Program Co-Chairmen)

Table of Contents

Deltatalk: An Empirically and Aesthetically Motivated Simplification of the Smalltalk-80 Language

Alan Borning
Computer Science Department, FR-35
University of Washington
Seattle, Washington 98195
U.S.A.

Tim O'Shea[1]
System Concepts Laboratory
Xerox Palo Alto Research Center
3333 Coyote Hill Road
Palo Alto, California 94304
U.S.A.

Abstract. The Smalltalk-80 system offers a language with a small and elegant conceptual core, and a highly interactive programming environment. We believe, however, that it could be made more learnable and usable by a relatively small set of changes. In this paper, we present the results of a series of empirical studies on learnability, and also some informal studies of large implementation projects. Based on these studies, we suggest a number of changes to the Smalltalk-80 language and system.

1 Introduction

The Smalltalk-80[2] system [8] is the fifth in a succession of object-oriented programming environments which have been produced as part of the long term research programme [13] of the System Concepts Laboratory (originally the Learning Research Group) at Xerox PARC. The first, Smalltalk-72 [7] was designed for "children of all ages," but successive implementations of Smalltalk have become larger and more complex, and have required increasing sophistication on the part of the user [9]. At the same time, successive Smalltalks offer better engineered environments [6] and increased efficiency; the Smalltalk-80 system can now be implemented on an increasingly diverse range of hardware.

The Deltatalk proposal is a way of organising a set of thoughts about improving the learnability and usability of the Smalltalk-80 system. Our starting point in writing this paper is that the object-oriented programming style is particularly attractive for a very wide range of applications, and that the Smalltalk-80 language is the best of the various object-oriented languages that are currently available. In our view it has easily the most usable environment, and the language is based on a small, elegant and mostly consistent conceptual core. However, Smalltalk is obviously not perfect, and we believe that it could be made more learnable and more usable without sacrificing any expressive power or any useful features of the environment. In this paper, we primarily address Smalltalk as a language, and more peripherally Smalltalk as an environment and as an integrated system. Many of the linguistic suggestions we make are taken from the earlier implementations, especially Smalltalk-76 [12].

In general we are willing to trade more text and verbosity in programs against a smaller number of basic constructs. The overall spirit of this paper is to identify small (i.e. "delta") changes from the current Smalltalk-80 system, where there is some genuine evidence that the change might be beneficial. We have pruned our set of recommendations to ensure that they are mutually compatible, and have forced ourselves to not make proposals here (for example with respect to inheritance or blocks and methods) that would change the fundamental character of Smalltalk.

---

[1] Visiting from Institute of Educational Technology, Open University, Milton Keynes, MK7 6AA, United Kingdom.
[2] Smalltalk-80 is a trademark of the Xerox Corporation.

2 Background

The line of modest development from the Smalltalk-80 system suggested in this paper was initially motivated by a series of empirical studies on learnability [15]. The subjects included over thirty experts with substantial experience in the design and implementation of one of the versions of Smalltalk or one of the object-oriented extensions of Lisp. The experts were asked to make predictions about learnability, and these predictions were compared with the results of a study of over fifty teachers, students, and autonomous learners. The data collection methods included questionnaires (administered by post and by electronic mail), structured interviews, and the completion (by autonomous learners) of daily inventories. The inventories included questions on failures, misconceptions, and known areas of difficulty. The chronological inventory data was used to focus interviews with struggling students and to guide the analysis of student programs and project reports. The different data sources taken together revealed a consistent picture. No single source of learnability problems dominates the data, but a small number of difficulties (with a variety of causes) impacted the learning trajectories of nearly every student. The study also has a number of very positive results with regard to the Smalltalk-80 system. Students and teachers are enthusiastic about it, they can discuss all but one of the core concepts cogently and accurately, and they make effective use of the programming interface, particularly the browser.

It is important not to confuse learnability with usability. The learnability studies described above do not shed any light on how accomplished programmers use Smalltalk or what they can sensibly use it for. In order to shed some light on usability, we considered five large systems implemented primarily at Xerox PARC. These systems are ThingLab [2,3] (a simulation kit), Babar (an electronic mail interface), Rehearsal World [10,11] (an educational programming system for teachers), ARK [16, 17] (the Alternate Reality Kit—a visual programming language based on a physical metaphor), and, of course, the Smalltalk-80 environment itself. Considering these five systems made it possible for us to look at issues regarding programming-in-the-large and advanced programming techniques (e.g. programs that write programs). It became possible to collect statistical data regarding frequency of use of given language constructs in full scale applications. It also forced us to be realistic in considering issues such as sharing, version control, and change management.

Our discussion is also motivated by various aesthetic values that we would apply to the design of any language or environment. In order of importance, we value simplicity, uniformity, orthogonality, readability, economy, and tidiness. For example, in Smalltalk there is uniformity—every object is an instance of some class; simplicity—everything is an object; orthogonality—classes are first-class citizens; readability—with the use of unary message selectors; economy—through polymorphism and inheritance; and finally, tidiness—provided by the class hierarchy. In any attempt to apply these values to ameliorate learnability or usability problems one encounters design tradeoffs. To resolve these tradeoffs we apply various approaches, including one attributed to Alan Kay, viz. "in programming language design similar constructs should either be made identical or they should be made clearly dissimilar." Another principle that we try to follow is the "zero-one-infinity" notion [14], viz., that something in a language should be forbidden entirely, that exactly one occurrence of the thing is permitted, or that it should be possible to use arbitrary numbers of the thing. For example, in Smalltalk there are no methods that don't return a value; every object is an instance of exactly one class; and identifiers can contain an indefinitely large number of characters. An example of a language feature that does not fit this notion is the restriction in FORTRAN that identifiers have at most 6 characters.

We believe that learnability is an important issue in language design generally, and quite crucial if a wide community of users is to be established for languages that are built on innovative models of computation (such as the object model). We believe that it is foolish not to build on past experience and systems, and that one should take great pains to avoid the new language syndrome (i.e. only invent a major new language when one is really forced to).

3   Recommendations Arising from Empirical Studies

3.1   Metaclasses

We identified various learnability problems, but by far the most acute were associated with meta-classes. All the students and teachers reported that they were unable to understand metaclasses, and that they could not bring themselves to stop worrying about where the seemingly endless chain of metaclasses stopped. The solution to this problem is either to remove metaclasses or to find some way of illuminating their creation and operation.

3.2   System Size

Students all reported problems with the size of the system. Although they found the browser helpful for dealing with the class hierarchy, they often got lost and generally felt uneasy about the large number of classes (over 200) and huge number of methods (5,000) that they knew existed in the license version of the system. Limited studies of students working with LOOPS do not indicate that "dynamic browsing" would be helpful. The obvious solution is to introduce some form of layering through the use of modules. (Many students used a "spaghetti" metaphor for the existing system, so we are proposing a shift to "lasagne.")

3.3   Inheritance

Students also had difficulty with nonstandard forms of inheritance (super) and with abstract super-classes.[3] Within our self-imposed confines of delta-sized changes, there does not appear to be a good linguistic solution; so we favour environmental solutions that illuminate inheritance in the browser. However, students did master the general notions of object, message, class, subclass, and method inheritance without difficulty.

3.4   Other Difficulties

Some "minor" matters of syntax and convention turned out to cause numerous problems. The precedence rules and the significance of capitalisation taxed students, as did the variation in the tone and content of error messages. Students also had difficulty in keeping track of the variety of scoping rules in the language. The solution is to simplify the parsing, rigidify conventions where possible, and reduce the number of scoping rules.

Two other possible problem areas (for which we have no strong empirical support) concern keyword parameters and assignment. Keyword parameters might bring up images of more generality than actually exists in the language—that the keywords of a message can be given in any order, and that keywords can be elided and a default value supplied. (These properties hold, for example, for keyword parameters in Ada.) From studies of the difficulties experienced by learners of other languages, we know that assignment is often a source of confusion. In Smalltalk, the operation of assignment is defined as in other imperative languages and hence hidden from the student; one would instead prefer that it be handled via message-passing, as are other Smalltalk operations.

The empirical studies are reported in detail elsewhere. In this document we have confined ourselves to results that could in principle be acted on by making small changes to Smalltalk. Other courses of action include the elaboration of new teaching materials and making major changes to the language (such as removing the object-class distinction).

---

[3]An abstract superclass is like any other class as far as the Smalltalk language and environment are concerned. However, by convention, its purpose is only to define protocol and useful methods that can be inherited by concrete subclasses, and not to be instantiated. An example from the current Smalltalk-80 language is class Collection.

4   Recommendations Arising from Large Implementations

In addition to the insights arising from empirical studies, we have also accumulated (in a less formal manner) a number of recommendations regarding the language based on the experiences of implementors of large systems in Smalltalk.

4.1   Programs as Data

A number of applications, such as ThingLab, ARK, and Programming by Rehearsal, compose and install Smalltalk methods, and also store fragments of Smalltalk code that can be manipulated in a variety of ways. This is not particularly convenient in the Smalltalk-80 system. (Lisp provides an example of a language in which these sorts of activities are much easier.)

We examine ThingLab to pinpoint some of the problems. In early versions of ThingLab [2], code was stored as text strings. New methods were composed by concatenating these strings, adding parentheses, selectors, temporaries, and so forth as needed. The string that represented the new method was then given to the compiler. It was straightforward to compose methods in this way, but very difficult to analyze and transform code fragments. Because of these problems, ThingLab now stores code as parse trees. The parse tree classes built into Smalltalk make it easy to inspect and manipulate code. Nevertheless, it remains much less convenient to manipulate code than in Lisp. One problem is that the expressions to build pieces of parse tree are verbose (although straightforward to write). Another problem is that parse tree objects, as currently implemented, are tied to a particular method. For example, moving a part of a tree into a method for a different class requires that new literal nodes be created and noted in the literal dictionary for the new method.

4.2   Modules and Scoping Rules

Regarding modules and scoping rules, an obvious problem with the current system is that there is a single global name space for classes and global variables. When combining several large application packages, one can run up against conflicting class names. A related problem is that there is no way to create private messages for a class or a group of cooperating classes—there is a convention of providing a "private" category in the browser, but access to these private messages is not restricted by the language.

It has regularly been noted that there are too many kinds of variable names in Smalltalk: global, pool, class variable, instance variable, method argument, temporary, and block argument. In addition to variable names, there are selector names. Accompanying these names are a variety of scope rules. Global names are, of course, in a single global name space. Pool variables are shared by all classes that name the given pool, and can also be inherited down the subclass hierarchy. Class and instance variables are inherited down the subclass hierarchy. Method argument and temporary names are local to the given method. Block arguments are known only within the given block, but space for them is stored in the method context, resulting in blocks that are not reentrant.

For the novice, this plethora of kinds of names and scopes presents a learning problem; experts can learn to work with the kinds of names and scopes. One difficulty that does arise for experts is that these rules increase the difficulty of having programs that manipulate programs. For example, since there is no general hierarchical, lexical scoping method, one cannot easily do inline expansion of method invocations.

4.3   Blocks

Blocks are fundamental in supporting extensible control structures in Smalltalk, and also have more sophisticated uses (e.g. in process creation). However, they have some anomalous properties. Block arguments are not stored local to the block activation, but rather with the method activation, leading to various bugs and restrictions. As noted above, blocks are not reentrant. As an example of another bug, consider the following code:

```
1 to: 10 do: [:i | [Transcript show: i] fork].
```

One would expect the digits 1 to 10 to be printed on the transcript (perhaps in some permuted order due to process priorities). Instead, if the forked processes have lower priority than the creating process, 10 will be printed 10 times, since i is not local to the iterated block. Another annoying limitation of blocks is that they cannot have temporary variables of their own. Following Alan Kay's principle mentioned above, on aesthetic grounds, blocks and method bodies are similar enough that they ought to be the same.

4.4   Multiple Inheritance

Multiple inheritance is a thorny issue. Borning and Ingalls [4] designed and implemented a straight-forward multiple inheritance mechanism for the Smalltalk-80 system. This was subsequently included in the release system, but without environmental support. It has received almost no use. Whether this is because it is inadequate, not well supported by the environment, or both, is not known. Looking at other object-oriented systems, multiple inheritance is used extensively in e.g. Flavors in ZetaLisp [5]. Flavors is a system for experts only, and our informants tell us that the more unusual modes of method combination receive little use even by them, since it is difficult to predict how a combined method will behave. More generally, there is no consensus in the object-oriented programming community regarding what sort of multiple inheritance, if any, should be supported. It does seem that single inheritance, as used pervasively in Smalltalk, is a powerful mechanism for constructing object taxonomies and for doing "differential programming." Multiple inheritance, when used, seems better at a different role, namely combining many small packages of behaviour to make a new kind of object. Multiple inheritance works better when the behaviours can be made relatively independent, as in window systems, and not as well when they interact strongly, as in defining different kinds of collections.

4.5   Super

As noted in the previous section, super is confusing to novices. In the Deltatalk spirit, we considered simply eliminating it. Rather than writing super zork, one would need to define a method with a different name in the superclass, and invoke that method. To investigate the feasibility of that route, we gathered statistics on the use of super in a large system—namely the Smalltalk system itself. The current research version of the Smalltalk-80 system has a total of 8826 methods. Of this total, 428 methods use super. Of these 428, 81 methods send some selector to super other than the selector for that method. We concluded from inspecting these methods that eliminating super would result in a blowup in the number of method names (in a system with too many different method names already). There would also be some code that was less clear. Regarding sending super to some other selector, many methods did so for dubious reasons, but there were some legitimate uses. We therefore conclude that some mechanism like super should remain in the language.

4.6   Literals

Our last two recommendations are much finer-grained. The Smalltalk-80 language supports integer, float, string, symbol, and array literals. Some additional sorts are needed. For readability and editability, one would like bitmap literals. These should be seen and edited as bitmaps, not as strings that can be used to create the bitmaps. Parse tree literals would ease a few of of the problems listed above regarding programs that write programs. Classes are too "heavy" in the current system for some applications. One would like support for anonymous, in-line class definitions for simple classes, so that for example one could package up a pair of objects and return them as an appropriate unit. A notation for literal classes would handle this. Minor increases in efficiency could be gained if point and rectangle literals were supported. Regarding literals other than bitmaps, one could build each of them into the language, but one would regularly come up with some new sort of literal that should be supported as well. Therefore, we instead recommend that there be a language construct that instructs the compiler to evaluate an expression at compile time and include the result as a literal. If a more convenient set of messages for constructing classes and parse trees is devised, this should handle the remaining cases, and also support such things as constant expressions in code.

4.7 Naming Conventions

Finally, to some programmers who have used a variety of languages, the Smalltalk conventions for building long names are peculiar. For example, in Smalltalk one would write a long instance variable name in a manner such as veryLongName. In most other languages, one could write very_long_name, which we regard as more readable. We therefore recommend that underscores be allowed as part of a token, and (as noted in the previous section), that case not be significant in names.

5 Recommendations Regarding the Environment

This paper is concerned primarily with changes to the Smalltalk-80 language. However, our studies have some implications for the programming environment as well, and so we believe that it is worth noting some areas for improvement and simplification.

Both the empirical studies and surveys of experts indicate that the Smalltalk browser is a major win. A few improvements would be useful, however. There should be support for an indefinite number of levels of class categories, rather than just one as at present. This support should be integrated with the proposed module mechanism. (The current naming conventions in effect result in two levels of classification—for example, in the current system there is in effect a category *Graphics* with subcategories such as *Editing* and *Text*, although the browser doesn't know about the two levels.) There should be a mode that, if desired, allows inherited methods to be seen in the list of methods for a class. There should be support for reorganising chunks of the class hierarchy, as well as for adding and editing classes. Some have argued that there should be explicit "protocol objects" representing the protocols that classes must obey, rather than just having a less formal category in the third browser pane.

Code viewing and display is tied a bit too tightly to the text strings typed in by the programmer. For example, if one views code in a browser with different width than the one in which it was created, lines will sometimes wrap around, with a loss of the clues given by indentation. Similarly, when typing comments, carriage returns and tabs must be inserted manually if the comments are to be indented properly; when the comment is edited, the formatting must be adjusted. To remedy these problems, we recommend that methods be stored as parse trees, and that they be presented using a pretty-printer. It should be possible to attach a comment node to any other node in the parse tree; comments should be formatted appropriately. However, formatting should not be completely automatic; for example, if the user indicates that two short statements are to be printed on the same line, this should be remembered and obeyed. Similarly, while case would not be significant in looking up names, the system should remember the particular way a name was written by the programmer in a given method, and show the name in that way when the code is displayed, rather than (say) showing everything in lower case.

The set of tools and conventions for handling concurrency is inadequate. A comprehensive remedy is well beyond the scope of Deltatalk. However, experience with e.g. the Sun and Cedar environments shows that associating a process with each window considerably enhances programmer productivity. In these environments, one can start up a long file-in process in one window, and then go on to read one's mail in another window while the file-in continues. Support for this modest level of concurrency is recommended. Nearly all of the necessary primitives are already available within the system (an obvious exception is reentrant blocks); what is needed is a consistent set of tools and conventions that make use of them.

The Smalltalk-80 environment provides the Model-View-Controller mechanism (MVC) for constructing user interfaces. MVC provides a toolkit of classes and conventions for user interface design, in which there is a clear separation between the underlying object (the model) and views on the model. The basic goals of MVC are clearly appropriate. In practice, however, MCV has proven difficult for both both novices and experts to use; it should be replaced. Finally, there are parts of the system that have grown and changed over the years, perhaps having been translated automatically from Smalltalk-76, and which are due for an overhaul.

6   Principal Language Changes Involved in Deltatalk

As described in the introduction, our starting point is a feeling that the Smalltalk-80 language is mostly right, and that a number of relatively small changes would improve the language considerably. In this section the proposed changes are outlined. The language would otherwise remain as specified in [8].

6.1   Metaclasses

In our empirical studies, metaclasses were regarded as the most significant barrier to learnability by both students and teachers. We propose that they be eliminated. We have explored various alternatives to metaclasses, such as the use of prototypes [1]. However, for Deltatalk we simply propose that the language revert to the situation in Smalltalk-76. Every class would be an instance of class Class. New instances would be created by sending the new message, and come with fields initialised to nil. Thus, one could create a new point using the expression

    Point new x: 10 y: 20

(Of course, the language would continue to support infix creation of points using e.g. 10@20.)

Two of the reasons that metaclasses were included in the Smalltalk-80 language were to avoid uninitialised instance variables, and to have a convenient place for messages that access or initialise information common to all instances of a class. (Examples of the latter include the message pi to Float, and messages to initialise class variables.) Regarding uninitialised instance variables, some evidence indicates that these errors aren't that frequent, and when they do occur, they are very easy to track down. There is in fact some advantage to having nil in the x field of a point that one has neglected to initialise, rather than say 0, since the error will be discovered earlier. For novices, a protocol that allows them to inquire what parts need to be initialised could be provided. Regarding messages that access or initialise shared information, sending a class variable initialisation message to 0.0 instead of Float is admittedly odd, but isn't hard to understand.

6.2   Variable Length Classes

Variable length classes are another source of complexity, although the novice need not encounter them as soon as metaclasses. We recommend that the language be simplified by removing the option of creating classes with both named and indexed fields. Instead, one could have classes with only named fields, or only indexed fields. (To achieve the effect of a class with both, one would instead create an ordinary class with named fields, with one field pointing to an object with indexed fields.)

6.3   Super

The reserved word super is confusing to novices. (Apparently self is confusing to some as well. However, others have an "Aha!" experience when they finally understand self, and we regard it as essential to object-oriented programming.) In addition to the data regarding novice confusion around super, it does have some peculiar properties. For example,

    super zork.

behaves differently than

    temp ← super. temp zork.

The problem is that super does not denote an object in the same way as other identifiers in Smalltalk. Rather, it denotes self, and at the same time causes the interpreter to go into a special mode. To prevent the sort of anomaly illustrated above, we recommend that super be allowed only as the receiver of a message. This is not a complete solution to the problem, since super remains different from other variables in the system. However, all of the other alternatives that we explored had disadvantages of their own.

6.4 Multiple Inheritance

As noted above, multiple inheritance is a thorny issue, on which we went back and forth several times. In the Deltatalk spirit, we propose that it be omitted, in favour of tried-and-true single inheritance.

6.5 Blocks

As also noted above, there are a number of problems with blocks: their small differences from method bodies, the lack of local state for block activations, and the general problem of too many kinds of variables and scope rules. We sought a comprehensive solution to all these problems[4], but decided that we were moving beyond Deltatalk. Here, we take a conservative view and suggest that blocks be retained, with three modifications. First, block arguments should be stored local to the block activation. Second, temporary variables in blocks should be supported, and should again be stored local to the block activation. A reasonable syntax for block temporaries is to include the temporaries between a pair of vertical bars; if no temporaries are used, the bars could be elided. (This is exactly analogous to the syntax for temporary variables in methods.) Third, the language should support arbitrary nesting of blocks, with block arguments and temporaries lexically scoped.

6.6 Naming Conventions

Capitalisation should not be significant in either variable or selector names. Underscores should be allowed as a way of building long names.

6.7 Modules

A module mechanism should be included in the system; we suggest that a relatively simple mechanism be used, based on some proven design from e.g. Modula-2. The global name space should consist just of module names. There would be no nested modules or submodules. Within a module are classes and other kinds of objects. Names can be exported or hidden (including selector names). Names must also be explicitly imported, although there would also be a mechanism for importing all the names that a given module exports. The module mechanism should subsume pool variables, and should be well supported by the programming environment.

6.8 Literals

As noted in the previous section, some additional literals would be useful. We recommend that bitmap literals be fully supported by the environment. To handle the other kinds of literals, we

---

[4]Two schemes showed some promise. In the first, method bodies would be made exactly the same as blocks; arguments for both methods and blocks would be labelled with keywords. (A method's selector would be separate from the keywords.) In the second, blocks would be replaced with inline definitions of objects that understood a single message.

suggest that the construct
```
{ ... an expression ... }
```
instruct the compiler that the expression in brackets be evaluated at compile time, and that its value should then be included as a literal at that point. To take advantage of this construct, we should devise compact message protocols to create new anonymous classes, and to build various sorts of parse tree fragments.

6.9 Programs as Data

Finally, we recommend some changes to the parse tree classes to make it easier to manipulate programs as data. Historically, these classes were developed for use by the compiler. Later, they were used as well by the decompiler, and then by other applications that manipulate programs as data. They should be cleaned up to make them more suitable as general vehicles. One change is to devise some more compact message protocols for parse node creation. Another is to remove the dependence of parse nodes on a particular method and literal dictionary. Instead, a literal node would just contain the literal; the indexing of literals and construction of the literal table would take place during the code generation phase.

7 Conclusions

This paper has reported a *gedanken* experiment in which we have sought to improve the learnability and usability of the Smalltalk-80 system with a package of deletions and small tweaks. Ideally, any version of Deltatalk could be described by a version of [8] with a few sections blanked out and a few small inserts. We believe that a version of Smalltalk that was only a "delta" change could be usefully implemented, and see no reason why it would not be used by all the current types of user of the Smalltalk-80 system. The main virtue of the proposal sketched out here is that modest effort would be followed by a fairly certain gain in learnability and hence in the size of Smalltalk programmer community. The enthusiasm exhibited by learners for the key ideas of the language and the quality of the large systems that have been implemented in it to date suggest to us that a collection of improvements in overall learnabilty could have a dramatic positive effect.

Acknowledgments. We gratefully acknowledge the financial and intellectual help of Xerox PARC during the course of the research which led to this paper. We are particularly grateful to David Robson, Randall Smith, and Frank Zdybel for ideas, helpful advice and constructive criticism. The authors are, of course, entirely responsible for any inconsistencies or errors in the views expressed in this paper.

References

[1] A. H. Borning. Classes versus Prototypes in Object-Oriented Languages. In *Proceedings of the ACM/IEEE Fall Joint Computer Conference*, pages 36–40, ACM and IEEE, Dallas, Texas, Nov. 1986.

[2] A. H. Borning. The Programming Language Aspects of ThingLab, A Constraint-Oriented Simulation Laboratory. *ACM Transactions on Programming Languages and Systems*, 3(4):353–387, Oct. 1981.

[3] A. H. Borning. *ThingLab—A Constraint-Oriented Simulation Laboratory.* PhD thesis, Stanford, March 1979. A revised version is published as Xerox Palo Alto Research Center Report SSL-79-3 (July 1979).

[4] A. H. Borning and D. H. H. Ingalls. Multiple Inheritance in Smalltalk-80. In *Proceedings of the National Conference on Artificial Intelligence*, pages 234–237, American Association for Artificial Intelligence, Pittsburgh, Pennsylvania, Aug. 1982.

[5] H. I. Cannon. *Flavors.* Technical Report, MIT Artificial Intelligence Lab, 1980.

[6] A. Goldberg. *Smalltalk-80: The Interactive Programming Environment.* Addison-Wesley, 1984.

[7] A. Goldberg and A. C. Kay. *Smalltalk-72 Instruction Manual.* Technical Report SSL-76-6, Xerox Palo Alto Research Center, 1976.

[8] A. Goldberg and D. Robson. *Smalltalk-80: The Language and its Implementation.* Addison-Wesley, 1983.

[9] A. Goldberg and J. Ross. Is the Smalltalk-80 System for Children? *Byte*, 6(8):348–368, Aug. 1981.

[10] L. Gould and W. Finzer. *Programming by Rehearsal.* Technical Report SCL-84-1, Xerox Palo Alto Research Center, May 1984.

[11] L. Gould and W. Finzer. Programming by Rehearsal. *Byte*, 9(6):187–210, June 1984.

[12] D. H. H. Ingalls. The Smalltalk-76 Programming System: Design and Implementation. In *Proceedings of the Fifth Annual Principles of Programming Languages Symposium*, pages 9–16, ACM, Tucson, Arizona, Jan. 1978.

[13] A. C. Kay and A. Goldberg. Personal Dynamic Media. *Computer*, 10(3):31–42, March 1977.

[14] B. J. MacLennan. *Principles of Programming Languages.* Holt, Rinehart and Winston, second edition, 1987.

[15] T. O'Shea. The Learnability of Object-Oriented Programming Systems. In *Proceedings of the ACM Conference on Object-Oriented Programming Systems, Languages, and Applications*, page 502, ACM, Portland, Oregon, Sep. 1986.

[16] R. B. Smith. Experiences with the Alternate Reality Kit: An Example of the Tension between Literalism and Magic. In *Proceedings of CHI+GI 1987*, pages 61–67, ACM, Toronto, Canada, Apr. 1987.

[17] R. B. Smith. The Alternate Reality Kit: An Animated Environment for Creating Interactive Simulations. In *Proceedings of the 1986 IEEE Computer Society Workshop on Visual Languages*, IEEE, Dallas, Texas, June 1986.

Reversible Object-Oriented Interpreters

Henry Lieberman

Artificial Intelligence Laboratory, Massachusetts Institute of Technology
Cambridge, Mass. 02139 USA
Electronic mail (Arpanet): `Henry@AI.AI.MIT.Edu`

Abstract

The "programs are data" philosophy of Lisp uses Lisp's *S-expressions* to represent programs, and permits a program written in Lisp itself to implement the interpreter for the language. Object-oriented languages can take this one step further: we can use *objects* to represent programs, and an *object-oriented interpreter* takes the form of responses to a protocol of messages for evaluating programs. Because objects are a richer data structure than simple S-expressions, the representation of programs can have more built-in intelligence than was feasible using simple list manipulation alone.

This paper surveys techniques and applications for object-oriented interpreters. We focus particularly on object-oriented interpreters that are *reversible*, those that, unlike conventional interpreters, remember their history of evaluation. We illustrate the techniques involved with two applications of reversible object-oriented interpreters: a reversible stepper for Lisp, and a programming environment which constructs Lisp programs from examples.

---

1. Representing programs as active objects is a key to increased power in programming environments

As we strive to embed more intelligence in the programming environment, it is inevitable that we must change the way we think about programs. If the machine is to be more helpful in the design, coding, debugging, maintenance and documentation of programs, it must move beyond considering a program as simply a text string, denoting constructs in a programming language. The obvious place to locate the more sophisticated knowledge and behavior we will require of our programs is to distribute it in active objects representing the components of the programming language itself. The responses to messages received by objects representing programs will constitute a new generation of interpreters, some of which will exhibit novel properties.

To illustrate some techniques for exploiting object-oriented representations for programs, we will discuss interpreters that are *reversible*, those that maintain a *history* of the computation as they interpret programs. These interpreters, in addition to conventional program execution, also make it possible to run programs *backwards*, and provide new power for incremental program construction and debugging.

2. Representing programs as objects: the basics

To convey the flavor of the technique, we start by describing the structure of a relatively conventional interpreter for a Lisp-like language, then move on to consider more radical departures. We will show the structure of a simple interpreter based on responses of programming language objects to EVAL messages, which ask the objects to evaluate themselves. Whereas the Lisp interpreter is a monolithic function, the object-oriented interpreter is *distributed* by the response of the various objects to messages like EVAL or APPLY. Alternative interpreters can co-exist with the standard one, based on introducing messages other than EVAL. They may make use of the behavior provided by EVAL if they wish.

A major advantage of using an object-based representation for programs over Lisp lists is that behavior-sharing mechanisms such as *inheritance* can be used to capture commonalities between programming constructs. New kinds of program objects can be defined to inherit the behavior of previously existing objects, and add new behavior for EVAL or other messages.

The root of the hierarchy for all objects representing programs is an object called FORM [after the Lisp terminology for an argument to the Lisp EVAL function]. For many interpreters, this object may not have much interesting behavior by itself, but at least serves to identify those objects which have procedural semantics from those that do not. Built directly upon FORM are the "atomic" constructs of the language. Numbers, text strings, and "self-evaluating constants" are all instances of the object CONSTANT. When a CONSTANT receives an EVAL message, it returns itself.

A VARIABLE is an object that has one [instance] variable, its NAME, a symbol or text string. [Note that we don't include the *value* of the variable, since we're talking about unevaluated variables]. The argument to the EVAL message is an ENVIRONMENT object, an object that accepts LOOKUP messages to retrieve the value of a VARIABLE. When a VARIABLE receives an EVAL message, it sends a LOOKUP method to the ENVIRONMENT.

Composite program objects are either FUNCTION-CALLs, SENDs, [if these differ in syntax], or SPECIAL-FORMS which represent other syntactic constructs. Each of these contains a list of ARGUMENTS, each of which is another FORM object.

The response of a FUNCTION-CALL object to an EVAL message is the guts of the interpreter. Its responsibility is to send EVAL messages to each FORM object in its list of arguments. They ultimately send an APPLY message to an object representing the DEFINITION of the function, as a LAMBDA object which sends EXTEND messages to the ENVIRONMENT to bind variables, and evaluates its BODY. Message SENDs work analogously, with MESSAGE objects, and METHODs.

Each of the special forms needs to have its own kind of object. Conditionals evaluate their TESTS, then evaluate their THEN or ELSE parts depending on the outcome of the test. Macros invoke their definitions and initiate another round of evaluation.

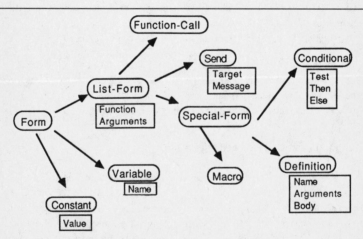

Figure 2-1: The object hierarchy for programs

The object protocol is transparent to control structure decisions in the interpreter. The object interpreter could rely on the stack of the host language, or explicitly create objects for continuations or activation records.

3. FORM objects respond to interpreters other than EVAL

Once we have a suitable object representation for programs, interpreters driven by messages other than EVAL play an important role. They can mediate between the object representation and other representations. Chief among them are the interpreters that correspond to the functions of READ and PRINT. These perform coercions in both directions between the object representation and either text strings or conventional Lisp S-expressions, in a distributed fashion. Each FORM object responds to messages asking it to convert a text string or S-expression to a program object, or to deliver a string or S-expression representation of itself.

These coercions are important, as they allow nonstandard object-oriented interpreters to coexist in a programming environment with more conventional interpreters. An object-oriented interpreter such as is described above may perhaps be slower than a conventional Lisp interpreter by factors of hundreds. But the ability to dynamically and incrementally convert between program representations means that at any point we can "boil away" object representation to produce a representation acceptable to conventional interpreters and compilers. This means that we needn't pay a permanent efficiency penalty for the use of object-oriented interpreters to enhance interactive programming environments.

4. Applications of object-oriented interpreters: A reversible object-oriented stepper

ZStep [Zstep] is a stepping debugger for Lisp designed to provide explicit support for the task of *localizing* bugs which appear in a large body of code, especially in cases where the investigator cannot make good guesses as to where the bug might be. ZStep's goals contrast with traditional debugging tools such as tracing and breakpoints, which are oriented toward the *instrumentation* of suspect pieces of code.

ZStep presents evaluation of a Lisp expression by visually replacing the expression by its value, conforming to an intuitive model of evaluation as a substitution process. The control structure of ZStep allows a user to "zoom in" on a bug, examining the program first at a very coarse level of detail, then at increasingly finer levels until the bug is located. ZStep keeps a history of evaluations, and can be run either forward or backward.

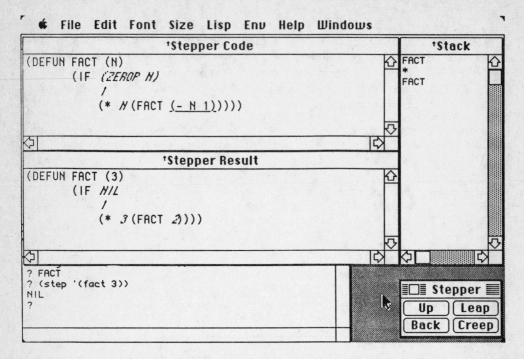

Figure 4-1: A reversible stepper displaying evaluation as substitution

When ZStep presents an expression for evaluation, the user is given a choice about whether to next view the details of evaluation [the *creep* command], or simply see the result of evaluation [the *leap* command]. Successive creep commands create a *linear* structure of incrementally generated evaluation events, whereas the leap commands induce a *tree* structure on the history of evaluations.

Either command can be invoked either in the forward or reverse direction at any point. Thus, the interpreter that generates the successive displays as the program is executed must be a *reversible* interpreter. We will show how the technique of object-oriented interpreters makes this easy to implement an interpreter that runs in parallel with Lisp's, and provides the necessary reversibility property.

An important property of a debugger like ZStep is that the control structure of the stepper must be *decoupled* from the control structure of the program being debugged. The traditional technique for implementing steppers is to piggyback the stepper's control structure onto the control structure of the program, using hooks into the interpreter provided by the EVALHOOK feature of Common Lisp [CommonLisp]. This won't work for a debugger like ZStep, where the control structure of the program always runs "forward", recursively, despite the fact that the debugger may run, iteratively, in either direction.

5. EVENTs provide a reversible representation of evaluation steps

The basic kind of object manipulated by ZStep is called an EVENT. Different kinds of EVENT objects represent different states the interpreter can be in. An EVAL-EVENT is produced when the interpreter is just about to evaluate a form, while a RESULT-EVENT says the interpreter is just about to return a value for a form. Similar objects exist for APPLY.

Events are linked in four ways: First, every event is doubly linked to its "leap" event, EVAL-EVENTs to EVAL-RESULT-EVENTs and vice versa. Every form thus knows its value and every value knows what form produced it. Every EVENT is linked to its UP-EVENT, the one for which it is evaluating a form, or to which it is returning a value. The chain of UP-EVENTs thus constitutes the "stack".

Each event is linked to its CREEP and PREVIOUS events, strictly in the order of "single-stepping" evaluation. The CREEP events are computed lazily; The first time an event receives a CREEP message, it computes the next step of the interpreter, then stores it to answer future CREEP queries.

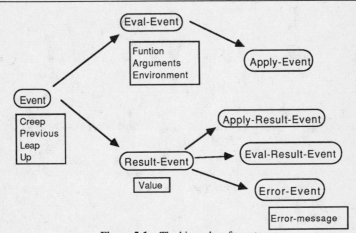

Figure 5-1: The hierarchy of events

The ZStep object-oriented interpreter is a distributed one, working by responses of each FORM object to a SINGLE-STEP message. It takes an event as argument, and returns the next event in the sequence of evaluation, if it has not already been computed. This becomes the next event accessed by the creep command, and initialization of the event object automatically links the event objects in both directions.

To illustrate the flavor of the interpreter code, we present the response of a FUNCTION-CALL object to a SINGLE-STEP message.

```
If I'm a FUNCTION-CALL object, and I get a SINGLE-STEP message,
 with an EVENT, asking me to produce the next EVENT:
  If I don't have any ARGUMENTS,
   I return a new APPLY-EVENT
    whose FUNCTION and ARGUMENTS are copied from mine.
  Otherwise, I return a new EVAL-EVENT
   evaluating the first element of my ARGUMENTS list,
   with an ARGUMENT-EVALUATION object
    that will eventually evaluate
    all the other ARGUMENTs and apply the FUNCTION.
  I copy the ENVIRONMENT and APPLY-EVENT for the new event
   from the old EVENT,
   and the UP-EVENT for the new event is the old EVENT.
```

Figure 5-2: Part of a reversible single-stepper

Argument evaluation objects are like continuations, in that they receive control after values are returned, and initiate the remainder of the computation. They carry any state that must be preserved over the recursive evaluation of argument expressions.

6. Objects representing errors are another example of unconventional interpretation techniques

When evaluating some code with ZStep, if the code causes an error, instead of substituting the value for the code in the result window, ZStep *substitutes the error message for the code which caused the error*. This is important because it makes visually clear the context in which the error happened. The user can use the commands which browse the event structure to discover the cause of the error.

Obviously, if an error occurs in the program being debugged, we don't want a corresponding error to happen in the debugger! This is a grave problem for traditional debuggers that couple the control structure of the debugger to that of the target program. To deal with this, we introduce *objects explicitly representing errors* into the language.

ERROR-EVENTs are similar to RESULT-EVENTs, except that they hold an error message instead of a returned value. They also must be linked to their corresponding EVAL-EVENTs. The rule for propagation of error events says that if any expression contains an error event, that expression must itself yield an error event, including the back pointers that maintain the reversibility of all ZStep events. Error events linked by the UP-EVENT link preserve the "stack" at the time of the error, leaving the potential for fixing and resuming the computation at any point.

Tinker, the example oriented programming system described below, also makes use of error objects, albeit somewhat differently, to implement non-standard semantics for error situations.

7. A reversible object-oriented interpreter provides the means for implementing example-based programming

Tinker [Seeing], [Aisbed] is a novel programming environment which synthesizes Lisp programs from examples. To write a program with Tinker, a user presents an example of data the program is to operate on, and demonstrates the steps of the computation on the example data. As each step is performed, the results in the concrete example are displayed, and the step is also remembered to become part of the final program. By indicating which objects represent arguments to the procedure to be constructed, the user informs Tinker what generalizations to make. A "teaching sequence" of examples may be presented, each building upon the partial definition constructed from previous examples. When several examples are presented, Tinker asks the user to provide criteria for distinguishing between them, resulting in procedures containing conditionals. Tinker has a menu-based graphical interface, as shown below.

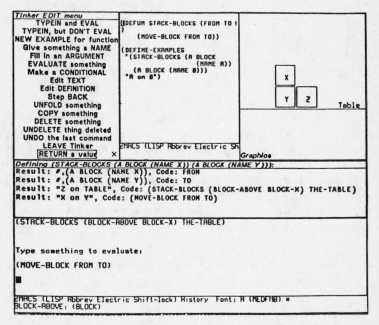

Figure 7-1: Writing a blocks world program by example with Tinker

The heart of Tinker, like ZStep, is a reversible object-oriented interpreter. While ZStep's interpreter starts by running forward, beginning with Lisp code and unfolding the sequence of events that take place for a particular computation, Tinker's *normally runs backward*. Starting with an example computation, Tinker's interpreter eventually generates Lisp code that corresponds to the user's intended program.

Values are input to Tinker in one of two ways: either by evaluating typed Lisp expressions, or as the result of demonstrative actions like menu selections. In any case, Tinker converts the expression to a FORM object. The evaluation of this FORM object via EVAL messages produces what Tinker calls a RESULT object. This object contains both the value, and the original FORM that produced it. Both the value and code are displayed for each such object, appearing in the center window of the Tinker screen.

More complex expressions are built out of simple ones by utilizing the RESULT objects as arguments in further computation. The user can point to an already-computed value, and pass it as an argument to some other function, using the menu operation **Fill in an argument**. The function will be executed using the indicated value, but the RESULT object produced will contain the code that created the value instead of the value itself. Thus every Tinker computation represented by a RESULT object records a complete history of its computation, which is finally read out in the opposite direction when Tinker constructs the final program. While conventional interpreters analyze expressions from the outside in, Tinker builds up an expression "inside out".

Tinker has no need of the doubly-linked linear history of events produced by ZStep. But Tinker does have another novel data structure for interpretation of programs, motivated by the need to handle multiple examples. A RESULTS object is similar to the RESULT object introduced earlier, but records the correspondence between a piece of code and its execution in *more than one environment*. As multiple examples are presented to Tinker for the same function, a RESULTS object is sent a MERGE message to incorporate each successive example. The RESULTS object contains a list of VALUES and ENVIRONMENTS, instead of just a single value and environment. For subexpressions where the examples differ, Tinker assumes the user intended to generate a conditional. The set of values and environments for that subexpression becomes *split*, with one subset following the THEN part of the conditional, and the other subset following the ELSE part.

8. Object-oriented interpreters have application in language design

One reason object-oriented languages are popular among system developers is that they provide a good substrate for further experimentation in developing new languages and systems. A major category of applications of object-oriented interpretation techniques is in the implementation of new languages on top of existing object-oriented ones. One can use an object-oriented representation of programs in the embedded language, and define an interpreter which implements the semantics of the language by "unfolding" it into the implementation language. This is another kind of reversibility that can appear in object-oriented interpreters. Scripter [ApiarySimulator] and its successor Pract [Pract] interpret actor programs by transforming them from a recursively nested expression form to unidirectional message passing using generated *continuation* objects. Symbolic evaluators, "code walkers", indexers, and partial evaluators are also examples of alternative evaluators that can profit from implementation in an object-oriented fashion.

The idea of representing programs as objects, by itself, is not new. The most radical object-oriented languages, such as the actor languages [Coop] and Smalltalk [SmalltalkLanguage] represent *everything* as objects, and so have no choice if they wish to represent programs at all. The actor languages have long had object-oriented interpreters written in the manner we describe. Smalltalk-80, a compiler-based system, lacks an interpreter, but implements its compiler through compilation messages, though perhaps not as accessibly as one would like.

It has been pointed out that the *denotational semantics* technique for defining the meaning of programming languages [DenSem] bears some conceptual similarity to object-oriented interpretation techniques. Syntactic categories of language constructs are the "objects", and equations involving them constitute the "interpreter". However, these formalisms are weak on dynamic representations, don't explicitly consider reversibility, and have little to say about the consequences for programming environment issues such as incremental program construction and debugging.

The examples presented here far from exhaust the uses of reversible object-oriented interpreters. We hope that these examples give some indication of the power and utility of the techniques. Computer programs are complex entities which can be viewed in many different ways, and object-oriented representation of programs provides a convenient and effective means of realizing some of the possibilities.

9. Acknowledgments

Major support for this work was provided by by the System Development Foundation. Related work at the MIT AI Lab was sponsored by DARPA under ONR contract N00014-80-C-0505.

References

1. Adele Goldberg and David Robson. *Smalltalk-80: The Language and its Implementation.* Addison-Wesley, Reading, Mass., USA, 1983.

2. Henry Lieberman. An Object Oriented Simulator for the Apiary. AAAI-83, American Asociation for Artificial Intelligence, Washington, D. C., USA, August, 1983.

3. Henry Lieberman. Steps Toward Better Debugging Tools for Lisp. Proceedings of the Fourth ACM Conference on Lisp and Functional Programming, Austin, Texas, USA, August, 1984.

4. Henry Lieberman. "Seeing What Your Programs Are Doing". *International Journal of Man-Machine Studies 21*, 4 (October 1984).

5. Henry Lieberman. "An Example Oriented Environment for Beginning Programmers". *Instructional Sciences 14* (1986), 277-292.

6. Carl Manning. Traveler: the Apiary Observatory. ECOOP-87 [this volume], Paris, France, June, 1987.

7. Guy Steele, et. al.. *Common Lisp: The Language.* Digital Press, Maynard, Mass., USA, 1984.

8. Joseph Stoy. *Denotational Semantics.* MIT Press, Cambridge, Mass., USA, 1977.

9. A. Yonezawa and M. Tokoro, eds.. *Concurrent Object Oriented Programming.* MIT Press, Cambridge, Mass., USA, 1987.

Using Types and Inheritance in Object-Oriented Languages

Daniel C. Halbert   Patrick D. O'Brien

Digital Equipment Corporation, Object-Based Systems Group
HLO 2-3/M08, 77 Reed Road
Hudson, Massachusetts 01749, USA

Abstract

If the object-oriented style of programming hopes to live up to its potential as an improved methodology for software programming, a clear understanding of how to use types and inheritance is essential. Our experiences with using object-oriented languages and teaching object-oriented techniques to other programmers have shown that effective use of types and inheritance may be problematic. There are no concrete guidelines to assist programmers, and the existing aphorisms often create interpretation problems for novice object-oriented programmers. In this paper we look at how types, subtyping, and inheritance are used in object-oriented languages. We discuss the different ways that types and type hierarchies can be used to structure programs. We illustrate appropriate use of these concepts through examples and develop guidelines to assist programmers in using the object-oriented methodology effectively.

1 Introduction

The object-oriented style of programming offers an improved methodology for software development. Types[1], type hierarchies, and inheritance are fundamental concepts of object-oriented programming, and mastery of these concepts is essential if the benefits of the object-oriented style of programming are to be realized. We will describe the different ways types and inheritance can be used to structure programs and present some guidelines for proper use.

The Object-Based Systems Group at Digital has developed an object-oriented language called Trellis/Owl[2] [Schaffert *et al*]. Over the past three years we have been using the Trellis/Owl language to build several large applications, including the Trellis programming environment, a window management system, and a project manager's workstation. We have also introduced object-oriented programming to several groups within our company. Our experience has shown that the object-oriented methodology increases programmer productivity by enhancing the maintainability, extensibility, and reusability of software.

To achieve this increase in productivity, types and inheritance must be used effectively. Types are the major organizing principle in object-oriented programming, and inheritance enables one to specify important relationships between types. But using these concepts appropriately is a difficult skill to master. Furthermore, the lack of existing guidelines to assist programmers exacerbates the problem. We believe that guidelines and heuristics need to be developed to aid both novice and experienced programmers[3]. In this paper we will discuss some problems object-oriented programmers encounter and develop some guidelines they can use in programming.

Different languages provide types and inheritance in different ways. Consequently, when these concepts are discussed, the reasons for how and why they are used are often couched in terms of a particular implementation. We will concentrate on types and inheritance in general, and not just how they can be used in one particular language.

In the next section we review types and inheritance as they relate to object-oriented programming. Section 3 discusses the use of types in more detail and points out some common difficulties that novices encounter. It also presents some guidelines for structuring code using types. Section 4 discusses the uses of inheritance and the different ways that inheritance can be used with types to structure code. It also describes some uses that should be avoided and presents more desirable alternatives. Section 5 presents a

---

[1]In this paper, we use the words *type* and *class* synonymously. The same holds for *fields* and *instance variables*, *operations* and *methods*, *operation names* and *selectors*, and *procedure calls* and *messages*.

[2]Trellis is a trademark of Digital Equipment Corporation.

[3]Novice and experienced refer to the user's familiarity with the object-oriented style of programming. Most of our novice users were experienced programmers.

detailed example that illustrates some of the guidelines and principles developed in this paper. We conclude with a summary and recommendations in section 6.

2 Foundations

In object-oriented programming, computation proceeds by objects sending messages amongst themselves. Objects encapsulate both state and behavior. Types capture the common characteristics of objects and can be related hierarchically through inheritance. Inheritance enables types to share various characteristics. Abstract types, which are used to group characteristics and do not have any instances, are useful when utilizing inheritance.

2.1 Types

Object-oriented programming combines descriptions of data and procedures within a single entity called an *object*. The data in an object consists of *fields* which may reference other objects. The *operations* associated with an object collectively characterize its *behavior*. Every object has a *type* and the object is referred to as an *instance* of that type. The type mechanism provides a means of classifying similar objects and capturing the common characteristics of those objects. An object's type determines the set of operations that can be applied to it.

Object-oriented programming differs from conventional *control-based* programming. It encourages the programmer to concentrate on the data to be manipulated rather than the code that does the manipulation. This emphasis helps to maintain a balance between data and control flow. Since types are commonly used to model entities in the application domain, they provide a natural basis for modularization in a program. In control-based programming, one is forced to modularize programs based on procedural criteria. This often leads to program structures that are radically different from the structures in the application domain. Since types model application entities, the structures in object-oriented programs can more closely resemble the structures in the application domain.

Types are the major organizing principle in object-oriented programming. A program with a well-designed type structure will minimize and localize the interdependencies among types, thus enhancing maintainability and extensibility.

2.2 Subtyping and inheritance

An object-oriented language often provides a *subtyping* mechanism in its type system. One type may be a subtype of another, with the implication that if B is a subtype of A, an object of type B may be used wherever an object of type A may be used. In other words, objects of type B are also of type A. Some languages permit a subtype to have multiple parent types (*supertypes*). The relationships between the types define a *type hierarchy*, which can be drawn as a graph:

In this example, both B and C are subtypes of A.

Intimately connected with subtyping is the concept of *inheritance*. A subtype may share or *inherit* various characteristics of its supertype(s). The subtype in turn may pass on its own or its inherited characteristics to its subtypes. The characteristics that can be inherited usually include the storage representation of the supertype and the operations provided by the supertype.

Frequently, the inherited characteristics may be changed, or *overridden*. A subtype may respecify the storage representation or give new definitions for operations inherited from a supertype. Different languages allow varying degrees of control over what can be inherited and what can be overridden. For instance, in Smalltalk-80[4] [Goldberg & Robson], operations defined in a supertype are always inherited and may be reimplemented in a subtype. The storage representation of an instance, as defined in the supertype, is

---

[4]Smalltalk-80 is a trademark of Xerox Corporation.

also inherited, and may be augmented by defining additional storage fields. By comparison, in Trellis/Owl, operations and fields may be declared to be *public* or *private*. Private declarations are visible within but not outside the type, and, therefore, a subtype cannot use a supertype's private operations and fields.

The definition of an operation consists of two pieces: the *interface* and the *implementation*. The interface describes the external characteristics of the operation, such as the operation name, the type of the return value, and what arguments the operation takes. The implementation contains the actual code for the operation.

Although most languages allow an existing implementation of an operation to be overridden by a subtype, they often restrict how an interface can be respecified. For example, in Trellis/Owl, which is a *type-safe* language, an interface can be overridden only in specific ways. These restrictions guarantee that the type checking implied by the interface declarations can always be done at compile-time.

2.3 Abstract types

An abstract type is a type for which no instances are created. Abstract types characterize common behavior and pass on those characteristics to their subtypes. Often, an abstract type just describes the interface to the operations of the type, or is a partial implementation of those operations. The complete implementation is left to one or more subtypes. Other times, an abstract type describes a complete implementation of some data type, but the type is useful only when it is combined with other types in a new subtype. Even if a language does not distinguish in its syntax between abstract and non-abstract types, programmers will often use abstract types and indicate so through coding conventions.

In Smalltalk parlance, one often says that a class obeys a certain *protocol*. This means that the class has defined methods for a particular set of selectors, and that these methods obey a certain semantics. For example, instances of Integer and Point both obey comparison protocol; that is, both classes provide methods for <, >, etc. A class can obey more than one protocol; for instance, Integer will also obey arithmetic protocol by providing methods for +, -, and so forth.

Although the term "protocol" is used informally, the idea can be crystallized and made formal through the use of abstract types. An abstract type that contains operation interfaces, but no implementations, defines a protocol. If some implementations are included, the abstract type defines a protocol with default implementations. Several protocols can be combined by inheriting definitions from multiple supertypes.

Some languages can guarantee that a type implements a certain protocol. For instance, Trellis/Owl checks at compile-time for operations that are unimplemented in a non-abstract subtype. Therefore, one can be certain that a subtype has completely implemented an abstract supertype. In Smalltalk-80 this check is done only by a run-time convention: operations in an abstract supertype that do not supply a useful default implementation instead provide an implementation that generates a run-time error. The error indicates that the operation should have been implemented in a subtype.

We have now introduced the concepts of types, which capture common characteristics of objects; inheritance, which enables types to share various characteristics; and abstract types, which group behavior but have no instances. In the next section we begin looking at how types can be used to structure code.

3 Using types

To the novice user, designing a program using types can be a formidable task. A lack of clear guidelines has compounded the problem, and the fuzzy principles which have been proposed often lead to confusion and misinterpretation. A clearer understanding of how to use types will result in better structured programs and also shorten the time it takes to become adept at using the object-oriented style of programming. We will first discuss a few misconceptions often held by beginning object-oriented programmers, and then will develop some general guidelines for using types effectively.

3.1 Process versus data

As we mentioned earlier, object-oriented programming encourages the programmer to concentrate on data rather than procedures. This emphasis sometimes presents problems for novice object-oriented programmers. Novice programmers generally understand *data abstraction*: that is, they understand grouping data and the operations on that data into a type. But they then believe that modelling a process as an object goes against the grain of the object-oriented paradigm. By a process we are referring to a procedural mechanism as opposed to a concrete entity. For example, payroll is probably thought of as a process, but employees are considered concrete entities. Should payroll be modelled as an operation on employee entities, or should it be modelled as an independent process defined as a separate type? Both approaches seem plausible: choosing one or the other will depend on the details of payroll and employees.

As another example, consider a lexical scanner which is a front-end process for a parser. The scanner accepts strings, and, according to a set of rules, constructs tokens which it passes to the parser. We could define the scanner process as an operation on the type String, since it operates on strings and generates tokens from the strings. But to consider the scanner as an operation on the type String does not capture the desired abstraction, nor does it improve the structure of the program. A better design would be to create a distinct type for the scanner: this packages the abstraction properly by focusing on the scanner itself and not the strings it takes as input.

Processes can and should be modelled as separate types. This is not contrary to the object-oriented style of programming. Later in this section we will discuss reasons to separate behavior into distinct types and reasons to keep behavior within an existing type.

3.2 Correspondence to the application domain

Novices encounter another difficulty, related to the common aphorism that objects should be used to model entities in the application domain. This is a useful guideline, but novice users sometimes interpret this guideline to mean that the *only* types that should exist are ones that model the external view of the application.

A program can be viewed as a model of the real world. In moving from real world to computer system, entities are introduced that do not necessarily correspond to visible real world entities. There is nothing wrong with this: it simply reflects deeper levels of implementation. The higher levels of the program still model the application closely.

For example, in a window management system there is often an intangible object called the "window manager." The window manager directs I/O traffic between the physical display device and the windows the user sees on the screen. But the concept of a window manager is artificial, and was introduced only to help us code the application. It does not intuitively correspond to a real world entity; it is merely an artifact of how we model a portion of our application.

3.3 What's in a type?

Code written in an object-oriented language is normally associated with a particular type. When a programmer adds new code, there are two alternatives: the new code can be added to an existing type or a new type can be defined. Usually the choice is obvious, but sometimes it is not. Making this decision correctly, however, is very important: it affects the structure of the program and has important consequences for further evolution of the program.

To decide where to add new code, one must consider whether the behavior being added is better modelled as one or more operations on an existing type, or as an independent concept which can stand on its own. If a new type is created, would the new type be a meaningful abstraction that groups behavior in a useful way? For example, an operation to clear a window on the screen would naturally be provided in the type Window itself. But suppose we want to draw a clock in a window. Since clocks are not germane to windows, and since a clock can be thought of as an independent and useful concept, we would probably create a new type, Clock, to capture this specialized behavior.

Now, consider the process of enrolling a student in a course. Should this be an operation on the student or the course? The choice depends on our perspective. Another alternative is to create an Enrollment type to model the relationship between students and the courses they are taking. This would be important if we later wanted the enrollment relationship to capture other information, such as the grade a particular student received. Enrollment is related to other types (Student and Course), but it can be modelled as an independent concept and thus can stand on its own as a separate type.

There is no firm rule that can be applied in all cases to decide where to add behavior. But we can suggest criteria that should be considered when associating new behavior with types. The programmer should look at certain aspects of the behavior: its reusability, complexity, applicability, and its knowledge of representation details. Each of these criteria will be examined in detail.

If the behavior can be shared by several types, we suggest creating a separate type. This is analogous to factoring out code into procedures that can be reused by other procedures. For example, consider the concept of a rectangle. Rectangles are useful for describing the boundaries of windows, and are also useful for describing graphical shapes that can be displayed inside windows. By factoring out the concept of a rectangle into a separate type, we can use the abstraction in both windows and graphical shapes. If we had imbedded the behavior of rectangles within Window, we would have to duplicate the code within graphical shapes. Reusability is an important consideration when deciding how to structure code. Structuring types for reusability provides leverage when adding new program functionality. This is sometimes referred to as the "building block" approach to system development.

If the algorithm for implementing some particular new behavior is quite complex, we might factor out the code into a separate type, to avoid cluttering up the original type. For instance, calculating the area of a rectangle is a simple and straightforward algorithm, so we would put this operation in type Rectangle itself. On the other hand, text hyphenation and justification is a much more complex task, so we would create a new type to do text formatting, instead of putting the behavior in the text type.

One should also consider the general applicability of the behavior: in other words, will most users of the type want to use the behavior? The more specialized the behavior is, the more sensible it is to factor it out into a separate type. For example, the capability of converting strings to uppercase is generally useful, and would likely be included in the String type. Conjugating a regular French verb is quite specialized, and even though it is a simple operation on a string, it would make more sense to put the behavior into a different type.

Lastly, one should consider how much the new code needs to know about the representation details of the type. If the behavior needs to know a great deal, it should be included in the type. For instance, an operation that makes a copy of a given object should be implemented in the object's type. When making a copy of an object, one has to know whether the object and its copy can share the values of various fields, or whether the copy will have its own copies of certain field values. Thus, the code implementing the copy operation will need to have access to the representation and should therefore be associated with the type. We should point out that if a behavior does not need to know very much about representation details, this does not necessarily imply that we should create a new type: it merely means that it is less important for the operation to be implemented in the existing type. In all cases, the programmer should try to minimize and localize interdependencies between types.

These criteria must be used in concert to decide where to place new behavior. In many cases applying the different criteria will give conflicting results. One should weigh each criterion individually, and then decide which criteria take priority in a particular circumstance.

Consider a more involved example. Suppose we want to sort arrays of objects. We can either define this behavior as an operation on arrays or create a new type. Since sorting is a complex operation, and since it does not need to know very much about the representation of the objects being sorted, we decide to create a type that is a *sorter* object. The primary operation of the sorter would be sort, which would take an array and return a sorted version of it. We would also define an abstract type Ordered which would define operations like greater_than, less_than, and equal. The sort operation would take arrays of Ordered objects. Therefore, types that we want to sort, like strings and integers, are declared to be subtypes of Ordered. The Ordered type is created because it groups behavior that is required by the sort operation.

The applicability criterion suggests that the sort behavior should be associated with the array type, since sorting is a generally useful operation which most users of array would want to use. We chose to stress the complexity criterion and thus factored out the sort behavior. A shortcoming of this approach is that the sort algorithm cannot be easily modified based on the type of object being sorted. For example, we might want to sort arrays of integers and arrays of strings using different algorithms. To do this we would have to write code within the sort type to choose a particular algorithm based on the type of object passed to it.

A better way to accomplish this would be to introduce another abstract type, Sortable. The type Array[Ordered][5] would be a subtype of Sortable. Sortable would define the operation sort, and this operation would be inherited by all subtypes of Array[Ordered], such as Array[Integer] and Array[String]. The default implementation of sort would be similar to the sort operation on the Sorter type described earlier.

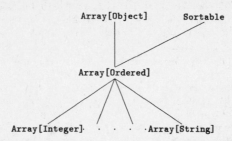

The advantage of the second approach is that the property of sortability is associated with the objects that possess this property: arrays of Ordered objects. Sortability is not separated out somewhere else. Moreover, each type that inherits the properties of Sortable can specialize the behavior and thus replace the default sort algorithm if desired. By factoring out the sort code into Sortable, we adhere to the complexity rule. But by using inheritance, we can factor the sort behavior back into the array type, and thus adhere to the applicability rule.

This example shows one of several ways that inheritance can be used to improve the structure of code. In the next section, we will take a closer look at the effect that inheritance has on decisions for grouping behavior within types.

4 Using inheritance

In this section, we will discuss how the programmer can turn concepts and implementations into type hierarchies. We will first describe the general design methodology that subtyping promotes, and then cover the different ways of using subtyping.

4.1 Subtyping as a design methodology

One of the major problems in designing and implementing large software systems is organizing the complex relationships that exist among objects in the application domain. Types provide natural criteria for modularization, and thus help shape the strategy for decomposing a program into modules. Subtyping enhances the type system's ability to cope with this inherent complexity. Subtyping affects the strategy used in determining the overall organization of programs, in contrast to techniques such as structured programming, which affect the style of writing small segments of code.

The seminal idea of subtyping is that a program can be constructed by first modelling, in terms of types, the most general concepts in the application domain, and then proceeding to deal with special cases through more specialized subtypes. Subtyping thus provides a general design methodology based on "stepwise refinement by specialization." This methodology can be compared with the well-known methodology of "stepwise refinement by decomposition" [Wirth].

Stepwise refinement by decomposition can be applied to both procedural and data abstractions. At each level of abstraction, the problem is subdivided into smaller components which are in turn subdivided. For procedural abstraction this subdividing process is achieved by creating procedures which call lower-level procedures. The program ends up as a hierarchy of procedures.

When decomposition is used to develop layers of data abstractions, the programmer creates a high-level data type and describes the operations on it. Then the programmer breaks down the top-level data type into its constituent components, breaks down each of those, and so forth. For example, consider a payroll database as a top-level data type. When broken down, one component of the payroll type might

---

[5]Arrays are defined as *parameterized* types[Schaffert *et al*].

be a collection of employee records. Each employee record could be broken down into fields describing the number of hours worked, the hourly wage, the deductions requested, and so forth. Together, these data types would form an aggregation hierarchy that describes the structure of the top-level payroll data type.

Some early uses of stepwise decomposition did not use procedures to preserve the series of abstractions that was created. Instead, the components of each decomposition were substituted in-line for the higher-level abstraction they implemented. Thus, the final program flattened out the design: it did not preserve the hierarchy of abstractions through which it was created. The result was that maintaining or enhancing a program developed by decomposition was not necessarily simpler than it would have been for a program developed in any other way [Shaw].

Similarly, before the introduction of data abstraction into programming languages, abstract data types were also flattened out. Complex data types were explicitly encoded in terms of simple ones, and only the encodings were visible, not the abstractions. For instance, records with named components were frequently encoded as simple arrays with numbered elements. The introduction of programmer-defined data types helped a great deal by explicitly presenting levels of data abstraction.

Coding a program with data abstractions, but without subtyping, can result in a flattened data type design along another dimension, namely the subtype hierarchy. Natural progressions from general data types to more specialized ones are obscured. Frequently, the programmer ends up overloading a type to represent more than one kind of object. In a language with subtyping, the programmer can factor out the common behavior in two or more types into a common supertype. But without subtyping the programmer must maintain several types with very similar code, or instead must combine several similar types into one, keeping track of the variants using some kind of tag.

For instance, in the payroll example given above, there may be hourly, weekly, and salaried employees whose pay information is quite different, but who otherwise have many properties in common, such as age, badge number, and so forth. In a language with subtyping, one could create an Employee type to hold the common information, and create subtypes for each category of employee. Without subtyping, the hierarchy would become encoded in a tag. If there were further divisions, such as temporary and permanent hourly employees, more tags would be needed.

Thus the lack of subtyping makes the data types harder to understand and obscures the natural hierarchy. When subtyping is present, it can be used to implement and preserve data abstraction hierarchies, just as procedures can preserve procedural hierarchies.

With decomposition, one rarely designs strictly in a top-down fashion, even though the methodology in its purest form calls for it. Sometimes one codes certain lower levels of the program first, to see how their design will affect higher-level aspects of the program, such as what data must be passed between parts of the program. Similarly, one does not always design types in a type hierarchy by starting with a supertype and then creating the subtypes. Frequently, the programmer creates several seemingly disparate types, realizes they are related, and then factors out their common characteristics into one or more supertypes. In either case, there is nothing wrong with this bottom-up or middle-out design; several passes up and down are usually required to produce a complete and correct program design.

In the next section we begin to look at different reasons for using subtyping.

4.2 Subtyping for specialization

As we implied above, subtyping is most frequently used for modelling conceptual hierarchies. Sometimes the hierarchy produced is a model of the real world. For instance, Jet and Turboprop might be subtypes of Airplane. Employee might be a subtype of Person. Input device might be the common supertype for Mouse, Tablet, and Keyboard:

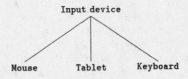

Other times, the programmer will use type hierarchies to model intangible concepts that are neverthe-less external to the program. For instance, a hierarchy might model the relationship between algebraic groups, rings, and fields. Finally, subtyping can be used to describe concepts that are particular to the program itself. For example, the supertype `Command` might describe behavior common to `Batch_command` and `Interactive_command`.

In all these cases, a subtype describes a type that is more specific than that of the supertype. Thus the subtype is a *specialization* of the supertype. Conversely, one could say that a supertype is the *generalization* of its several subtypes. Which term is used depends on one's point of view. A programmer could realize that several types share common characteristics, and factor out the commonality to produce a more general type which would be a supertype. Or, the programmer might need a more specific description of something, and so would create a subtype to specialize an existing type.

Another way of viewing specialization is to think of types as describing sets of values. The supertype defines a possible set of objects, and the subtype restricts the definition in order to define a subset of that set. Thus the term *restriction* could be used to describe specialization.

The supertype in a specialization hierarchy is frequently, but not always, an abstract type. The supertype may have factored out the common characteristics of its subtypes, but standing by itself it is an incomplete description, incapable of describing any useful object. Subtypes will add behavior that turns the abstract type into something useful. For example, the `Input_device` type described above would be incomplete, and so this type would undoubtedly be abstract.

A supertype is also usually abstract if the subtypes partition the instance space of the supertype. For example, in the `Airplane` example given above, if all kinds of airplanes of interest can be described using one subtype or another (e.g. `Jet` or `Turboprop`), there is no need to create instances of type `Airplane` itself, even though `Airplane` might be a perfectly reasonable non-abstract type. If a new kind of airplane needs to be described, a new subtype can be added.

4.3 Subtyping for implementation

Another common use for subtyping is to guarantee that types present a certain interface, that is, they obey a certain protocol. The programmer can define an abstract supertype that specifies certain operations. Many of the operations may be unimplemented. The programmer will then define several non-abstract subtypes that implement the behavior specified in the abstract supertype. For instance, the programmer may define an abstract type, `Dictionary`, and then implement this type in two ways, say, `Hash_table` and `Property_list`.

Here, the subtypes are not specializations of an existing supertype, but are *realizations* of the abstract supertype. The type hierarchy in this case reflects implementation only: there is no interface change from supertype to subtype.

4.4 Subtyping for combination

Until now we have been talking about types with single immediate supertypes. When a subtype has multiple supertypes, they combine to form a type with the behavior of all the supertypes.

In some instances, types of relatively equal importance are combined. For example, one might define a type `Teaching_assistant` with supertypes `Teacher` and `Student`. Here the supertypes seem to add together equally to form the subtype. In other cases, one combines a primary supertype with other supertypes that add ancillary functionality. For example, consider a type `Text_window`, which is a subtype of `Window`. `Text_window` is also a subtype of `Keyboard_handler`, which adds operations to permit keyboard input to the window. Here we would consider `Window` to be the main supertype. We might even draw these two hierarchies differently:

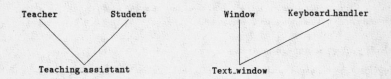

As with other kinds of subtyping, the supertypes may or may not include complete implementations for the types they define. In the examples above, `Teacher` and `Student` probably include complete implementations, but `Keyboard handler` may be an abstract type that just specifies the interface for the type-in operations, and does not provide any implementations. Thus, as mentioned before, a supertype can be used to guarantee that a subtype provides a certain interface; multiple supertypes just make this capability easier.

Since multiple supertypes can be used to merge implementations together, programmers are tempted to use supertyping even when it is inappropriate. For instance, we could create a type `Airplane` out of the supertypes `Wings`, `Fuselage`, `Engine`, and `Tail`:

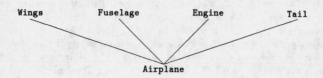

But a conceptual error is being made here. An airplane is *composed* of these parts: it is not the sum of the behavior of these parts. Multiple supertypes allow us to view an instance of a subtype as being an instance of any of its several supertypes. But we are not trying to view an airplane in such a way: we don't really want to think of an airplane as a more sophisticated way of viewing an engine or a fuselage.

We should not use subtyping for accomplishing this kind of aggregation. We already have an excellent mechanism: object fields. In our example, `Airplane` should have fields that contain the wings, fuselage, engine, and tail objects. Achieving aggregation through fields instead of through inheritance also allows more than one instance of a particular type of object, since a subtype cannot inherit a supertype more than once. If our airplane had more than one engine, or if we wanted `Wings` to be broken down into two instances of `Wing`, we could not use subtyping for aggregation.

To take another example, suppose we would like to keep track of the order in which windows are created. It would make sense to keep the windows on a linked list. We could define a type `Linked list node`, which defines a "next on the list" field, and make it one of the supertypes of `Window`. Windows would then have as part of their behavior the ability to be linked together in a list. But we do not necessarily want to view a window sometimes as a window and sometimes as a node in a linked list. Instead, we should make the linked list node a field defined in `Window`, or even better, we should keep a completely separate list of windows. Then, we could also put a window on more than one linked list, since the list behavior would not have been added by inheritance.

Nevertheless, it is often hard to decide when to combine types using supertyping, and when to use aggregation. For example, in our applications, we have coded the type `Rectangle` and the type `Window`. `Rectangle` implements operations such as `overlaps?`, `includes_point?`, `upper_left`, and so forth. Now, since windows are rectangular areas on the screen, should `Window` be a subtype of `Rectangle` or should it have a field that is a `Rectangle`? Choices like this are a toss-up. We have chosen one and then later the other, based on how `Window` was used by other code, and not based on anything inherent only to `Rectangle` and `Window`.

4.5 Nonstandard subtyping

In the uses for subtyping we have discussed so far, concepts from the abstract design of the program are closely reflected in the type hierarchy. We will now discuss some uses for subtyping that are driven mostly by implementation, not design considerations.

4.5.1 Subtyping for generalization

Subtyping for generalization is the opposite of subtyping for specialization. Here, a subtype extends a supertype to create a more general kind of object. For instance, `Ellipse` could be implemented as a subtype of `Circle`. A circle would be described by a single center point (focus) and a radius. An ellipse can be described by adding another focus. Or consider a `Plain_window`, which displays its contents on a simple white background. The programmer could create a subtype of Plain_window, Color_window, which allows the background color to be other than white, by adding an additional field to store the color, and by changing the inherited window display code so the background was drawn in that color.

In these examples, the conceptual hierarchy we would expect does not correspond to the actual type hierarchy. For instance, circles are special cases of ellipses, not the other way around. Nevertheless, the hierarchy specified by the programmer allows useful implementations to be inherited from supertype to subtype, and can save much recoding.

The programmer should be wary of disassociating the conceptual and implementation hierarchies in this way, since it goes against intuition, and may make the subtypes unduly dependent on the implementation of the supertype. If the hierarchies are dissimilar solely for reasons of implementation expediency, the programmer should consider whether there is a way to rearrange the implementation hierarchy to make it match the conceptual dependencies. For instance, Circle, above, might better be described as an Ellipse in which the two foci are identical.

On the other hand, casually trying to match the conceptual and implementation hierarchies can cause other problems. In the window example above, one alternative is to make Plain_window be a subtype of Color_window, with the background color restricted always to be white. This causes problems, however, if the color of a Color_window can be changed at runtime, since an attempt to change the color of a Plain_window should be detected as an error by code in Plain_window. We can avoid the possibility of such a runtime error by factoring out the common behavior of windows into an abstract type Window, and then creating the new types Fixed_color_window and Varying_color_window, with Plain_window being a subtype of Fixed_color_window:

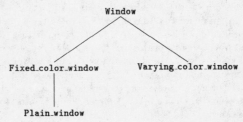

In some cases, this sort of restructuring may be more trouble than it is worth. Keeping the original implementation hierarchy is easier, even it does not correspond to the conceptual hierarchy.

Subtyping for generalization may also be unavoidable if the programmer does not have complete control of the type hierarchy. For instance, the programmer may wish to create a generalization of some type in the system library, but to do so would mean creating a new type that is a supertype of the system type. If such changes to the library are not permitted, the reasonable alternative is to subtype the system type.

4.5.2 Subtyping for variance

Subtyping for variance is similar to subtyping for generalization: the conceptual hierarchy does not match the implementation hierarchy. In the case of variance, however, there is no direct hierarchical relationship between the supertype and the subtype. Instead, the types are likely to be cousins or siblings in the conceptual hierarchy.

For instance, in the Input_device example given earlier, the implementations of Mouse and Tablet may be nearly identical. One could then make Mouse a subtype of Tablet, or vice versa, to allow all the common code to be reused.

As with subtyping for generalization, there may be a better way to structure the types. In the example above, factoring out the common code into an abstract type, say Pointing_device, is conceptually cleaner. And as with subtyping for generalization, an inability to change an existing type hierarchy might make subtyping for variance necessary, though not the most desirable choice.

5 Types and inheritance: an extended example

To illustrate the ideas and principles we have presented in the previous sections, we will describe a more involved example, and show how our design choices are influenced by these guidelines.

We will consider the design of an inspector facility. An inspector displays debugging information about an object in a window designed for that purpose. The information displayed includes various aspects of the object's state, such as the contents of some or all of its fields, and perhaps some computed values as well. Different types of inspectors are needed for different kinds of objects. For instance, all the interesting information about a point can be displayed at once in a simple format, whereas a large two-dimensional array might best be displayed as a matrix which can be scrolled. Such type-specific data display can greatly speed up the debugging process.

We should first decide where to put the behavior of the inspector. Should we put it in the type of the object to be inspected, or in a new, separate type? An inspector window is a visible, concrete entity, and seems to be a good abstraction in its own right. On the other hand, the information the inspector will display is closely related to the object being inspected. Because we have conflicting indications about where inspector behavior should go, we will consider the guidelines discussed in section 3.3 in more detail.

We will first consider the general applicability of inspector behavior, and also how much the inspector must know about the representation of the object it will display. Since every type of object should be inspectable, and since debugging is a common task, inspector behavior is generally useful, and is applicable to every type. An inspector must also have intimate knowledge about the type of the object being inspected, because it needs to know what values to display, and what kind of display is most suitable for that type of object. Thus, both of these criteria imply that we should define inspector behavior within each type whose objects can be inspected.

But this conclusion conflicts with what the criteria of reusability and algorithm complexity would suggest. Many types of objects will be displayed in the same way. If we implement the display code in each type separately, we would end up with a lot of duplicated code. Instead, we should put the common code in a separate type; then the behavior could be shared by all the types that use it. In addition, handling the display of the debugging information on the screen is a complex task, and will probably require quite a lot of complicated code. Many aspects of this code have nothing to do with the type of the object being inspected. For reasons of modularity, this code should be put in a separate type.

The subtyping guidelines presented in section 4 also suggest that inspector behavior should be implemented in a separate type. Different types of objects will be displayed in different ways, but the variations from one type of display to another may be slight. Different kinds of inspectors will still have a great deal of behavior in common. We can therefore factor out this common behavior into a few supertypes, and create subtypes to handle the variations of different kinds of inspectors.

Since we have concluded that some aspects of object inspection are closely associated with the object itself, and others are not as germane, we should split the behavior for inspectors along this division. Thus, we will implement inspectors as separate types, but we will include an interface in each object type that allows an inspector to look at the internals of the object in a systematic way. We will also provide an operation in every type that creates and displays the proper kind of inspector for objects of that type.

Our new type, Inspector, will handle the actual display of debugging information. Inspector will have subtypes that define different kinds of inspectors, such as Matrix_inspector and Bitmap_inspector. An inspector will be given an object to be displayed. But the inspector will get information about the object through an inspector_data operation which is defined on the type Object. The default implementation of this operation in Object will return the names of all the fields in the object and their values. Each type, however, will be able to reimplement this operation to return whatever names and values are appropriate. Special-purpose inspectors may need more information, and will require that the objects they can inspect provide the information through additional operations. Thus we continue to follow our guidelines by associating the knowledge of what is to be displayed with individual types, and yet breaking off the details of the display into separate inspector types.

Next, we need to describe how a specific type of inspector gets associated with a particular kind of object. Recall that we want to specify this behavior on a type by type basis. We can do this by defining another operation on Object, called inspect. The default implementation for inspect will simply create and display a default kind of inspector. Again, types can override this implementation if they want a specific type of inspector to be created. For example, a hash table might display a Dictionary inspector instead.

Finally, we should consider the structure of the type hierarchy used for the different kinds of inspectors. At first glance, we might consider defining the default Inspector as the top supertype. Types such as Matrix_inspector and Dictionary_inspector would be subtypes of this type. But in this type structure, subtyping is used largely for variation. A better structure might be one in which there is an abstract supertype `Abstract_inspector`, with subtypes `Default_inspector`, `Matrix_inspector`, `Dictionary_inspector`, and so forth.

In this type hierarchy, the common behavior is clearly in `Abstract inspector`. In the earlier hierarchy, the common code is mixed in with the code that is specific for the default inspector. A programmer may end up coding a new inspector in a way that makes the new one unduly dependent on the implementation of `Inspector`. The whole hierarchy would therefore be less maintainable and extensible.

The example we have presented here illustrates applying some of the principles we described earlier in the paper. But these guidelines are not a panacea, and are not hard and fast rules. Creativity and clear-headed thinking are still the most important ingredients of design. Nevertheless, we hope that the ideas we have presented allow the design to proceed in a more methodical way than might otherwise be expected.

6 Conclusion

In this paper, we have looked at typing, subtyping, and inheritance as they are used in object-oriented languages. We have discussed what types should represent, how to distribute program behavior among types, how to design programs that use subtyping and inheritance, and the different ways in which inheritance can be used. We have tried to draw out issues and codify principles which the programmer should consider when making these decisions.

Any one particular object-oriented language will influence how types and inheritance are used in the program to be written. Nevertheless, the programmer should think about the design of the types in the program in more general terms before constraining the design to fit onto a particular language.

When properly applied, object-oriented languages can significantly enhance the maintainability, extensibility, and reusability of the code in a program. But the proper and careful use of types and inheritance is critical to the success of programs built in an object-oriented way. In this paper, we have presented a number of guidelines for using types and inheritance; we hope they will contribute to good object-oriented program design.

References

[Borgida]   Alexander Borgida. Features of languages for the development of information systems at the conceptual level. *IEEE Software* **2**(1), January 1985.

[Curry *et al*]   Gael Curry, Larry Baer, Daniel Lipkie, and Bruce Lee. Traits: an approach to multiple-inheritance subclassing. *Proceedings of the SIGOA Conference on Office Information Systems*. Philadelphia, 1982.

[Goldberg & Robson] Adele Goldberg and David Robson. *Smalltalk-80: The Language and its Implementation*. Addison-Wesley, Reading, Massachusetts, 1983.

[O'Brien]   Patrick O'Brien. *Trellis Object-Based Environment: Language Tutorial*. Digital Equipment Corporation technical report DEC-TR-373, November 1985.

[Schaffert *et al*] Craig Schaffert, Topher Cooper, and Carrie Wilpolt. *Trellis Object-Based Environment: Language Manual*. Digital Equipment Corporation technical report DEC-TR-372, November 1985.

[Schaffert *et al2*] Craig Schaffert, Topher Cooper, Bruce Bullis, Mike Kilian, and Carrie Wilpolt. An Introduction to Trellis/Owl. *Proceedings of the ACM Conference on Object-Oriented Programming Systems, Languages, and Applications*. Portland, Oregon, 1986.

[Shaw]   Mary Shaw. Abstraction techniques in modern programming languages. *IEEE Software* **1**(4), October 1984.

[Wirth]   Niklaus Wirth. Program development by step-wise refinement. *Communications of the ACM* **14**(4): 221-227, April 1971.

Inheritance and Synchronization in Concurrent OOP

Jean-Pierre BRIOT*   Akinori YONEZAWA

Dept. of Information Science, Tokyo Institute of Technology
Ookayama, Meguro-ku, Tokyo 152, Japan

Abstract

This paper discusses knowledge sharing (inheritance) mechanisms for Object-Oriented Programming (OOP) in the context of concurrent (distributed) languages. We review three different schemes: *inheritance*, *delegation* and *copy*. A fourth model, called *recipe-query*, is presented and all are compared and criticized. Techniques relying on the shared memory assumption are rejected. We point out the conflict between distributing knowledge among objects and the synchronization of concurrent objects.

Keywords:

objects, classes, actors, message passing, knowledge sharing, inheritance, subclassing, delegation, proxies, code sharing, copy, synchronization, atomicity, distributed systems.

1 Introduction

1.1 Knowledge Sharing for Modularity and Classification

Knowledge sharing (or inheritance) is a mechanism intensively used in OOP. Its basic idea is the reuse of object descriptions. After defining an object, we would often like to refine it into a more specialized one. Rather than defining a new object from scratch, we could define it by inheriting the specification of the previous one.

The first main advantage of knowledge sharing is the increase of *modularity* it brings to OOP rather than duplicating similar knowledge. The second advantage is the introduction of *classification* among objects. It is used to hierarchically (or almost hierarchically) structuring knowledge, and it makes knowledge searching more efficient [Touretzky 86].

From an implementation point of view, knowledge sharing is also a very good means to share code efficiently. However, *code sharing* is only one of the implementation model [Borning 86]. We will also present other strategies based on a copy approach.

1.2 Strategies, Assumptions and Compromises

The *Smalltalk inheritance* scheme is just one of the strategies to specify and implement knowledge sharing. But the preeminence of inheritance among the majority of OOP languages gave this term a generic meaning. *Delegation* [Lieberman 86b] is another strategy we discuss as well. Delegation is discussed in the framework of the *Actor* model of computation [Hewitt 76,Lieberman 81]. Other models presenting various knowledge sharing and classification mechanisms include *frames languages* (e.g., FRL [Roberts & Goldstein 77] and KRL [Bobrow & Winograd 77]) and *(parallel) semantic network languages* (e.g., NETL [Fahlman 79]).

We note that there are many different description and implementation strategies for knowledge sharing, but usually they are compromises between full dynamicity and full recopy. Also many systems rely on strong assumptions. The most usual assumption is the existence of shared memory. This allows to gain efficiency by following the inheritance links which are implemented by simple pointers. In contrast, we like to explore

---

*also LITP, University Paris VI, 4 place Jussieu, 75005 Paris, France

the strategies of inheritance in more general memory models, i.e., general distributed models, because we are concerned with concurrency and flexibility. (America's paper [America 87] on the same topic emphasizes reliability issues through the separation of inheritance from subtyping.)

1.3   Plan of the Paper

As the background of our discussion, we will first review the two main schemes used in object-oriented systems, namely inheritance and delegation, in Section 2 and Section 3 respectively. We will compare them, following [Briot 84] and [Lieberman 86a]. Only the delegation scheme is flexible enough to be free from the shared memory assumption, so we will examine and criticize it in the distributed memory context. We will show in section 4 that delegation can conflict with synchronization. Section 5 will then present an alternative to delegation based on a synchronous approach, but unfortunately this scheme (called the *recipe-query* scheme) also suffers from some deficiencies. The last scheme we will discuss in Section 6 is a *copy* approach. We will discuss the tradeoff between flexibility and efficiency in this approach and present some techniques to increase flexibility.

2   The Smalltalk Inheritance Scheme

The *Smalltalk inheritance* scheme (also often called *subclassing* and pioneered in Simula-67 [Dahl et al. 70]) was proposed in Smalltalk-76. This scheme has been followed by most OOP languages.

In this scheme, knowledge is shared among *classes*. A class can be declared as a *subclass* of another class, called the *superclass*. The subclass will then inherit the structure and properties of its superclass. This *subclass/superclass* hierarchy is usually represented as a tree, which is called the *inheritance tree*. (It could be a more general graph in case of *multiple inheritance*. We won't discuss it here.)

2.1   Variables and Methods

This inheritance scheme is strongly related to the *class* notion of Smalltalk and its implementation decisions. The designer of Smalltalk has separated the inheritance of the data-base of an object, called the *variable dictionary*, from that of its method-base, called the *method dictionary*. The first one is of the static nature whereas the second one of the dynamic nature.

The variable dictionary of an object is split in two parts. The class owns the ordered set of variables (or the index to them), while every *instance* of the class owns its corresponding values. The class code is shared by all its instances, thus an instance needs a link to its class and the isomorphism between variables and values must be maintained. As a consequence, the set of variables owned by the class should not vary over time and is determined at the time of defining the class. The inheritance of variables of a class is *static* and performed only once when the class is created. (The list of variables of a class inheriting from its *superclass* is set by concatenating the list of variables of the superclass before the variables of the class.)

On the other hand, the inheritance of the method dictionary is dynamic. When one activates a method which is not explicitly specified in the definition of the class, the lookup process for the method begins in the method dictionary of the class the object belongs to. Then it propagates along the subclass/superclass hierarchy until the method is found.

2.2   Flexibility versus Efficiency

This is one of the main tradeoffs in knowledge sharing. The Smalltalk inheritance scheme is a good tradeoff. The inheritance of the variable dictionary is static thus efficient, but the changes in the subclassing relations won't propagate unless there is an automatic updating mechanism. The link between a class and its superclass is "hard-wired," which is usually implemented as pointers for the efficiency purpose in the same way as the link between an object and its class. The inheritance of the method dictionary is dynamically performed at run time, which often slows down system performance. But this dynamicity gives us a greater degree of flexibility. Our main comment is that this inheritance scheme using hard-wired links is not suitable for distributed memory models.

3   Delegation

The *delegation* scheme has been proposed in the Act-1 language [Lieberman 81]. An object (called an *actor* in this computation model [Hewitt 76] where the *class* concept is absent) knows about another object called a *proxy*. The object will (at runtime) delegate to its proxy the messages that it cannot recognize. This proxy can in turn delegate the message to its own proxy. The proxy will handle the message in place of the initial receiver of the message. The intuitive account might be: "I don't know how to respond to this message, can you respond for me?" [Lieberman 81].

3.1   Delegation versus Inheritance

In contrast to the Smalltalk inheritance scheme, in the delegation scheme the inheritance of the variable dictionary is dynamic. In fact, accessing (read or write) a variable in the variable dictionary is like invoking an accessing method associated with this variable. There is no merging of the data-bases as in the Smalltalk scheme. The delegation scheme enjoys the uniformity of the communication protocol: the delegation to the proxy of an object is performed by message passing, not by a system primitive through the hard-wired physical link (pointer). Thus delegation can be fully designed at the user-language level and it can be locally customized by the user easily. This scheme is independent of the assumption of shared memory and is perfectly suitable for distributed (memory and computation) models. It also allows full dynamicity and modularity.

In examining this scheme, two issues, namely efficiency and synchronization, must be addressed. Efficiency can be gained by interpreter optimization such as caching [Deutsch & Schiffman 84,Lieberman 86b]. But as we will see in Section 4, synchronization can conflict with recursion and the problem is not simple. There seems to be a tradeoff between distributing knowledge and synchronizing its access in concurrent models.

3.2   Access to Variables through Message Passing

In the delegation scheme, variable consultation as well as method activation should be performed through message passing because both can be delegated to another object (the proxy). Thus there is no direct variable reference, but an indirect access through message passing in order to be independent of variable location. Accessing to a variable in an object corresponds to a message sent to the object itself. The simplest and most natural way is to identify the name of the variable with the pattern (selector) of the message to access it.

3.3   From a Serial to a Parallel World

In order to present the delegation scheme, we will first restrict it to a functional and serial world. We will then move to a parallel world and point out the difficulty of synchronization which emerges. A simple example will help us to illustrate this point.

Thus we first identify message passing with function call as in most of OOP extensions of Lisp. Let **ask** denote the primitive to send a message and return the evaluation of the method activated. Then to consult the variable **x** is equivalent to perform a function call: (**ask self 'x 'get**). To update the value of **x** is equivalent to: (**ask self 'x 'set** *new-value*).

3.4   Implementation of Variables

There are several strategies to implement variables. We will present two such strategies, with different level of object *granularity*, i.e., size of objects.

3.4.1   Variables as Methods

The first strategy considers each variable as a method (with the same name as the variable) with an optional argument. This optional argument represents the new value in case of updating. Each *variable-method* is implemented by a closure to store and protect its value. The distinction between consulting and updating the variable can be made through the test of this optional argument. However we chose to explicitly specify the operation name (get or set) in the message for the readability purpose.

In CommonLisp, such variables could be defined with:

```
(defun make-variable-method (value)
  #'(lambda (operation &optional new-value)
      (if (eq operation 'set) (setq value new-value) value)))
```

In this implementation model, variables are directly invoked through method calls.

3.4.2 Variables as Objects

Another strategy, proposed by Henry Lieberman [Lieberman 86a], represents each variable by an object. Each such *variable-object* owns the two methods that handle two kinds of messages: one to consult the variable (get), and the other to update it (set). In contrast to the previous strategy, we need to explicitly redirect the access message to the variable-object. Now the *script* of any object (i.e., the behavior of the object when it receives a message) needs to distinguish a method invocation from a variable access. If no method is applicable, the script checks the existence of a variable with same name in order to redirect the accessing message to it, otherwise the unrecognized message is delegated to the proxy.

Table 1 shows in column 2 how to access a variable of an object through message passing to the object. This is common to both strategies. On the other hand, column 3 (message passing to the variable-object) is specific to this second strategy. All the discussion in the rest of the paper is independent of the strategy choice.

variable reference	message to the object	message to the variable
read x	(ask self 'x 'get)	(ask x 'get)
update x with *new-value*	(ask self 'x 'set *new-value*)	(ask x 'set *new-value*)

Table 1. Variable accessing through message passing.

(Remark that we omit here the description and the solution to the *self problem*, i.e., how to handle correct recursion, which is described in [Lieberman 86b].)

4 Delegation and Synchronization

4.1 Variable Access and Atomicity

The delegation scheme relies on message passing to access variables, as previously shown. The ask primitive using a function call model synchronizes such accesses. However in some concurrent models such as the Actor model, message passing is asynchronous and unidirectional. There is no implicit synchronization. As a consequence, variable access is no more atomic and could be mishandled.

To present this problem, we now consider the delegation scheme in a parallel world. The functional call (synchronous) ask primitive is replaced by the asynchronous send primitive. The optional :reply-to keyword allows the specification of a *continuation* or *customer*[1].

A simple example will illustrate a synchronization problem when accessing a variable. This example doesn't involve delegation but it shows that the requirement of the delegation scheme, namely accessing to variables through message passing, conflicts with an atomic access to variables.

---

[1] A *customer* is an object which encodes all the behavior necessary to resume a computation after reception of an answer to a question [Hewitt 76,Lieberman 81].

4.2 The Counter Example

Suppose that we define a simple object, named `counter`, which owns only one variable, named `contents`. We now explain how `counter` will increment its `contents`.

When `counter` is requested to increment, the first thing to do is the reading of its `contents` variable. Because message passing is unidirectional, we need to explicitly specify an object which will receive the value of `contents` and increment it. We dynamically create a *customer* object called `incrementor` dedicated to the incrementation. (Such a customer could also be automatically created by a compiler such as Scripter [Lieberman 83].) The `incrementor` object will receive the value of `contents`, add 1 to it, and then send a message to `counter` to update `contents` with that new value. Figure 1 shows the `counter` and `incrementor` objects, and their message exchanges.

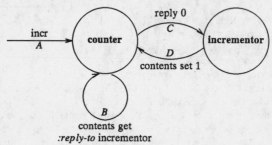

Figure 1. Incrementation of `counter`.

Table 2 shows the computation of the `incr` method. Four message passings are performed and they are ordered from (A) to (D) by their causality. (A) is the initial increment message (`incr`) sent to `counter`. We assume the value of `contents` is initially 0.

(A)	`(send counter 'incr)`	*from* top-level
(B)	`(send counter 'contents 'get :reply-to incrementor)`	*from* counter
(C)	`(send incrementor 'reply 0)`	*from* counter
(D)	`(send counter 'contents 'set 1)`	*from* incrementor

Table 2. Incrementation of `counter`: causality of messages.

4.3 Message Ordering Issue

Suppose that we send consecutively two `incr` messages to `counter`. We cannot ensure that the value of `contents` will be 2, because the `incr` method is not atomic. Messages can interfere during the processing of the `incr` method, because this method reduces to several message passings. As a consequence, the two `incr` computations may overlap and the first assignment may be shadowed by the second one. The second `incr` message (A') will create three new message transmissions (B') to (D'). If the second message (B') consulting the `contents` variable happens to reach `counter` before the first assignment message (D) caused by the first `incr` message, the first incrementation will be shadowed by the second one. Then the value of `contents` becomes 1. The problem is the ordering of messages which cannot be predicted.

4.4 Fairness and Recursion

In an asynchronous message passing model, the messages sent to an object O are ordered (in a queue) following the ordering of their arrivals to O. It is assumed that two messages cannot arrive at the same time. An arbiter orders them. This arbiter must be *fair* [Clinger 81]. As a consequence, in case of recursion (the object O sends a message to itself), the ordering of this recursive message and another message sent to O cannot be predicted. Meanwhile we would like to handle recursive messages at first to regain the atomicity for variable access, but then it would conflict with fairness.

We may lock `counter` to avoid it to process some other messages before the end of the `incr` method computation. But the problem is not simple because, on the other hand, `counter` needs to accept the recursive messages (sent by itself) and even messages sent by local customers such as `incrementor`, while temporarily rejecting other incoming ones. It is possible to implement such a mechanism but the scheme becomes very complicated, which is opposed to its intuitive foundation.

A way is to use a *waiting mode* or/and a *synchronous* message passing type, such as the *now* type of the ABCL model [Yonezawa et al. 86]. In this model, the order of message transmission from one object to another object is preserved in the message arrival order. We may also simulate a waiting mode with *insensitive actors* [Agha 84] in the new Actor model. However, in any case we cannot rely on synchronous calls in case of recursion, because we get a deadlock. If we use a synchronous approach, the delegation model should be replaced by another scheme, the *recipe-query* scheme, we present in Section 5.

4.5   The Replacement Actor Scheme

We notice that the latest Actor model [Agha 85] relies on *atomic* objects. In this model, there is no side effect. In order to allow changing states, an actor must specify its *replacement actor* which could have a different state. As soon as this replacement takes place (using the primitive *become*), the replacement actor begins to process the next message in the mail queue, thus allowing a pipelining of incoming messages. There is no delegation proposed in the Actor model of [Agha 85]. It seems complicate to combine this replacement scheme with delegation scheme because the replacement action should be delegated to proxies, but the state changing of an object and that of its proxies must be synchronized (through transition to insensitive actors) in a proper manner. The next section will show another strategy to synchronize delegation messages by explicitly ordering the messages through a manipulation of communication channels (streams).

4.6   Synchronization through Stream Manipulation

In the Vulcan language [Kahn et al. 86], the basic computation model is similar to the replacement Actor model of Agha. A "perpetual" object is implemented in a Concurrent Logic Programming Language [Shapiro & Takeuchi 83] as the illusion of a *perpetual process*, i.e., an *ephemeral* process that continually reincarnates itself in another process with the same functor and consuming the remainder of the message stream. A state change is represented by a new incarnation of the object replacing the old one. The new process owns a new state instead of the old one. The stream (used as a communication channel) is passed along from process to process in order to provide a perpetual identity to the object.

A delegation scheme is proposed[2] in Vulcan. The explicit manipulation of the communication stream avoids the serialization problem we pointed out above. Recursion will operate on *self* so that any message sent to *self* during the delegation will arrive before those sent externally. This technique allows a good handling of recursion and delegation, because the communication channel is unique and explicitly declared. But the issue of ordering preservation in case of stream merging is not addressed. In case of a *fair* merge of streams, any kind of insertion could occur, so the problems of overlapping we pointed out could reemerge.

The delegation scheme is conceptually natural and flexible. However, the synchronization issue must be carefully taken care of because accessing variables is performed through message passing.

5   An Alternative Scheme to Delegation

We now present another scheme, which we will call the *recipe-query* or "reverse" scheme, because it intuitively works in the reverse way of the delegation scheme.

5.1   Recipe-Query Scheme

Rather than delegating an unrecognizable message, the receiver object will ask another object (proxy) for the "recipe," i.e., the method of how to answer to the message. In that case, the receiver object waits for the

---

[2]In Vulcan, a class model is adopted. An inheritance mechanism is implemented by a recopy of the inherited code. A delegation mechanism is also proposed in order to define delegation from an object to its components (parts). This was previously introduced in [Shapiro & Takeuchi 83] and [Yonezawa 83].

proxy to send back the method associated to the message. Then using that method, the original message will be processed. Figure 2 compares *delegation* and *recipe-query* schemes.

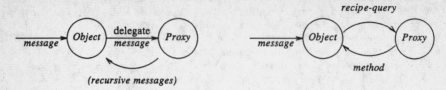

Figure 2. Delegation vs. Recipe-Query.

This scheme relies on some assumptions. Every object should understand the message: "What is your recipe for that message?". This pattern must be primitive and default to the set of methods of any object. We could also introduce a special type of message to get a method's body. In both cases it decreases the uniformity.

The second assumption is concerned with how to send back the recipe method to the initial receiver. Without the shared memory assumption, we cannot just send the address of the code. A solution to this problem is to copy the code body of the recipe method and to send it back. Then the body is executed. This operation might be rather expensive in terms of memory allocation. Another solution assumes that methods are themselves objects. Then the address (or name) of the selected recipe object can be sent back. The initial receiver object will then send an "eval" request to this method and wait for acknowledgment of its termination. Unfortunately, the method object may need to access a variable in the receiver object by sending a message to the receiver object which has been already locked. Once again it is difficult to avoid deadlock. This scheme, as delegation, does not fully satisfy our needs.

If however, we are allowed to send the environment of the object with the "eval" request, variables could be accessed directly, and no deadlock will occurs. Thus the above problem will be resolved. But the number of message transmission will become very large (to get all the variables distributed along the proxies-chain), which might not be appetizing to those who are seriously concerned with the current states of the art in computer architecture. Note that the number of message transmission can be reduced if the inheritance of variables is disallowed.

5.2 Object-Based Inheritance Scheme

We recently discovered the existence of a scheme which is very close to ours. The object-based inheritance proposed by Hailpern and Nguyen [Hailpern 86,Nguyen & Hailpern 86] has some similarity with an "autoload" library concept. They consider two kinds of methods: *simple* methods and *inherited* methods. A *simple* method contains the actual code to be executed. An *inherited* method contains pointers (hard-wired links) to other objects which would contain the code. Two types of messages are provided: the usual type is called *request*, and the other is called *inheritance* which is used to access *inherited* methods. A copy of the body of the inherited method is sent back and evaluated in the name-space of the initial receiver. Message passing is synchronous, and messages are serialized to each object except for inheritances which could be processed in parallel because memory is not affected. Memory allocation problem seems to be significant in this scheme.

6 The Copy-Everything Scheme

In order to avoid the difficulties met with either delegation or recipe-query schemes, we can adopt a very simple scheme in which both variable dictionaries and method dictionaries of inherited objects are all copied and installed into the inheriting object when it is created or compiled. The advantages of this approach are the efficiency of execution and the atomicity of processing a message, thus avoiding serialization problems. This approach is usually chosen in static (compiled) OOP languages.

The two deficiencies associated with this approach should be pointed out. First, the code size becomes very large because of all the recopies, specially in the case of very general objects being inherited by a large number of objects. The second deficiency is the staticity of inheritance, i.e., once copied, a change to the initial object won't affect the new ones. It is possible to use some techniques to reduce these two weaknesses. We review them below.

6.1 Memory Occupation

In languages with inheritance, there is usually a class called `Object`. This usual default superclass represents the most common (or default) behavior and is the root of the inheritance tree. As a consequence, every object will recognize the methods specified by this *root* class, unless they are shadowed somewhere in the hierarchy. We cannot use such a basic object in our copy scheme. If we do so, its code will be copied into *every* object. To alleviate this problem, basic (default) methods should be declared as global (or at least on each machine). Their activation will rely on a default mechanism, not on the usual inheritance scheme. Then the uniformity of inheritance will be lost. One way is to store default knowledge about a message with the message itself, as suggested in [Lieberman 86b]. Anyway the use of inheritance should be restricted to objects which have a small number of light offsprings otherwise the copy-everything scheme is too heavy.

6.2 Updating Problem

An automatic updating mechanism can be easily added in order to remedy the second shortcoming. Such a facility is used in the inheritance of the Flavors system [Moon & Weinreb 80]. We assume that objects won't change too often, and again that their offsprings are not too many. (In the Flavors system, a change made to the *Vanilla* flavor, the root of the hierarchy, will start a recompilation of the entire system!). [Borning 86] proposes a definition of inheritance by augmenting a copy mechanism with a *constraint* mechanism to support classification and updating. Unfortunately solving the updating problem doesn't solve the memory occupation problem.

7 Conclusion

In this paper, we have reviewed and discussed the main strategies proposed for inheritance (knowledge sharing) in object-oriented concurrent programming [Yonezawa & Tokoro 87]. We remarked that the attempts to increase the flexibility of inheritance by widely distributing functions and knowledge among objects complicates the synchronization issues. The tradeoff between the distribution for the sake of flexibility and the atomicity for the sake of synchronization appears to be fundamental in concurrent (distributed) computation. Alternatives based on synchronous communication tend to restrict the degree of concurrency that is the primary concern in concurrent computation and increase the deadlock risks. More static approaches based on the copy scheme solve these problems but inheritance should be restricted to avoid memory overloading. Delegation seems to be the most promising approach for knowledge sharing in distributed systems, but we must be very careful in combining the requirements of the delegation approach with the necessity of synchronization. We now need to find good compromises which are derived from both the characteristics of application domains and the underlying architectural supports for object-oriented concurrent programming.

Acknowledgments

We would like to thank Pierre Cointe, Brent Hailpern, Henry Lieberman, Etsuya Shibayama, as well as the reviewers for various fruitful discussions or comments.
Part of this research was carried out while the first author was visiting RIMS at Kyoto University.

References

[Agha 85] Agha, G., Actors: A Model of Concurrent Computation in Distributed Systems, MIT Press, Cambridge MA, USA, December 1985.

[Agha 84] Agha, G., Semantic Considerations in the Actor Paradigm of Concurrent Computation, *Seminar on Concurrency*, LNCS, Springer-Verlag, No 197, pp. 151-179, Carnegie-Mellon, Pittsburgh PA, July 1984.

[America 87] America, P., Inheritance and Subtyping in a Parallel Object-Oriented Language, *ECOOP'87*, P. Cointe and H. Lieberman (ed.), Springer-Verlag, Paris, France, 15-17 June 1987.

[Bobrow & Winograd 77] Bobrow, D.G., Winograd, T., An Overview of KRL, A Knowledge Representation Language, *Cognitive Science*, Vol. 1, No 1, pp. 3-46, January 1977.

[Borning 86] Borning, A.H., Classes Versus Prototypes in Object-Oriented Languages, *Proceedings of the Fall 86 Joint Computer Conference*, pp. 36-39, November 1986.

[Briot 84] Briot, J-P., Instanciation et Héritage dans les Langages Objets, *(thèse de 3ème cycle)*, *LITP Research Report*, No 85-21, LITP - Université Paris-VI, Paris, France, December 1984.

[Clinger 81] Clinger, W.D., Foundations of Actors Semantics, *Phd thesis*, *AI-TR-633*, MIT, Cambridge MA, USA, May 1981.

[Dahl et al. 70] Dahl, O-J., Myhrhaug, B., Nygaard, K., Simula-67 Common Base Language, *SIMULA information*, S-22 Norvegian Computing Center, Oslo, Norway, October 1970.

[Deutsch & Schiffman 84] Deutsch, L.P., Schiffman, A.M., Efficient Implementation of the Smalltalk-80 System, *11th ACM Symposium on POPL*, pp. 297-302, Salt Lake City UT, USA, Jan 1984.

[Fahlman 79] Fahlman, S.E., NETL: A System for Representing and Using Real-World Knowledge, MIT Press, Cambridge MA, USA, 1979.

[Hailpern 86] Hailpern, B., Object-based Inheritance, *(position paper)*, *OOPSLA'86*, Portland OR, USA, November 1986.

[Hewitt 76] Hewitt, C.E., Viewing Control Structures as Patterns of Message Passing, *AI Memo*, No 410, MIT, Cambridge MA, USA, December 1976.

[Ingalls 78] Ingalls, D.H., The Smalltalk-76 Programming System Design and Implementation, *5th ACM Symposium on POPL*, pp. 9-15, Tucson AR, USA, January 1978.

[Kahn et al. 86] Kahn, K., Dean Tribble, E., Miller, M.S., Bobrow, D.G., Objects in Concurrent Logic Programming Languages, *OOPSLA'86*, Special Issue of SIGPLAN Notices, Vol. 21, No 11, pp. 242-257, Portland OR, USA, November 1986.

[Lieberman 81] Lieberman, H., A Preview of Act1, *AI Memo*, No. 625, MIT, Cambridge MA, USA, June 1981.

[Lieberman 83] Lieberman, H., An Object-Oriented Simulator for the Apiary, *Proceedings of the AAAI-83*, pp. 104-108, Washington DC, USA, August 1983.

[Lieberman 86a] Lieberman, H., Delegation and Inheritance - Two Mechanisms for Sharing Knowledge in Object-Oriented Systems, *3rd AFCET Workshop on Object-Oriented Programming*, J. Bezivin and P. Cointe (ed.), Globule+Bigre, No 48, pp. 79-89, Paris, France, January 1986.

[Lieberman 86b] Lieberman, H., Using Prototypical Objects to Implement Shared Behavior in Object Oriented Systems, *OOPSLA'86*, Special Issue of SIGPLAN Notices, Vol. 21, No 11, pp. 214-223, Portland OR, USA, November 1986.

[Moon & Weinreb 80] Moon, D.A., Weinreb, D., Flavors: Message Passing In The Lisp Machine, *AI Memo*, No. 602, MIT, Cambridge MA, USA, November 1980.

[Nguyen & Hailpern 86] Nguyen, V., Hailpern, B., A Generalized Object Model, *Proceedings of the Object-Oriented Workshop*, SIGPLAN Notices, Vol. 21, No 10, pp. 78-87, Yorktown Heights NY, USA, June 1986.

[Roberts & Goldstein 77] Roberts, R.B., Goldstein, I.P., The FRL Manual, *AI Memo*, No. 409, MIT, Cambridge MA, USA, 1977.

[Shapiro & Takeuchi 83] Shapiro, E., Takeuchi, A., Object Oriented Programming in Concurrent Prolog, *New Generation Computing*, Vol. 1, No 1, pp. 25-48, Ohmsha, Tokyo, Japan - Springer-Verlag, Berlin, West Germany, 1983.

[Touretzky 86] Touretzky, D.S., The Mathematics of Inheritance Systems, *Research Notes in Artificial Intelligence*, Pitman, London, UK - Morgan Kaufman, Los Altos CA, USA, 1986.

[Yonezawa 83] Yonezawa, A., On Object-Oriented Programming, *Computer Software*, Vol. 1, No 1, Iwanami Publisher, Japan, April 1983.

[Yonezawa et al. 86] Yonezawa, A., Briot, J-P., Shibayama, E., Object-Oriented Concurrent Programming in ABCL/1, *OOPSLA'86*, Special Issue of SIGPLAN Notices, Vol. 21, No 11, pp. 258-268, Portland OR, USA, November 1986.

[Yonezawa & Tokoro 87] Yonezawa, A., Tokoro, M., (ed.), Object-Oriented Concurrent Programming, MIT Press, Cambridge MA, USA, May 1987.

On Including Part Hierarchies in Object-Oriented Languages, with an Implementation in Smalltalk.

Edwin Blake & Steve Cook

Department of Computer Science, Queen Mary College,
London University, Mile End Road, London, E1 4NS.
Email: edwin@qmc-cs.UUCP

§1. Introduction.

In very many situations we consider objects to be constructed from parts. The parts in their turn may consist of smaller, simpler parts. And so forth. In engineering design we speak of assemblies and subassemblies; in science we describe things in terms of their components. However, when we want to model objects consisting of parts in Smalltalk, and many other object-oriented languages, we are confronted with a dilemma: either sacrifice the data encapsulation properties of the language or utterly flatten the whole-part hierarchy.

In this paper we describe what a part hierarchy is and why it is so important (§1.1). We then show how many object-oriented languages fail to provide this hierarchy (§1.2). After reviewing previous work (§1.3) we sketch how we added the structure to the Smalltalk (§2). The simple implementation details are outlined in an appendix. We discuss where in our experience the part hierarchy was useful and where it fails (§3). Lastly we stand back and examine the broader implications of adding a part hierarchy, and how a part hierarchy interacts with a single and multiple inheritance class hierarchy (§4).

It may roughly be said, to give a taste of the conclusions, that parts and wholes address a different dimension of generalization from that addressed by classes. Classes, like sets, provide a partial ordering structure which can be read as "is-a-kind-of" or "belongs-to", while parts and wholes provide a much more complicated "is-a-part-which-fits- there" structure.

1.1 What is meant by a Part Hierarchy and Why is it Important?

Things are often described in terms of parts and wholes; the way the division into parts is made depends on the purpose of the analysis. A part is a part by virtue of its being included in a larger whole. A part can become a whole in itself, which can then be split into further parts. In this way we build up a hierarchy of parts and wholes, which we have called the *part hierarchy*. Rather than attempt a formal description of part-whole relations [Smith, 1982] we shall present a series of illustrative examples.

We distinguish between a mere *collection,* or additive whole, or heap, (e.g., a bag of marbles, a pile of electronic components) and a more *structured whole* (e.g., an animal, a wired-up electronic circuit). To the former we apply set theory, to the latter a part hierarchy.

It is also useful to distinguish between extensive *parts* — components, fragments, constituents, pieces — and non-extensive *attributes* — features, aspects, moments. For example: a table is made up out of a flat top and four identical legs placed in the corners; these are the parts. A table also has a colour, which is an attribute rather than a part. We shall be more concerned with parts than attributes.

Part-whole analysis is crucial to science and technology. Pirsig [1974] provides a very good example of the hierarchical description of the assemblies and subassemblies used in engineering:

> A motorcycle may be divided for purposes of classical rational analysis by means of its component assemblies and by means of its functions.

If divided by means of its component assemblies, its most basic division is into a power assembly and a running assembly.

The power assembly may be divided into the engine and the power-delivery system. The engine will be taken up first.

The engine consists of a housing containing a power train, a fuel-air system, an ignition system, a feedback system and a lubrication system.

The power train consists of cylinders, pistons, connecting rods, a crankshaft and a flywheel.

The ignition system consists of an alternator, a rectifier, a battery, a high-voltage coil and spark plugs. ... etc.

That's a motorcycle divided according to its components. To know what the components are for, a division according to functions is necessary ...

Parts are also met in the those branches of computation where physical objects are represented, for example, *model-based computer vision* and *computer graphics*. We shall be testing our implementation with an example which straddles these two fields: a stick figure [Marr & Nishihara, 1978] (see figure 1). The particular stick figure we shall discuss, called "joe", has numerous parts arranged hierarchically. For example, joe's legs have feet which have toes, and toes consist of phalanges.

Model-based vision draws upon the work on knowledge representation in artificial intelligence [e.g., Brooks 1981]. *Frame-based* representation [Fikes & Kehler 1985] has similarities to the object-oriented approach. Frames describe parts and attributes by means of *slots*.

One of the standard texts on computer graphics [Foley & van Dam 1982] devotes a chapter to "Modelling and the Object Hierarchy". The proposed new graphics standard PHIGS (Programmer's Hierarchical Interactive Graphics System) [1986] organizes objects in a structure hierarchy. Both *structure hierarchy* and *object hierarchy,* as used above, are synonyms for our part hierarchy.

PHIGS also has the novel concept of *inheritance* on a part hierarchy where attributes of the whole are inherited by the parts. E.g., the legs of the table could inherit the colour of the whole. The requirement is not quite as general as it at first appears. This "inheritance" is only used when the whole structure is traversed from the root down in order to display it, thus the wholes are always accessed before the parts and the attributes can therefore be stacked.

We adopt the policy that information is stored in the part hierarchy at its corresponding logical level: information about the whole is not stored in the parts, information about the parts which is not modified by the whole remains with the parts. Ideally the whole knows the parts but the parts do not know of the whole.

1.2 The Dilemma Posed by Parts in Object-Oriented Languages.

Data abstraction is a fundamental aspect of object-oriented languages. Data abstraction can be summarized as meaning explicit interface protocols and a hidden local state. When an object is assembled from its parts these parts are no longer independent. A part belongs to the local state of the whole and the interface is mediated by the owner.

If this requirement is strictly interpreted the existence of the parts should become invisible to the users of the whole. The whole protocol which a part understands, some of which it may implement perfectly adequately, will have to be reimplemented as the protocol of the whole. The net result is that the part hierarchy is replaced by a single monolithic whole as far as the external world is concerned.

On the other hand, if we did not include parts in the local state of the whole, external users could explicitly request the part and then modify it. The resulting changes could violate the integrity of the whole. The response of a part would also be independent of its position in the whole.

This is the dilemma. We would like the parts to remain visible, while at the same time access is mediated by the owner.

1.2.1 An Example of the Dilemma in Smalltalk.

Parts can be identified with a particular kind of instance variable, that can be accessed via messages to read and assign the parts. In standard Smalltalk the parts can be accessed by putting together the message selectors of the various parts.

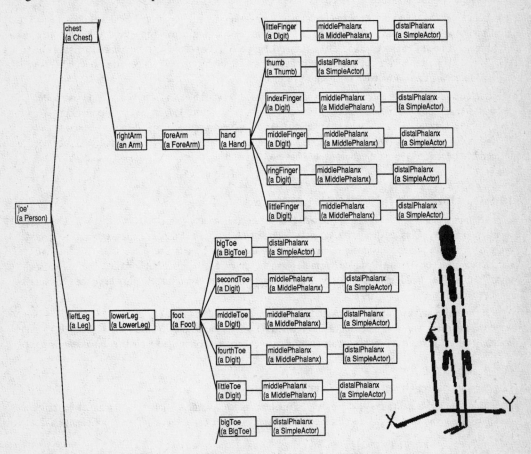

Figure 1. The part hierarchy for a stick figure implemented in Smalltalk. The boxes contain the name of the part and the default class to which it belongs. The figure itself is rendered on the right (without fingers and toes).

In our example of a stick figure (figure 1) we define the following classes:

Person with instance variables: chest, leftLeg, etc.
Foot has instance variables: bigToe, secondToe etc..

then:

> joe ← Person new.   "Create an instance of Person called 'joe'"
> joe leftLeg.   "Return contents of the left leg instance variable."
> joe leftLeg lowerLeg foot.   "Return the left foot."
> joe leftLeg lowerLeg foot bigToe wiggle.   "Wiggle left big toe."

This standard syntax has the disadvantage that the actual instance variable objects themselves are handed out and the sender of the message can modify them at will. This subverts the idea that objects can hide and control their local state.

The alternative is to disallow the direct part access messages; but then the top level object needs to implement the whole message protocol for all its parts. For example, to wiggle the left big toe the class Person would need a message like 'leftLegLowerLegFootBigToeWiggle' in its instance message protocol. This collapsed message completely flattens the part hierarchy and so removes the conceptual advantages of factoring that knowledge in an intuitive manner.

One could attempt to intermix direct access to instance variables in "safe" cases, and use collapsed messages (e.g., leftLegLowerLegFoot) when access must be controlled, in an *ad hoc* manner. This is really worse, because the external world needs to know when to send collapsed messages and when not. If 'joe' in our example above, gets his foot encased in plaster then a collapsed message would be needed instead of direct access and all callers would have to know this.

1.2.2 Class Hierarchies Do Not Provide Part Hierarchies.

Neither single nor multiple class inheritance seem to have any bearing on the part-whole dilemma mentioned above. Classes deal with specializations of objects. In single inheritance we have a partial ordering which provides the same structure as can be expressed by sets and subsets. Even with multiple inheritance only one set of instance variables can be inherited for each superclass. Thus, even if the class "Table" inherited legs four times over along different paths, it would still only have the characteristics of one leg.

If multiple inheritance were extended so that the instance variable data were somehow kept separate, the parts would still be defined at the same level as the whole. That is, the same object would contain both the complete part protocols and the protocols corresponding to their structured interaction.

1.3 Parts in Object-Oriented Programming.

The standard Smalltalk system provides for objects to have dependants. The normal operation is that parts are given backpointers to their owners, and the owner can then be informed of changes. However:

- Parts have to know which changes are significant to the owner. (i.e., high level knowledge at lower levels).

- If parts forward all changes indiscriminately to the owner object then the owner must again contain the equivalent of the protocols of all the parts.

- It creates circular structures, with attendant maintenance problems.

This system of storing knowledge of the whole in a part which is then handed out, is useful where the part hierarchy is shallow and where it is simpler to hand out parts to the external world. An example of such a "part" is the *model* in the Smalltalk model-view-controller mechanism.

Part-whole relations are not often catered for in object-oriented languages: Loops' *composite objects* [Stefik & Bobrow, 1985] being one of the few examples. ThingLab [Borning 1979, 1981] is a

Smalltalk based system for simulating physical objects (e.g., geometric shapes, bridges, electrical circuits, documents, calculators). In ThingLab, objects consist of parts. The major contribution is a system for representing and satisfying constraints which exist between the parts. Multiple class inheritance hierarchies, and *part-whole hierarchies* are used to describe the objects and their interrelations. Parts are referred to symbolically by means of *paths* that name the nodes to be visited in proceeding down the part hierarchy. Our work extracts, analyses, and refines the concept of a part hierarchy first encountered in ThingLab and draws a clearer distinction between class hierarchies and part hierarchies.

1.3.1 Prototypes and Delegation.

As will be seen in section 2, our *implementation* of a part hierarchy makes use of message forwarding. Message forwarding is a powerful general notion which can also be used to implement delegation, which has long been used in actor languages in preference to the notion of class [Agha 1986]. This means that an object's message protocol includes those messages which can be delegated to prototypes or exemplars [Borning 1986; Lieberman 1986; LaLonde, Thomas & Pugh 1986]. For example, if we were modelling horses, the Platonic ideal horse would be a prototype and a particular nag in the field would delegate the responses to some of its messages to that ideal horse.

It is in this sense that multiple inheritance was implemented by means of parts in ThingLab. This creates a rather blurred distinction between a part hierarchy and a class hierarchy which we want to avoid in this paper. The notion of class is retained, as is the possibility of multiple class inheritance.

§2. A Mechanism for Modelling Objects with Parts.

We have given a concrete example of incorporating parts using standard Smalltalk (§1.2.1). This provides the motivation for making a small change to the standard syntax (§2.1) which does allow a full part hierarchy to coexist with data encapsulation. The implementation of the extended language (§2.2) is achieved by a rather simple modification to the standard system.

For the rest of this section we shall be concerned with Smalltalk, but many of the remarks will apply to other object-oriented languages.

2.1 A Syntax and Semantics for Manipulating Parts in Smalltalk.

We want to recognize that parts are objects in their own right — active first class objects. But *without violating the principle of encapsulation*. A whole is allowed to hide its parts, even pretend it has parts which do not in fact exist as such. The whole has additional properties arising from the interaction of the parts, which should not be stored in the parts.

Our solution uses the notion of censored access. The whole forwards messages, possibly censored, to parts, and returns answers, also possibly censored, from parts. This necessitates a new kind of message selector: a *compound message selector* and a new concept: *message forwarding* of possibly censored messages.

Let us call the message selectors of standard Smalltalk simple selectors, whether they be unary, binary or keyword selectors. A compound selector is then a <path>+"."+<simple-selector>. The path is a series of one or more part names also separated by full stops ("."). Part names always begin with a lower case letter. The first part name in a path (its head, if it were a list) is called the prefix. A path provides a way of referring to a part further down the part hierarchy.

Our example (§1.2.1) then becomes:

        joe leftLeg. "Return the left leg instance variable."
        joe leftLeg.foot.bigToe. "Return the left toe."
        joe leftLeg.foot.bigToe.wiggle. "Wiggle left big toe."

The semantics associated with the construct is one of message forwarding. Either a class understands a full compound message selector or it does not. If it does then the method corresponding to the compound selector is executed and the result returned; this may involve sending a censored version of the message to the part.

If the compound message is not part of the protocol of the object then the prefix is stripped off. The rest of the (possibly compound) message is forwarded to the instance variable named by the prefix. In that case the answer to the forwarded message is also the answer to the compound message as a whole. This definition is clearly recursive.

If the Smalltalk convention of *private* messages is accepted as providing adequately strict encapsulation, then parts can always be accessed by means of automatically generated private messages. The message is then forwarded not to an instance variable, but to the *answer* returned by sending a part access message. This means that the parts need not necessarily be instance variables. They can be generated as and when needed. This could provide multiple views of the same object without storing all versions explicitly. This further extends the principle of information hiding.

2.3 Implementing the Part Hierarchy (see also appendix).

To implement the part hierarchy the following changes are needed:

1)   Change the compiler to allow compound messages.

2)   Extend the message selector class (Symbol) to provide access to the various parts of the compound messages.

3)   Implement the mechanism for forwarding messages to parts.

4)   (Optional) Add a class initialization method to add private messages automatically to access all parts.

The extended Smalltalk with multiple inheritance [Borning and Ingalls, 1982] is widely distributed. This provides (1) and most of (2) above, while (4) is an elementary exercise.

It is (3) which is the heart of the system. It uses a powerful general mechanism: message forwarding. When a compound message is initially sent it is only understood if the object needs control over that aspect of its part structure which the message accesses. If the compound message is not understood then the part named by the message prefix can safely handle the message. A method is then compiled just to forward the message. If the same message is sent again the code already exists and the message will be understood.

The forwarding of messages can be overridden in a completely natural way if it is later decided that an object *does* need control over that aspect of its parts. The controlling method is simply added with the compound selector which names the part, and it replaces the forwarder.

§3. Experience with Using the Part Hierarchy.

The importance of a part hierarchy in computer graphics and vision has been mentioned in the introduction, as was the example of a stick figure. The part hierarchy described the structured figure rather well (§3.1) but it is not designed for a collection of stick figures (§3.2).

3.1 Results from Modelling a Single Stick Figure.

A moving stick figure and camera was implemented using the part hierarchy defined above. The following points arose from this experiment:

1) Parts are compatible with the existing multiple inheritance implementation.

2) For deep hierarchies the message selectors become rather lengthy.

3) Some, more or less elaborate, form of typing is required for the parts of an object.

4) The class inheritance hierarchy can interact in unexpected ways with the part hierarchy.

The second point means we might require some more syntactic sugar by way of abbreviations. In the case of parts which are common to a number of subclasses it is, at present, possible to define an abbreviation explicitly in the superclass. For example, all limbs of the stick figure have a proximal joint which implements the local coordinates. A common message to the proximal joint is to alter its orientation, thus the superclass of limbs implemented the abbreviation "orientation:" for the compound message "proximalJoint.orientation:".

The third point, concerning typing, uncovers an active area of current research, which is beyond the scope of this paper. The need for an instance variable type arises when a new object is created and its parts have to be instantiated. In order to instantiate the parts their classes have to be known. This can be coded as an initialization message to the new instance, but a more general solution is to associate a default class with each instance variable. When a new object is then created, the creation message is also forwarded to these classes in order to create the parts.

The fourth point concerns the interaction between the class inheritance hierarchy and the part (or modelling) hierarchy. Message forwarders are treated as normal methods, they apply to a whole class and are inherited by subclasses. This means that all instances in the same class are forced to have the same relationship to their subparts. Another problem arises when message forwarders are created in the class of the receiver of the compound message and not in the (super) class where the instance variable is actually defined. If the superclass is then modified to intercept the compound message it will have no effect in those subclasses which have already acquired message forwarders. In our implementation this problem was alleviated by making message forwarders visible to the user in a special category of message. A fairly effective solution to this problem would be to place the message forwarder in the method dictionary of the highest class in the hierarchy which possesses the relevant instance variable, rather than in the method dictionary of the original recipient of the compound message.

3.2 Elements of a Collection are not Parts.

In our experimental implementation of stick figures the one situation where the part hierarchy was at a distinct disadvantage was with collections of stick figures. This is perhaps not too surprising since wholes are meant to be more structured than sets. The collection itself has an associated coordinate system in which the figures are embedded, it may even have a graphical appearance. Thus the collection is a kind of "Actor", and is in some ways a whole just like a single stick figure.

The problem with using parts is two fold:

- The representation of a variable number of parts is rather difficult.

- The requirement that parts have explicit names, otherwise such an advantage, is here a liability. Objects in a collection are nameless, or at least their names change.

Representing a variable number of parts can be achieved in a number of more or less messy ways: a class for each cardinal number, allowance for empty part slots, or having indexed anonymous parts. All these options were attempted but had to be rejected. If classes are dispensed with and prototypes used instead, some of these objections might be met. Each particular collection with a fixed number of elements could perhaps have its own part access messages.

However, an appropriate solution is provided by multiple inheritance of both a *Collection* to provide access to the objects and a basic class of figure *(Actor)* to convey the appearance and position of the collection. This was the strategy adopted. The individuals in the collection were accessed with the normal messages used on collections.

§4. Implications of the Part Hierarchy for Object-Oriented Languages.

At this stage of the paper we have established the general importance of part hierarchies in natural philosophy and engineering. We have shown how a simple extension of Smalltalk can provide, fairly elegantly, a part hierarchy mechanism. This mechanism has been illustrated and criticized by means of examples drawn from three-dimensional modelling. We are now going to characterize the results of this effort.

4.1 Part Hierarchies and Class Inheritance Hierarchies.

When it comes to a single inheritance language, the question is really how orthogonal the concepts of part hierarchy and class hierarchy are. That the *implementations* can have mutual dependencies has already been seen.

The class hierarchy can be taken to express an "IS-A" relation [Brachman, 1983]. Thus an integer IS-A number. More specifically in our view, if the inheritance hierarchy is anything more than an implementation tool then it exemplifies the "IS-A-KIND-OF" relation: integer IS-A-KIND-OF number. The part hierarchy on the other hand expresses an "IS-A-PART-OF" relation, or more accurately since the part does not know its owner it expresses the reversed "HAS-A-PART" relation.

If we adopt this view then the two concepts are orthogonal. The class hierarchy provides generalization and specialization, this has nothing to do with structured building up of objects from parts, except that general objects may sometimes have fewer parts than their specialized subclasses.

It has already been said that delegation provides an inheritance mechanism. Message forwarding, which we use to access parts, can be used for delegation. Therefore message forwarding can be used to implement multiple inheritance [Borning, 1986]. If we retain the notion of class (or maintain a distinction between prototypes and other objects), then we can regard this as an implementation issue and not a fundamental relation.

Multiple inheritance is preferred when objects are unstructured collections. When objects have a fixed structure, or when parts are subservient to the emergent properties of the whole, then a part hierarchy is better. A part hierarchy is thus a valuable extension to both single and multiple inheritance object-oriented languages.

4.2 Part Hierarchies and Encapsulation.

At first sight it might appear that part hierarchies violate the principle of data encapsulation and information hiding, because they provide access to the parts of an object. In our view the opposite is actually the case. Part Hierarchies provide better control over access to the parts than is found in many object-oriented languages.

It is true that the internal structure of the object is made visible. But this is strictly mediated by messages. These messages allow full control and even allow the whole to pretend it has parts, by providing messages which mimic the behaviour of parts without actually implementing them explicitly.

The need to see structure of an object is similar to the need for "grey-boxes" rather than "black-boxes" in engineering. Depending on the level at which we are designing we need more or less of the structure of our wholes to be visible.

§5. Conclusion.

Part hierarchies have been incorporated in object-oriented languages in a way which strengthens the data abstraction properties of these languages. Such part hierarchies are most useful in simulation, where we are concerned with structured physical objects.

Part hierarchies provide facilities not provided by class hierarchies. This is because class hierarchies provide less structure than part hierarchies, they provide the structure of sets, and sets contain no notion of relative position or multiplicity. Part hierarchies are less useful for describing sets and collections and multiple inheritance may be needed to deal with these. Part hierarchies can be regarded as being an orthogonal notion to class inheritance hierarchies.

5.1 Further work: Multiple Views.

Part hierarchies can implement multiple representations of knowledge without requiring there to be an independent object for each representation. For example: consider a point defined in either Cartesian coordinates or in polar coordinates. If we wish to implement both views then the polar coordinates can always be calculated from the Cartesian coordinates, even though no such "parts" are actually stored [Borning, 1979, "virtual parts"].

Multiple views are used in certain kinds of knowledge representation. Philosophers [e.g., Pirsig 1974] emphasize that the division into parts is arbitrary and depends on the purpose of the analysis. It does seem that a small number of alternate views (e.g., polar vs. Cartesian coordinates) can be accommodated, but whether it is a general extensible mechanism requires further investigation.

Appendix: Implementing a Part Hierarchy in Smalltalk.

We assume that the Smalltalk has been extended allow multiple inheritance [Borning & Ingalls, 1982]. This provides the changes to the parser which allows compound messages and the basic modification to the class Object's instance method for the message "doesNotUnderstand:". This sends a message to the class of the receiver with the selector "tryCopyingCodeFor:".

The class method "tryCopyingCodeFor:" is the one we override in the super (meta) class of all objects which are to have parts. If the message sent was not compound or was sent as part of the multiple inheritance implementation we treat it as before. If it is a compound selector and the prefix starts with a lower case letter (excluding "super" and "all") we compile a message forwarder.

The message forwarder is simply a method which has as selector the complete compound message with all the keywords and arguments. The method sends the prefix to self and then the rest of the compound message. The answer of the method is that result. For example:

To forward:
    joe leftLeg.lowerLeg.foot
the method is:
    ↑self leftLeg lowerLeg.foot

These methods are synthesized and compiled without saving the source code by using the class message "compileUnchecked:". They are classified as 'message forwarders' for access in the browser. It is not essential for message forwarders to be visible in the browser, but if they are not it can make the behaviour of programs rather non-obvious to the programmer. The appropriate class messages are "organization classify:under:".

The remaining class methods are equally simple. These are methods to compile code to access parts (instance variables) by name automatically. In this case it is useful to save the source code, since fast compilation is no longer important. A dictionary which associates instance variable names with default classes should also be created and stored as a class variable. This dictionary can be used when parts belonging to a whole have to be instantiated.

References.

Agha, G. (1986) *SIGPLAN Notices* **21,** 10 58-67. "An overview of actor languages."

Borning, A.H. (1979) *ThingLab: A constraint-oriented simulation laboratory. Xerox Palo Alto Research Center report SSL-79-3,* **a revised version of** Stanford University PhD. thesis, Stanford Computer Science Department Report STAN-CS-79-746.

Borning, A.H. (1981) *ACM trans. Programming Languages and Systems* **3,** 4 353-387. "The programming language aspects of ThingLab, a constraint-oriented simulation laboratory."

Borning, A.H. (1986) *IEEE/ACM Fall Joint Computer Conf., Dallas, Texas,* Nov 1986. pp. 36-40 "Classes versus prototypes in object-oriented languages."

Borning, A.H. & Ingalls, D.H.H. (1982) *Proc. Nat. Conf. Artificial Intelligence, Pittsburgh, PA.* pp. 234-237. "Multiple inheritance in Smalltalk-80."

Brachman, R.J. (1983) *Computer* **16,** 10 30-36. "What IS-A is and isn't: an analysis of taxonomic links in semantic networks."

Brooks, R.A. (1981) *Artificial Intelligence* **17** 285-348. "Symbolic reasoning among 3-D models and 2-D images."

Fikes, R. & Kehler, T. (1985) *Comm. ACM* **28** 904-920. "The role of frame-based representation in reasoning."

Foley, J.D. & van Dam, A. (1982) *Fundamentals of Interactive Computer Graphics.* Addison-Wesley. Reading, Massachusetts.

LaLonde, W.R., Thomas, D.A. & Pugh, J.R. (1986) *OOPSLA'86: SIGPLAN Notices* **21,** 11 322-330. "An exemplar based Smalltalk."

Lieberman, H. (1986) *OOPSLA'86: SIGPLAN Notices* **21,** 11 214-223. "Using prototypical objects to implement shared behavior in object- oriented systems."

Marr, D. & Nishihara, H.K. (1978) *Proc.R.Soc.Lond. B* **200** 269-294. "Representation and recognition of the spatial organization of three- dimensional shapes."

Moon, D.A. (1986) *OOPSLA'86: SIGPLAN Notices* **21,** 11 1-8. "Object-oriented programming with Flavors."

PHIGS (1986) *Programmer's Hierarchical Interactive Graphics System.* ISO PHIGS revised working draft, 13 June 1986.

Pirsig, R.M. (1974) *Zen and the art of motorcycle maintenance: An enquiry into values.* The Bodley Head.

Smith, B. (1982) *Parts and Moments. Studies in Logic and Formal Ontology.* Philosophia Verlag. München.

Stefik, M. & Bobrow, D.G. (1985) *The AI Magazine.* **6,** 4 40-62. "Object-oriented programming: themes and variations."

What is "Object-Oriented Programming"?

Bjarne Stroustrup

AT&T Bell Laboratories, Murray Hill, New Jersey 07974, USA

ABSTRACT

"Object-Oriented Programming" and "Data Abstraction" have become very common terms. Unfortunately, few people agree on what they mean. I will offer informal definitions that appear to make sense in the context of languages like Ada, C++, Modula-2, Simula67, and Smalltalk. The general idea is to equate "support for data abstraction" with the ability to define and use new types and equate "support for object-oriented programming" with the ability to express type hierarchies. Features necessary to support these programming styles in a general purpose programming language will be discussed. The presentation centers around C++ but is not limited to facilities provided by that language.

1 Introduction

Not all programming languages can be "object oriented". Yet claims have been made to the effect that APL, Ada, Clu, C++, LOOPS, and Smalltalk are object-oriented programming languages. I have heard discussions of object-oriented design in C, Pascal, Modula-2, and CHILL. Could there somewhere be proponents of object-oriented Fortran and Cobol programming? I think there must be. "Object-oriented" has in many circles become a high-tech synonym for "good", and when you examine discussions in the trade press, you can find arguments that appear to boil down to syllogisms like:

> Ada is good
> Object oriented is good
> -----------------------------------
> Ada is object oriented

This paper presents one view of what "object oriented" ought to mean in the context of a general purpose programming language.

§2 Distinguishes "object-oriented programming" and "data abstraction" from each other and from other styles of programming and presents the mechanisms that are essential for supporting the various styles of programming.

§3 Presents features needed to make data abstraction effective.

§4 Discusses facilities needed to support object-oriented programming.

§5 Presents some limits imposed on data abstraction and object-oriented programming by traditional hardware architectures and operating systems.

Examples will be presented in C++. The reason for this is partly to introduce C++ and partly because C++ is one of the few languages that supports both data abstraction and object-oriented programming in addition to traditional programming techniques. Issues of concurrency and of hardware support for encapsulation are ignored in this paper.

2 Programming Paradigms

Object-oriented programming is a technique for programming – a paradigm for writing "good" programs for a set of problems. If the term "object-oriented programming language" means anything it must mean a programming language that provides mechanisms that support the object-oriented style of programming well.

There is an important distinction here. A language is said to support a style of programming if it provides facilities that makes it convenient (reasonably easy, safe, and efficient) to use that style. A language does not support a technique if it takes exceptional effort or exceptional skill to write such programs. For example, you can write structured programs in Fortran, write type-secure programs in C, and use data abstraction in Modula-2, but it is unnecessarily hard to do because these languages do not support those techniques.

Support for a paradigm comes not only in the obvious form of language facilities that allow direct use of the paradigm, but also in the more subtle form of compile-time and/or run-time checks against unintentional deviation from the paradigm. Type checking is the most obvious example of this; ambiguity detection and run-time checks can be used to extend linguistic support for paradigms. Extra-linguistic facilities such as standard libraries and programming environments can also provide significant support for paradigms.

A language is not necessarily better than another because it possesses a feature the other does not. There are many example to the contrary. The important issue is not so much what features a language possesses but that the features it does possess are sufficient to support the desired programming styles in the desired application areas:

[1] All features must be cleanly and elegantly integrated into the language.

[2] It must be possible to use features in combination to achieve solutions that would otherwise have required extra separate features.

[3] There should be as few spurious and "special purpose" features as possible.

[4] A feature should be such that its implementation does not impose significant overheads on programs that do not require it.

[5] A user need only know about the subset of the language explicitly used to write a program.
The last two principles can be summarized as "what you don't know won't hurt you." If there are any doubts about the usefulness of a feature it is better left out. It is *much* easier to add a feature to a language than to remove or modify one that has found its way into the compilers or the literature.

I will now present some programming styles and the key language mechanisms necessary for supporting them. The presentation of language features is not intended to be exhaustive.

Procedural Programming

The original (and probably still the most commonly used) programming paradigm is:

> *Decide which procedures you want;*
> *use the best algorithms you can find.*

The focus is on the design of the processing, the algorithm needed to perform the desired computation. Languages support this paradigm by facilities for passing arguments to functions and returning values from functions. The literature related to this way of thinking is filled with discussion of ways of passing arguments, ways of distinguishing different kinds of arguments, different kinds of functions (procedures, routines, macros, ...), etc. Fortran is the original procedural language; Algol60, Algol68, C, and Pascal are later inventions in the same tradition.

A typical example of "good style" is a square root function. It neatly produces a result given an argument. To do this, it performs a well understood mathematical computation:

```
double sqrt(double arg)
{
    // the code for calculating a square root
}

void some_function()
{
    double root2 = sqrt(2);
    // ...
}
```

From a program organization point of view, functions are used to create order in a maze of algorithms.

Data Hiding

Over the years, the emphasis in the design of programs has shifted away from the design of procedures towards the organization of data. Among other things, this reflects an increase in the program size. A set of related procedures with the data they manipulate is often called a *module*. The programming paradigm becomes:

> *Decide which modules you want;*
> *partition the program so that data is hidden in modules.*

This paradigm is also known as the "data hiding principle". Where there is no grouping of procedures with related data the procedural programming style suffices. In particular, the techniques for designing "good procedures" are now applied for each procedure in a module. The most common example is a definition of a stack module. The main problems that have to be solved for a good solution are:

[1] Provide a user interface for the stack (for example, functions push( ) and pop( )).

[2] Ensure that the representation of the stack (for example, a vector of elements) can only be accessed through this user interface.

[3] Ensure that the stack is initialized before its first use.

Here is a plausible external interface for a stack module:

```
// declaration of the interface of module stack of characters
char pop();
void push(char);
const stack_size = 100;
```

Assuming that this interface is found in a file called stack.h, the "internals" can be defined like this:

```
#include "stack.h"
static char v[stack_size]; // ``static'' means local to this file/module
static char* p = v;         // the stack is initially empty

char pop()
{
    // check for underflow and pop
}

void push(char c)
{
    // check for overflow and push
}
```

It would be quite feasible to change the representation of this stack to a linked list. A user does not have access to the representation anyway (since v and p were declared static, that is local to the file/module in which they were declared). Such a stack can be used like this:

```
#include "stack.h"

void some_function()
{
    char c = pop(push('c'));
    if (c != 'c') error("impossible");
}
```

Pascal (as originally defined) doesn't provide any satisfactory facilities for such grouping: the only mechanism for hiding a name from "the rest of the program" is to make it local to a procedure. This leads to strange procedure nestings and over-reliance on global data.

C fares somewhat better. As shown in the example above, you can define a "module" by grouping related function and data definitions together in a single source file. The programmer can then control which names are seen by the rest of the program (a name can be seen by the rest of the program *unless* it has been declared static). Consequently, in C you can achieve a degree of modularity. However, there is no generally accepted paradigm for using this facility and the technique of relying on static declarations is rather low level.

One of Pascal's successors, Modula-2, goes a bit further. It formalizes the concept of a module, making it a fundamental language construct with well defined module declarations, explicit control of the scopes of names (import/export), a module initialization mechanism, and a set of generally known and accepted styles of usage.

The differences between C and Modula-2 in this area can be summarized by saying that C only *enables* the decomposition of a program into modules, while Modula-2 *supports* that technique.

Data Abstraction

Programming with modules leads to the centralization of all data of a type under the control of a type manager module. If one wanted two stacks, one would define a stack manager module with an interface like this:

```
class stack_id;  // stack_id is a type
                 // no details about stacks or stack_ids are known here

stack_id create_stack(int size);// make a stack and return its identifier
destroy_stack(stack_id);        // call when stack is no longer needed

void push(stack_id, char);
char pop(stack_id);
```

This is certainly a great improvement over the traditional unstructured mess, but "types" implemented this way are clearly very different from the built-in types in a language. Each type manager module must define a separate mechanism for creating "variables" of its type, there is no established norm for assigning object identifiers, a "variable" of such a type has no name known to the compiler or programming environment, nor do such "variables" do not obey the usual scope rules or argument passing rules.

A type created through a module mechanism is in most important aspects different from a built-in type and enjoys support inferior to the support provided for built-in types. For example:

```
void f()
{
    stack_id s1;
    stack_id s2;
```

```
        s1 = create_stack(200);
        // Oops: forgot to create s2

        char c1 = pop(s1,push(s1,'a'));
        if (c1 != 'c') error("impossible");

        char c2 = pop(s2,push(s2,'a'));
        if (c2 != 'c') error("impossible");

        destroy(s2);
        // Oops: forgot to destroy s1
    }
```

In other words, the module concept that supports the data hiding paradigm enables this style of programming, but it does not support it.

Languages such as Ada, Clu, and C++ attack this problem by allowing a user to define types that behave in (nearly) the same way as built-in types. Such a type is often called an *abstract data type*†. The programming paradigm becomes:

> *Decide which types you want;*
> *provide a full set of operations for each type.*

Where there is no need for more that one object of a type the data hiding programming style using modules suffices. Arithmetic types such as rational and complex numbers are common examples of user-defined types:

```
    class complex {
        double re, im;
    public:
        complex(double r, double i) { re=r; im=i; }
        complex(double r) { re=r; im=0; }    // float->complex conversion

        friend complex operator+(complex, complex);
        friend complex operator-(complex, complex);    // binary minus
        friend complex operator-(complex);             // unary minus
        friend complex operator*(complex, complex);
        friend complex operator/(complex, complex);
        // ...
    }
```

The declaration of class (that is, user-defined type) complex specifies the representation of a complex number and the set of operations on a complex number. The representation is *private*; that is, re and im are accessible only to the functions specified in the declaration of class complex. Such functions can be defined like this:

```
    complex operator+(complex a1, complex a2)
    {
        return complex(a1.re+a2.re, a1.im+a2.im);
    }
```

and used like this:

---

† I prefer the term "user-defined type": "*Those types are not "abstract"; they are as real as* int *and* float." – Doug McIlroy. An alternative definition of *abstract data types* would require a mathematical "abstract" specification of all types (both built-in and user-defined). What is referred to as types in this paper would, given such a specification, be concrete specifications of such truly abstract entities.

```
complex a = 2.3;
complex b = 1/a;
complex c = a+b*complex(1,2.3);
// ...
c = -(a/b)+2;
```

Most, but not all, modules are better expressed as user defined types. For concepts where the "module representation" is desirable even when a proper facility for defining types is available, the programmer can declare a type and only a single object of that type. Alternatively, a language might provide a module concept in addition to and distinct from the class concept.

Problems with Data Abstraction

An abstract data type defines a sort of black box. Once it has been defined, it does not really interact with the rest of the program. There is no way of adapting it to new uses except by modifying its definition. This can lead to severe inflexibility. Consider defining a type shape for use in a graphics system. Assume for the moment that the system has to support circles, triangles, and squares. Assume also that you have some classes:

```
class point{ /* ... */ };
class color{ /* ... */ };
```

You might define a shape like this:

```
enum kind { circle, triangle, square };

class shape {
    point center;
    color col;
    kind k;
    // representation of shape
public:
    point where()      { return center; }
    void move(point to) { center = to; draw(); }
    void draw();
    void rotate(int);
    // more operations
};
```

The "type field" k is necessary to allow operations such as draw( ) and rotate( ) to determine what kind of shape they are dealing with (in a Pascal-like language, one might use a variant record with tag k). The function draw( ) might be defined like this:

```
void shape::draw()
{
    switch (k) {
    case circle:
        // draw a circle
        break;
    case triangle:
        // draw a triangle
        break;
    case square:
        // draw a square
    }
}
```

This is a mess. Functions such as draw( ) must "know about" all the kinds of shapes there are. Therefore the code for any such function grows each time a new shape is added to the system. If you define a new shape, every operation on a shape must be examined and (possibly) modified. You are not able to add a new shape to a system unless you have access to the source code for every operation. Since adding a new shape involves "touching" the code of every important operation on shapes, it requires great skill and potentially introduces bugs into the code handling other (older) shapes. The choice of representation of particular shapes can get severely cramped by the requirement that (at least some of) their representation must fit into the typically fixed sized framework presented by the definition of the general type shape.

Object-Oriented Programming

The problem is that there is no distinction between the general properties of any shape (a shape has a color, it can be drawn, etc.) and the properties of a specific shape (a circle is a shape that has a radius, is drawn by a circle-drawing function, etc.). Expressing this distinction and taking advantage of it defines object-oriented programming. A language with constructs that allows this distinction to be expressed and used supports object-oriented programming. Other languages don't.

The Simula67 inheritance mechanism provides a solution. First, specify a class that defines the general properties of all shapes:

```
class shape {
    point center;
    color col;
    // ...
public:
    point where() { return center; }
    void move(point to) { center = to; draw(); }
    virtual void draw();
    virtual void rotate(int);
    // ...
};
```

The functions for which the calling interface can be defined, but where the implementation cannot be defined except for a specific shape, have been marked "virtual" (the Simula and C++ term for "may be re-defined later in a class derived from this one"). Given this definition, we can write general functions manipulating shapes:

```
void rotate_all(shape* v, int size, int angle)
// rotate all members of vector "v" of size "size" "angle" degrees
{
    for (int i = 0; i < size; i++) v[i].rotate(angle);
}
```

To define a particular shape, we must say that it is a shape (that is, derive it from class shape) and specify its particular properties (including the virtual functions).

```
class circle : public shape {
    int radius;
public:
    void draw() { /* ... */ };
    void rotate(int) {}    // yes, the null function
};
```

The programming paradigm is:

> *Decide which classes you want;*
> *provide a full set of operations for each class;*
> *make commonality explicit by using inheritance.*

Where there is no such commonality data abstraction suffices. The amount of commonality between types that can be exploited by using inheritance and virtual functions is the litmus test of the applicability of object-oriented programming to an application area. In some areas, such as interactive graphics, there is clearly enormous scope for object-oriented programming. For other areas, such as classical arithmetic types and computations based on them, there appears to be hardly any scope for more than data abstraction and the facilities needed for the support of object-oriented programming seem unnecessary.

Finding commonality among types in a system is not a trivial process. The amount of commonality to be exploited is affected by the way the system is designed. When designing a system, commonality must be actively sought, both by designing classes specifically as building blocks for other types, and by examining classes to see if they exhibit similarities that can be exploited in a common base class.

For attempts to explain what object-oriented programming is without recourse to specific programming language constructs see Nygaard[13] and Kerr[9]. For a case study in object-oriented programming see Cargill[4].

3 Support for Data Abstraction

The basic support for programming with data abstraction consists of facilities for defining a set of operations for a type and for restricting the access to objects of the type to that set of operations. Once that is done, however, the programmer soon finds that language refinements are needed for convenient definition and use of the new types. Operator overloading is a good example of this.

Initialization and Cleanup

When the representation of a type is hidden some mechanism must be provided for a user to initialize variables of that type. A simple solution is simply to require a user to call some function to initialize a variable before using it. For example:

```
class vector {
    int  sz;
    int* v;
public:
    void init(int size);    // call init to initialize sz and v
                            // before the first use of a vector
    // ...
};


vector v;
// don't use v here
v.init(10);
// use v here
```

This is error prone and inelegant. A better solution is to allow the designer of a type to provide a distinguished function to do the initialization. Given such a function, allocation and initialization of a variable becomes a single operation (often called instantiation) instead of two separate operations. Such an initialization function is often called a constructor. In cases where construction of objects of a type is non-trivial, one often needs a complementary operation to clean up objects after their last use. In C++, such a cleanup function is called a destructor. Consider a vector type:

```
class vector {
    int  sz;                    // number of elements
    int* v;                     // pointer to integers
public:
    vector(int);                // constructor
    ~vector();                  // destructor
    int& operator[](int index); // subscript operator
};
```

The vector constructor can be defined to allocate space like this:

```
vector::vector(int s)
{
    if (s<=0) error("bad vector size");
    sz = s;
    v = new int[s];    // allocate an array of "s" integers
}
```

The vector destructor frees the storage used:

```
vector::~vector()
{
    delete v;          // deallocate the memory pointed to by v
}
```

C++ does not support garbage collection. This is compensated for, however, by enabling a type to maintain its own storage management without requiring intervention by a user. This is a common use for the constructor/destructor mechanism.

Assignment and Initialization

Controlling construction and destruction of objects is sufficient for many types, but not for all. It can also be necessary to control all copy operations. Consider class vector:

```
vector v1(100);
vector v2 = v1;   // make a new vector v2 initialized to v1
v1 = v2;          // assign v2 to v1
```

It must be possible to define the meaning of the initialization of v2 and the assignment to v1. Alternatively it should be possible to prohibit such copy operations; preferably both alternatives should be available. For example:

```
class vector {
    int* v;
    int  sz;
public:
    // ...
    void operator=(vector&);   // assignment
    vector(vector&);           // initialization
};
```

specifies that user-defined operations should be used to interpret vector assignment and initialization. Assignment might be defined like this:

```
vector::operator=(vector& a) // check size and copy elements
{
    if (sz != a.sz) error("bad vector size for =");
    for (int i = 0; i<sz; i++) v[i] = a.v[i];
}
```

Since the assignment operation relies on the "old value" of the vector being assigned to, the initialization operation *must* be different. For example:

```
vector::vector(vector& a)    // initialize a vector from another vector
{
    sz = a.sz;               // same size
    v = new int[sz];         // allocate element array
    for (int i = 0; i<sz; i++) v[i] = a.v[i];    // copy elements
}
```

In C++, a constructor of the form X(X&) defines all initialization of objects of type X with another object of type X. In addition to explicit initialization constructors of the form X(X&) are used to handle arguments passed "by value" and function return values.

Ada does not support constructors, destructors, overloading of assignment, or user-defined control of argument passing and function return. This severely limits the class of types that can be defined and forces the programmer back to "data hiding techniques"; that is, the user must design and use type manager modules rather than proper types.

Parameterized Types

Why would you want to define a vector of integers anyway? A user typically needs a vector of elements of some type unknown to the writer of the `vector` type. Consequently the vector type ought to be expressed in such a way that it takes the element type as an argument:

```
class vector(typedef T) {        // vector of elements of type T
    T* v;
    int sz;
public:
    vector(int s)
    {
        if (s <= 0) error("bad vector size");
        v = new T[sz = s];        // allocate an array of "s" "T"s
    }
    T& operator[](int i);
    int size() { return sz; }
    // ...
};
```

Vectors of specific types can now be defined and used:

```
vector(int) v1(100);        // v1 is a vector of 100 integers
vector(complex) v2(200);    // v2 is a vector of 200 complex numbers

v2[i] = complex(v1[x],v1[y]);
```

Ada, Clu, and ML support parameterized types. C++ does not; the syntax used here is simply devised as an illustration. Where needed, parameterized classes are "faked" using macros. Parameterized classes would clearly be extremely useful in C++. They could easily be handled by the compiler, but the current C++ programming environment is not sophisticated enough to support them without significant overhead and/or inconvenience. There need not be any run-time overheads compared with a type specified directly.

Typically a parameterized type will have to depend on at least some aspect of a type parameter. For example, some of the vector operations must assume that assignment is defined for objects of the parameter type. How can one ensure that? One solution to this problem is to require the designer of the parameterized class to state the dependency. For example, "T must be a type for which = is defined". A better solution is not to; a compiler can detect a "missing operation" if it is applied and give an error message such as. For example:

```
cannot define vector(non_copy)::operator[](non_copy&):
        type non_copy does not have operator=
```

This technique allows the definition of types where the dependency on attributes of a parameter type is handled at the level of the individual operation of the type. For example, one might define a vector with a sort operation. The sort operation might use <, ==, and = on objects of the parameter type. It would still be possible to define vectors of a type for which '<' was not defined as long as the vector sorting operation was not actually invoked.

A problem with parameterized types is that each instantiation creates an independent type. For example, the type `vector(char)` is unrelated to the type `vector(complex)`. Ideally one would like to be able to express and utilize the commonality of types generated from the same parameterized type. For example, both `vector(char)` and `vector(complex)` have a `size()` function that is independent of the parameter type. It is possible, but not trivial, to deduce this from the definition of class `vector` and then allow `size()` to be applied to any vector. An interpreted language or a language supporting both parameterized types and inheritance would have an advantage here.

Exceptions

As programs grow, and especially when libraries are used extensively, standards for handling errors (or more generally: "exceptional circumstances") become important. Ada, Algol68, and Clu each support a standard way of handling exceptions. Unfortunately, C++ does not. Where needed exceptions are "faked" using pointers to functions, "exception objects", "error states", and the C library `signal` and `longjmp` facilities. This is not satisfactory in general and fails even to provide a standard framework for error handling.

Consider again the `vector` example. What *ought* to be done when an out of range index value is passed to the subscript operator? The designer of the `vector` class should provide a default behavior to handle this case. For example:

```
exception vector_range
/*
    define an exception called vector_range
    and specify default code for handling it
*/
{
    error("global: vector range error");
    exit(99);
}
```

Instead of calling an error function, `vector::operator[]()` can invoke the exception handling code, "raise the exception":

```
int& vector::operator[](int i)
{
    if (0<i || sz<=i) raise vector_range;
    return v[i];
}
```

This will cause the call stack to be unraveled until an exception handler for `vector_range` is found; this handler will than be executed.

Any function may specify its own code for handling the `vector_range` exception. A definition of an exception may be understood as a statement redefining it for the duration of the dynamic scope in which it is defined. For example:

```
void f() {
    vector v(10);
    exception vector_range {
        error("f(): vector range error");
        return;
    }
    // ...
    int i = g();    // g might cause a range error using some vector
    v[i] = 7;       // potential range error

}
```

There are many ways of defining exceptions and the behavior of exception handlers. The facility sketched here has deliberately been kept minimal, but flexible. A local exception handler does not establish a separate scope so the `return` is a return from the enclosing function `f()` not just from the exception handling code. The position of the exception declaration is considered significant so the `vector_range` code can access `v` but not `i`. This style of exception handling can be implemented so that code is not executed unless an exception is raised†.

---

† except possibly for some initialization code at the start of a program.

Could exceptions, as defined above, be completely "faked" in a language such as C++? Unfortunately, no. The snag is that when an exception occurs, the run-time stack must be unraveled up to a point where a handler is defined. To do this properly in C++ involves invoking destructors defined in the scopes involved. This is not done by a C longjmp and cannot in general be done by the user.

Coercions

User-defined coercions, such as the one from floating point numbers to complex numbers implied by the constructor complex(double), have proven unexpectedly useful in C++. Such coercions can be applied explicitly or the programmer can rely on the compiler to add them implicitly where necessary and unambiguous:

```
complex a = complex(1);
complex b = 1;              // implicit: 1 -> complex(1)
a = b+complex(2);
a = b+2;                    // implicit: 2 -> complex(2)
```

Coercions were introduced into C++ because mixed mode arithmetic is the norm in languages for numerical work and because most user-defined types used for "calculation" (for example, matrices, character strings, and machine addresses) have natural mappings to and/or from other types.

One use of coercions has proven especially useful from a program organization point of view:

```
complex a = 2;
complex b = a+2;   // interpreted as operator+(a,complex(2))
b = 2+a;           // interpreted as operator+(complex(2),a)
```

Only one function is needed to interpret "+" operations and the two operands are handled identically by the type system. Furthermore, class complex is written without any need to modify the concept of integers to enable the smooth and natural integration of the two concepts. This is in contrast to a "pure object-oriented system" where the operations would be interpreted like this:

```
a+2;    // a.operator+(2)
2+a;    // 2.operator+(a)
```

making it necessary to modify class integer to make 2+a legal. Modifying existing code should be avoided as far as possible when adding new facilities to a system. Typically, object-oriented programming offers superior facilities for adding to a system without modifying existing code. In this case, however, data abstraction facilities provide a better solution.

Iterators

It has been claimed that a language supporting data abstraction must provide a way of defining control structures[11]. In particular, a mechanism that allows a user to define a loop over the elements of some type containing elements is often needed. This must be achieved without forcing a user to depend on details of the implementation of the user-defined type. Given a sufficiently powerful mechanism for defining new types and the ability to overload operators, this can be handled without a separate mechanism for defining control structures.

For a vector, defining an iterator is not necessary since an ordering is available to a user through the indices. I'll define one anyway to demonstrate the technique. There are several possible styles of iterators. My favorite relies on overloading the function application operator ( )†:

---

† This style also relies on the existence of a distinguished value to represent "end of iteration". Often, in particular for C++ pointer types, 0 can be used.

```
class vector_iterator {
    vector& v;
    int i;
public:
    vector_iterator(vector& r) { i = 0; v = r; }
    int operator()() { return i<v.size() ? v.elem(i++) : 0; }
};
```

A `vector_iterator` can now be declared and used for a `vector` like this:

```
vector v(sz);
vector_iterator next(v);
int i;
while (i=next()) print(i);
```

More than one iterator can be active for a single object at one time, and a type may have several different iterator types defined for it so that different kinds of iteration may be performed. An iterator is a rather simple control structure. More general mechanisms can also be defined. For example, the C++ standard library provides a co-routine class.

For many "container" types, such as `vector`, one can avoid introducing a separate iterator type by defining an iteration mechanism as part of the type itself. A `vector` might be defined to have a "current element":

```
class vector {
    int* v;
    int  sz;
    int current;
public:
    // ...
    int next() { return (current++<sz) ? v[current] : 0; }
    int prev() { return (0<--current) ? v[current] : 0; }
};
```

Then the iteration can be performed like this:

```
vector v(sz);
int i;
while (i=v.next()) print(i);
```

This solution is not as general as the iterator solution, but avoids overhead in the important special case where only one kind of iteration is needed and where only one iteration at a time is needed for a vector. If necessary, a more general solution can be applied in addition to this simple one. Note that the "simple" solution requires more foresight from the designer of the container class than the iterator solution does. The iterator-type technique can also be used to define iterators that can be bound to several different container types thus providing a mechanism for iterating over different container types with a single iterator type.

Implementation Issues

The support needed for data abstraction is primarily provided in the form of language features implemented by a compiler. However, parameterized types are best implemented with support from a linker with some knowledge of the language semantics, and exception handling requires support from the run-time environment. I have little doubt that both can be implemented to meet the strictest criteria for both compile time speed and efficiency without compromising generality or programmer convenience.

As the power to define types increases, programs to a larger degree depend on types from libraries (and not just those described in the language manual). This naturally puts greater demands on facilities to express what is inserted into or retrieved from a library, facilities for finding out what a library contains, facilities for determining what parts of a library are actually used by a program, etc.

For a compiled language facilities for calculating the minimal compilation necessary after a change become important. It is essential that the linker/loader is capable of bringing a program into memory for execution without also bringing in large amounts of related, but unused, code. In particular, a library/linker/loader system that brings the code for every operation on a type into core just because the programmer used one or two operations on the type is worse than useless.

4 Support for Object-Oriented programming

The basic support a programmer needs to write object-oriented programs consists of a class mechanism with inheritance and a mechanism that allows calls of member functions to depend on the actual type of an object (in cases where the actual type is unknown at compile time). The design of the member function calling mechanism is critical. In addition, facilities supporting data abstraction techniques (as described above) are important because the arguments for data abstraction and for its refinements to support elegant use of types are equally valid where support for object-oriented programming is available. The success of both techniques hinges on the design of types and on the ease, flexibility, and efficiency of such types. Object-oriented programming simply allows user-defined types to be far more flexible and general than the ones designed using only data abstraction techniques.

Calling Mechanisms

The key language facility supporting object-oriented programming is the mechanism by which a member function is invoked for a given object. For example, given a pointer p, how is a call p->f(arg) handled? There is a range of choices.

In languages such as C++ and Simula67, where static type checking is extensively used, the type system can be employed to select between different calling mechanisms. In C++, two alternatives are available:

[1] A normal function call: the member function to be called is determined at compile time (through a lookup in the compiler's symbol tables) and called using the standard function call mechanism with an argument added to identify the object for which the function is called. Where the "standard function call" is not considered efficient enough, the programmer can declare a function `inline` and the compiler will attempt to inline expand its body. In this way, one can achieve the efficiency of a macro expansion without compromising the standard function semantics. This optimization is equally valuable as a support for data abstraction.

[2] A virtual function call: The function to be called depends on the type of the object for which it is called. This type cannot be determined until run time. Typically, the pointer p will be of some base class B and the object will be an object of some derived class D (as was the case with the base class `shape` and the derived class `circle` above). The call mechanism must look into the object and find some information placed there by the compiler to determine which function f is to be called. Once that function is found, say D::f, it can be called using the mechanism described above. The name f is at compile time converted into an index into a table of pointers to functions. This virtual call mechanism can be made essentially as efficient as the "normal function call" mechanism. In the standard C++ implementation, only three additional memory references are used.

In languages with weak static type checking a more elaborate mechanism must be employed. What is done in a language like Smalltalk is to store a list of the names of all member functions (methods) of a class so that they can be found at run time:

[3] A method invocation: First the appropriate table of method names is found by examining the object pointed to by p. In this table (or set of tables) the string "f" is looked up to see if the object has an f(). If an f() is found it is called; otherwise some error handling takes place. This lookup differs from the lookup done at compiler time in a statically checked language in that the method invocation uses a method table for the actual object.

For a virtual call, the compiler uses a table determined by the type of the expression referring to the object (this type is often a pointer to a class from which the object's class was derived).

A method invocation is inefficient compared with a virtual function call, but more flexible. Since static type checking of arguments typically cannot be done for a method invocation, the use of methods must be supported by dynamic type checking.

Type Checking

The shape example showed the power of virtual functions. What, in addition to this, does a method invocation mechanism do for you? You can attempt to invoke *any* method for *any* object.

The ability to invoke any method for any object enables the designer of general purpose libraries to push all responsibility for handling types onto the user. Naturally this simplifies the design of libraries. For example:

```
class stack {    // assume class any has a member next
    any* v;
    void push(any* p)
    {
        p->next = v;
        v = p;
    }
    any* pop()
    {
        if (v == 0) return error_obj;
        any* r = v;
        v = v->next;
        return r;
    }
};
```

It becomes the responsibility of the user to avoid type mismatches like this:

```
stack cs;
cs.push(new car);
plane* p = cs.pop();
p->takeoff();         // Oops! Run time error:
                      // a car does not have a takeoff method.
```

An attempt to use a `car` as a `plane` will be detected by the message handler and an appropriate error handler will be called. However, that is only a consolation when the user is also the programmer. The absence of static type checking makes it difficult to guarantee that errors of this class are not present in systems delivered to end users. Combinations of parameterized classes and the use of virtual functions can approach the flexibility, ease of design, and ease of use of libraries designed with method lookup without relaxing the static type checking or incurring measurable run time overheads (in time or space). For example:

```
class stack(shape*) shape_stack;

shape_stack ss;
ss.push(new circle);
shape* p1 = ss.pop();

p1->rotate(45);        // OK
p1->rotate(ss);        // Compile time error:
                       // type mismatch: stack passed, shape* expected
```

```
ss.push(new square);
plane* p2 = ss.pop();        // Compile time error:
                             // type mismatch: shape* assigned to plane*
p2->takeoff();
```

The use of static type checking and virtual function calls leads to a somewhat different style of programming than does dynamic type checking and method invocation. For example, a Simula or C++ class specifies a fixed interface to a set of objects (of any derived class) whereas a Smalltalk class specifies an initial set of operations for objects (of any subclass). In other words, a Smalltalk class is a minimal specification and the user is free to try operations not specified whereas a C++ class is an exact specification and the user is guaranteed that only operations specified in the class declaration will be accepted by the compiler.

Inheritance

Consider a language having some form of method lookup without having an inheritance mechanism. Could that language be said to support object-oriented programming? I think not. Clearly, you could do interesting things with the method table to adapt the objects' behavior to suit conditions. However, to avoid chaos, there must be some systematic way of associating methods and the data structures they assume for their object representation. To enable a user of an object to know what kind of behavior to expect, there would also have to be some standard way of expressing what is common to the different behaviors the object might adopt. This "systematic and standard way" would be an inheritance mechanism.

Consider a language having an inheritance mechanism without virtual functions or methods. Could that language be said to support object-oriented programming? I think not: the shape example does not have a good solution in such a language. However, such a language would be noticeably more powerful than a "plain" data abstraction language. This contention is supported by the observation that many Simula67 and C++ programs are structured using class hierarchies without virtual functions. The ability to express commonality (factoring) is an extremely powerful tool. For example, the problems associated with the need to have a common representation of all shapes could be solved. No union would be needed. However, in the absence of virtual functions, the programmer would have to resort to the use of "type fields" to determine actual types of objects, so the problems with the lack of modularity of the code would remain†.

This implies that class derivation (subclassing) is an important programming tool in its own right. It can be used to support object-oriented programming, but it has wider uses. This is particularly true if one identifies the use of inheritance in object-oriented programming with the idea that a base class expresses a general concept of which all derived classes are specializations. This idea captures only part of the expressive power of inheritance, but it is strongly encouraged by languages where every member function is virtual (or a method). Given suitable controls of what is inherited (see Snyder[15] and Stroustrup[16]), class derivation can be a powerful tool for creating new types. Given a class, derivation can be used to add and/or subtract features. The relation of the resulting class to its base cannot always be completely described in terms of specialization; factoring may be a better term.

Derivation is another tool in the hands of a programmer and there is no foolproof way of predicting how it is going to be used – and it is too early (even after almost 20 years of Simula67) to tell which uses are simply mis-uses.

Multiple Inheritance

When a class A is a public base of class B, a B inherits the attributes of an A; that is, a B is an A in addition to whatever else it might be. Given this explanation it seems obvious that it might be useful to have a class B inherit from two base classes A1 and A2. This is called multiple

---

† This is the problem with Simula67's inspect statement and the reason it does not have a counterpart in C++.

inheritance[19].

A fairly standard example of the use of multiple inheritance would be to provide two library classes `displayed` and `task` for representing objects under the control of a display manager and co-routines under the control of a scheduler, respectively. A programmer could then create classes such as

```
class my_displayed_task : public displayed, public task {
    // my stuff
};

class my_task : public task {  // not displayed
    // my stuff
};

class my_displayed : public displayed {  // not a task
    // my stuff
};
```

Using (only) single inheritance only two of these three choices would be open to the programmer. This leads to either code replication or loss of flexibility – and typically both.

There appear to be wide agreement that multiple inheritance is useful and that it is quite difficult to implement and/or quite expensive to use. Unfortunately, there does not appear to be a wide agreement on the details of what multiple inheritance is. However, experimental use of multiple inheritance in C++[18] demonstrates that at least some variations of multiple inheritance do not impose significant overheads compared to single inheritance.

Encapsulation

Consider a class member (either a data member or a function member) that needs to be protected from "unauthorized access". What choices can be reasonable for delimiting the set of functions that may access that member? The "obvious" answer for a language supporting object-oriented programming is "all operations defined for this object"; that is, all member functions. A non-obvious implication of this answer is that there cannot be a complete and final list of all functions that may access the protected member since one can always add another by deriving a new class from the protected member's class and define a member function of that derived class. This approach combines a large degree of protection from accident (since you do not easily define a new derived class "by accident") with the flexibility needed for "tool building" using class hierarchies (since you can "grant yourself access" to protected members by deriving a class).

Unfortunately, the "obvious" answer for a language oriented towards data abstraction is different: "list the functions that needs access in the class declaration". There is nothing special about these functions. In particular, they need not be member functions. A non-member function with access to private class members is called a `friend` in C++. Class `complex` above was defined using `friend` functions. It is sometimes important that a function may be specified as a `friend` in more than one class. Having the full list of members and friends available is a great advantage when you are trying to understand the behavior of a type and especially when you want to modify it.

Here is an example that demonstrate some of the range of choices for encapsulation in C++:

```
class B {
                        // class members are default private
    int i1;
    void f1();
protected:
    int i2;
    void f2();
```

```
public:
    int i3;
    void f3();

friend void g(B*);    // any function can be designated as a friend
};
```

Private and protected members are not generally accessible:

```
void h(B* p)
{
    p->f1();      // error: B::f1 is private
    p->f2();      // error: B::f2 is protected
    p->f3();      // fine:  B::f1 is public
}
```

Protected members, but not private members are accessible to members of a derived class:

```
class D : public B {
public:
    void g()
    {
        f1();     // error: B::f1 is private
        f2();     // fine:  B::f2 is protected, but D is derived from B
        f3();     // fine:  B::f1 is public
    }
};
```

Friends have access to private and protected members just like a member function:

```
void g(B* p)
{
    p->f1();      // fine: B::f1 is private, but g() is a friend of B
    p->f2();      // fine: B::f2 is protected, but g() is a friend of B
    p->f3();      // fine: B::f1 is public
}
```

Encapsulation issues increase dramatically in importance with the size of the program and with the number and geographical dispersion of its users. See Snyder[15] and Stroustrup[16] for more detailed discussions of language support for encapsulation.

Implementation Issues

The support needed for object-oriented programming is primarily provided by the run-time system and by the programming environment. Part of the reason is that object-oriented programming builds on the language improvements already pushed to their limit to support for data abstraction so that relatively few additions are needed†.

The use of object-oriented programming blurs the distinction between a programming language and its environment further. Since more powerful special- and general-purpose user-defined types can be defined their use pervades user programs. This requires further development of both the run-time system, library facilities, debuggers, performance measuring, monitoring tools, etc. Ideally these are integrated into a unified programming environment. Smalltalk is the best example of this.

---

† This assumes that an object-oriented language does indeed support data abstraction. However, the support for data abstraction is often deficient in such languages. Conversely, languages that support data abstraction are typically deficient in their support of object-oriented programming.

5 Limits to Perfection

A major problem with a language defined to exploit the techniques of data hiding, data abstraction, and object-oriented programming is that to claim to be a general purpose programming language it must

[1] Run on traditional machines.

[2] Coexist with traditional operating systems.

[3] Compete with traditional programming languages in terms of run time efficiency.

[4] Cope with every major application area.

This implies that facilities must be available for effective numerical work (floating point arithmetic without overheads that would make Fortran appear attractive), and that facilities must be available for access to memory in a way that allows device drivers to be written. It must also be possible to write calls that conform to the often rather strange standards required for traditional operating system interfaces. In addition, it should be possible to call functions written in other languages from a object-oriented programming language and for functions written in the object-oriented programming language to be called from a program written in another language.

Another implication is that an object-oriented programming language cannot completely rely on mechanisms that cannot be efficiently implemented on a traditional architecture and still expect to be used as a general purpose language. A very general implementation of method invocation can be a liability unless there are alternative ways of requesting a service.

Similarly, garbage collection can become a performance and portability bottleneck. Most object-oriented programming languages employ garbage collection to simplify the task of the programmer and to reduce the complexity of the language and its compiler. However, it ought to be possible to use garbage collection in non-critical areas while retaining control of storage use in areas where it matters. As an alternative, it is feasible to have a language without garbage collection and then provide sufficient expressive power to enable the design of types that maintain their own storage. C++ is an example of this.

Exception handling and concurrency features are other potential problem areas. Any feature that is best implemented with help from a linker is likely to become a portability problem.

The alternative to having "low level" features in a language is to handle major application areas using separate "low level" languages.

6 Conclusions

Object-oriented programming is programming using inheritance. Data abstraction is programming using user-defined types. With few exceptions, object-oriented programming can and ought to be a superset of data abstraction. These techniques need proper support to be effective. Data abstraction primarily needs support in the form of language features and object-oriented programming needs further support from a programming environment. To be general purpose, a language supporting data abstraction or object-oriented programming must enable effective use of traditional hardware.

7 Acknowledgements

An earlier version of this paper was presented to the Association of Simula Users meeting in Stockholm. The discussions there caused many improvements both in style and contents. Brian Kernighan and Ravi Sethi made many constructive comments. Also thanks to all who helped shape C++.

8 References

[1] Birtwistle, Graham et.al.: *SIMULA BEGIN*. Studentlitteratur, Lund, Sweden. 1971. Chartwell-Bratt ltd, UK. 1980.

[2] Bobrow, D. and Stefik, M.: *The LOOPS Manual*. Xerox Parc 1983.

[3] Dahl, O-J. and Hoare, C.A.R.: *Hierarchical Program Structures*. In *Structured Programming*. Academic Press 1972.

[4] Cargill, Tom A.: *PI: A Case Study in Object-Oriented Programming*. SIGPLAN Notices, November 1986, pp 350-360.

[5] C.C.I.T.T Study Group XI: *CHILL User's Manual*. CHILL Bulletin no 1. vol 4. March 1984.

[6] Goldberg, A. and Robson, D.: *Smalltalk-80: The Language and its Implementation*. Addison-Wesley 1983.

[7] Ichbiah, J.D. et.al.: *Rationale for the Design of the Ada Programming Language*. SIGPLAN Notices, June 1979.

[8] Kernighan, B.W. and Ritchie, D.M.: *The C Programming Language*. Prentice-Hall 1978.

[9] Kerr, Ron: *Object-Based Programming: A Foundation for Reliable Software*. Proceedings of the 14th SIMULA Users' Conference. August 1986, pp 159-165. An abbreviated version of this paper can be found under the title *A Materialistic View of the Software "Engineering" Analogy* in SIGPLAN Notices, March 1987, pp 123-125.

[10] Liskov, Barbara et. al.: *Clu Reference Manual*. MIT/LCS/TR-225, October 1979.

[11] Liskov, Barbara et. al.: *Abstraction Mechanisms in Clu. CACM vol 20, no 8, August 1977, pp 564-576.*

[12] Milner, Robert: *A Proposal for Standard ML*. ACM Symposium on Lisp and Functional Programming. 1984, pp 184-197.

[13] Nygaard, Kristen: *Basic Concepts in Object Oriented Programming*. SIGPLAN Notices, October 1986, pp 128-132.

[14] SIMULA Standards Group, 1984: *SIMULA Standard*. ASU Secretariat, Simula a.s. Post Box 150 Refstad, 0513 Oslo 5, Norway.

[15] Snyder, Alan: *Encapsulation and Inheritance in Object-Oriented Programming Languages*. SIGPLAN Notices, November 1986, pp 38-45.

[16] Stroustrup, Bjarne: *The C++ Programming Language*. Addison-Wesley, 1986.

[17] Stroustrup, Bjarne: *An Overview of C++*. SIGPLAN Notices, October 1986, pp 7-18.

[18] Stroustrup, Bjarne: *Multiple Inheritance for C++*. Proceedings of the Spring'87 EUUG Conference. Helsinki, May 1987.

[19] Weinreb, D. and Moon, D.: *Lisp Machine Manual*. Symbolics, Inc. 1981.

[20] Wirth, Niklaus: *Programming in modula-2*. Springer-Verlag, 1982.

[21] Woodward ,P.M. and Bond ,S.G.: *Algol 68-R Users Guide*. Her Majesty's Stationery Office, London. 1974.

Object Representation of Scope During Translation

S. C. Dewhurst

AT&T, Summit, New Jersey 07901, USA

ABSTRACT

Languages, such as C++, that combine static type checking with inheritance pose a challenge to the compiler writer: the flexibility of the type and scope system implies that a compiler must be able to cope with data structures of a complexity far exceeding what is needed for traditional languages. Fortunately, they also supply the means for coping with this complexity. This paper describes the strategies devised for representing and manipulating C++ scopes and the storage management techniques employed to make these representations efficient. The techniques have been used to implement a C++ compiler in C++.

1 Introduction

Scope is typically represented at translation time exclusively as an attribute of a name, either explicitly as a field within the name or implicitly by the presence of the name in a data structure that implements the compile-time semantics of scope. The data structures that maintain the relationship between name and scope are traditionally monolithic; that is, all scope information is contained within a single structure. This structure is modified as the program is translated to reflect the changing scope.

This organization is well-suited to the translation of traditional block-structured languages in which the "current" scope changes rather slowly as the program text is analysed. Since scope changes slowly, the modifications of the data structure used to represent it are relatively restrained. However in C++ and a number of other modern languages the combination of static type checking and inheritance produce a scope structure too complex and volatile to be easily and efficiently represented with traditional compiler symbol table structures. The solution developed for the C++ compiler represents scope as an object and the dynamic nature of scope during translation as a dynamic graph of these scope objects. In addition to simplifying the task of maintaining scope information, this approach permits efficient translation-time storage management and provides opportunity to interface to environment tools to save and restore compilation states, and to avoid recompilation of common program pieces.

Section 2 shows how language features affect the structure of scope during translation, section 3 describes the implementation of the object-oriented solution, section 4 shows how this approach allows for efficient translation-time memory management, and section 5 describes some applications this style of memory management makes practicable. Because these techniques were developed for a C++ compiler they are motivated by examples from the C++ language. However, the examples are of minimal complexity and should not require prior knowledge of C++.

2 Effect of Language Features on Scope Structure

For the purposes of the present discussion, a class in C++ can be considered to be simply a record type containing both data and function members. The body of a member function occurs in the scope of the class of which it is a member. Figure 1 has an example of a member function:

```
int i;

class B {
        int i;
        void f();
};

void B::f() { ... = i; }
```

Figure 1

The syntax B::f uses the scope operator :: to indicate that f is a member of class B. The i referenced in the function body of f refers to the member i, not the global one. Functions can also be defined within a class body:

```
int i;

class B {
        int i;
        void f() { ... = i; }
        friend void f() { ... = i; }
};
```

Figure 2

In Figure 2, class B has two members: the integer i and the function f. The friend designation of the non-member function f is related to the data hiding features provided by C++ and is beyond the scope of this paper. It is sufficient to note that the friend function is not a member of class B, and so the reference to i in its body is a reference to the global i. Note also that both functions may be referred to through the same identifier because they are defined in different scopes; the member function is in the scope of class B, while the non-member function is at global scope. The semantics of the member function f in Figure 2 are identical to those of the member function in Figure 1. These examples show that lexical and semantic scope are separate in C++; that is, lexical nesting does not imply semantic nesting.

C++ accomplishes type inheritance through the mechanism of class derivation. The derived class inherits the members of its base class in addition to its own members. However, a member of the base class is hidden in the scope of the derived class if its identifier has been reused in the derived class.

```
class B {
    public:
        int i, j;
};

class D : B {
        int i;
        void f() { i = j; }
};
```

Figure 3

In Figure 3, class D is derived from class B. The keyword public, like friend, is related to the data hiding features of the language. The body of member function f assigns the value of the base class member j to the derived class member i. A derived class occurs in the scope of its base class. Note that this "enclosing" scope is unaffected by the scope in which the individual classes are defined:

```
class B { ... };

void g() {
        class D2 : B { ... };
}
```

Figure 4

The enclosing scope of class D2 is still that of B even though D2 is defined in the scope of the function g. These examples show that in C++ there is not necessarily a relationship between enclosing scope and scope of definition of a name, except, of course, that the lifetime of the enclosing scope must at least include that of the scope of definition. This is always the case.

The practical effect of class derivation (type inheritance) on scope is the production of a very complex scope structure and a very volatile notion of the "current" scope. The following example combines the concepts outlined above and will serve to motivate the approaches discussed in the following section:

```
class B {
        int m1();
};

class D1 : B {
        int m2();
};

int f1() {
        class D2 : B {
                friend int f2() { ... }
                int m3() { ... }
        };
}

int D1::m2() { ... }
```

Figure 5

3   Object Representation of Scope

Fortunately, while the features of languages like C++ produce these translation difficulties they also provide the means to solve them through support for the object-oriented programming paradigm. The strategy employed by the C++ compiler is to define a general "scope object" class which contains references to the objects that represent its enclosing scope and routines that implement the semantics of the scope (such as lookup and insertion).

As each scope is entered, a corresponding object is created and its enclosing scope references set to the objects that represent its enclosing scope. When the scope is no longer accessible its scope object is deleted. In this way, as scopes are entered and deleted the compiler maintains a graph of scope objects that reflects the scope structure of the program being translated.† Figure 6 shows the graph that is produced by the example in Figure 5 at the point during which the body of function m3 is being translated.

---

† In the absence of multiple inheritance, each scope object will contain at most one reference to an enclosing scope object and the graph will always be a tree.

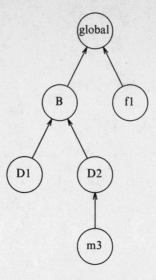

Figure 6

Figure 7 is a finer-detailed view of the structure in Figure 6. It shows the separation of scope of definition and enclosing scope. Names are represented as labeled boxes and scope objects as ellipses. The scope object that is an attribute of a given name is indicated by a solid arrow from the name to the scope object. The dashed arrows show the scope hierarchy illustrated in Figure 6.

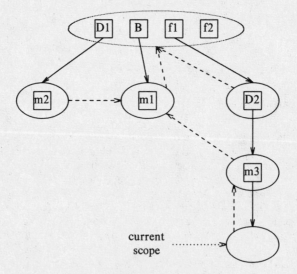

Figure 7

In effect this scheme uses the complexity of the program under translation to build and maintain the scope graph. Thus the burden of complexity is abstracted from the program and the compiler needn't anticipate all the combinations of scoping situations that could arise. For example consider Figure 5 above. Although the scope of definition of D2 is the scope of f1 (that is, the name of D2 is entered in f1's scope) the scope of f1 is not interposed within the scope hierarchy formed by D2 and B. Because all scope information about f1 is represented in a single object, the separation of lexical and semantic scope is accomplished simply by positioning f1's scope object in the correct position in the graph. No complex algorithm is needed to bypass the scope of f1 when referencing a name in the scope of D2.

The current scope is represented at any given time by a single node in the scope graph. The current scope is the set of graph nodes reachable from the current node.† For example, the scope current while translating the body of function m3 in Figure 5 is represented in Figure 6 by the list of scope nodes labeled "m3", "D2", "B" and "global". Because the current scope is represented by a single node in the scope graph, the volatile nature of current scope can be handled easily and efficiently by stacking references to nodes. For example, referring again to Figure 5, when the friend function f2 is encountered, the current scope (labeled D2) is pushed on a "lexical scope" stack, and the current scope is set to a new scope node for f2, with global enclosing scope. At the end of translation of f2, the stack is popped to restore the old scope. The definition of the member function m2 at the end of the figure is handled in a similar way; the current (global) scope is pushed and the new current scope is set to a new node for m2, with the parent as D1.

The C++ compiler partitions scopes into three categories: global, class and function. Each category is represented by a class derived from the general scope class, and is tailored to suit the characteristics of the scope in question. The global and class scope types both implement "flat" scopes,† but the global scope type is optimized to handle a larger number of names than the class scope type. The function scope type implements a block-structured scope. Additionally, each type implements a number of scope-specific operations that are not present in the others. The conventional implementation of scope as a monolithic data structure with complex access and insertion rules is replaced by a collection of simpler objects that need concern themselves only with their own structure and the locations of their enclosing scope. This simplicity is a typical advantage of an object-oriented solution.

The decision as to what constitutes a scope is as flexible as the translation task requires. For instance, the C++ compiler does not consider a block within a function as creating a scope; rather, block structure is an attribute of function scope. The rationale for this is that the flexibility of the object approach is not required within a function, where conventional techniques for maintaining block structure are clear and efficient. Additionally, certain translation information, such as activation record layout, is naturally associated with an object that represents an entire function, rather than a collection of block objects.

Another advantage of the object-oriented approach is that of being robust in the face of change. The C++ language is still evolving, and the localization of semantic routines to individual object types allows new semantics to be added without incident. Likely additions to the language, such as multiple inheritance, can be accommodated without significant disruption of the structure of the current compiler.

4 Efficient Translation-Time Memory Management

The logical locality implied by an object also permits an easy implementation of physical locality, either as contiguous memory or in easily accessible locations. That is, if every language feature is associated with a given scope, then the compiler data structure used to translate an instance of that feature can be associated with a given scope object. The lifetime of the data structure should be identical to that of the scope object, just as the lifetime of the feature instance is no greater than that of the scope in which it appears. As an example consider a function definition at global scope. At the exit of the function scope, the scope object of the function may be freed. Note that because the name of the function is not in the function scope, this action will not remove information required for translation to continue. If all the data structures

---

† In the absence of multiple inheritance the scope is represented by a simple list of nodes.
† That is, a scope in which an identifier always refers to exactly one name.

associated with the function scope object are removed along with it, then the remaining data structures will be left in a consistent state, and translation can continue.

The approach used in the C++ compiler is to associate a different memory space with each active function scope and with the global scope. Class scope objects are allocated in the memory space of the scope that is current at the time of their creation. When a function or global scope object is created, a new memory space is set up and the scope object is allocated within it. All subsequent compiler data structures *within that scope* are allocated in that memory space. At the end of the function or global scope the memory for the scope is freed, removing the scope object from the scope graph and leaving the compiler data structures in a consistent state. Figure 8 shows how the C++ compiler would segment memory for the program example of Figure 5, during the translation of the friend function f2. Each dotted boundary encloses a separate memory space associated with an active global or function scope.

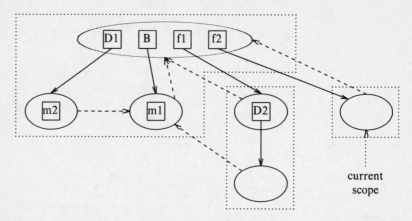

Figure 8

In addition to the efficiency gained by essentially constant time memory management, this segmentation of memory by scope has the advantage of leaving the memory spaces of all active scope objects available at all times. It was shown earlier that a friend function like f2 of Figure 5, although lexically within function f1, is actually defined in the global scope. Consider the difficulties this would present to a stack allocation scheme. The memory associated with global scope would be below that of the function f1, and the name of the friend f2 would be allocated within the memory associated with f1. Of course, the name of the friend function would still be entered in the global scope, but on popping the function information off the allocation stack at the end of f1, the compiler data structures would be in error, as the friend name will have been removed. More flexible methods of memory management with finer granularity of control can be employed, but these typically have concomitant penalties in performance and complexity.

In associating patterns of memory management with the scope graph, memory management inherits the scope scheme's simplicity while allowing the program under translation to drive the construction of the complex memory management. Each scope object has a memory descriptor. The (unique) allocation routine uses the descriptor of the current scope object to determine the memory space from which to allocate. In the example above, the current descriptor is set to the global descriptor before f2 is translated and then restored to that of f1. In this way, the name of the friend function f2 is allocated in the global memory space. After the translation of f2, the current scope is reset to f1 and the current memory space is reset from f1's descriptor.

5 Applications of Scope-Segmented Memory Management

A side effect of this memory allocation scheme is the ability to process multiple program files in sequence with little overhead. Many compilers (including early versions of the C++ compiler) process only a single file per invocation because, due to the way memory is managed, cleanup between files would be prohibitively expensive. The C++ compiler solves this problem by creating an object that represents the scope that exists before and between file compilations. Its memory space contains invariant data that is created on compiler initialization (but no names). At the end of each file the global scope object is deleted to re-initialize the compiler. In avoiding loading and initialization for each file, the compiler realizes significant gains in translation time for compilations that comprise several files.

Other, as yet unimplemented, applications which could make use of this strong association between memory space and scope are perhaps best viewed as compiler support for programming environment tools. For example, this organization would simplify an implementation that minimizes recompilation of common file prefixes.

Consider the problem of compiling a sequence of files, each of which has a common initial part. If no external effect is produced during the compilation of the common prefix (such as code generation) then the effect of the translation to that point is to move the compiler from its initial configuration to a given compilation state. If this state can be restored easily, the common part need be compiled only once for the sequence of files.

In most compilers the state of compilation is represented entirely within the compiler's data structures. If the memory allocation scheme described above is used, these are contained within the memory spaces of a collection of scope objects. Thus, just as earlier we were able to restore the initial compiler state by deleting all scope objects but the initial "between file" object, it is possible to restore any intermediate compilation state through judicious segmentation and deletion of scope objects. (Note that there needn't be a one-to-one relationship between scopes and scope objects.) The ease with which this can be accomplished is highly language dependent. For example, the C++ compiler could easily implement delayed code generation (expanding the class of code prefixes it could handle) because much of that capability is required for inline function expansion. On the other hand, in C++ the definition of a name may be begun at one point in the compilation and added to at a remote point. (For example, a function prototype may add default argument initializers.) In order to handle prefixes containing definitions of this kind it would be necessary to record and undo effects of this sort that occur after the prefix.

Once the case of the single common prefix can be handled, a number of additional opportunities arise. Perhaps the most obvious of these is the stacking of compilation states. In this way the prefix dependancies of a set of files to be compiled can be arranged into a DAG and the files compiled in such an order that by pushing and popping the scope objects representing compilation states minimal recompilation is performed. Additional gains can be obtained by the ability to save an external representation of a compilation state in a program database.

6 Summary

The C++ compiler deals with the complex and volatile scope structures that arise during translation by abstraction to a graph structure; a scope is represented as a node and an enclosing scope relationship as an edge. The logical encapsulation of scope as object eases the task of representing the complex nature of scope in languages like C++, and permits both reduction in complexity and increased flexibility. In extending the logical encapsulation implied by an object to physical encapsulation, the C++ compiler implements efficient and simple translation-time memory management. In effect, the compiler uses the complexity of the program being translated to guide the building and maintenance of a complex data structure composed of simple components.

The simplicity of the resultant compilation structures permits further optimization of the translation process, including multiple file compilation and intelligent interface to program environment tools in order to avoid recompilation of common code pieces.

7 Acknowledgements

The author wishes to thank Bjarne Stroustrup for invaluable advice on organization and content of this paper, and Kathy Stark, Laura Eaves and Barbara Moo for many valuable discussions and comments.

[1] B. Stroustrup, *The C++ Programming Language*, Addison-Wesley, Reading, Massachusetts, 1986.

Dynamic Grouping in an Object-Oriented Virtual Memory Hierarchy

Ifor Williams,* Mario Wolczko,* Trevor Hopkins

Department of Computer Science, The University, Manchester M13 9PL, UK.

ifor@uk.ac.man.cs.ux, mcvax!uk!man.cs.ux!ifor
miw@uk.ac.man.cs.ux, mcvax!uk!man.cs.ux!miw
trevor@uk.ac.man.cs.ux, mcvax!uk!man.cs.ux!trevor

Abstract

Object oriented programming environments frequently suffer serious performance degradation because of a high level of paging activity when implemented using a conventional virtual memory system. Although the fine-grained, persistent nature of objects in such environments is not conducive to efficient paging, the performance degradation can be limited by careful grouping of objects within pages. Such object placement schemes can be classified into four categories — the grouping mechanism may be either static or dynamic and may use information acquired from static or dynamic properties. This paper investigates the effectiveness of a simple dynamic grouping strategy based on dynamic behaviour and compares it with a static grouping scheme based on static properties. These schemes are also compared with near-optimal and random cases.

1   Introduction

Virtual memory enables programs much larger than primary memory to be implemented without the need for explicit management of primary memory by the user program. Virtual addresses are usually mapped onto a two-level hierarchy of memory devices consisting of primary random access memory and secondary disk memory. Contiguous portions of virtual memory (termed 'pages') are swapped between primary and secondary memory as required by the program. Pages are typically several thousand bytes long and page sizes are carefully chosen to minimise the amount of paging. When programs occupy contiguous sections of store large in comparison with page sizes, the virtual memory system performs well. However, in *Smalltalk-80*[1] [GR83] the unit of locality is a fine-grain object (50 bytes on average [Ung84]) small in comparison to page size. Consequently *Smalltalk-80* suffers serious performance degradation on conventional paging systems.

Applications are often developed by incrementally grafting new objects into a persistent environment, so that the static locality inherent in conventional programs is lost. The re-use of code is encouraged by the inheritance mechanism, which enables an application to use any portion of a large persistent environment. In contrast, conventional programs are limited to the code that represents the program text (with the exception of library routines and the operating system). In addition, conventional programs have statically bound procedure calls, whilst in *Smalltalk-80* binding is performed at run time.

The cumulative effect of such properties of object oriented systems is poor paging performance on conventional paging systems. To reduce the inefficiencies, various object grouping strategies may be employed. In general, several related objects are placed together on a page; the fundamental aim of this process is to maximise the useful content of a page when it is brought in from secondary storage. Ideally, when a page is brought in from secondary memory, it should be full of objects that will be required in the near future which are not already in primary memory. Similarly, a page to be swapped out to secondary memory should contain objects that will not be required for some time. In swapping out a page, any object in primary memory can be selected and included on the page to be transferred into secondary memory. However, when a page is brought in from secondary memory, it is much more efficient if objects contained within the page

---

*Supported by the Science and Engineering Research Council
[1] *Smalltalk-80* is a trademark of Xerox Corp.

reside on adjacent disk blocks. Therefore it is impractical to satisfy the ideal grouping for both fetching and ejecting a group of objects from primary memory.

2 The Experiment

The purpose of this experiment was to investigate the effectiveness of two different grouping schemes. A *static* grouping scheme based on static information was compared with a *dynamic* grouping scheme based on dynamic behaviour. The comparison was performed by simulating the respective memory models and animating the simulations with long memory reference traces gathered on a *Smalltalk-80* system. These memory reference traces were obtained by modifying the *Smalltalk-80* virtual machine emulator to write all object memory accesses, object creation and garbage collection information onto a file. The trace file was then read by the memory model simulation which provided statistics to evaluate the effectiveness of the model. No compression of memory traces was necessary, as sufficient memory space and processor power was available to perform a realistic simulation.

The memory traces used to exercise the memory model simulation were derived from typical interactive sessions using *Smalltalk-80*. There were four traces, each representing approximately 4 000 000 bytecodes of activity. Trace 1 to trace 3 were 4M, 3.5M and 5.5M bytecodes in length respectively and consisted of compiling, browsing and editing activity and execution of some examples. Trace 4 was derived from a 19M bytecode session which involved the filing in and compilation of a 24Kbyte source file and the re-compilation of the hierarchy rooted at StandardSystemView.

In order to ease the capture of long traces, the virtual machine executing the sample sessions wrote event information onto a file. Another virtual machine implementation was then driven by these event traces and generated the memory reference traces. If the virtual machine used in executing the sample sessions traced all memory accesses, the reduction in performance would limit the length of obtainable traces. Since large and representative traces were required to provide an accurate simulation, this indirect method of generating memory reference traces was used.

3 Grouping Categories

In a static grouping scheme, objects are re-grouped whilst the system is in a 'frozen' state; this is done by creating an 'initial placement' that locates objects related in some way close to each other in memory. For example, *Smalltalk-80* has a facility whereby a 'snapshot' of the whole state of the system is taken and an 'image' created. The *Smalltalk-80* virtual machine can load the image into its memory and re-create a state identical to the state of the environment when the image was created. When the virtual machine loads the image it may arrange the objects in memory such that related objects are close together, thereby statically grouping objects.

Conversely, dynamic grouping is performed while the system is running and is inherently more complex because of the need to maintain memory integrity. In the incremental copying garbage collectors [Ste75,LH83] for example, objects are copied from one area in memory to another whilst the system is running. The principal aim is to identify unreferenced objects, but by incrementally copying related objects into a new area of memory dynamic grouping is performed.

Grouping strategies can be further categorised by the nature of the information used to group objects. Information from static relationships, such as from the graph formed by pointers from objects, may be used with either static or dynamic grouping. For example, these pointers may be followed in either a 'depth-first' or 'breadth-first' manner. Similarly, grouping based on dynamic behaviour can also be used — for example, a 'least recently accessed' mechanism. This gives a total of four categories for classifying grouping strategies.

4 Static Grouping

Static grouping involves the generation of an initial placement of objects within virtual memory. The initial placement may be determined by a wide variety of factors leading to many different initial placement schemes. However, a previous study of static grouping schemes [Sta84] showed that there is no appreciable difference between different object groupings. In the study, several static grouping schemes were compared and the results did not indicate a scheme which performed convincingly better than others. Thus it appears that the choice of static grouping strategy is not critical; hence a simple depth-first ordering is considered here.

The model used to simulate a conventional paged memory system is specified formally in Appendix A. Note that the assignment of objects to virtual addresses does not change after the initial placement. Except for objects created or deleted during the simulation run, a page will always contain the same set of objects. When an object not in primary memory is accessed, the page on disk containing the object is brought into primary memory. If primary memory is full, a page must be purged to create space for the required page. In the model, page replacement is achieved by a true 'least recently used' (LRU) purging policy; this approach is considered reasonable as most conventional paging systems use an LRU approximation.

When an object is created, a best fit algorithm is employed to allocate a free space to the object. A list is maintained of the free spaces in memory and new objects are allocated into the smallest contiguous space that will contain them. If no free space is available then an existing page must be purged from primary memory. Additionally, for the purposes of simulation, the memory within a page is effectively compacted after an object is deleted from that page; fragmentation within a page is not modelled. Deleting objects by request from the reference counting garbage collector is immediate and the freed space is added to the free list.

5 Dynamic Grouping

As mentioned earlier, an effective grouping of objects to be purged is not necessarily the best grouping for objects to be fetched from secondary memory. Identifying the group of objects not in primary memory that are to be accessed in the immediate future is clearly impossible; in general, it is also difficult to find an adequate approximation. In contrast to this, assessing which objects are least likely to be used in the future is equally impossible but has a more readily realisable approximation in the form of a 'least recently used' heuristic. Consequently, the dynamic grouping scheme based on dynamic information modelled here will be in the form of a 'least recently used' (LRU) purging algorithm.

5.1 Least Recently Used Grouping

For an efficient implementation, a dynamic grouping scheme requires pointer-offset object addressing. In many *Smalltalk-80* implementations, virtual addresses are used to directly access objects [UP83] thus saving an object table indirection. However, when objects are dynamically relocated in memory, the object table indirection is clearly invaluable. There are two possible levels of implementation for the object table indirections. First, the object table may translate pointers into virtual addresses for the underlying machine or alternatively, the pointers may be translated into real primary or secondary memory addresses. This experiment assumes that the object table translates onto real addresses.

Accessing an object not in primary memory causes the secondary memory page containing the object to be fetched. Purging primary memory is achieved by swapping out pages of objects into secondary memory. Grouping objects onto the page to be ejected is achieved by constructing a collection of least recently used objects whose cumulative size is not greater than the page size. When objects are created during the simulation run, space is reclaimed in primary memory by ejecting objects into secondary memory. Also, the garbage collector reclaims space occupied by an object by marking the object as garbage and adding it to the free list.

5.2 Random Grouping

To give some indication of the effectiveness of the LRU dynamic grouping scheme, a random dynamic grouping scheme is also simulated. Purging involves identifying a random group of objects to be swapped into secondary memory. This is achieved by pseudo-random probing into the object table until sufficient objects have been collected to fill a page.

5.3 Near-Optimal Grouping

A near-optimal dynamic grouping strategy is also simulated to measure the effectiveness of the LRU dynamic grouping scheme. An optimal scheme is not realisable in practice but, given a complete memory trace where 'future' memory references may be analysed, it may be approximated with a reasonable amount of accuracy.

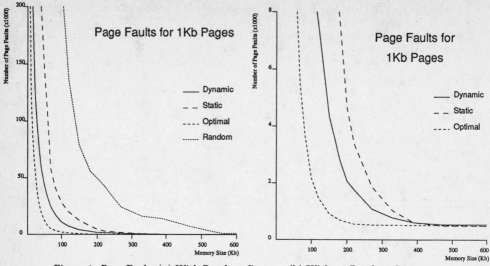

Figure 1: Page Faults (a) With Random Curve (b) Without Random Curve

In the ideal case, if a group of X objects are to be swapped into primary memory, the group would contain the next X objects to be accessed that are currently not in primary memory. However, for the purpose of simulation, $X = 1$ since it is assumed that the secondary memory has no latency. If all objects are the same size and primary memory is full, fetching an object from secondary memory necessitates ejecting an object from primary memory. The object to eject is obviously the one that is next needed furthest in the future. This object can be identified by scanning the memory traces forward in time from the faulted reference until references to $N - 1$ different objects in primary memory have been observed (where N is the number of objects in primary memory). However, due to the varying sizes of objects, the Nth object is not necessarily the optimal choice of object to purge.

6 Discussion

The four models are implemented in C and driven with the memory reference traces gathered from a *Smalltalk-80* system. Three models provide near-optimal, random and LRU dynamic grouping whilst a fourth static grouping scheme is included for comparison. Near-optimal static grouping and random static grouping are not included since they have no implication on the dynamic grouping scheme and have been covered in a previous study [Sta84]. An attempt has been made to keep the models simple without introducing inaccuracies that may bias the results. However, there are several points which deserve mention:

- In the static grouping scheme on a conventional paging system, the model is generous in that it assumes a true LRU page purging policy. However, studies have shown that LRU approximations are sufficiently effective for this to be realistic [EF79].

- For the same amount of primary memory, it is more difficult to approximate LRU purging for objects than for page purging. This is due to the smaller granularity of object-based LRU purging.

- In the dynamic grouping scheme, when a group of objects are brought in from secondary memory, they are considered to be a group of 'most recently used' objects. Altering the position of the newly fetched group in the LRU selection may improve the effectiveness of the dynamic grouping scheme. Clearly, considering a newly fetched group of objects as least recently used may lead to their premature ejection.

- All objects are smaller than the page size — large *Smalltalk-80* objects which do not fit onto a page are dealt with as special cases by the simulator. Objects do not cross page boundaries.

- For simplicity, only one static grouping scheme is modelled. It is considered that previous studies of static grouping schemes [Sta84] are conclusive in that there is no single scheme which is identifiably more effective than any other.

- No 'dirty bit' is included in the conventional paging model. Thus, unchanged pages are purged in the same way as modified pages. This is in accordance with the dynamic grouping scheme which does not create space by deleting unmodified objects.

- The memory reference traces do not include accesses to bitmaps and accesses to class fields by the someInstance or nextInstance primitives.

- The garbage collection scheme used conforms to the definition of the virtual machine [GR83] and is the same for all memory traces.

7   Results

For the three main traces, each combination of grouping scheme and page size had 15 primary memory sizes. Given that four page sizes were simulated for four grouping schemes, this gives a total of 720 points for all three main traces. The traces represented approximately four million bytecodes and 40 million memory references of *Smalltalk-80* activity each, with a fourth, 19 million bytecode trace being run with much fewer points. No statistical manipulation is attempted, relative comparisons are not made and the results are presented in their absolute form. Results are only presented from trace 1. The graphs obtained from traces 2-4 were very similar to those from trace 1. The simulations predict how real implementations with similar memory and image sizes behave with a reasonable amount of accuracy. However, it is unknown whether the results scale to larger memory and image sizes.

7.1   Page Faults

The graph in Figure 1(a) shows the page faults obtained for trace 1 for 1Kbyte pages. Note that each curve falls towards a constant level which represents the page activity caused by starting and terminating the simulations with all objects on the disk. The random figures are an order of magnitude worse than figures for static, dynamic and near-optimal grouping. Figure 1(b) shows the same graphs on a different scale without the random curve. With 200 Kbytes of main memory the dynamic grouping scheme pages 45% as much as the static grouping scheme. At 56 Kbytes of main memory, dynamic grouping activity is 31.5% of static grouping. When paging occurs during *Smalltalk-80* activity (not including that caused by startup or shutdown), the graph indicates that dynamic grouping is always better than static grouping — the curves only meet when no paging is performed.

The graphs in Figure 1 show only 1Kbyte pages. Other graphs were plotted for different page sizes, and Figure 2 shows curves for all the page sizes for static and dynamic grouping with trace 1. For the range of page sizes simulated, all the dynamic grouping simulations performed better than the corresponding static grouping simulations.

7.2   Page Activity

Whilst graphs of the page fault totals are useful for comparing the effectiveness of various paging schemes, it is interesting to observe the page fault activity in order to gain an insight into the effect of paging schemes on interactive response. Figure 3(a) illustrates one of the activity traces taken for a 200 Kbyte main memory with 1 Kbyte pages for trace 1. Many of the paging peaks for dynamic grouping are of similar magnitude, but are generally shorter in duration compared with the static grouping trace. Relating the peaks of page activity with new applications being run in the *Smalltalk-80* image shows that the dynamic grouping scheme changes the working set much more rapidly than static grouping. Figure 3(b) shows a section of the same activity graph expanded.

8   Conclusion

Dynamic grouping works well for the given combinations of image and memory sizes. It is unknown whether the results will scale to larger images and memory sizes, and it is not envisaged that any accurate predictions

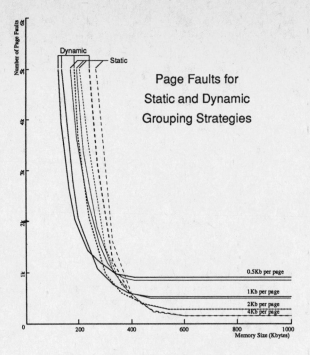

Figure 2: Page Faults for Different Page Sizes

may be made until large applications are available. Future research will concentrate on investigating practical implementations of pointer-addressed dynamic grouping virtual memory and simulating such memories in order to estimate and compare cost and performance with conventional paging hardware.

9   Acknowledgements

The authors would like to thank Cliff Jones for commenting on the formal specification in Appendix A. Thanks also go to the Department for the provision of computing facilities.

References

[EF79]   Malcom C. Easton and Peter A. Franaszek. Use bit scanning in replacement decisions. *IEEE Transactions on Computers*, 28(2):133–141, 1979.

[GR83]   Adele Goldberg and David Robson. *Smalltalk-80: The Language and its Implementation*. Addison-Wesley, 1983.

[Jon86] Cliff B. Jones. *Systematic Software Development Using VDM*. Prentice-Hall International, 1986.

[LH83]   H. Lieberman and C. Hewitt. A real time garbage collector based on the lifetimes of objects. *Communications of the ACM*, 26(6):419–429, June 1983.

[Sta84] J. W. Stamos. Static grouping of small objects to enhance performance of a paged virtual memory. *ACM Transactions on Computer Systems*, 2(2):155–180, May 1984.

[Ste75] G. L. Steele. Multiprocessing compactifying garbage collection. *Communications of the ACM*, 18(9):495–508, September 1975.

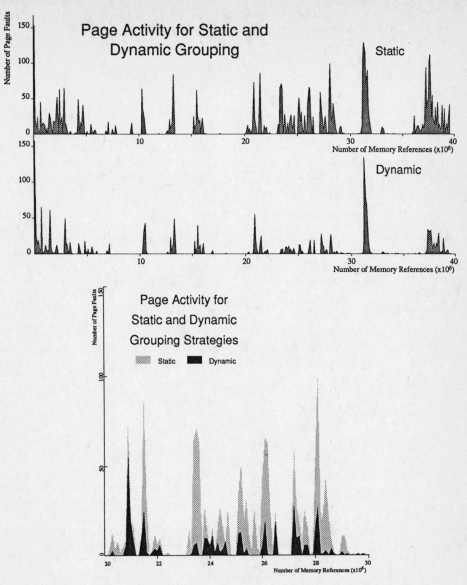

Figure 3: (a) Page Activity for Trace 1 (upper) (b) Expanded Section (lower)

[Ung84] David Ungar. Generation scavenging: A non-disruptive, high performance storage reclamation algorithm. In *Proc. Software Engineering Symposium on Practical Software Development Environments*, pages 157–167, ACM SIGSOFT/SIGPLAN, Pittsburgh PA, May 1984.

[UP83] D. M. Ungar and D. A. Patterson. Berkeley Smalltalk: Who knows where the time goes? In Glenn Krasner, editor, *Smalltalk-80: bits of history, words of advice*, pages 189–206, Addison-Wesley, 1983.

Appendix A

This appendix contains formal specifications written in VDM [Jon86] of the models used to simulate both static and dynamic grouping schemes. Two specifications are given of both models, the second specification being a more detailed refinement of the first (the refinements have been proved to model the abstract specifications, but the proofs are not included for brevity).

Conventional Paging

The simplest specification is that of the conventional paging system where the primary memory is modelled as a set of pages. Pages are classed as being either in or out of primary memory. A reference to a page in memory does not affect the state of the system, whilst a reference to a page not in memory causes the required page to be included into primary memory. Clearly, if the primary memory is not full then no purging is required.

Mem :: PS : set of Pg

where

$inv\text{-}Mem(mk\text{-}Mem(ps))$ $\triangle$ card $ps \leq store\_size\_in\_pages$

$REFCE$ $(p{:}Pg)$

ext wr m : Mem

post if $p \in PS(\overleftarrow{m})$ then $m = \overleftarrow{m}$ else if card $PS(\overleftarrow{m}) = store\_size\_in\_pages$
$$\text{then } PS(m) - PS(\overleftarrow{m}) = \{p\}$$
$$\wedge \text{ card}\,(PS(m) \cap PS(\overleftarrow{m})) = store\_size\_in\_pages - 1$$
$$\text{else } PS(m) = PS(\overleftarrow{m}) \cup \{p\}$$

Conventional Paging—LRU

By adding the concept of sequence to pages in real memory, least recently used purging can be specified. The sequence of pages reflects the sequence of references — the head of the sequence contains the least recently referenced page. If the referenced page is not in primary memory, the LRU page is ejected and the required page fetched.

Mem_{LRU} :: PL : seq of Pg

where

$inv\text{-}Mem_{LRU}(mk\text{-}Mem_{LRU}(pl))$ $\triangle$ len $pl \leq store\_size\_in\_pages \wedge$ card rng $pl = $ len pl

LRU_REFCE $(p{:}Pg)$

ext wr m : Mem_{LRU}

post if $p \in$ rng $PL(\overleftarrow{m})$ then $PL(m) = remove\_pg(p, PL(\overleftarrow{m}))$ $\frown$ $[p]$
    else if len $PL(\overleftarrow{m}) = store\_size\_in\_pages$
        then $PL(m) = $ tl $PL(\overleftarrow{m})$ $\frown$ $[p]$
        else $PL(m) = PL(\overleftarrow{m})$ $\frown$ $[p]$

$remove\_pg : Pg \times \text{seq of } Pg \to \text{seq of } Pg$

$remove\_pg(p, pl) \triangleq \text{if } pl = [] \text{ then } [] \text{ else if } p = \text{hd } pl$
$$\text{then tl } pl$$
$$\text{else hd } pl \frown remove\_pg(p, \text{tl } pl)$$

Object Swapping

Object swapping groups objects to be purged onto a page to be ejected into secondary memory. In statically grouped systems, the content of a page is the same in primary memory as in secondary memory. With the dynamic grouping scheme, secondary memory is divided into pages whose contents are static. When pages are brought from secondary memory, the objects they contain are scattered into free spaces in primary memory. Similarly, pages being written to secondary memory are composed dynamically by selecting the appropriate objects to purge from primary memory.

The existence of an auxiliary function, $size: Obj \to \{1, \ldots, pg\_size\}$, is assumed. This gives the size (in words) of a particular object.

$Obj\_mem ::\ Disk\ :\ \text{set of } Pg$
$$Mem\ :\ \text{set of } Obj$$

where

$inv\text{-}Obj\_mem(mk\text{-}Obj\_mem(d, m)) \triangleq$
$$is\_disjoint(m, \bigcup\{OS(p) \mid p \in d\})$$
$$\wedge \sum_{obj \in m} size(obj) \leq store\_size$$
$$\wedge\ is\_prdisj(d)$$

$Pg ::\ OS\ :\ \text{set of } Obj$

where

$inv\text{-}Pg(mk\text{-}Pg(os)) \triangleq os \neq \{\} \wedge \sum_{obj \in os} size(obj) \leq pg\_size$

The following function states that an object may not be on more than one page in a given set of pages, i.e. the sets which constitute each page are pairwise disjoint.

$is\_prdisj : \text{set of } Pg \to \mathbf{B}$

$is\_prdisj(d) \triangleq \forall d_1, d_2 \in d \cdot OS(d_1) = OS(d_2) \vee is\text{-}disjoint(OS(d_1), OS(d_2))$

$REFCE\ \ (p: Obj)$

ext wr $disk\ :\ \text{set of } Pg$
  wr $mem\ :\ \text{set of } Obj$

pre $p \in mem \cup \bigcup\{OS(p) \mid p \in disk\}$

post if $p \in \overline{mem}$

  then $mem = \overline{mem} \wedge disk = \overleftarrow{disk}$

  else $\exists pg\_in \in \overleftarrow{disk}, objs\_out \subseteq \overline{mem}, pgs\_out \in \text{set of } Pg \cdot$
$$p \in OS(pg\_in)$$
$$\wedge\ mem = \overline{mem} \cup OS(pg\_in) - objs\_out$$
$$\wedge\ objs\_out = \bigcup\{OS(p) \mid p \in pgs\_out\}$$
$$\wedge\ disk = \overleftarrow{disk} - \{pg\_in\} \cup pgs\_out$$
$$\wedge\ is\text{-}prdisj(pgs\_out)$$
$$\wedge \sum_{obj \in mem} size(obj) \leq store\_size$$

Object Swapping–LRU

The following specification is the same as the previous object swapping model, except for the inclusion of 'least recently used' (LRU) purging. LRU purging is specified by modelling primary memory as a sequence of objects which reflects the sequence of references to the objects. The head of the sequence contains the least recently referenced object and objects are added to the tail whenever they are accessed. When objects are brought in from the disk, they are also added to the tail of the sequence.

Obj_mem_{LRU} :: $Disk$: set of Pg
$\qquad\qquad\quad Mem$: seq of Obj

where

$inv\text{-}Obj\_mem_{LRU}(mk\text{-}Obj\_mem_{LRU}(d,m))$ $\triangle$
$\qquad inv\text{-}Obj\_mem(mk\text{-}Obj\_mem(d, \text{rng } m)) \wedge \text{len } m = \text{card rng } m$

LRU_REFCE $(p: Obj)$

ext wr $disk$: set of Pg
$\quad$ wr mem : seq of Obj

pre $p \in \text{rng } mem \cup \bigcup\{OS(p) \mid p \in disk\}$
post if $p \in \text{rng } \overleftarrow{mem}$

$\quad$ then $disk = \overleftarrow{disk} \wedge mem = remove\_obj(p, \overleftarrow{mem}) \frown [p]$

$\quad$ else $\exists pg\_in \in \overleftarrow{disk}, obj\_seq\_out, tmp\_mem \in \text{seq of } Obj,$
$\qquad\qquad pg\_seq\_out \in \text{seq of seq of } Obj, pgs\_out \in \text{set of } Pg \cdot$
$\qquad\quad p \in OS(pg\_in)$
$\qquad\quad \wedge \overleftarrow{mem} = obj\_seq\_out \frown tmp\_mem$
$\qquad\quad \wedge tmp\_mem \neq []$
$\qquad\quad \wedge obj\_seq\_out = \text{conc } pg\_seq\_out$
$\qquad\quad \wedge pgs\_out = \{mk\text{-}Page(\text{rng } p) \mid p \in \text{rng } pg\_seq\_out\}$
$\qquad\quad \wedge post\text{-}add\_to\_mem(OS(pg\_in), tmp\_mem, mem)$
$\qquad\quad \wedge disk = \overleftarrow{disk} - \{pg\_in\} \cup pgs\_out$
$\qquad\quad \wedge \sum_{obj \in mem} size(obj) \leq store\_size$
$\qquad\quad \wedge \forall i \in \text{dom } pg\_seq\_out \cdot$

$$\left(\left(\sum_{obj \in \text{rng } pg\_seq\_out(i)} size(obj)\right) + \begin{array}{l} \text{if } i = \text{len } pg\_seq\_out \\ \text{then } size(tmp\_mem(1)) \\ \text{else } size(pg\_seq\_out(i+1)(1)) \end{array}\right.$$

$$\left. > pg\_size\right)$$

The $remove\_obj$ function (signature $Obj \times \text{seq of } Obj \rightarrow \text{seq of } Obj$) removes an Obj from a sequence of Objs; it can be defined in a similar way to $remove\_pg$.

add_to_mem $(objs: \text{set of } Obj)$

ext wr mem : seq of Obj

post $mem = \overleftarrow{mem} \frown objlist \wedge \text{rng } objlist = objs \wedge \text{len } objlist = \text{card } objs$

Traveler: The Apiary Observatory

Carl R. Manning

Message Passing Semantics Group
MIT Artificial Intelligence Laboratory
Cambridge, Massachusetts USA

Abstract

Observing and debugging concurrent actor programs on a distributed architecture such as the Apiary poses new problems not found in sequential systems. Since events are only partially ordered, the chronological order of events no longer corresponds to their causal ordering, so the execution trace of a computation must be more structured than a simple stream. Many events may execute concurrently, so a stepper must give the programmer control over the order in which events are stepped. Because of the arrival order nondeterminism of the actor model, different actors may have different views on the ordering of events. We conquer these problems by recording the *activation ordering*, the *transaction pairing*, and the *arrival ordering* of messages in the Apiary and displaying the resulting structures in Traveler's window oriented interface under user control.

1. Introduction

Observing and debugging concurrent actor programs on a distributed architecture such as the Apiary poses new problems not found in sequential systems. Since events are only partially ordered, the chronological order of events no longer corresponds to their causal ordering, so the execution trace of a computation must be more structured than a simple stream. Many events may execute concurrently, so a stepper must give the programmer control over the order in which events are stepped. Because of the arrival order nondeterminism of the actor model, different actors may have different views on the ordering of events. We conquer these problems by recording the *activation ordering*, the *transaction pairing*, and the *arrival ordering* of messages in the Apiary and displaying the resulting structures in Traveler's window oriented interface under user control, either after the fact in case of a trace, or while the structure is incrementally constructed in a stepping session.

Actor programs are concurrent at a fine grain, the level of message passing. Each actor can process its messages concurrently with other actors using only its local state; thus concurrency is engendered whenever an actor sends more than one other actor a message. The Apiary architecture takes advantage of this property by migrating actors between the different processors of the architecture to balance the work load across the processors. Each processor in the Apiary keeps a queue of messages which need to be processed by the actors resident in it. The conceptual cycle of the worker is to take a message off the queue, deliver it to an actor which processes the message, and send any new messages to their target actors. Sending the new messages involves either sending a message over the network to another processor if the target of the message is resident there, or just enqueueing it locally if the target actor is local. A debugging system for the Apiary must deal with the fine level of concurrency and the distributed nature of the machine.

Actor programs are currently written in a core actor language called *Acore*. Acore syntax is much like that of Lisp, but expressions and commands in the same context (e.g. a command body or an argument list) may be performed concurrently. Acore forms are interpreted in a message passing style, so for example

```
(1 :+ 2)
```

sends the actor '1' the message ':+ 2'. Symbols in the keyword package (starting with ':') are interpreted as the selector of the message. Function calls are also interpreted as a short hand for message passing with the assumed selector ':do', so for example

```
(list 1 2) and (list :do 1 2)
```

mean the same thing: the target actor 'list' is sent the message ':do 1 2'. This syntax is used throughout this paper.

2. Observing Transactions

Traditionally, tracing a program involves setting up an output stream (say, the user's terminal) and printing a description of an event on the stream as it occurs. This is feasible because the sequential nature of the program means there is a single total ordering on events, and this ordering corresponds well to the causal ordering of events. In this ordering, any functions called by a procedure are called one at a time in sequence, and all the subroutines called by the function are completed before moving on to the next function. Thus each function call is completed before the next begins, and the source of each subroutine call is apparent. For example, see figure 2-1.

```
Procedure1 a b c
  Function1 a
    subroutine1 a
    <-- a'
    subroutine2 a'
    <-- a''
  <-- a''
  Function2 b
    subroutine3 b
    <-- b'
  <-- b'
  Function3 a'' b' c
  <-- (a'' b' c)
<-- (a'' b' c)
```

Figure 2-1: Traditional Trace

Since everything is sequential, showing events in chronological order produces a stream where causality is apparent; there is no question who called `subroutine3` or where the parameter b came from.

However, tracing a concurrent actor program cannot proceed so simply because messages sent to different actors may be processed concurrently. If we were to naively output the events to a stream as they happen, then the stream would only reflect the approximate chronological order of the events rather than the causal order. Since the events do not necessarily have a total ordering, their order may change from trace to trace. In a distributed architecture, not only will the order of concurrent events be nondeterministic, but the order in which descriptions of events arrive at the output stream will also be nondeterministic. Thus we sought a method of recording the causal order of events which could be implemented in a distributed fashion.

Given an object oriented distributed computing environment, the obvious thing to do was to build an object oriented distributed recording mechanism. A message and its target comprises a task; each task execution is a message reception and is considered an event. For every event, a task record is created which records the target and the contents of the message, the task record of the event which activated it (the activating event), and the task records of the events which it activates (the activated events). Thus the *causal* or *activation ordering* of a transaction is recorded in this doubly linked graph of task records. See figure 2-2.

In order to produce this graph while the program is running, each task in a transaction being recorded carries an extra parameter which holds information about recording. The Apiary emulator traps on the presence of information in this parameter and performs some special processing to record the task. If the parameter is empty, then the emulator does not trap, makes no recording, and runs at full speed.

A reference to the activating task record is passed using the recording parameter of the task. After a task is

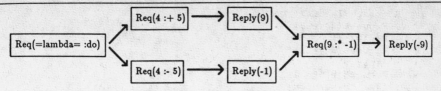

Figure 2-2: Graph of task records

This is the graph of task records for the computation performed by the expression

`((lambda () ((4 :+ 5) :* (4 :- 5))))`

`:Do` is the selector used for function calls.

---

dequeued, but just before it is delivered to the target actor, a task record for the task is created. The passed task record is the activating task record for the new task record. A message is sent to the activating task record to link it with the new task record. Finally the message is delivered to the actor with the new task record in the recording parameter; this will be passed onto any new tasks the actor creates.[1]

Now that the causal ordering of the tasks in a transaction is recorded, the question arises about how to display it. Since the traditional trace displayed only a single sequence of events and we wanted to display a partially ordered graph of events, it seemed logical to try to find a graphical way of using the screen and somehow gain another dimension to the display. A *Tree display*, which showed the graph as a tree of event nodes connected by lines representing the causal links, was tried; a simple display looked somewhat like figure 2-2 rotated 90° clockwise (except that joins were not displayed; see footnote). An *Actor Lifelines display*, which looked something like the event diagrams in [Clinger 81] and [Agha 86] rotated 90° counterclockwise, was also tried. These graphs were fine for showing the parallelism and structure in the computations, but they failed to be useful debugging tools because they obscured too much information about what the computation was doing and why. With all the nodes and lines, there wasn't much room to display much information about what actors were receiving messages, or what the content of the messages was. Another major problem was that these displays did not correspond to the abstractions made by the programmer in the program. The programmer thinks in terms of function and method calls and the results returned by these; in the event graphs there was little to link the requesting event with the corresponding reply, and the display wasn't suited to displaying it. In light of this experience, a display of the computation in terms of nested transactions, much like a traditional sequential trace, seems to be the answer.

Thus one goal was to create a display which looked something like a nested trace. For example, for the computation of figure 2-2, it might look something like figure 2-3.

There are several things to note about this format. The pairing of requests and replies makes it apparent which response corresponds to each request. The nesting of subtransactions preserves some of the causal information, but it does not show which of the subtransactions were performed concurrently and which must have been performed sequentially. However, we have found that the clues for debugging are generally found in the text of the descriptions (what is *that* actor doing here?, why did *that* function get called?) and in the nesting of transactions (what method was this called from?); causal relations between transactions within a method are much less important and are easily deduced from the source code (or they can be annotated on an individual task basis

---

[1] This method does not quite produce the graph shown in figure 2-2; in particular, of the tasks forming a join (e.g. the replies from the sum and difference), only the last to arrive will be linked as causing the continuation to continue (e.g. start the multiplication). The reason for this is that the replies are sent to a joining continuation actor, but the continuation actor just remembers the values previous to the last without activating any more tasks. Improving on this would require knowing how the joining continuation actor decided when to continue, an added complication we have been able to do well without so far.

```
Request(<lambda> :Do)
  Request(4 :- 5)
  Reply(-1)
  Request(4 :+ 5)
  Reply(9)
  Request(9 :* -1)
  [Tail Recursion]
Reply(-9)
```

Figure 2-3: Design of the Transaction Display

A possible transaction display for the computation `((lambda () ((4 :+ 5) :* (4 :- 5))))`.

from the Traveler's display).

This display seems to work well, but more information is needed before it can be generated from the recorded graph of the transaction. The pairing of requests with the corresponding response is crucial to the display, but the graph does not directly contain information linking pairs of requests with responses. A first attempt is to just indent a step for each request and outdent for a reply, but this approach doesn't work if there are tail recursive replies which close off more than one request.

Each request contains a *customer* to which the reply for the request should be sent. One way to make the pairing is to start with the request and search the activated graph for the reply which is sent to the customer of that request. However, such a search would consume large computational resources, especially in a large graph with many requests and replies, so a more efficient approach was needed. Thus we use *transaction customers* to put in a bit more effort to store the pairing information while recording.

The role of a transaction customer is to intercept the reply before it is sent to the real customer, record the information about the reply in a reply task record, link the reply task record with the request task record, and forward the reply to the real customer. Therefore, at the time a request task record is made (just before the request is delivered to the actor), a transaction customer is created with references to the request task record and the real customer, and substituted for the real customer in the request task. Thus the transaction customer masquerades as the real customer, and when it receives the reply, performs its duties and forwards the reply to the real customer.

With the transaction pairing links added by the transaction customers, the recording mechanism for transactions is complete, and generating a trace display is not difficult. A transaction display for Traveler is shown in figure 2-4.

The implementation of the transaction display for Traveler includes the ability to selectively open and close transactions to expose or hide subtransactions, giving the user control over the level of detail shown, much like outline processing in some modern word processors. Closed transactions (those whose subtransactions are hidden) are displayed in italics. Traveler also provides the ability to save a snapshot of the entire display in an editor buffer, so if the display is still too large to conveniently view on the screen even when irrelevant transactions are closed, it may be printed out.

The tracing facility provided by Traveler so far has proven to be very useful in localizing problems in small applications. Even when the program hangs, a trace of an incomplete transaction can be produced to find the reason for hanging. The ability to selectively open and inspect subtransactions has proven to be a great help in dealing with the complexity of small and medium small applications, but for larger applications it has become apparent that a form of selective tracing (e.g. displaying only messages to certain actors) is also needed to cut down even further on excess information.

```
(#<SPONSOR-REQUESTER Actor~6966758> :More-Sponsor-Ticks APIARY::REQUEST #<<Tc
  (#<DEFAULT-TOP-LEVEL-SPONSOR-SCRIPT Actor~9543323> :More-Sponsor-Ticks 50)
  +(:Value 50)
  (#<<TopLevelExpr> Actor~9543303> :Do)
    (#<RECURSIVE-FACTORIAL Loader-Forwarder~35667927> :Do 3)
      (#<RECURSIVE-FACTORIAL Actor~35667949> :Do 3)
        (3 :< 2)
        +(:V6 NIL)
        (Update (Script: #<RECURSIVE-FACTORIAL Cont Script 35668028>)))
        (3 :- 1)
        +(:V4 2)
        (#<RECURSIVE-FACTORIAL Loader-Forwarder~35667927> :Do 2)
        +(:V5 2)
        (3 :* 2)
        +[Tail Recursion]
        (Update (Script: #<RECURSIVE-FACTORIAL Cont Script 35668054>)))
      +[Tail Recursion]
    +[Tail Recursion]
  +[Tail Recursion]
+(:Value 6)
```

Figure 2-4: Transaction Snapshot

A snapshot of a Traveler screen showing the recursive factorial of 3. The transactions in italics have their subtransactions hidden.

---

3. Stepping Tasks and Transactions

Stepping in a sequential programming system is traditionally done either by modifying the compiled code of the program to be stepped to introduce breakpoints between statements, or by using an interpreted version of the program so it can be stepped with an interpreter. Both of these pose problems in a concurrent system where the program may be shared — modifying the program to introduce breakpoints or replacing the compiled version with the interpreted version also affects anything else which calls the program concurrently. Although an interpreted stepper can afford a source code oriented view of the stepping process, it cannot step compiled code. Yet it may be important to see how a compiled system actor interacts with other actors, so it would be nice if there was a way to step compiled programs without modifying them.

Actor programs on the Apiary already have a set of built-in breakpoints: each time a message is sent, the message may potentially need to be transmitted to another processor. Therefore there is a break each place a message is sent, and it becomes natural to step by messages. The acceptance of a message by an actor (the processing of a task) is an event; as the result of processing the message, new messages may be sent. Since message passing occurs at the level of function and method calls, message events have proven to be a small enough step size.

In order to step by event without modifying compiled code, we again make use of the recording parameter of tasks and the trap which checks it. To step a single task, an actor called a *collector* is placed in the recording parameter; the idea is that all new tasks created when the stepped task is performed will be sent to the collector instead of being delivered to their targets. When the recording trap finds a collector in the recording parameter, it sets a flag in the parameter before running the task. The recording parameter is passed on to all new tasks created by the actor; just before these tasks are delivered, they will also trigger the recording trap. This time, since the flag is set, the recording trap sends the tasks to the collector instead of delivering the message to the target actor.

Thus, by using collectors, we can build a stepper which starts with a task, steps it by sending it with a collector, and then displays the new tasks returned to the collector. When another unstepped task is stepped, the cycle is repeated.

Concurrency in the program means that many tasks will be available for stepping simultaneously. If several of these concurrent transactions interact with the same history sensitive actors, it may be important to test different orders of execution. To control the order tasks are performed, the user must be able to select which task to step next from the pool of unstepped tasks.

Stepping concurrent programs also introduces a problem of presentation – how can the pool of unstepped tasks be displayed so that their relation to the operation of the program isn't lost? A traditional stepper displays the stepping process as an incomplete trace in progress. With a little effort we can take advantage of a dynamic window interface to display stepping concurrent programs as a concurrent trace in progress. The display dynamically expands as more activated transactions are filled in between the outer transactions.

In Traveler the same display is used displaying a trace as displaying the stepping progress, so once a transaction is completely stepped, the display which results is the same as if the program had simply been traced. See figure 3-1. Since the same display is used, the facilities for opening and closing transactions are still available to control the display.

```
(#<<TopLevelExpr> Actor~12747712> :Do)
   (4 :+ 5)
   ←[No response for this transaction]
   (4 :- 5)
   ←[No response for this transaction]
 ←[No response for this transaction]
```

Figure 3-1: Snapshot of the Stepper Display

This is a snapshot of the stepper in the middle of computing the value of

(**(lambda** () **((4 :+ 5)** :* **(4 :- 5)))))**

Unstepped tasks are shown in boldface and may be stepped by selecting them with the mouse.

Traveler also provides stepping by transaction, but with a new twist. Steppers usually allow you to step through a procedure call in one step, so you don't have to waste time stepping through procedures which you think are working fine. Traveler provides this capability by allowing you to step through a transaction in one step, so you can step from a request to its corresponding reply without stepping through the subtransactions needed to compute the reply. The difference is that the transaction is recorded, so that if the reply does not turn out as expected, you can open the transaction and examine its trace to find out what happened.

Displaying the stepped tasks as a trace and stepping by transaction both pose problems in implementation: how do you catch the response for a transaction and display it correctly in the trace? To solve this problem we use the same technique we used in building the trace, the transaction customer. When we step a request, we insert a transaction customer to take care of the reply. The transaction customer keeps track of the correct location in the screen's transaction structure for the reply, so when it receives the reply it is displayed in the correct place ready for stepping.

This stepping facility has proven to be very useful for small and medium small applications, but as we move into larger applications, we have found that there is too much careful but tedious stepping just to get to the problematic parts of the program. A breakpoint mechanism is needed so that we can start stepping in the middle of a program.

4. Viewing Lifelines

When there are history sensitive objects in a concurrent computing system, the ordering of events at an object becomes important to observe. We noted above that it is important to be able to control the ordering of concurrent transactions which interact with a common, history sensitive actor; when examining a trace, it sometimes becomes important to know how things happened from a particular actor's viewpoint. For example, there may be many concurrent transactions dealing with the same bank account, and we think we've constrained the ordering of the transactions so that no withdrawals will bounce, but if we find that a transaction occasionally does bounce it is useful to find out in what order the transactions really did arrive at the bank account so we can figure out what went wrong. We record this *arrival order* of recorded tasks at an actor in the actor's *biography*; the display of this biography is called a *lifeline*.

Recording the biography is fairly straightforward; each time we create a task record, we add it to the corresponding target actor's biography. The only subtle point is that we store a copy of the target actor's state in the task record rather than just a reference to the target actor; thus when we look back at the biography we can see a history of states as well as a history of tasks, and better understand why the actor behaved as it did as it evolved into its current state.

Displaying the biography is also straightforward; we display the list of tasks in the order the arrived. Traveler provides a few conveniences: users may change the level of detail with which a task is displayed, or they may hide the events between disparate events in the lifeline to juxtapose them for better comparison. See figure 4-1 for an example lifeline.

```
This actor was born as a a #<ACCOUNT Actor~12758330> with Acquaintance:
    Balance: 0
---- Start of Lifeline ----
(Request •   (:Balance) #<DEFAULT-TOP-LEVEL-SPONSOR-SCRIPT Actor 12759896> #<RETURN-TO-LISP-CUS
(Request •   (:Deposit 3000) #<DEFAULT-TOP-LEVEL-SPONSOR-SCRIPT Actor 12761918> #<RETURN-TO-LIS
(Update •·· (Balance: 3000))
(Request •   (:Deposit 500) #<DEFAULT-TOP-LEVEL-SPONSOR-SCRIPT Actor 12764083> #<RETURN-TO-LISP
(Update •   (Balance: 3500))
(Request •   (:Withdrawal 50) #<DEFAULT-TOP-LEVEL-SPONSOR-SCRIPT
(Update •   (Balance: 3450))
   . . .
(Request •   (:Withdrawal 50) #<DEFAULT-TOP-LEVEL-SPONSOR-SCRIPT
(Update •   (Balance: 2350))
    This actor became a #<ACCOUNT Actor~12758330> with Acquaintan
       Balance: 2350
(Request •   (:Withdrawal 5000) #<DEFAULT-TOP-LEVEL-SPONSOR-SCRIP
(Update  •)
----- End of ·Lifeline -----
```

```
Activating Event
Make Concise
Hide Above
Hide Event
Hide Below
Examine Task
Display Transaction
```

```
Lifeline   Lock   Decache   Snapshot   History
Mouse-L, -M, -R: Show only activating event.
[Wed 7 Jan 2:22:50]   CarlManning          CL-USER:    Tyi                    Lisp Machi
```

Figure 4-1: Lifeline Snapshot
This is the lifeline of a bank account; the ellipses indicate portions of the lifeline are hidden to juxtapose different parts of the lifeline.

In our experience so far, lifelines haven't been used as often as transaction traces or even stepping, but they were very helpful when they were needed. The small programs we've tried so far are probably not complex enough for arrival ordering to get too far out of hand, and I expect lifelines may come into more use as more complex programs are tried. However, lifelines are useful for studying actors which arise as history sensitive managers as programs become more complex. The current format of displaying only the arriving tasks in the lifeline has also been a limitation on their use; it would be a better idea to present a lifeline of transactions where possible so that not only can you find what messages arrived, but you can study what the actor did with each message.

5. Summary and Future Work

Traveler is an integrated set of tools for examining actors and actor computations built on a window interface. In addition to the transaction and lifeline displays mentioned here, the current state of an actor may be examined simply by mousing any actor in the display. Traveler's panes can be reconfigured in several sizes to fit the task at hand, and each of the work panes can hold any transaction, lifeline, or examination.

All communication with actors to determine their state and for printing them is done through message passing. However, since debugging tools need to work even when there are problems with locked serialized actors (especially if the locking is the problem), communication with the user's actors is done with special system-requests which bypass the normal locks and handlers. Thus the debugging system bypasses fragile and possibly broken user code while still taking advantage of the distributed message passing nature of the system while it is investigating.

Of course, all this recording does come at a price. While recording, what is normally just two events, a request and a reply, now expands into at least 4 additional events to link the records. Three actors are created: the request record, the reply record, and the transaction customer. Because of this overhead, in our current emulation system programs can take from 5 to 20 times as long to run. Most of this overhead is due to the paging that goes on because of the high memory allocation rate.

Traveler has proven to be a very useful tool for observing and debugging concurrent actor programs on the Apiary. The strategy of recording a concurrent transaction and then examining the record is successful: transaction oriented tracing and stepping have been a huge leap forward over the chronological tracing and stepping facilities which existed before it, allowing us to observe and debug more complex programs. As we develop even larger programs, we are finding a few improvements and additions can be made; in particular, selective tracing and breakpoints are needed.

For the future, we plan to make the improvements I've suggested, as well as work on other tools. In particular, a source-oriented stepper (based on earlier work of Henry Lieberman) is under development. This stepper will display source code and allow concurrent expressions and commands within the code to be stepped by selection; when a value is produced, it replaces the expression which produced it in the code. An interpreter for our core actor language, Acore, is also under development to support this stepper.

Acknowledgements

Many thanks to the members of the Message Passing Semantics Group, who continue to serve as a user community, providing ideas and feedback on Traveler, and especially to Chun Ka Mui, who did much of the early work on Apiary debugging tools. This work was supported by a grant from the System Development Foundation.

References

[Agha 86]   G. Agha.
             Actors: A Model of Concurrent Computation in Distributed Systems.
             MIT Press, Cambridge, Mass., 1986.

[Clinger 81]   W. D. Clinger.
                Foundations of Actor Semantics.
                AI-TR- 633, MIT Artificial Intelligence Laboratory, May, 1981.

Classification of actions
or Inheritance also for methods

Bent Bruun Kristensen,
Institute of Electronic Systems, Aalborg University Centre, Aalborg, Denmark

Ole Lehrmann Madsen,
Computer Science Department, Aarhus University, Aarhus, Denmark

Birger Møller-Pedersen,
Norwegian Computing Center, Oslo, Norway.

Kristen Nygaard,
Institute of Informatics, University of Oslo, Oslo, Norway

Abstract

The main thing with the sub-class mechanism as found in languages like C++, SIMULA and Smalltalk is its possibility to express *specializations*. A general class, covering a wide range of objects, may be specialized to cover more specific objects. This is obtained by three properties of sub-classing: An object of a sub-class inherits the attributes of the super-class, virtual procedure/method attributes (of the super-class) may be specialized in the sub-class, and (in SIMULA only) it inherits the actions of the super-class.

In the languages mentioned above, virtual procedures/methods of a super-class are specialized in sub-classes in a very primitive manner: they are simply *re-defined* and need not bear any resemblance of the virtual in the super-class. In BETA, a new object-oriented language, classes and methods are unified into one concept, and by an extension of the virtual concept, virtual procedures/methods in sub-classes are defined as *specializations of the virtuals* in the super-class. The virtual procedures/methods of the sub-classes thus inherits the attributes (e.g. parameters) and actions from the "super-procedure/method".

In the languages mentioned above only procedures/methods may be virtual. As classes and procedures/methods are unified in BETA this gives also *virtual classes*. The paper demonstrates, how this may be used to parameterize types and enforce constraints on types.

1. Introduction

One of the key language concepts associated with object-oriented programming is the notion of classes and sub-classes.

The essence of sub-classing is that objects of any sub-class of a class C to some degree have the properties of C-objects. To some degree, because sub-classes may introduce properties, that are "in contradiction" with the intention of the super-class. Languages supporting classes/sub-classes do not prevent programmers from making such sub-classes, but in various ways they support, that objects of sub-classes behave like objects of the super-class.

One such support is that an object of a sub-class *inherits* the attributes (in terms of variables and procedures/methods) of the super-class. If MessageWindow is a sub-class of Window, it is known that a

Part of this work has been supported by NTNF, The Royal Norwegian Council for Scientific and Industrial Research, grant no. ED 0223.16641 (the Scala project) and by the Danish Natural Science Research Council, FTU Grant No. 5.17.5.1.25.

MessageWindow object has at least the same attributes as Window-objects. For languages with qualified references this is essential for the possibility of checking uses of references. A reference qualified by Window may only denote objects of class Window and of sub-classes to Window. When denoting an object by a Window qualified reference, then we are sure that the object has the attributes of Window, even if the object is a MessageWindow-object.

Most object-oriented languages support *virtual* attributes. A procedure attribute in e.g. SIMULA [SIMULA67] and C++ [Stroustrup] has to be declared explicitly as a virtual (in order to be a virtual attribute), while all methods in Smalltalk [Smalltalk] and Flavors [Cannon83] are virtual attributes.

Attributes declared in sub-classes are attributes, that objects of the sub-classes have *in addition to* those of the super-class, while virtual procedures/methods are both procedures/methods of the super-class and of the sub-classes. If an object is known to be a C-object or an object belonging to *some* sub-class of C, it will have at least the C-attributes, but no assumptions are made about the extra attributes of sub-classes. But it is assumed that a virtual procedure/method of C may be specialized in a sub-class so that it reflects the intention of this, and that this specialization is used when the virtual procedure/method is executed, even when it is used within the super-class.

Some object-oriented languages support objects with individual action sequences in addition to attributes. In SIMULA and BETA ([BETA83a], [BETA85], [BETA87]) objects have, in addition to attributes, an action sequence. In case of inheritance in these languages, the sub-class objects inherits the actions of the super-class. The details of how this is done will be given below.

When defining classes, sub-classes and especially virtuals, an element of abstraction called *generalization/specialization* is used. A super-class is a generalization, that is common for a set of classes, and sub-classes are specializations of this class to cover different special situations. One way of specializing is to add attributes in the sub-classes, but the most powerful mechanism is virtuals. By means of virtuals it is possible to specialize procedures/methods, that are attributes of the general class, so that they cover situations appropriate for the special sub-classes.

Even though this is the most common use of virtuals, most object-oriented languages with virtuals do not support, that definitions of virtuals in sub-classes may be specializations of the virtual definitions in the super-class. A sub-class method in Smalltalk and Flavors need not have more than the identifier in common with the corresponding method in the super-class. A recent improvement of SIMULA has made it possible to specify the parameters that all procedure definitions in sub-classes shall have. But apart from that, a definition of a virtual in a sub-class consist of a pure *re-definition* of the virtual definition in the super-class.

In the use of these languages it has, however, been recognized that a pure re-definition of the virtual is not always what is wanted. When (re)defining a virtual in a sub-class, the definition (or effect) of the virtual in the super-class is also wanted. In Smalltalk this is obtained by simply sending the message to the super-class (from within the method of the sub-class), so that the method of the super-class will be performed. Flavors provides a more sophisticated scheme (e.g. before and after methods). In SIMULA the virtual definition in the super-class is simply not accessible as part of or after a binding of the virtual.

In this paper it is demonstrated that by an extension of the virtual concept and by a unification of classes and methods, it is possible to use the sub-class mechanism when specializing virtual procedures/methods in sub-classes. This implies, that virtual procedures/methods in sub-classes are defined as *sub-procedures/methods* of the procedure/method in the super-class.

Section 2 describes the unification of classes and methods. This is a result of a more general unification covered by the notion of *pattern* in the object-oriented language BETA. Section 3 describes the virtual concept based on the general notion of pattern, and section 4 gives a series of examples on the use of virtual patterns.

2. The notion of pattern and sub-pattern in BETA

BETA is a language based on one abstraction mechanism, the *pattern*, covering concepts like classes, methods and types found in other languages.

A BETA program execution consists of a collection of *objects*. An object consists of an *attribute-part* and an *action-part*. Objects are described by *object descriptors*.

BETA supports objects of different *kinds*. *System* objects execute their actions in *concurrency* with other system objects, *component* objects execute their actions *alternating* (that is at most one at a time and interleaved at well-defined points) with other components, while *item* objects are executed as part of systems, components or other items. For the purpose of this paper only item objects are covered. For a description of concurrency and alternation in BETA see [BETA85, BETA87].

Even though objects may be of different kinds, there is only one form of object descriptor.

```
(#
    Decl1; Decl2; ...; Decln
enter In
do Imp
exit Out
#)
```

where $Decl_1; Decl_2; ... Decl_n$ are declarations of the attributes. The action part of an object consists of an enter-part, a do-part and an exit-part. The do-part, *Imp*, is an imperative that describes the actions of the object. Prior to the execution of an object, a value may be entered into the enter-part, *In*. After the execution of an object, a value may be delivered from the exit-part, *Out*. The enter-part corresponds to a value-parameter and the exit-part to a result-parameter.

A *pattern* is described by a *name* and an object descriptor:

```
P:  (#
        Decl1; Decl2; ...; Decln
    enter In
    do Imp
    exit Out
    #)
```

Objects generated according to P will have the *structure*, that is the same set of attributes, the same enter-part, the same do-part and the same exit-part. The kind of an object is not specified as part of its descriptor, but as part of its generation. We will say, that an object generated according to P is a P-object or an object of P.

A pattern may be a *specialization* (or a *sub-pattern*) of another pattern. This is specified by *prefixing* the object descriptor of the sub-pattern with the name of the super-pattern:

```
P1: P (#
        Decl'1; Decl'2; ...; Decl'm
    enter In'
    do Imp'
    exit Out'
    #)
```

A P1-object will have the attributes declared in P and those declared in P1. Execution of a P1-object will consist of executing the actions of P, specified by *Imp*. Execution of the special imperative **inner** in the actions of P imply the execution of the actions of P1, specified by *Imp´*.

The **inner** construct is the mechansim, that is provided for specialization of actions. According to [Thomsen] specialization of actions may be obtained in two ways: as a specialization of the effect of the general action or as a specialization of the partial ordered sequence of part-actions, that constitue the general action. The **inner** mechanism supports the last form of specializations. Examples will be given below.

Attributes of objects in BETA may be part objects, references to other objects and patterns. As an example consider a general pattern Window in a window system :

```
Window: (# UpperLeft,LowerRight:@ Point;
             Next: ^ Window;
             Display: (# ... #);
         #)
```

A Window object will have the part objects (@) UpperLeft and LowerRight (of the pattern Point), a reference (^) Next to someWindow object and a pattern attribute Display.

In case pattern attributes are used to generate and execute item objects, they correspond to local procedures in SIMULA and to methods in Smalltalk and Flavors. As BETA has a general sub-pattern concept, also covering item objects acting as local operations, we have in Smalltalk terms "classes and sub-classes of methods".

It is not a new idea to use the class/sub-class mechanism for methods. In 1975 Vaucher proposed prefixed procedures as a structuring mechanism for operations [Vaucher]. In BETA this is a consequence of a more general notion of pattern/sub-pattern. As Vaucher has demonstrated, a class/sub-class mechanism for methods is useful in itself. In the next section the notion is used in the specification of virtuals.

As an example of the usefulness of specialization of action, consider a pattern defining a small set of integers. The pattern attribute ForAll defines a general scanning of the elements of the set:

```
SmallIntSet:
  (# A:[100] @ Integer;
     Top:@ Integer;
     ...
     ForAll:
        (# Index:@ Integer;
           Current: (#exit S[Index] #)
        do 1 → Index;
           Loop:
           (if (Index ≤ Top)
           // true then
               inner;
               Index + 1 → Index;
               restart Loop
           if)
        #);
  #);
```

Given a SmallIntSet-object S, a specialization of ForAll of S is obtained by prefixing with S.ForAll:

```
do . . .; S.ForAll(# do Current →DoSomething #); . . .
```

For each execution of **inner** in the general S.ForAll, the specialization, that is Current → DoSomething, is executed, doing something for each element in the set.

3. Virtual patterns

A pattern attribute may be specified *virtual*. This implies almost the same thing as for methods in Smalltalk and Flavors: Any generation and execution of objects according to a virtual pattern implies the generation and execution of objects according to a possible definition (or *bindin*g) of the virtual in the actual sub-pattern.

BETA has an extension of this known scheme: *a virtual pattern is qualified with a pattern*, and any binding of the virtual pattern (in sub-patterns of the pattern with the virtual pattern attribute) must be a *sub-pattern of the qualifying pattern*. This has the consequence that objects of a virtual pattern are known to be objects of at least the qualifying pattern. This makes it easier to preserve the intention of a virtual attribute in sub-patterns. It may also be used for checking purposes and for generating more efficient code for generation and execution of objects according to the virtual pattern.

A pattern attribute V of pattern P is declared as virtual by:

```
P: (# V:< Q #)
```

Q is the name of a pattern and is the qualification of V. In sub-patterns of P, the virtual V may only be bound to a sub-pattern of Q. So even though V may be defined differently in different sub-patterns of P, it is still in P known to be at least a Q. The bindings of a virtual pattern in different sub-patterns are thus enforced to be specializations of the definition in the super-pattern.

In P-objects and in objects of sub-patterns of P with no binding of V, the qualifying pattern Q is the definition of V. So the qualifying pattern is also *default-binding*.

A *further* binding of V in sub-patterns of P is specified by:

```
P1: P (#  V::< Q1  #)
```

where Q1 is a sub-pattern of Q. Q1 does not have to be an immediate sub-pattern of Q. Q1 is both the binding of V and the the qualification of the (still) virtual V.

A shorthand is provided so the qualification does not have to be a separate pattern:

```
P: (#  V:< (# X,Y:@ Real#)  #)
```

The binding of V in

```
P1: P (#  V::< (# Z:@ Real #)  #)
```

is a shorthand, that binds V to a sub-pattern of the qualification, so in P1 a V-object will have the attributes X,Y and Z.

A further binding as specified above, that is V::< Q1, specifies that V is also virtual in the sub-pattern P1. If V is bound by a *final binding*, of the form

```
P1: P (#  V:: Q1  #)
```

then V is not virtual in P1 and it is not possible to bind V in sub-patterns of P1.

4 Examples on specialization of actions and virtual patterns

4.1 Why specialization of virtuals

As a very general pattern in a window system we may have the pattern Window:

```
Window:
(#
  UpperLeft,LowerRight:@ Point;

  Display:(#  { display the border of the  Window } #);
#)
```

As described here, a Window object may be displayed by executing an object of the local pattern attribute Display, and it will only display the border of the window.

Suppose that we have the following specializations of Window:

```
WindowWithLabel: Window (# Label:@ LabelType  #)

MessageWindow: Window (# Message:@ Text #)
```

We would like windows and their Display attribute to have two properties:

1. All objects of sub-patterns of Windows may be displayed, independently of which sub-pattern and independently of how a sub-pattern will be displayed. For example a WindowWithLabel will display the

label at a special position in the window, while a MessageWindow will display the message in some form. Given an object of pattern Window or of any sub-pattern, it shall be assured, that it has a Display attribute, and that this is the one defined especially for the actual sub-pattern of Window.

```
SomeWindow.Display
```

shall lead to the Display defined in the pattern of the object currently denoted by SomeWindow. SomeWindow is an object reference qualified by Window, which means that it may denote Window-objects or objects of sub-patterns to Window.

2. Display of sub-patterns of Window shall, in addition to displaying the information special for the sub-pattern, also display the border of the window. That is the Display attributes of sub-patterns shall be specializations of the Display of Window.

The former is obtained by declaring the Display attribute of Window as a virtual pattern. Then any generation and execution of Display objects will imply the generation and execution of Display objects according to the definition of Display in the actual sub-pattern. This is the same as for methods in Smalltalk.

The latter is obtained by declaring Display in Window not only virtual, but also give it a qualification, in this case a descriptor as part of the Display, describing the displaying of the border:

```
Window:
   (#
    UpperLeft,LowerRight:@ Point;

    Display:< (# do { display the border }; inner  #);
   #)
```

By this declaration Display is specified as a virtual that at least displays the border. This means that in sub-patterns of Window, the Display may be given a descriptor which is appropiate for the actual sub-pattern of Window, but this descriptor will be a specialization of Display in Window.

```
WindowWithLabel:
    Window (# Label:@ LabelType;

             Display::< (# do { display Label }; inner  #)
          #);

MessageWindow:
    Window (# Message:@ Text;

             Display ::< (# do { display Message }; inner  #)
          #)
```

When e.g. Display of a MessageWindow is executed then the action of its super-pattern is executed, displaying the border of the window. Execution of **inner** will lead to the actions of the Display for MessageWindow and will display the message. MessageWindow and WindowWithLabel may be used as super-patterns and the Display may then be further specialized.

In Smalltalk the same would be done by sending the message Display to the super-class (from Display in the sub-class). The responsibility for preserving the property of Display defined in the super-class also in sub-classes is left to the sub-classes, while in BETA the super-pattern defines what is to be preserved of its virtual attributes in all sub-classes.

4.2   Specialization of Initialization

A well-known problem in Smalltalk-like languages is the "initialization procedure/method problem". Consider a class C with a virtual procedure/method Init. In sub-classes of C it is desirable that Init may be defined, so that it incorporates the Init of C. In Smalltalk it is necessary to send Init explicitly to the super-class.

In BETA the Init of the sub-patterns will be sub-patterns of the Init in C, and they will thus have as part of them (as super-pattern) the Init in C.

Consider a pattern defining point objects:

```
Point: (# X,Y:@ Integer;
           Init:< (# do 0 → X; 0 → Y; inner #);
        #)
```

The specification of Init indicates that it is a virtual pattern. A sub-pattern of Point may bind Init to a descriptor that is a sub-descriptor of the Init in Point:

```
ThreeDPoint: Point (#  Z:@ Integer;
                        Init::< (# do 0 → Z; inner #);
                    #)
```

When executing the Init of ThreeDPoint, the actions of its super-pattern are performed, assigning 0 to both X and Y. Execution of the **inner** in Init of Point implies the execution of the actions in a possibly sub-pattern; in this case the assignment of 0 to Z. In case of a ThreeDPoint-object, the **inner** following 0 → z is an empty action, but in case ThreeDPoint is used further to define e.g. FourDPoint, then the **inner** would imply execution of initialization special for FourDPoint.

4.3   Type parameters

In the following example the SetType pattern local to SmallWindowSet does not define a method local to SmallWindowSet, but define (data) objects constituting a set of Windows.

```
SmallWindowSet:
    (#
        SetType:< Window;
        A:[100]@ SetType;
        Top:@ Integer;

        DisplaySet:
            (# do (for Inx:Top repeat A[Inx].Display  for)   #);
        ...
    #)
```

The type of the elements in the set is the virtual pattern SetType. The qualifying pattern Window says that the elements will at least be Window-objects. SetType may be bound to different sub-patterns of Window in different sub-patterns of SmallWindowSet, thereby obtaining specialized sets.

DisplaySet displays the whole set. As the elements of the set are known to be at least Window-objects, they will have a Display attribute.

A WindowWithLabel set is obtained by binding SetType to WindowWithLabel:

```
SmallWindowWithLabelSet:
    SmallWindowSet (# SetType::< WindowWithLabel  #)
```

All windows objects in this set will be WindowWithLabel objects. Note that while the bindings of Init in the previous example were to descriptors local to the sub-pattern (as it also are for re-definitions of methods in Smalltalk), SetType is here bound to a non-local pattern WindowWithLabel.

As Display of Window is a virtual pattern, then the DisplaySet as described in SmallWindowSet will also work for SmallWindowWithLabelSet. Execution of Display in

```
(for Inx:Top repeat A[Inx].Display  for)
```

will now be the execution of Display of WindowWithLabel.

4.4   Generics, polymorphism

A thorough comparison of generics (as found in e.g. Ada) and inheritance is found in [Meyer]. The following example demonstrates how constrainted genericity as defined in [Meyer] may be obtained by means of virtual patterns.

Consider the problem of writing a function Minimum, that is to work for two objects of any type. The constraint on the types in this situation is that a LessThan operation is defined. By use of virtuals this may be obtained by defining LessThan as a virtual pattern attribute of a pattern Type, and enforce the parameters of Minimum to be objects of at least the pattern Type. Type is assumed to be a general pattern. Objects of pattern Type wil e.g. be assignable. For the purpose of this example only the property that a LessThan operation is defined on Type objects is covered.

```
Type: (# OpType:< Type;
           ...
         LessThan:< (# Parameter:@ OpType;
                        Result:@ Boolean;
                      enter Parameter
                      do inner
                      exit Result
                      #);
       #);


Minimum:
    (#
       T:< Type;
       A,B,Result:@ T;
     enter (A,B)
     do
        (if  A → B.LessThan
        //True  then A → Result
        //False then B → Result
        if)
     exit Result
     #);
```

Notice, that as B is at least a Type object, it has a LessThan attribute, and A may be entered as a parameter. This is valid for for all bindings of T, as it may only be bound to sub-patterns of Type. The general Minimum, as described here, may therefore be checked independently of the binding of T.

All patterns that are to be assignable (and in this case comparable by LessThan) will be sub-patterns of Type. The binding of the virtual LessThan will for each sub-pattern give the implementation of LessThan for the appropriate type. As an example, Integer will be a sub-pattern of Type:

```
Integer: Type (# OpType:: Integer;
                 LessThan::
                      (# {implementation of LessThan for integers } #);
               #)
```

A Minimum function for integers is obtained by binding the virtual T of Minimum to Integer. The following specifies the execution of an object that has a descriptor prefixed with Minimum. The only thing specified in the sub-descriptor is the binding of the virtual T to Integer:

```
(I,J) → Minimum(# T::Integer #) → K;
```

The values of I and J are entered into the enter-part of the object prior to execution and the result is assigned to K after execution of the object.

4.5   Procedures/methods as parameters

Many languages allow parameters to procedures to be procedures. A procedure P with a formal procedure Fp is specified by

```
procedure P(Fp); procedure Fp;
begin
      ... ; Fp(1,2); ... ; Fp(3,4); ...
end;
```

When calling P with a procedure ActualFp

```
P(ActualFp)
```

the procedure ActualFp is passed, and all calls of Fp in the execution of P will be calls on ActualFp. ActualFp must then be a procedure with formal parameters that corresponds to the actual parameters (1,2) and (3,4), e.g.

```
procedure ActualFp(x,y); real x,y; begin ... end;
```

The actual procedure may be different in different calls of P. In simple cases a compiler may check that all possible actual parameters to P satify the requirements on the formal parameter, but in general this mechanis implies that each call of the formal parameter must be checked at execution time for correspondance between formal and actual parameters. An alternative is to specify as part of Fp the requirements on the actual procedure parameters.

In BETA the effect of a procedure as parameter is obtained by a virtual pattern, that is used to generate and execute item objects.

```
P: (#
      Fp:< Fpar
   do
      ...; (1,2) → Fp; ... ; (3,4) → Fp; ...
   #)
```

The qualification of Fp is a pattern, that defines the parameters:

```
Fpar:(# X,Y:@ Real enter(X,Y) #);
```

By qualifying with a pattern, that defines the parameters, it is assured, that all bindings of the virtual pattern Fp are to sub-patterns of Fpar. All bindings will thus have these parameters, and this may be checked at compile-time.

The calling of P with an actual procedure parameter is obtained by executing an item object according to a descriptor prefixed by P and with a binding of the virtual Fp:

```
do  ...; P (# Fp:: ActualFp #); ...
```

where ActualFp is a sub-pattern of Fpar and therefore has the parameters X,Y:

```
ActualFp: Fpar (# ... do ... #)
```

5. Conclusion

It has been demonstrated that by a slight extension of the virtual concept known from virtual procedures in SIMULA and methods in Smalltalk-like languages, a language may offer better support for specialization, in the sense that a method in a sub-class may be a specialization of the method in the super-class.

In BETA this is obtained by a generalization of langauge concepts like class, procedure, method, function and types into one concept, the pattern. Specialization of patterns in general thus implies specialization for patterns that act as methods. A pattern attribute, that is specified virtual and defined as an operation on the object, of which it is an attribute, works like a Smalltalk method. By requirering that a virtual pattern only may be bound to sub-patterns of a pattern qualifying the virtual pattern, it is enforced that all bindings in different sub-patterns are specializations of the qualifying pattern.

This mechanism may also be applied to languages, that do not have a generalization like the pattern concept. In e.g. Smalltalk the only requirement would be, that a method may be a specialization of a more general method - that is the sub-class mechanism should be applied also to methods and not only to classes.

Acknowledgements

We would like to thank Knut Barra, Axel Hagemann and Claus Nørgård for commenting the paper.

References

[BETA83a] B.B. Kristensen, O.L. Madsen, B. Møller-Pedersen, K. Nygaard: *Abstraction Mechanisms in the BETA Programming Language*. Proceedings of the Tenth ACM Symposium on Principles of Programming Languages, 1983.

[BETA83 b] O.L. Madsen, B. Møller-Pedersen, K. Nygaard: *From SIMULA 67 to BETA*. Proceedings of the Eleventh SIMULA User's Conference, 1983

[BETA85] B.B. Kristensen, O.L. Madsen, B. Møller-Pedersen, K. Nygaard: *Multi-sequential Execution in the BETA Programming Language*. Sigplan Notices, Vol. 20, No. 4 April 1985

[BETA87] B.B. Kristensen, O.L. Madsen, B. Møller-Pedersen, K. Nygaard: *The BETA Programming Language*. To appear in: *Research Directions in Object Orienetd Programming*. Edited by B. Shriver and P. Wegner. MIT Press Spring 1987.

[Cannon83] H. Cannon: Flavors, A Non-Hierarchical Approach to Object-Oriented Programming. Draft 1982

[DELTA75] E. Holbæk Hansen, P. Haandlykken, K. Nygaard: *System Description and the DELTA Language*. Norwegian Computing Center, Oslo 1975

[Meyer] B. Meyer: *Generisity versus Inheritance*. In *OOPSLA, Object-Oriented Programming Systems, Languages and Applications*. Conference Proceedings, Sigplan Notices Vol.21 No.11 November 1986.

[SIMULA67] O.J. Dahl, B. Myhrhaug & K. Nygaard: *SIMULA 67 Common Base Language*, Norwegian Computing Center, 1968, 1970, 1972, 1984

[Smalltalk] A. Goldberg, D. Robson: *Smalltalk 80: The Language and its Implementation*. Addison Wesley 1983.

[Stroustrup] B. Stroustrup: *The C++ Programming Language*. Addison Wesley 1986.

[Thomsen] K.S. Thomsen: *Multiple Inheritance, a Structuring Mechanism for Data,Processes and Procedures*. DAIMI PB-209, Aarhus University, April 1986.

[Vaucher] J. Vaucher: Prefixed procedures: *A structuring Concept for Operations*. Infor, Vol 13, no.3, October 1975.

Semantics of *Smalltalk-80**

Mario Wolczko[†]

Dept. of Computer Science, The University, Manchester M13 9PL, United Kingdom

miw@uk.ac.man.cs.ux, mcvax!ukc!man.cs.ux!miw

Abstract

A formal model of the *Smalltalk-80* programming language is introduced. The semantics of much of the *Smalltalk-80* language are described using the denotational style. A poorly-designed feature of Smalltalk is highlighted, and alternative semantics are presented for the language feature.

1 Introduction

Smalltalk-80 is the archetypal object-oriented programming environment. All code within the *Smalltalk-80* system is written in the *Smalltalk-80* programming language (hereafter referred to as "Smalltalk"). Smalltalk has several characteristics that are common in object-oriented langauges, and others that distinguish Smalltalk from other languages: a uniformly-applied object model; an inheritance hierarchy of classes; and message-sending as the sole inter-object communication mechanism.

A formal model of Smalltalk would be useful in describing what Smalltalk is, and how it differs from other languages. Also, as many non-object-oriented languages have been described through formal models, it would help to illustrate how the object-oriented paradigm differs from other programming paradigms[5]. Furthermore, since a formal model is likely to be more concise and succinct than, say, an interpreter for the language[2], it would provide a convenient framework for discussion of language semantics. This is because a formal model would be at the right level of abstraction for such discussions: implementation details (e.g., the garbage collection strategy) would not appear in the formal model.

This paper introduces a formal model of Smalltalk. As Smalltalk is a non-trivial language, the complete model cannot be presented in the limited space available; the remainder will appear elsewhere[7]. However, the major parts of a simplified model are presented here. This simplified model also serves as an introduction to the more complicated model. Using the model as a basis, the design of Smalltalk is discussed, and weaknesses in the design are highlighted. In particular, the block evaluation mechanism is found to be inadequate, and an alternative design for this feature is presented.

2 A Formal Model of Smalltalk

The formal description technique used will be that of denotational semantics[1,3,6], "sugared" with a VDM-like syntax[4]. Several simplifications are made to keep the semantics tractable, and to preserve the right level of abstraction:

1. In a Smalltalk-80 system there a number of processes (conceptually) executing in parallel. Due to the lack of any protection mechanisms, these processes, which reside in a single address space, could interfere with each other. By convention, most methods in the Smalltalk-80 system assume that no interference is taking place, and the use of concurrency is limited to a few places in the system. To simplify the model we have assumed that no concurrency is present, and therefore that no interference can take place.

2. Non-local variables, i.e., global, class and pool variables, have been omitted. These could all be simulated in Smalltalk by sending messages to the appropriate dictionary.

Smalltalk-80 is a registered trademark of Xerox Corp.

[†]Work supported by the Science and Engineering Research Council

3. The only forms of literal dealt with are integers and blocks. It would be straightforward to deal with other forms, such as Floats and Strings, but the treatment would be similar to that for integers, and is therefore omitted for brevity.

4. All the integer classes (SmallInteger, LargePositiveInteger, LargeNegativeInteger) have been replaced by a single class, Integer, instances of which are integers of arbitrary size.

5. A block in Smalltalk can be directed to return to the place that invoked its execution, or to the place that invoked its creation, which need not be the same. The semantics presented here only deal with the former case.

6. A block in Smalltalk can access all the variables of its enclosing method. This means that the activation record of a method that contains a block cannot be discarded when the corresponding method is exited. As a simplification, the semantics presented here restrict blocks so that they cannot access the temporaries of the enclosing method. However, they can access the arguments of the method and the instance variables of the receiver.

3 The Abstract Syntax of Smalltalk

A "program" in Smalltalk is composed of a set of class definitions. Each definition states: (i) how the class relates to other classes by inheritance, (ii) the instance variables that are defined by that class, and (iii) the messages that instances of that class respond to, and how. Formally, this can be stated thus:

$Program = Class\_map$

$Class_map = $ map $Class\_name$ to $Class\_body$

$$Class\_body :: \quad Instvars : \text{ set of } Id$$
$$Super : Superclass$$
$$Methods : \text{ map } Selector \text{ to } (Method\_body \cup Primitive\_method)$$

In the single inheritance scheme supported by the Smalltalk Virtual Machine, each class can have zero or one superclasses:

$Superclass = [Class\_name]$

For the purposes of this paper, we shall restrict ourselves to the single inheritance scheme supported by the Smalltalk Virtual Machine.

A selector can be a single postfix identifier (a *unary* selector), an infix (*binary*) selector, or a *keyword* selector:

$Selector = Unary \cup Binary \cup Keyword$

$Unary = Id$

$Binary = \{+, -, *, /, <, \ldots\}$

$Keyword = \text{ seq of } Id$

Later we will use a function, $nargs: Selector \rightarrow \mathbf{N}$, which returns 0 for unary selectors, 1 for binary selectors, and len s for a keyword selector s.

Each method body declares a number of arguments and temporary variables, and has a list of expressions as the executable part of the method.

$$Method\_body :: \quad Args : Ulist(Id)^1$$
$$Temps : \text{ set of } Id$$
$$Exprs : Expression\_list$$

$Expression_list = $ seq of $Expression$

An *Expression* can be one of four things: an assignment to a variable, an object name, a message send, or a literal object (integer or block):

$Expression = Assignment \cup Object\_name \cup Message\_list \cup Literal\_object$

$Assignment ::\ LHS\ :\ Id$
$\qquad\qquad\quad RHS\ :\ Expression$

$Object\_name = Id \cup \{\textsc{Self}, \textsc{Super}, \textsc{Root}\}$

SELF is the name of the receiver. SUPER is also an alias for the receiver, but messages sent to SUPER are searched for differently. ROOT is a global object guaranteed to be in the system. It plays the part of the global dictionary, Smalltalk.

A *Message_list* consists of an expression which evaluates to a receiver object, and a list of messages to be sent to the receiver (cascaded messages, to use the *Smalltalk-80* terminology).

$Message\_list ::\ Rcvr\ :\ Expression$
$\qquad\qquad\qquad Msgs\ :\ $ seq of $Message$

$Message ::\ Sel\ :\ Selector$
$\qquad\qquad\quad Args\ :\ Expression\_list$

A *Literal_object* is a 'constant' (i.e., immutable) object. Here, we only consider integers and blocks.

$Literal\_object = \mathbf{Z} \cup Block\_body$

One can consider a block to be a nameless method; it is activated by sending it the **value** message. Bound blocks are first-class objects. To emphasize the similarity between methods and blocks, we use the same abstract syntax for both:

$Block\_body ::\ Args\ :\ Ulist(Id)$
$\qquad\qquad\qquad Temps\ :\ $ set of Id^2
$\qquad\qquad\qquad Exprs\ :\ Expression\_list$

An extra field required in the full model, *RetHome*: $\mathbf{B}$, has been omitted. A Smalltalk block differs from an anonymous method in one important way: it can return to one of two different places. The normal return route is to the method that activated the block by sending it the **value** message. However, control may also return to the method that activated the textually enclosing method (i.e., the method in which the block was bound). This is indicated by placing an uparrow before the last statement in a Smalltalk block. In the latter case, the activation of methods is not LIFO. The inclusion of this feature would complicate the semantics enormously, and so has not been covered in this limited exposition.

Context conditions stating exactly which programs are considered to be legal are to be found in the appendix.

4   The Object Model in Smalltalk

Smalltalk methods operate on objects which reside in a single, persistent store. This store, or object memory, contains all the objects that exist in a Smalltalk system, including methods, classes, and "primitive objects" such as integers. Note also that method activation records, or *contexts* in Smalltalk terminology, also reside in the object memory. However, for simplicity our semantics does not place contexts in the object store.

$Object_memory = $ map Oop to $Object$

We shall usually denote values of *Object_memory* by σ.

Every object is identified by a unique internal name, or *object pointer* (here contracted to *Oop*). Every object is an instance of a class:

$Object ::\ Class\ :\ Class\_name$
$\qquad\qquad Body\ :\ Object\_body$

---

[1] The type *Ulist*(X) models a list with no duplicate elements. Formally, $Ulist(X) = $ seq of X, where $inv\text{-}Ulist(X)(l) \triangleq$ len $l = $ card rng l.

[2] Actually, Smalltalk does not allow blocks to have temporaries. The absence of temporary variables from blocks was a curious omission in the design of Smalltalk. Later we shall meet other strange features of blocks.

$Object\_body = Plain\_object \cup Primitive\_object$

$Primitive\_object = \mathbf{Z} \cup Block$

Primitive objects have no instance variables and are therefore immutable: their internal state cannot change.[3]

Plain_objects are instances of user-defined classes. They contain references to other objects. In Smalltalk, the instance variables of an object are exactly those declared in its class and superclasses (except for indexed instance variables). This leads naturally to the following model of *Plain_objects*:

$Plain\_object = \mathsf{map}\ Id\ \mathsf{to}\ Oop$

Smalltalk implementations linearise the instance variables, so that each is assigned a unique integer, leading to the following model:

$Plain\_object = \mathsf{seq\ of}\ Oop$

However, this creates severe problems when multiple inheritance is involved. For the moment, we shall choose the former model, and introduce indexed instance variables later.

5 Environments

In the semantic equations that follow we use two structures that we term "environments". The *static environment* describes the textual context of a method with respect to the rest of the program. This is constant for any particular method within a program. The *dynamic environment* describes the local state of an invocation of a method (it is anologous to a Smalltalk **MethodContext**). It changes during the invocation of a method, and each invocation has its own local dynamic environment. In addition to these there is the object memory which is global. One can consider these to be, from an operational point of view, the environment known at compile-time, the local values known at method invocation time, and the store, respectively.

5.1 The Static Environment

A static environment, denoted by ρ, contains the "text" of all the methods, and an indication of which class the current method is in (required by the **super** mechanism):

$$SEnv :: \begin{array}{ll} Class & : & Class\_name \\ P & : & Program \end{array}$$

5.2 The Dynamic Environment

A dynamic environment, denoted by δ, records the state of the computation local to a method invocation:

$$DEnv :: \begin{array}{lll} Rcvr & : & Oop \\ Args & : & \mathsf{map}\ Id\ \mathsf{to}\ Oop \\ Temps & : & \mathsf{map}\ Id\ \mathsf{to}\ Oop \end{array}$$

The receiver and arguments of a method are determined when a method is bound to a message, and do not change during the execution of the method. Temporaries, however, are initialised to nil and are usually assigned to within the method.

6 The Semantic Function for Methods

In our semantics, methods and blocks are functions which transform the object memory. In reality, they are encoded into **CompiledMethods**, which are first-class objects interpreted by the Smalltalk Virtual Machine. As mentioned earlier, this has been ignored in the existing semantics, and methods no longer reside in the *Object_memory* as full objects.

A *Method* takes a receiver and a list of arguments, and returns a result object, transforming the object memory as a side-effect:

$Method = Oop \times \mathsf{seq\ of}\ Oop \times Object\_memory \rightarrow Oop \times Object\_memory$

---

[3]Most Smalltalk implementations take advantage of this by encoding the value of an integer object into its object pointer.

A *Block* is similar, but the associated receiver is the block-object (see later section on blocks).

$$Block = Oop \times \text{seq of } Oop \times Object\_memory \rightarrow Oop \times Object\_memory$$

An initial object memory will contain not only the methods and blocks specified by the Smalltalk program, but also so-called "primitive" methods, which cannot be expressed in Smalltalk[2]. Such primitive methods include those for integer arithmetic and comparison, and special methods for activating blocks. This is why the *Methods* field of a *Class_body* can map a *Selector* to a "pre-compiled" method, known as a *Primitive_method*.

$$Primitive\_method = Method$$

We now present the semantic function for methods. It takes a method definition, in its static environment, and returns a method denotation.

$$MMethod\_body : Method\_body \rightarrow SEnv \rightarrow Method$$

$MMethod\_body[\![mk\text{-}Method\_body(args, temps, exprs)]\!]\rho \;\; \triangle$
$\quad \lambda rcvr, arglist, \sigma \cdot$
$\qquad \text{let } \delta = mk\text{-}DEnv(rcvr, \{args(i) \mapsto arglist(i) \mid i \in \text{dom } args\}, \{id \mapsto \text{NilOop} \mid id \in temps\}) \text{ in}$
$\qquad \text{let } (result, \delta', \sigma') = MExpression\_list[\![exprs]\!]\rho\delta\sigma \text{ in}$
$\qquad (result, \sigma')$

The result value of a list of expressions is the result of the last expression in the list.

$$MExpression\_list : Expression\_list \rightarrow SEnv \rightarrow DEnv \rightarrow Object\_memory$$
$$\rightarrow Oop \times DEnv \times Object\_memory$$

$MExpression\_list[\![exprs]\!]\rho\delta\sigma \;\; \triangle$
$\quad \text{let } (oop, \delta', \sigma') = MExpression[\![\text{hd } exprs]\!]\rho\delta\sigma \text{ in}$
$\quad \text{if len } exprs = 1 \text{ then } (oop, \delta', \sigma') \text{ else } MExpression\_list[\![\text{tl } exprs]\!]\rho\delta'\sigma'$

7 The Semantic Function for Expressions

7.1 Assignment

Expressions change the local state of the computation by altering the dynamic environment. An assignment can only alter the values of temporaries or instance variables; arguments are read-only.

$$MExpression : Expression \rightarrow SEnv \rightarrow DEnv \rightarrow Object\_memory \rightarrow Oop \times DEnv \times Object\_memory$$

$MExpression[\![mk\text{-}Assignment(id, rhs)]\!]\rho\delta\sigma \;\; \triangle$
$\quad \text{let } (result, \delta', \sigma') = MExpression[\![rhs]\!]\rho\delta\sigma \text{ in}$
$\quad \text{if } id \in \text{dom } Temps(\delta)$
$\quad \text{then } (result, \mu(\delta', Temps \mapsto Temps(\delta') \dagger \{id \mapsto result\}), \sigma')$
$\quad \text{else } (result, \delta', \sigma' \dagger \{Rcvr(\delta) \mapsto \mu(\sigma(Rcvr(\delta)), Body \mapsto Body(\sigma(Rcvr(\delta))) \dagger \{id \mapsto result\})\})$

7.2 Variables

$MExpression[\![id]\!]\rho\delta\sigma \;\; \triangle \quad \text{if } id \in \text{dom } Temps(\delta)$
$\qquad\qquad\qquad\qquad \text{then } (Temps(\delta)(id), \delta, \sigma)$
$\qquad\qquad\qquad\qquad \text{else if } id \in \text{dom } Args(\delta)$
$\qquad\qquad\qquad\qquad\quad \text{then } (Args(\delta)(id), \delta, \sigma)$
$\qquad\qquad\qquad\qquad\quad \text{else } \Big(Body(\sigma(Rcvr(\delta)))(id), \delta, \sigma\Big)$

7.3 Pseudo-variables

$MExpression[\![\text{Self}]\!]\rho\delta\sigma \;\; \triangle \quad (Rcvr(\delta), \delta, \sigma)$

$MExpression[\![\text{SUPER}]\!]\rho\delta\sigma \quad \triangleq \quad (Rcvr(\delta), \delta, \sigma)$

ROOT is present in all object memories, and therefore has a constant Oop, ROOTOOP.

$MExpression[\![\text{ROOT}]\!]\rho\delta\sigma \quad \triangleq \quad (\text{ROOTOOP}, \delta, \sigma)$

7.4 Integer Constants

$MExpression[\![int]\!]\rho\delta\sigma \quad \triangleq$
  let $(oop, \sigma') = find\_or\_make\_int(int, \sigma)$ in
  (oop, δ, σ') for $int \in \mathbf{Z}$

The $find\_or\_make\_int$ function, given an integer and an object memory, returns the Oop of an integer object that has the integer as its value. It is specified as a VDM operation in such a way that duplicate integer objects are allowed (to give an implementor freedom).

$find\_or\_make\_int$ $(int: \mathbf{Z})$ $obj: Oop$
ext wr σ : $Object\_memory$
post $\sigma(obj) = mk\text{-}Object(\text{Integer}, int) \wedge (\sigma = \overleftarrow{\sigma} \vee \sigma \lhd \{obj\} = \overleftarrow{\sigma})$

7.5 Message Sending

Sending messages is the only way in Smalltalk for objects to communicate with each other. Smalltalk messages are synchronous: the sender waits for the receiver to return a value before continuing. A Smalltalk message can therefore be considered to be a dynamically bound procedure call; the particular method to be executed in response to a message is determined by the class of the receiver. When a message is received by an object a search is performed for a corresponding method, starting at the class of the receiver, and working up through its superclasses.

Additionally, in Smalltalk there is an alternative starting point for the search, indicated by an object sending a message to itself with the special designation **super**. This starts the search in the superclass of the class in which the message is being sent from. This allows a class to override the behaviour of an inherited method but still have access to that method.

In the formal semantics, these searches are distinguished by different bindings of the *find* function. The super search is based entirely on the static environment, and can therefore be bound at compile-time, whereas the usual search cannot.

$MExpression[\![mk\text{-}Message\_list(rcvr, msgs)]\!]\rho\delta\sigma \quad \triangleq$
  let $(rcvr\_object, \delta', \sigma') = MExpression[\![rcvr]\!]\rho\delta\sigma$ in
  let $search_fn = $ if $rcvr = \text{SUPER}$
      then $find(Super(P(\rho)(Class(\rho))), \rho)$
      else $find(Class(\sigma'(rcvr\_object)), \rho)$
    in
  $MMessage\_list[\![msgs]\!]\rho\delta'(search\_fn, rcvr\_object, \sigma')$

The method search may fail to find a method corresponding to a particular message selector, in which case the search function returns nil (i.e., a VDM nil, not to be confused with the Smalltalk nil object).

$Search\_function = Selector \to [Method]$

$find$: $[Class\_name] \times SEnv \to Search\_function$

$find(class, \rho)sel \quad \triangleq$
  if $class = nil$ then nil else if $sel \in$ dom $Methods(P(\rho)(class))$
          then if $Methods(P(\rho)(class))(sel) \in Primitive\_method$
            then $Methods(P(\rho)(class))(sel)$
            else $MMethod\_body[\![Methods(P(\rho)(class))(sel)]\!]\mu(\rho, Class \mapsto class)$
          else $find(Super(P(\rho)(class)), \rho)sel$

Sending a list of messages to an object consists of evaluating the arguments of the first message, sending the first message, then sending the rest of the messages in the list.

$MMessage\_list : seq\ of\ Message \rightarrow SEnv \rightarrow DEnv \rightarrow (Search\_function \times Oop \times Object\_memory)$
$\qquad \rightarrow (Oop \times DEnv \times Object\_memory)$

$MMessage\_list[\![msgs]\!]\rho\delta(search\_fn, rcvr, \sigma) \quad \triangle$
$\quad$ let $(v, \delta', \sigma') = MMessage[\![hd\ msgs]\!]\rho\delta(search\_fn, rcvr, \sigma)$ in
$\quad$ if len $msgs = 1$ then (v, δ', σ') else $MMessage\_list[\![tl\ msgs]\!]\rho\delta'(search\_fn, rcvr, \sigma')$

$MMessage : Message \rightarrow SEnv \rightarrow DEnv$
$\qquad \rightarrow (Search\_function \times Oop \times Object\_Memory) \rightarrow (Oop \times DEnv \times Object\_Memory)$

$MMessage[\![mk\text{-}Message(sel, arglist)]\!]\rho\delta(search\_fn, rcvr, \sigma) \quad \triangle$
$\quad$ let $(actuals, \delta', \sigma') = MAll\_Expression\_list[\![arglist]\!]\rho\delta\sigma$ in
$\quad$ let $(result, \sigma'') = perform(rcvr, sel, actuals, search\_fn, \sigma')$ in
$\quad (result, \delta', \sigma'')$

$MAll\_Expression\_list$ evaluates a list of expressions, returning a list of results.

$MAll\_Expression\_list : seq\ of\ Expression \rightarrow SEnv \rightarrow DEnv \rightarrow Object\_Memory$
$\qquad \rightarrow seq\ of\ Oop \times DEnv \times Object\_Memory$

$MAll\_Expression\_list[\![el]\!]\rho\delta\sigma \quad \triangle$
$\quad$ if $el = [\,]$
$\quad$ then $([\,], \delta, \sigma)$
$\quad$ else let $(val, \delta', \sigma') = MExpression[\![hd\ el]\!]\rho\delta\sigma$ in
$\qquad$ let $(val\_list, \delta'', \sigma'') = MAll\_Expression\_list[\![tl\ el]\!]\rho\delta'\sigma'$ in
$\qquad ([val] \frown val\_list, \delta'', \sigma'')$

If a particular method search fails, the special message doesNotUnderstand: must be sent to the receiver. A method corresponding to the doesNotUnderstand: message is searched for in the same way. This allows a class to override the behaviour of doesNotUnderstand:.

$perform : Oop \times Selector \times seq\ of\ Oop \times Search\_function \times Object\_memory \rightarrow Oop \times Object\_Memory$

$perform(rcvr, sel, args, search\_fn, \sigma) \quad \triangle$
$\quad$ let $first\_search\_result = search\_fn(sel)$ in
$\quad$ if $first\_search\_result \neq$ nil
$\quad$ then $first\_search\_result(rcvr, args, \sigma)$
$\quad$ else let $second\_search\_result = search\_fn(\text{doesNotUnderstand:})$ in
$\qquad$ let $(message, \sigma') = create\_message(sel, args, \sigma)$ in
$\qquad second\_search\_result(rcvr, [message], \sigma')$

Note that for the result of the *perform* function to be defined should the original message not be understood, there *must* exist a method corresponding to the doesNotUnderstand: selector.

The *create_message* function creates an instance of class **Message** that records the selector and arguments of the message that was not understood.

7.6 Blocks

The implementation of blocks in Smalltalk does not work as one might expect. When a block is bound to its surrounding context, an instance of **BlockContext** is created that records the binding. The **BlockContext** also has memory reserved for the workspace required when the block is activated. Unfortunately, blocks can be activated re-entrantly. This means that most Smalltalk implementations fail in unexpected ways when presented with re-entrant blocks, because the workspace of one activation is overwritten by another. For example, the following Smalltalk code, which looks reasonable at first sight, would not work on most systems:

```
factBlock ← [ :n |
    n=0 ifTrue: [1]
        ifFalse: [n * (factBlock value: n−1)]].
factBlock value: 2
```

The solution to the problem is to make a clean separation between the acts of binding the block to its surrounding context, and activating a bound block. To this end, we propose that binding a block create an instance of a new class, Closure. The Closure would be a first-class object. To activate the block, the special value message would be sent to the Closure. This leads to the following semantics:

$$MExpression[\![block]\!]\rho\delta\sigma \quad \triangle$$
$$\text{let } (closure, \sigma') = make\_closure(block, \rho, \delta, \sigma) \text{ in}$$
$$(closure, \delta, \sigma') \qquad \text{for } block \in Block\_body$$

When the closure is created the block is bound to the dynamic environment in existence at the time.

$$make\_closure \; (block: Block\_body, \rho: SEnv, \delta: DEnv) \; closure: Oop$$

$$\text{ext wr } \sigma \; : \; Object\_Memory$$

$$\text{post } \sigma(closure) = mk\text{-}Object(\text{Closure}, MBlock\_body[\![block]\!]\rho\delta) \wedge (\sigma = \overleftarrow{\sigma} \vee \sigma \triangleleft \{closure\} = \overleftarrow{\sigma})$$

As mentioned earlier, a block is bound in such a way that it has access to the receiver of the method in which it was bound, and the arguments of the enclosing method (and any enclosing blocks) but not to the temporary variables of enclosing methods/blocks. Access to these would require dynamic environments to outlive their associated invocations, complicating the model somewhat.

Note also that a block must check at run-time that it was invoked with the same number of arguments that it had in its definition. If this is not the case, an error message is sent.

$$MBlock\_body : Block\_body \rightarrow SEnv \rightarrow DEnv \rightarrow Block$$

$$MBlock\_body[\![mk\text{-}Block\_body(args, temps, exprs)]\!]\rho\delta(closure, arglist, \sigma) \quad \triangle$$
$$\text{let } (result, \delta'', \sigma') =$$
$$\quad \text{if len } arglist = \text{len } args$$
$$\quad \text{then let } \delta' = mk\text{-}DEnv(Rcvr(\delta), Args(\delta) \cup \{args(i) \mapsto arglist(i) \mid i \in \text{dom } args\},$$
$$\quad\quad\quad \{id \mapsto \text{NilOop} \mid id \in temps\}) \text{ in}$$
$$\quad\quad MExpression\_list[\![exprs]\!]\rho\delta'\sigma$$
$$\quad \text{else } MMessage[\![mk\text{-}Message(mk\text{-}Unary(\text{wrongNumberOfArguments}), [\,])]\!]\rho\delta$$
$$\quad\quad\quad (find(Class(\sigma(closure)), \rho), closure, \sigma)$$
$$\quad \text{in}$$
$$(result, \sigma')$$

8 Primitives

Every Smalltalk system has to have a complement of primitive operations provided. In this section, we outline how the semantics of such primitives can be described within our model. There are far too many primitives in Smalltalk to cover here, but many are provided purely for efficiency purposes, and many are similar to each other. We will only describe a few: the value: primitive for activating blocks, the new primitive for creating objects, an arithmetic primitive, and the perform: primitive for computed selectors.

8.1 The value: primitive

The value: primitive activates a block with one argument. The other forms of value for zero, and two or more arguments would be similar.

$$value\_primitive : Method$$

$$value\_primitive \quad \triangle \quad \lambda closure, [arg], \sigma \cdot Body(\sigma(closure))(closure, [arg], \sigma)$$

8.2　The new primitive

Up to now we have not dealt with the fact that in Smalltalk, classes are objects. We shall simply state that an initial object memory should contain representations of the classes in the static environment, and that a function is required to map the representation of the class to its abstract syntax. The operation presented here, which creates a new instance of a class, is passed the abstract syntax of the class as an argument.

$new\_primitive$　($class: Class\_name$) $new\_oop: Oop$
ext wr σ : $Object\_Memory$
　rd P : $Program$
post $new\_oop \notin$ dom $\overleftarrow{\sigma}$
　$\wedge\, \sigma = \overleftarrow{\sigma} \cup \{new\_oop \mapsto mk\text{-}Object(class, \{id \mapsto \text{NILOOP} \mid id \in inst\_vars(class, P)\})\}$

A definition of $inst\_vars$ can be found in the appendix.

8.3　An Arithmetic Primitive

As an example of one of the many arithmetic primitives, we present the primitive for integer addition. Rather than model the Smalltalk Virtual Machine concept of primitive failure[2], we choose to return nil if the argument to the primitive is not an Integer.

$plus\_primitive : Method$

$plus\_primitive$　$\triangleq$
　$\lambda rcvr, [arg], \sigma \cdot$
　　　let $addend = Body(\sigma(rcvr))$ in
　　　let $augend = Body(\sigma(arg))$ in
　　　if $augend \in \mathbf{Z}$
　　　then $find\_or\_make\_int(addend + augend, \sigma)$
　　　else (NILOOP, σ)

8.4　The perform: Primitive

The perform: primitive takes a Symbol representing a selector, and sends a message to an object using that selector as the name of the message. As with the new primitive, we have not explicitly stated that selectors have representations in the object memory, but we assume that a mechanism exists for deriving the abstract syntax of the selector from its stored representation. The following operation assumes that its selector is a unary selector.

$perform\_primitive$　($obj: Oop, sel: Selector$) $result: Oop$
ext wr σ : $Object\_Memory$
　rd ρ : $SEnv$
post $(result, \sigma) = perform(obj, sel, [\,], find(Class(\overleftarrow{\sigma}(obj)), \rho), \overleftarrow{\sigma})$

9　Indexed Instance Variables

Thus far we have not mentioned indexed instance variables. We now outline how the model can be adapted to include indexed instance variables.

Firstly, a class can either define that all its instances may have indexed instance variables, or inherit the property from its superclass. This requires the addition of a field, $Has\_indexed: \mathbf{B}$, to the definition of $Class\_body$. One can then determine whether a class' instances may have indexed instance variables with the following function:

$has\_indexed : Class\_name \times Class\_map \to \mathbf{B}$

$has\_indexed(class, class\_map)$　$\triangleq$　$Has\_indexed(class\_map(class))$
　$\vee\, (Super(class\_map(class)) \neq$ nil $\Rightarrow has\_indexed(Super(class\_map(class)), class\_map))$

Secondly, the definition of *Plain_object* has to be modified to include the integer indices into the domain of the map:

$$Plain\_object = \text{map } Id \cup \mathbf{N}_1 \text{ to } Oop$$

Next, the new: primitive is provided so that objects with indexed instance variables may be created:

new:_primitive (*class*: *Class_name*, *size*: $\mathbf{N}_1$) *new_oop*: *Oop*

ext wr σ : *Object_memory*

   rd P : *Program*

pre *has_indexed*(*class*, *P*)

post *new_oop* $\notin$ dom $\overleftarrow{\sigma}$

   $\wedge\, (\sigma = \overleftarrow{\sigma} \cup mk\text{-}Object(class, \{name \mapsto \text{NILOOP} \mid name \in instvars(class, P) \cup \{1, \ldots, size\}\}))$

Finally, the at: and at:put: primitives have to be provided to allow access to the indexed instance variables:

at_primitive : *Method*

at_primitive $\triangleq$ $\lambda obj, [index], \sigma \cdot$ if *in_bounds*(*obj*, *index*, σ)

                then ($Body(\sigma(obj))(index), \sigma$)

                else *bound_error*(*obj*, *index*, σ)

atput_primitive : *Method*

atput_primitive $\triangleq$

   $\lambda obj, [index, value], \sigma \cdot$

      if *in_bounds*(*obj*, *index*, σ)

      then ($value, \sigma \dagger \{obj \mapsto \mu(\sigma(obj), Body \mapsto Body(\sigma(obj)) \dagger \{index \mapsto value\})\}$)

      else *bound_error*(*obj*, *index*, σ)

in_bounds : $Oop \times Oop \times Object\_Memory \rightarrow \mathbf{B}$

in_bounds(*obj*, *index*, σ) $\triangleq$ $Body(\sigma(index)) \in \text{dom } Body(\sigma(obj))$

The *bound_error* function sends an appropriate error message; it will not be defined further here.

10 Discussion

We have presented semantics for most of the Smalltalk language. A number of things have been omitted:

1. Concurrency has been omitted because it would severely complicate the existing model. In fact, it is doubtful whether the existing approach can deal satisfactorily with concurrent processes at all.

2. Classes, selectors and methods do not appear as objects in the object memory; this is purely to make the model more understandable.

3. Blocks are not allowed to perform non-local returns and do not have access to non-local temporaries. Introducing non-local returns requires the use of continuation semantics[3,6] to carry around the extra possible return path. It also introduces a class of programming error whereby one can return to a context that has already been returned from.

Allowing access to non-local temporaries requires a more sophisticated mechanism to release contexts. In the Smalltalk-80 system each context is a full object, and because a method context can be referenced by a block context, it cannot be released automatically upon return. To keep the semantics simple we avoided non-local references to temporaries. However, they can be done away with quite easily by adding an indirection object to methods that contain blocks that access a non-local variable, and changing all references to the temporary to go via the indirection object instead. For example,

```
| i |
i ← 1.
[i < 10] whileTrue: [i ← i + 1]
```

can be rewritten as:

```
| i |
i ← Indirection on: 1.
[i value < 10] whileTrue: [i value: i value + 1].
```

where the following Indirection class is assumed to exist:

class	Indirection
superclass	Object
instance variables	object

class methods

on: anObject
↑self new value: anObject

instance methods

value
↑object

value: anObject
↑object ← anObject

In this case, the value of i accessible to the blocks in the whileTrue: statement is determined when the blocks are bound; essentially it is an extra argument to the blocks. The semantics are changed by altering the creation of the dynamic environment in *MBlock_body* to use the following expression:

$$\delta' = mk\text{-}DEnv(Rcvr(\delta), Args(\delta) \cup Temps(\delta) \cup \{Args(i) \mapsto arglist(i) \mid i \in \text{dom } args\},$$
$$\{id \mapsto \text{NilOop} \mid id \in temps\})$$

The context condition for blocks (see Appendix) is similarly modified so that non-local temporaries appear as arguments.

This transformation, together with the removal of non-local returns enables us to have LIFO contexts. The implications for implementations of the Smalltalk Virtual Machine are large, and may lead to significant performance gains. However, whether the loss of non-local returns significantly hampers programming style has yet to be determined. Clearly, the loss of access to non-local temporaries is not a problem; a pre-processor could mechanically transform existing code to use indirection objects.

11   Conclusions

The semantics of a large subset of Smalltalk have been presented. It is believed that discussion of language features is greatly aided by basing such discussion on formal semantics. Further work has to be done to cope with more of the language (parallelism, multiple inheritance); this work is the subject of current research. From the viewpoint of the formal semantics presented here it is felt that a better understanding of Smalltalk and other object-oriented languages will be gained, leading to improved designs in the future.

12   Acknowledgements

Numerous discussions with Cliff Jones helped shape the ideas in this paper. Many thanks to Michael Fisher for his careful reading and useful suggestions.

References

[1] D. Bjørner and C. B. Jones. *Formal Specification and Software Development*. Prentice-Hall, 1983.

[2] A. Goldberg and D. Robson. *Smalltalk-80: The Language and its Implementation*. Addison-Wesley, 1983.

[3] M. J. C. Gordon. *The Denotational Description of Programming Languages*. Springer-Verlag, 1979.

[4] C. B. Jones. *Systematic Software Development Using VDM*. Prentice-Hall International, 1986.

[5] C. Minkowitz and P. Henderson. A formal description of object-oriented programming using VDM. In D. Bjørner, C. B. Jones, M. M. an Airchinnigh, and E. J. Neuhold, editors, *VDM '87: VDM—A Formal Method at Work*, pages 237–259, Springer-Verlag, Brussels, Belgium, March 1987.

[6] J. E. Stoy. *Denotational Semantics: The Scott-Strachey Approach to Programming Language Theory*. MIT Press, 1977.

[7] M. Wolczko. *Specification and Implementation of Object-Oriented Systems (working title)*. PhD thesis, Department of Computer Science, University of Manchester, forthcoming.

A Context Conditions

In this appendix we state the context conditions defining which programs are well-formed.

The static environment required by the context conditions simply records which identifiers are in scope, and what sort of variable they denote.

$$CCEnv = \text{map } Id \text{ to } Var\_Type$$

$$Var\_Type = \{\text{INSTVAR}, \text{ARG}, \text{TEMP}\}$$

A *Program* is well-formed if the graph of classes is well-founded, and each individual class is well-formed with respect to its superclasses:

$$WFProgram : Program \rightarrow \mathbf{B}$$

$$WFProgram[\![class\_map]\!] \quad \triangleq \quad non\_circular(class\_map)$$
$$\wedge \; \forall class\_id \in \text{dom } class\_map \cdot$$
$$\quad Super(class\_map(class\_id)) \in \text{dom } class\_map \cup \{\text{nil}\} \wedge$$
$$\quad \text{let } inh\_iv = inherited\_inst\_vars(class\_id, class\_map) \text{ in}$$
$$\quad WFClass[\![class\_map(class\_id)]\!]\{id \mapsto \text{INSTVAR} \mid id \in inh\_iv\}$$

$$non\_circular : Class\_map \rightarrow \mathbf{B}$$

$$non\_circular(class\_map) \quad \triangleq \quad \forall s \subseteq \text{dom } class\_map \cdot s \neq \{\} \Rightarrow \exists class \in s \cdot Super(class\_map(class)) \notin s$$

$$inherited\_inst\_vars : Class\_name \times Class\_map \rightarrow \text{set of } Id$$

$$inherited\_inst\_vars(class, class\_map) \quad \triangleq$$
$$\quad \text{if } Super(class\_map(class)) = \text{nil then } \{\} \text{ else } inst\_vars(Super(class\_map(class)), class\_map)$$

$$inst\_vars : Class\_name \times Class\_map \rightarrow \text{set of } Id$$

$$inst\_vars(class, class\_map) \quad \triangleq \quad Instvars(class\_map(class)) \cup inherited\_inst\_vars(class, class\_map)$$

A class is well-formed if it does not redeclare any inherited instance variables, and all its methods are well-formed.

$$WFClass : Class\_body \rightarrow CCEnv \rightarrow \mathbf{B}$$

$$WFClass[\![mk\text{-}Class\_body(iv, super, meths)]\!]\theta \quad \triangleq \quad \text{is-disjoint}(iv, \text{dom } \theta)$$
$$\quad \wedge \; \forall sel \in \text{dom } meths \cdot$$
$$\quad\quad meths(sel) \notin Primitive\_method$$
$$\quad\quad\quad \Rightarrow \; nargs(sel) = \text{len } Args(meths(sel))$$
$$\quad\quad\quad\quad \wedge \; WFMethod[\![meths(sel)]\!](\theta \cup \{id \mapsto \text{INSTVAR} \mid id \in iv\})$$

A method is well-formed if none of its instance variables, arguments or temporaries are multiply declared, if it has at least one expression,[4] and all its expressions are well formed.

$WFMethod : Method\_body \rightarrow CCEnv \rightarrow \mathbf{B}$

$WFMethod[\![mk\text{-}Method\_body(args, temps, exprs)]\!]\theta \quad \triangleq \quad all\_disjoint([\operatorname{dom}\theta, \operatorname{rng}args, temps])$
$\quad \wedge \operatorname{len} exprs \geq 1$
$\quad \wedge \forall e \in \operatorname{rng} exprs \cdot$
$\quad\quad WFExpression[\![e]\!](\theta \cup \{id \mapsto \textsc{Arg} \mid id \in \operatorname{rng} args\} \cup \{id \mapsto \textsc{Temp} \mid id \in temps\})$

$all\_disjoint : \operatorname{seq} \operatorname{of} \operatorname{set} \operatorname{of} Id \rightarrow \mathbf{B}$

$all\_disjoint(ss) \quad \triangleq \quad \forall i, j \in \operatorname{dom} ss \cdot i \neq j \;\Rightarrow\; is\_disjoint(ss(i), ss(j))$

Now we shall enumerate by cases the well-formedness condition for each type of *Expression*.

An assignment is well-formed if it assigns to a variable (not an argument) that is in scope, and its RHS is well-formed.

$WFExpression : Expression \rightarrow CCEnv \rightarrow \mathbf{B}$

$WFExpression[\![mk\text{-}Assignment(id, rhs)]\!]\theta \quad \triangleq$
$\quad WFExpression[\![rhs]\!]\theta \wedge id \in \operatorname{dom}\theta \wedge \theta(id) \in \{\textsc{InstVar}, \textsc{Temp}\}$

$WFExpression[\![id]\!]\theta \quad \triangleq \quad id \in \operatorname{dom}\theta \quad \text{for } id \in Id$

$WFExpression[\![\textsc{Self}]\!]\theta \quad \triangleq \quad \text{true}$

$WFExpression[\![\textsc{Super}]\!]\theta \quad \triangleq \quad \text{true}$

$WFExpression[\![\textsc{Root}]\!]\theta \quad \triangleq \quad \text{true}$

$WFExpression[\![mk\text{-}Message\_list(rcvr, msgs)]\!]\theta \quad \triangleq \quad WFExpression[\![rcvr]\!]\theta \wedge \operatorname{len} msgs \geq 1$
$\quad \wedge \forall m \in \operatorname{rng} msgs \cdot$
$\quad\quad \operatorname{len} Args(m) = nargs(Sel(m)) \wedge \forall arg \in \operatorname{rng} Args(m) \cdot WFExpression[\![arg]\!]\theta$

$WFExpression[\![int]\!]\theta \quad \triangleq \quad \text{true} \quad \text{for } int \in \mathbf{Z}$

$WFExpression[\![mk\text{-}Block\_body(args, temps, exprs)]\!]\theta \quad \triangleq$
$\quad WFMethod[\![mk\text{-}Method\_body(args, temps, exprs)]\!](\theta \rhd \{\textsc{InstVar}, \textsc{Arg}\})$

If, as discussed in the text, we allow a block to have read-only access to non-local temporaries, the definition becomes:

$WFExpression[\![mk\text{-}Block\_body(args, temps, exprs)]\!]\theta \quad \triangleq$
$\quad WFMethod[\![mk\text{-}Method\_body(args, temps, exprs)]\!](\theta \rhd \{\textsc{InstVar}, \textsc{Arg}\})$
$\quad\quad \cup \{id \mapsto \textsc{Arg} \mid id \in \operatorname{dom}\theta \wedge \theta(id) = \textsc{Temp}\}$

---

[4]Smalltalk *does* allow empty methods and empty blocks. However, the former are equivalent to ↑self, and the latter return nil. We therefore insist that all methods and blocks have at least one expression.

The Construction of User Interfaces and the Object Paradigm

Joëlle Coutaz
Laboratoire de Génie Informatique (IMAG)
BP 68, 38402 St-Martin-d'Hères, France
UUCP ...!mcvax!inria!imag!joelle

Abstract : This article concerns generic tools for the construction of user interfaces: Application Frameworks and User Interface Management Systems (UIMS's). In this article, we propose a new taxonomy for these tools, identify their limitations and show how the object paradigm can be exploited to overcome the current deficiencies such as support for generality, context and distribution. This taxonomy is the result of our own experience in designing MOUSE, an object-oriented UIMS based on a general model, PAC, that can be applied at any level of abstraction of a user interface. PAC structures any component of an interactive application into three parts: the Presentation which defines the external behaviour, the Abstraction which corresponds to internal concepts and the Control which bridges the gap between the syntax and the semantics.

Keywords: User Interface, User Interface Management System, Object-Oriented Programming.

1. Introduction

Issues pertinent to user interface design can be discussed from two points of view: that of the application programmer and that of the end user. Here, we are concerned with the problems of the programmer, concentrating on principles and tools that facilitate the construction of user interfaces. One fundamental principle is the separation of the functions of an interactive application from its user interface. The functions of an application define the tasks that it is able to accomplish whereas the user interface mediates between the functions and the user. In reality, this division which is the direct application of the principle of modularity, is not easy to achieve. Indeed, mediation implies communication, communication implies I/O and I/O is naturally distributed throughout the application. It is not surprising then that the code which handles the interaction is intermixed with the code which implements the functions of the application. In these conditions, it is difficult or even impossible to put into practice a second important principle in user interface design, the iterative refinement of the user interface. In this paper, we are concerned with tools that encourage the separation between the functions of an application and its user interface: generic systems.

Generic systems, such as user interface management systems, automatically provide a standard user interface framework upon which the functional components of applications can be encrafted. The next section proposes a classification that identifies the advantages and the limitations of these building tools. Section 3 shows how the object-oriented paradigm can circumvent some of the unsolved problems in generic systems. Section 4 describes how the notion of object has been exploited in MOUSE, our own User Interface Management System.

2. Generic Systems

Generic systems include two types of tools: application frameworks and User Interface Management Systems (UIMS's). These categories are examined in the following two paragraphs.

2.1 Application Frameworks

Application frameworks like MacApp [Schmucker 86a], EZWin [Lieberman 85] and Apex [Coutaz 86] package the code that implements most of the user interface into a reusable and extensible skeleton. The implementor's task consists in filling the blanks of the skeleton, adding new functions or overriding parts that do not fit the application domain. Code extensibility, reusability and overriding are naturally supported by object-oriented programming techniques as MacApp, EZWin and Apex demonstrate.

2.1.1 MacApp and EZWin

MacApp is implemented in Object Pascal, an object-oriented extension of Pascal [Schmucker 86b]. It models an interactive application as an instance of the class TApplication which is responsible for tasks that are common to all of the applications such as launching and opening documents. A document is also an instance of a class, TDocument, with methods for manipulating files. The class Tview takes care of the content of a document displayed in a window for things such as selection and refreshing.

EZWin is implemented on a Symbolics 3600, using ZetaLisp with the object-oriented Flavors package. It models an application as an editor for presentation objects. A presentation object is a visual representation of a domain entity. It takes care of both input actions from the end user and output feedback. EZWin is based on three types of objects that Lieberman observed as common in structure and behaviour across applications. These are: the presentation objects, the command objects which represent the end user's actions, and the EZWin object corresponding to the entire user interface to an application. The system maintains a set of presentation objects that can be created, deleted or modified through command objects.

2.1.2 Apex

Apex is implemented in C on top of the Macintosh toolbox. As shown in the figure 1, the architecture of an Apex interactive application is comprised of two components: the Application part which implements the functions (i.e. the semantics of the dialog) and the Interface part which implements the presentation (i.e. the syntax of the dialog). The Application contains the code that is specific to the domain whereas the Interface is domain independent and contains the reusable code.

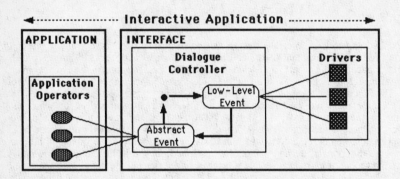

Figure 1: An Interactive Application built with Apex. (Thick arrows illustrate the control flow, thin lines represent procedural calls and • indicates the entry point of the cycle)

The reusable code is organized around two classes of objects: the dialog controller which contains the top level loop and acts essentially as a message dispatcher, and drivers such as window, menu and form drivers, each specialized in the processing of a predefined set of messages. A message may contain either a low level event generated by the underlying system, or an abstract event exchanged between a driver and the Application. A low level event, such as a window update or a scrolling request, is handled by a driver object as far as possible. If the driver cannot fully process a low level event, (for exemple, a mouse click in a window area that is not handled by the window driver) it generates an abstract event for further semantic processing. This abstract event, which is an enriched version of the low level event, is then sent to the Application (for example, the mouse event mentioned above would generate an "InContent" abstract event). The Application behaves like a semantic server with predefined operators such as "inContent", and may send messages to manipulate drivers such as create a window or read/write on the serial port.

Apex and EZWin are very similar in their goal of separating what is domain dependent from what is common to applications. In MacApp, this distinction is not made clear. Domain dependent notions tend to be diluted across various classes. As a result, the MacApp user needs to pay attention to the definitions of the various classes instead of concentrating his attention on a single piece of code (as is the case with the Apex Application).

2.1.3 Motivation for Application Frameworks and Evaluation

Application frameworks have been introduced to overcome problems with the use of toolboxes. Toolboxes generally provide the programmer with a wide range of powerful abstractions for implementing user interfaces. This diversity of services makes toolboxes flexible but hard to use. It requires the programmer to discover the right glue for assembling the pieces from the toolbox. Not only may this task be a tremendous technical barrier for the first time developer but also it must be carried out for each application. It is not surprising then that a strong interest has recently emerged for a tool that provides the implementor with both an implementation model and reusable code.

The existence of an implementation model and the availability of reusable code have several related side-effects: the implementor can concentrate on the functions of the application, user interface consistency is improved and application development time can be reduced by a factor of four or five [Schmucker 86a]. The experience described in [Garret 86] about the use of MacApp for the construction of a large scale application is an eloquent testimony to the advantages of application frameworks.

Our own experience with Apex leads us to believe that an application framework is not expensive to develop on top of a powerful toolbox. Our first version of Apex which included only drivers for windows and menus, has been developed in three months by a graduate student who had no previous knowledge of the Macintosh toolbox. The delicate part for him was to apply the object-oriented paradigm of which he had book-knowledge only. A more important and fundamental problem was to determine which abstractions should be implemented and how to organize them into a consistent model.

To solve this problem, we first defined five practical guidelines: first, any domain dependent code must be outside of Apex and made accessible through standard entry points; second, any domain independent code must be in Apex and structured according to functional criteria; third, closely related functions must constitute a unit (i.e. a driver); fourth, each unit must augment the functionality and hide the complexity of the services provided by the toolbox; fifth, Apex must be expandable in order to enrich and add services as required by a potentially wide range of applications.

When putting these principles into practice, it became natural to define the Application as an object whose methods implement a predefined set of semantic operators; in the Interface, each driver is a class whose methods implement a predefined set of operators dealing with a particular aspect of the user interface; although Apex is not a pure object-oriented system (there is no way to create instances of the class Application nor is it possible to create new classes) we have made extensive use of the principle of modularity along with the message passing mechanism promoted by the object-oriented programming. By doing so, it has been possible to implement a first simple version of Apex with a minimum of standard drivers and to then extend it easily as new applications were constructed. Clearly, the object-oriented approach is vital to the design of Apex.

In spite of their advantages, application frameworks still require the application implementor to deal with the underlying toolbox for appending code or modifying subroutines. Unlike UIMS's presented in the next paragraph, application frameworks impose a low level programming interface on the implementor.

2.2 User Interface Management Systems (UIMS's)

UIMS's, automatically generate an executable interactive application from a specification provided by the implementor. For doing so, a UIMS is comprised of a run time kernel whose architecture is similar to an application framework and a tool for processing the specification. This specification is usually a textual description using a special purpose language [Hayes 83] or an extended notation of an existing formalism such as petri-nets [Barthet 86], BNF [Bleser82, Olsen 83] or transition networks [Wasserman 85]. The specification is made easier when it is carried out through an interactive tool as in Flair [Wong 82], Menulay [Buxton 83], SOS [Hullot 86] and Peridot [Myers 86].

The UIMS model has served as the basis for a number of tools for dialogue specification and dialogue generation. The next section proposes a classification for these tools, indicates which design choices are desirable as well as identifies deficiencies in current UIMS's. It will also show how some of these limitations can be overcome with the object-oriented paradigm.

3. Taxonomy for UIMS's and Benefits from the Object Paradigm

UIMS's have been classified according to three design choices [Hayes 85]: the level of abstraction at which the specification is performed, the localization of the control of the dialogue and the expression of the ordering of events. In the next paragraphs, we propose a taxonomy with five additional criteria: adaptiveness, support for concurrency, context, distribution and generality.

3.1 Level of Abstraction

The level of abstraction defines the unit of exchange between the application and the UIMS. This unit can range from low-level tokens such as keystrokes, to the level of abstraction manipulated by the application such as complete and syntactically correct commands. Low-level abstractions concern the events at the user-visible interface whereas high-level abstractions are application-dependent.

The level of abstraction defines the effectiveness of the separation between the semantics and the syntax, i.e between the functions and the presentation of the application. Consequently, it determines the extent to which the implementor is able to concentrate on the logical functioning of the application. In order to facilitate the implementor's task, it is desirable that the information exchanged between the application and the UIMS be application concepts. The object-oriented paradigm provides a natural mechanism for representing information at the desired level of abstraction.

3.2 Localization of the Control

The control of the dialogue may be internal, external or mixed [Tanner 83]. The control is internal when it resides in the application. It is external when it is maintained by the UIMS. It is mixed when it is alternatively handled by the application and the UIMS. Internal control presents two serious drawbacks: first, it may lead to situations where an application traps the user in a kind of local mode by forcing him to reply right away to a question without allowing a new request that would help in the choice of the correct alternative. Second, by being rooted in the application, internal control does not enforce a clean separation between functions and presentation.

Conversely, when the UIMS maintains the control, the application is viewed as a semantic server. This technique entails a clean separation between functions and presentation. It opens the way to more modular programs although it may impose a style of programming on the implementor. We believe that the external control of the dialogue should lead to fewer arbitrary constraints on the user, constraints that may be unnecessarily imposed by an application implementor unaware of the basic "do's and don'ts" in user interface design. At the opposite of the internal control, external control operates in accordance with a user-driven style.

Between the two extremes, mixed control allows the implementor to switch freely between internal and external modes. This flexibility is useful for applications that need to notify the UIMS of asynchronous events (such as the ringing of the alarm clock) or for functions which dynamically require the user to specify some parameter before processing can continue (such as print commands in "more" mode, or expert systems which typically ask the user to provide additional information to resolve conflicts). However, mixed control may induce software maintenance problems (just like the goto statement). External control with hooks for mixed control seems to be a reasonable choice. In section 4.4, we indicate how the object paradigm can be applied to implement these hooks.

3.3 Ordering of Events

Ordering of events may be frozen in a declarative manner as with BNF and ATN based specification tools. The number of allowed actions (for example, the description of the free ordering of command parameters) and exceptional conditions must be anticipated exhaustively. This task may become difficult if the specification has to be performed at a low level of abstraction such as keystroke or mouse level. In addition, it is not clear how these tools account for parallel events.

The difficulty with ATN and BNF tools comes from the mismatch between the way they model the user and the behaviour of the real user. They model the user as a parsable sequential input file whereas the user is essentially unpredictable. A reasonable solution to this problem is the combination of an external control with high level abstractions which moves the problem of event ordering outside of the implementor's view. Paragraph 4.2 shows how the object paradigm is appropriate for the management of the user's unpredictable behaviour.

3.4 Adaptiveness

Adaptiveness is the abiliy to adjust to new or modified surroundings. For a computer system, adaptiveness is concerned with the multiple sources of variation in the environment: hardware, operating systems, languages and users. Here, we are concerned with the adaptiveness of the user interface to the user.

A user interface may be adaptable or adaptive. An adaptable user interface may be customized by hand on an explicit intervention of either the implementor or the user. In most cases, a modification to the user interface requires the recompilation of whole code. In the best case, as in the Macintosh, the user is able to perform cosmetic changes without recompilation. These changes, although superficial, are made possible on account of the object-oriented paradigm.

At the other end of the spectrum, an adaptive user interface behaves like an intelligent observer who automatically adapts the user interface to the habits and expertise of the user without being too intrusive. Experiments have been attempted in this direction, in particular for tutorials, but none have been undertaken in the framework of UIMS's. Given that knowledge can be modelled as a network of concepts, it seems reasonable to distribute the knowledge about the user across Loops-like objects [Bobrow 83] where rules would allow the object to alter his behaviour according to the user's actions.

3.5 Concurrency

Broadly speaking, concurrency refers to the existence of multiple activities. In the area of user interface, concurrency has three complementary facets: simultaneous use of multiple input and output devices, simultaneous interaction between a user and multiple applications, and simultaneous interaction between multiple users (e.g. teleconferencing),

Interaction between multiple users introduces a new dimension in the area of user interface: the social dimension which, so far, has not been the subject of significant study. The first two types of concurrency is becoming common on workstations supporting multitasking. In particular, the switchboard model [Tanner 86], based on rapid intertask message passing, provides UIMS's with a powerful tool for supporting parallel input. Interestingly, like Smalltalk objects, the switchboard tasks are small entities communicating through synchronous messages.

3.6 Context and Distribution

A context is a data structure that determines the meaning of a situation. This notion has been widely exploited in software engineering in particular for operating systems and programming languages. In the area of user interface, it is considered as an essential notion for helping the user to determine "where he is, where he can go and where he has come from". Although important, this notion is still not well integrated in current UIMS's.

One possible explanation of the situation is that context is inherently distributed and that current UIMS's do not support distribution well. Every component of a computer system manages a context. Unfortunately, context items are still defined without paying attention to the need of the end-user or are not made available to other components. As a result, the end-user is not well informed of the current state of the system nor is he well informed of his semantic errors. We believe that the object-oriented paradigm is the appropriate vehicle for distributing and communicating contextual information across objects and computers. However, the object paradigm does not solve the important problem of defining what is useful to the end-user!

3.7 Generality

Generality refers to the range of applications that a particular UIMS is able to support. The variety of applications results in a tremendous diversity of requirements. To simplify the situation, one can distinguish applications that require a fine grained control over I/O devices such as document formatters or graphic systems as opposed to applications for which information exchange does not require sophisticated services.

No UIMS claims to be fully general. Either it supports a specific class of applications as does Cousin [Hayes 83], or it provides the implementor with hooks for accessing the underlying toolbox as does ADM [Schulert 85]. A new trend is to provide application implementors with an object-oriented environment containing an extensible set of abstractions for the expression of the user interface. The difficulty is to define the appropriate basic set, determine the right organization through the composition and/or inheritance mechanism, and nearly as important, make the environment easy to use and learn.

(Larry Tesler in [Tesler 86] reports that most of the learning time of such an environment may go to mastering the extensive class library)

To summarize, the desirable criteria for a UIMS are the following: high level abstraction, external control with hooks for mixed control, implicit event ordering, adaptability, support for concurrency, contextual information and distribution. The next section shows how some of these design criteria have been integrated in MOUSE.

4. MOUSE, an Object Oriented UIMS

The architecture of MOUSE is based on a general object-oriented model, called PAC, that can be applied at any level of abstraction in a user interface. The following paragraphs describe PAC, identify its advantages and compare it with other object based models.

4.1 PAC, the Design Model

In MOUSE, an interactive application is comprised of three parts: Presentation, Abstraction and Control.

The Presentation defines the concrete syntax of the application, i.e. the input and output behaviour of the application as perceived by the user. The Abstraction part corresponds to the semantics of the application. It implements the functions that the application is able to perform. The Control part, called the MOUSE controller, maintains the mapping and the consistency between the abstract entities involved in the interaction and implemented in the Abstract part, and their presentation to the user. It embodies the boundary between semantics and syntax.

For example, the application "Clock" implements and involves two abstract entities in the dialogue : the data structure "Time" and the function "SetTime". "Time" may be presented as a digital or a dial clock, SetTime may be explicitly presented as a button or implicitly presented through the direct manipulation of the needles of the dial clock. The job of the Control part is to invoke SetTime on specific user's actions and provoke the update of the dial clock when the application (i.e the Abstract part) makes a request.

The Presentation of an application is implemented with a set of entities, called interactive objects, specialized in man-machine communication. As for applications, an interactive object is organized according to the PAC model. Consider for example the pie chart shown in the figure 2.

 1.The Presentation is comprised of:
  • for output, a circular shape and a colour for each piece of the pie;
  • for input, the mouse actions that the user can perform to change the relative size of the pieces.
 2.The Abstraction is comprised of an integer value within the range of two integer limits.
 3.The Control maintains the consistency between the Presentation and the Abstraction. For example, if the user modifies the size of one piece, Control provokes the update of the integer value. Conversely, if the application or another interactive object modifies the value of the integer, the size of the pieces is automatically adjusted.

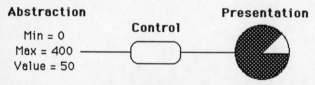

Figure 2: An elementary Interactive Object

Compound objects can be built from elementary interactive objects. They also adhere to the PAC model. Consider, for example, the super pie chart shown in the figure 3. It is made from two elementary objects: the pie chart described above and a numerical string which shows the current abstract value of the pie chart. If Control C receives a message notifying him of the modification of the abstract value, it notifies both C1 and C2 of the alteration. Conversely, if the user changes the size of a piece of the pie with the mouse, C1 reflects the modification to C who, in turn notifies C2. A sketch of the code for these objects is given in the appendix.

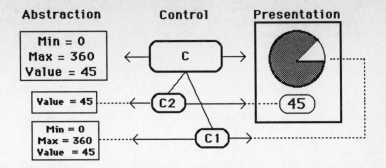

Figure 3: A Compound Interactive Object composed of an object of the class Pie Chart illustrated in the figure 2 and of an object of the class string.

In summary, as shown in the figure 4, everything in MOUSE is a PAC object from the elementary interactive object to the whole application. This recursive object-oriented organization presents some advantages which are described in the following paragraphs.

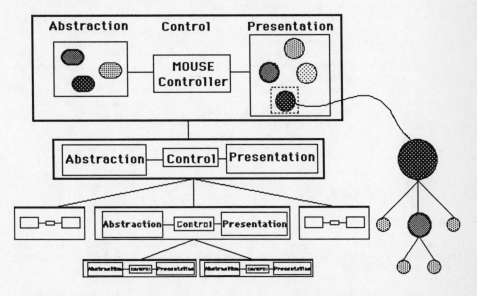

Figure 4: The Design Model. The upper rectangle represents the whole interactive application as a PAC entity. Its Abstraction involves three concepts in the dialogue. The MOUSE Controller bridges the gap between the Abstraction and the Presentation. The Presentation is made of 4 interactive objects. The second lower rectangle shows the PAC structure of the compound interactive object represented as a black circle. This object is built from two elementary PAC objects and one compound object which, in turn, is composed of two elementary PAC objects.

4.2 The Interest of the PAC Model

The interest of the PAC model is three-fold:

1. It defines a consistent framework for the construction of user interfaces that is applicable at any level of abstraction. As a direct consequence, the units of exchange between the application (i.e. the Abstract part) and the UIMS (i.e the MOUSE controller) are application concepts, not low-level details semantically irrelevant to the application.

2. It cleanly distinguishes functional notions from presentation policies but introduces the control part to bridge the gap between the abstract and the concrete worlds. The role of the control part may be extended from consistency maintenance between the two worlds, to the management of local contextual information that may be useful for help, error explanation and automatic adaptation to the user.

3. It takes full advantage of the object-oriented paradigm with the notion of interactive object. Let us develop this last point.

An *interactive object is an active entity* . It evolves, communicates and maintains relationships with other objects. Such activity, parallelism and communication are automatically performed by the Object Machine, the generic class of the interactive objects. The Object Machine defines the general functioning that is made common to all of the interactive objects by means of the inheritance mechanism. In particular, each object owns a private finite state automaton for maintaining its current dialogue state. On receipt of a message, an object is thus able to determine which actions to undertake according to its current state. In particular, The MOUSE controller at the top of the hierarchy of controllers, maintains the global state of the dialogue with the application.

Interactive objects implement the dialogue in a distributed way. This feature can serve as a basis for the implemention of facilities related to the notion of context. It also provides the necessary grounds for concurrent multiple I/O in the following way. The set of automata (one automaton per interactive object) defines the global state of the interaction between the user and the application. The control of the interaction is therefore distributed in an evolutive network of interactive objects. Dialogue control is not handled by a unique monolithic dialogue manager difficult to maintain, extend and implement, in particular when one wants a pure user-driven style of interaction. Conversely, since interactive objects are able to maintain their own state, it is easy to let the user switch between objects in any order. Thus, an object-oriented approach provides for free the maintenance of the user's arbitrary manipulations.

Interactive objects are easily customizable. Object-oriented programming languages support data abstraction which makes it possible to change underlying implementations without changing the calling programs. In the present case, this principle allows the internal modification of an interactive object without changing its presentation and abstract interfaces. Interestingly, it also allows the modification of one interface without any side-effect on the other interface. For example, one can modify the presentation of an interactive object (such as attaching a different key translation table to an interactive object of type string) without reflecting on its abstract behaviour. This property makes it possible fine grained dynamic adjustments of the user interface without questioning the presentation of the whole application.

The application of the object-oriented paradigm to the construction of user interfaces is rather new but not specific to MOUSE. The following paragraph presents similar works.

4.3 Related Work

Other models than PAC rely on the notion of object and make the distinction between functions and presentation. These are the Smalltalk MVC model [Golberg 84], Ciccarelli's PPS model [Ciccarelli 84], EZWin [Lieberman 85] and GWUIMS [Sibert 86].

Model, View and Controller are three Smalltalk classes. A Model implements some functions, a View is the output rendering of a Model and a Controller is the input driver of a Model. PAC and MVC differ in two points:

1. PAC distinguishes but encapsulates functions and presentation into an object. A local controller encompasses the boundary between local semantics and local syntax. At the opposite, MVC makes an explicit use of three Smalltalk objects which must maintain their consistency through message passing. In MVC, the notion of control is diluted across three related objects whereas it is explicitly centralized in PAC.

2. PAC combines input and output behaviour into one component whereas MVC distributes them across two objects. The distribution has the advantage of flexibility (one can change the input syntax without disturbing the component dealing with the output syntax). Unfortunately, it is often the case that, at the fine grained level of the interaction, input events are strongly related to immediate output feedbacks.

PPS is organized around a network of Presenters and Recognizers that manipulate two types of data bases. An Application data base defines some functions and a Presentation data base presents the Application data base. A Presenter builds a Presentation data base from an Application data base. The user modifies a Presentation data base, the associated Recognizer interprets the user's actions and modifies the corresponding Application data base. As in MVC, PPS makes a dichotomy between input and output behaviour but, at the opposite of MVC, these behaviours are not carried out by objects. PPS objects are passive entities manipulated by Presenters and Recognizers.

EZWin objects are close to PAC interactive objects: both combine input and output policies. The originality of PAC objects is the existence of the Control part which lays the ground for the implementation of distributed notions related to the notion of control. In particular, the Control part can maintain a context (e.g. current status, validity, defaults) that can be usefully exploited during interaction to provide the end user with dynamically tuned informative feedback.

GWUIMS revolves around five types of objects: A-objects embody the semantics of the application; I-Objects bridge the gap between A-Objects and R-objects. R-objects control the presentation. They are at the boundary between the lexical and syntactic levels of a UIMS. Lexical input is carried out by T-objects whereas lexical output is performed by G-objects. An elementary PAC object is functionally equivalent to the combination of a R-Object with a T-Object and a G-Object, and the MOUSE Controller is functionally equivalent to I-Objects.Clearly, PAC and GWUIMS are closely related in their overall organizatio although GWUIMS splits the presentation into input and output objetcs.

4.3 Current State of the Project and Future Evolution

MOUSE is currently under development in C on top of the Macintosh toolbox. The whole code of an interactive application is executed in a single Macintosh process. The MOUSE run time kernel is being extended to support coroutines in order to provide the application implementor with hooks for mixed control. The MOUSE controller will then be able to process READ messages issued by the Abstract part without forcing the end-user to directly satisfy the request. Consequently, the user may invoke several functions of the application (which may in turn issue READ requests) before replying to the initial request. For doing so, on reception of a READ message, the MOUSE Controller creates a request object and activates the interactive objects that represent the abstract entities referenced in the READ message. The request object watches the interaction between the user and the interactive objects and detects when the user has satisfied or cancelled the READ. When the READ operator is completed, control automatically returns to the instruction following the READ.

Once the run time kernel has been fully implemented and a reasonable data base of interactive objects been constructed, we need to build a programming environment for the construction of user interfaces. This environment will include an editor and a manager for automatically handling versions of user interfaces for a particular application. The editor will allow the implementor to interactively build new interactive objects and to define the presentation of the application.

5. Conclusion

The object paradigm allows for the construction of highly interactive user interfaces. It naturally leads the way to the definition of UIMS's where the user interface is implemented as small manageable units rather than as a single monolithic system. In addition, it makes it possible to distribute the semantic, syntactic and lexical levels of a user interface at various levels of abstraction rather than defining a rigid unique boundary. This distribution allows a UIMS to handle the user's arbitrary manipulations and parallel I/O more easily, to provide the user with useful explanation about his semantic errors and to facilitate fine grained dynamic customization.

It is only recently that object oriented programming has been applied to user interface design. As a result, a standard technique for organizing user interface software in terms of objects has not yet evolved. This is illustrated by the fact that each of the tools presented above has its own method for exploiting the object paradigm. More experience is needed in order for a general model to emerge.

Acknowlegment. This work is part of the project GUIDE, an object oriented distributed system, which is being designed at the Laboratoire de Génie Informatique (IMAG, University of Grenoble). It sets the foundation of the user interface for the GUIDE workstations.

Appendix

Some operators for the object Pie. A C-like notation is being used. Method names are in bold.The prefix **pie** is used for message selectors. Methods prefixed with **pie** are gathered in a single module that implements the Control part of a piechart. The prefixes pieAbs and piePres are used for methods that constitute the Abstract and the Presentation parts. In principle, they are callable from the Control part only.The prefix **obj** is used to denote methods of the class Object.

pieSetVal (whichPie, val, fromWhom)   *to change the current value*
   {pieAbsSetVal (whichPie, val);   *a method of the Abstract part to change the abstract value*
   valtoratio (val, ratio);   *a local procedure to translate the value to a ratio for the image*

```
        if (fromWhom != MYSELF)              image is updated only if the request doesn't come from the object itself
            piePresSetRatio (whichPie, ratio);}a method of the Presentation part to update the image according to the ratio
pieEvent (whichPie, theEvent)              to handle events from devices
    {case (theEvent.what)
        MOUSE: mouse (whichPie, theEvent);  .... }
mouse (whichPie, theEvent) a local procedure to process mouse events
    {case (wheremouse = mouseloc(whichPie, theEvent.where)
        INCONTENT:       a mouse event inside the circle signals a dynamic displacement
            if (objIsValid(whichPie,MOVE)) to determine whether the object currently accepts to be moved around
                pieMove(whichPie, theEvent.where);
        INNEEDDLE:       a mouse event inside the needle signals a dynamic displacement of the needle
            if (objIsValid(whichPie,MOVENEEDLE)) piePresTrackneedle(theEvent.where, ratio);
            if (piePreshaschanged(whichPie, ratio))
                {ratiotoval(ratio, val);      if the needle has moved, then the ratio has changed and the abstract
                pieAbsSetVal (whichPie, val, MYSELF)} value needs to be updated.
            if (objIsTalkative(whichPie)    returns true if the object has to signal ahanges of its abstract interface.
                { ... ;                      build msg to notify the ancestor of a change in the abstract interface
                ObjSendAncestor(whichPie, msg)};given a message and an object,  call the appropriate method of
                                             the object's ancestor ... }
```

One operator for the super pie chart described in 4.1

```
spieSetVal (whichSpie, val, fromWhom)      to set the current abstract value of a super pie chart
    {case (fromWhom)
        ANCESTOR:                            the request comes from the ancestor
        ... ;                                build appropriate message to update the value of son1 ( i.e. the pie chart)
        objSendSon(objSon(whichSpie, son1), msg);
        ... ;                                build appropriate message to update the value of son2 (i.e.  the string)
        objSendSon(objSon(whichSpie, son2), msg);
        SON:                                 the request comes from a son
        objSendSon(theotherson, msg);
        if (objIsTalkative) objSendAncestor(whichSpie, msg)}
```

References

[Barthet 86] M. F. Barthet; C. Sibertin-Blanc: La modélisation d'applications interactives adaptées aux utilisateurs par de réseaux de Petri à structure de donnée; Actes du 3eme Colloque-Exposition de Génie Logiciel, Versailles, mai 1986, 117-136

[Bleser 82] T. Bleser, J.D. Foley: Towards Specifying and Evaluating the Human Factors of User-Computer Interfaces; Huma Factors in Computer Systems Proceedings, march, 1982.

[Bobrow 83] D.G. Bobrow, M. Stefik: The Loops Manual; Tech. report KB-VLSI-81-13, Knowledge Systems Area, Xerox, Pal Alto Research Center, 1981.

[Buxton 83] W. Buxton, M.R. Lamb, D. Sherman, K.C. Smith: Towards a Comprehensive User Interface Management Systen Computer Graphics 17(3), July 1983, 35-42.

[Ciccarelli 84] E.C. Ciccarelli: Presentation Based User Interfaces, Technical Report 794, Artificial Intelligence Laboratory Massachusetts Intelligence Laboratory, August, 1984.

[Coutaz 86] J. Coutaz: La Construction d'Interfaces Homme-Machine, Rapport de Recherche IMAG-LGI, RR 635-I, nov. 1986.

[Garret 86] N. L. Garret, K. E. Smith: Building a Timeline editor from Prefabs Parts: The Architecture of an Object-Oriente Application; Proceedings OOPSLA'86, Sigplan Notices 11(21), November 1986, 202-213.

[Goldberg 84] A. Goldberg, D. Robson : Smalltalk-80 : The Interactive Programming Environment; Addison-Wesley Publ 1984.

[Hayes 83] P.J. Hayes, P. Szekely: Graceful Interaction through the Cousin Command Interface; International Journal of Ma Machine Studies 19(3), September 1983, 285-305.

[Hayes 85] P.J. Hayes, P. Szekely, R. Lerner: Design Alternatives for User Interface Management Systems Based on Experienc with Cousin; Proceedings of the CHI'85 Conference, The Association for Computing Machinery Publ., April 1985,169-175.

[Hullot 86] J.M. Hullot: SOS Interface, un Générateur d'Interfaces Homme-Machine, Actes des Journées Afcet-Informatique su les Langages Orientés Objet, Bigre+Globule, 48, Publ. IRISA, Campus de Beaulieu, 35042 Rennes, janvier, 1986, 69-78.

[Lieberman 85] H. Lieberman: There's More to Menu Systems than Meets the Screen; SIGGRAPH'85, 19(3), 181-189.

[Myers 86] B. Myers, W. Buxton: Creating Highly-Interactive and Graphical User Interfaces by Demonstration; SIGGRAPH'8(20(4), 1986, 249-257.

[Olsen 83] D.R Olsen, E.P Dempsey: Syngraph: A Graphical User Interface Generator; Computer Graphics, July 1983, 43-50.

[Schmucker 86a] K. Schmucker: MacApp: An Application Framework; Byte 11(8), 1986, 189-193.

[Schmucker 86b] K. Schmucker: Object-Oriented Languages for the Macintosh; Byte 11(8), 1986, 177-188.

[Schulert 85] A.J. Schulert, G.T. Rogers, J.A. Hamilton : ADM - A Dialog Manager; Proceedings of the CHI'85 Conference The Association for Computing Machinery Publ., April 1985, 177-183.

[Sibert 86] J.L. Sibert, W.D. Hurley, T.W. Bleser; An Object Oriented User Interface Management System; SIGGRAPH'8(20(4), 1986, 259-268.

[Tanner 83] P. Tanner, W. Buxton: Some Issues in Future User Interface Management Systems (UIMS) Development. IFI Working Group 5.2 Workshop on User Interface Management, Seeheim, West Germany, November 1983.

[Tanner 86] P. Tanner, S.A. Mackay, D. A. Stewart: A Multitasking Switchboard Approach to User Interface Managemen SIGGRAPH, 20(4), 1986, 241-248.

[Tesler 86] L. Tesler: Programming Experiences; Byte, 11(8), August 1986, 195-206.

[Wasserman 85] A. Wasserman: Extending State Transition Diagrams for the Specification of Human-Computer Interactior IEEE Transactions on Software Engineering, 11(8), August 1985.

[Wong 82] P.C.S. Wong, E.R. Reid: Flair- User Interface Design Tool; ACM Computer Graphics, 16(3), July 1982, 87-98.

The ZOO Metasystem:
A Direct-Manipulation Interface
to Object-Oriented Knowledge Bases

Dr. Wolf-Fritz Riekert
Siemens AG, K D ST SP 311, AI Programming Systems
Otto-Hahn-Ring 6, D-8000 München 83

Abstract

Transparency and adaptability are important criteria for the usability of computer systems. It is not easy to fulfill these criteria in ill-structured domains by using traditional software concepts. The object-oriented approach, however, allows the construction of metasystems which enable the user to understand and manipulate the underlying conceptual schemata of an application system.

ZOO[1] is a metasystem for the application expert. ZOO visualizes the contents of an object-oriented knowledge base in a graphic, spatial representation as a net of icons. ZOO allows its user to inspect, manipulate, create and delete the components of a knowledge base through direct manipulation of graphic objects.

1. Introduction

There is an increasing demand for computer solutions in ill-structured problem domains such as office automation, planning, design, or diagnosis. In general there is no formal description of the problem domain and the goals of operation are not well-defined. So it is hard or even impossible to find definite general methods for solving problems in these environments.

---

[1]The author was a member of the Research Group INFORM at the University of Stuttgart, when he developed the ZOO system. The Research Group INFORM is supported by the German Federal Ministry of Research and Technology (BMFT) under contract ITW8404A/4, as part of the joint project WISDOM. The development of the ZOO system was supported by the TA Triumph Adler AG, Nürnberg, West Germany.

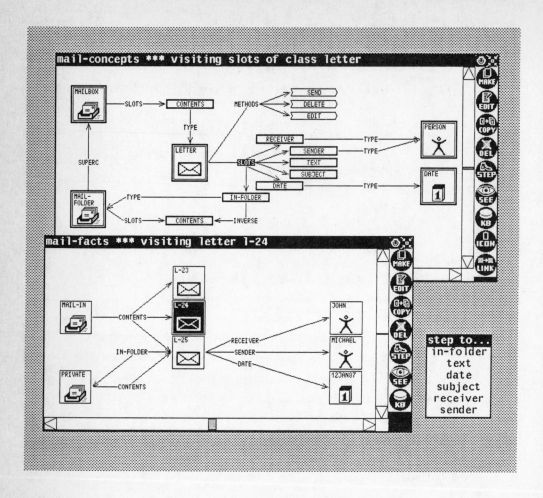

Figure 1: The ZOO metasystem

Therefore the usage of computer software for non-trivial problems in these domains imposes a lot of difficulties on the end user of the system.

- Due to the lack of well-defined goals and methods it is hard for a human to accept the solutions found by the computer. The user does not know the underlying conceptual model of the decisions made by a computer. The program documentation does not help, because it usually describes the software structure of the system rather than the concepts of the application domain.

- Since the application domain is not sufficiently formalized the computer software used is destined for incompleteness. The system designer can only follow heuristics which still have to be verified in the field. The use of the system will reveal new criteria which require a modification of the software by a software specialist. A permanent communication problem between the user and the programmer of the software is the result, taking a lot of time. Therefore most of the users would rather perform the necessary modifications by themselves.

So there are two criteria with increasing importance for the evaluation of complex software systems: the *transparency* and the *adaptability* of the system. These criteria are not fulfilled while using traditional application systems in ill-structured problem domains. The reason for this deficiency is the way knowledge is represented in traditional systems: Since the knowledge is encoded in a collection of procedures and data structures, its only use is the run of the application system. For all other purposes, the code of a program is a poor representation of knowledge: neither does it help much if we need documentation, explanation or help for the usage of the system nor does it support its augmentation or modification by itself.

Object-oriented application systems, however, offer a way out of this problem. The behavior of these systems is driven by a *knowledge base* consisting of objects rather than by a collection of procedures. There is no limit for the interpretation of the knowledge encoded in objects, so it is possible to design system components which access and manipulate the contents of an object-oriented knowledge base. Such system components operate on a higher level of abstraction than the underlying application system, therefore they are called *metasystems*[2]. Having access to the knowledge sources used by the application system, metasystems are able to explain and to control the behavior of an application system.

The ZOO[3] system presented in this paper is a metasystem which serves two purposes: It is both an instrument for inspecting the contents of an object-oriented knowledge base in a two-dimensional graphic representation and a tool for the modification of knowledge bases by direct manipulation of sensitive screen objects. Graphics is a very popular means used for problem specification and for the documentation of technical systems, so it is used in the ZOO system. ZOO intentionally appears to its user as simple as a system for the display and the construction of business graphics, whereas its functionality is much broader. Every graphic object displayed by the ZOO system represents an item of the system-internal knowledge base. Creating a new graphic object on the screen is a request for generating a new component of the knowledge base as well. Supporting the construction of a graphic diagram and a knowledge base at the same time, ZOO connects the processes

---

[2]The first knowledge-based metasystems were developed in Stanford: Typical examples are the systems EMYCIN/Teiresias and Meta-DENDRAL which are metasystems for the known expert systems MYCIN and DENDRAL [3]

[3]The name ZOO stands for a Zoo Of Objects.

of specification, implementation and documentation of knowledge-based systems in parallel. Thus ZOO may also be considered as a rapid-prototyping tool.

ZOO is running on a VAX 11/780 under Berkeley UNIX 4.2 and requires a BBN BitGraph terminal as communication device. ZOO makes use of the window-system WLISP [5] and the object-oriented language ObjTalk [13] which were both developed by members of the research group INFORM. The basic implementation language of all software components is Franz Lisp [7].

2. External Representation of Knowledge

In our software systems, we use ObjTalk [13; 14], an object-oriented language, for the representation of knowledge. ObjTalk is a language which combines the actor concept and the message passing paradigm of Hewitt [10] and the frame ideas of Minsky [12] in a way similar to KL-ONE [2] or LOOPS [1].

ObjTalk allows the representation of object-level knowledge about concrete facts as well as meta-level knowledge[4] about abstract concepts:

- Concrete facts about the real world may be represented by ObjTalk *objects* and their state. ObjTalk provides *slots* for every object in order to store properties and relations to other objects. ObjTalk allows the classification of objects: Every object belongs to a *class* of which it is called an instance.

- Abstract Concepts may be represented by a special kind of ObjTalk objects, called *conceptual objects*. Classes are conceptual objects representing the common properties of their instances. All classes are forming a specialization hierarchy. Classes provide *slot descriptions*, *rules* and *methods* which are conceptual objects as well.

For viewing and manipulating an object, we need an external representation for it. ObjTalk provides such a format, yet it is dedicated to programmers and consists of a Lisp-expression which would define the object when it is loaded or evaluated. This format is not suited for the end user of a system implemented in ObjTalk.

If there is a terminal with a high-resolution screen, there are new ways of displaying the internal objects and their state in a representation closer to the needs of the user. This was shown by the success of the new graphic user-interfaces which came up with Xerox' Star computer [17] and are a standard now in a lot of small computers. Objects and operations originating in an office environment are visualized by graphic symbols, so-called *icons* and may be activated and processed by *direct manipulation* [16; 11]. Icon-based

---

[4]The terms "object-level knowledge" and "meta-level knowledge" have been introduced by R. Davis [4]

direct-manipulation interfaces are very easy to learn and understand. A Star-like interface, however, does not fulfill all the needs of external knowledge representation:

- The Star interface is limited to the office world, while we want to represent objects of arbitrary domains.
- The Star interface supports only hierarchical relations, e.g. between a document and its folder, but a universal system should represent arbitrary relations between objects.
- It must be possible, to represent abstract concepts (such as the concept *folder*), not only concrete objects (such as the folder *XYZ*).

On the other side there are knowledge engineering tools which meet most of these requirements, but suffer from a poor use of graphics, such as the SMALLTALK-Browser [8]. KEE and LOOPS only display specialization and instantiation hierarchies of objects, they do not support other relations between objects. Moreover, their graphic representations cannot be changed through direct manipulation. KEE's SIMKIT system possesses a complete direct-manipulation interface, yet it is only useful for simulation applications. The idea behind the ZOO system described here is to combine the graphic capabilities of an icon-based system with the universality of a knowledge engineering system.

3. The ZOO Graphic Representation Format

Common objects and conceptual objects of the knowledge representation language ObjTalk may be represented in a graphic form by the ZOO system. For this purpose ZOO provides two kinds of graphic primitives: *icons* and *arrows*.

Icons are used for the graphic representation of *objects*. Usually such an icon has a square shape. It is labelled by the name of the object. It contains a graphic symbol which, in general, visualizes the class membership of the object. *Relations* to other objects are represented by labelled arrows pointing to the graphical representation of the corresponding objects while the label of the arrow contains the name of the relation. Figure 2 shows the graphic representation of an object, a German computer system, in relation to other objects. In summary, object-level knowledge appears as a network of icons as nodes and labelled arrows as links.

Meta-level knowledge consisting of a knowledge base of conceptual objects is represented basically the same way as object-level knowledge. *Classes* appear as icons which are surrounded by a fat border (see figure 3). By default, the graphic symbol used for the visualization of the class will be transmitted to its instances and to its inferiors in the specialization hierarchy. The specialization hierarchy of classes is represented internally by a relation with the name "superc", so it may be displayed using labelled arrows as described above. The other conceptual objects, such as slot descriptions, methods and rules are linked to the network of classes by labelled arrows representing the respective relations.

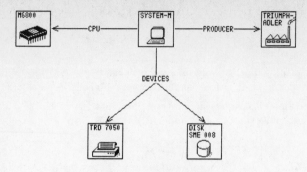

Figure 2: The object *System–M* in relation to other objects

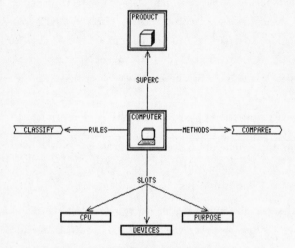

Figure 3: The class *computer* and its surrounding conceptual objects

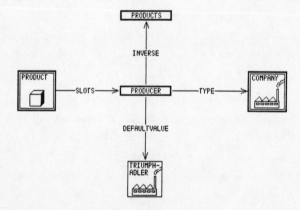

Figure 4: The slot description *producer* from class *product*

Slot descriptions appear as flat rectangles enclosing the name of the slot. Again there may be relation arrows originating from slot descriptions to other icons, displaying the type, the default value and the inverse relation (see figure 4). In a similar way ZOO visualizes *methods* and *rules* within the network of conceptual objects.

4. The ZOO metasystem

The ZOO metasystem may be considered as a user-interface to the whole knowledge represented by ObjTalk objects in a software system. The purpose of ZOO is to present the contents of a knowledge base in the graphic format described above, allowing the user to modify it through direct manipulation. ZOO is operating on the in-core representation of knowledge bases, so it is possible to make changes to a knowledge-based system at run-time. ZOO is able to access conceptual objects representing abstract concepts as well as concrete instances representing facts about the application domain.

The graphic representation of a knowledge base is displayed in a rectangular region on the screen, a so-called *zoo-window* (see figure 1). Each icon represents an object, each labelled arrow represents a relation between objects of the knowledge base. One of these graphic objects (icons or labelled arrows) may be selected by touching it with a pointing device (mouse). All object-specific operations apply to the selected item. The applicable operations are displayed on the border of the zoo-window as function-icons, which can also be activated with the mouse. Objects may be created by copying or instantiating the selected object, relations between objects may be established by drawing arrows from the selected object to other objects. The names of these relations may be selected from a pop-up menu, the contents of which is derived from the class of the selected object. In addition there are functions for storing and retrieving knowledge bases, for viewing objects, for deleting objects, for forgetting relations, and for changing the appearance and position of objects.

There is no central display manager for the graphic objects inside a zoo-window, the display management is done in an object-oriented way instead. Each icon and each labelled arrow is itself represented by an ObjTalk object, a so-called *interaction object* [9]. Interaction objects establish the link between internal objects and their graphic representation on the screen. Therefore interaction objects represent two kinds of knowledge:

- An interaction object possesses graphic knowledge, it describes the position and the appearance of a screen object. This knowledge will be used for the purposes of displaying and activating the graphic objects.

- An interaction object possesses knowledge about the existence of an internal object or about one of its properties. Interaction objects provide methods for the manipulation of their internal counterparts.

Within a zoo-window there are different classes of interaction objects which are used for the graphic presentation of the various kinds of knowledge base objects and their interrelations as described in section 3. The function-icons on the border of a zoo-window do not visualize the objects of the target knowledge base; they represent the functions of the ZOO system instead. Most of these functions apply to the selected graphic object inside the zoo-window. The effect of these functions depends on the class of the selected interaction object. Because of this context-dependent behavior, the number of functions may be kept small, making the user-interface simple and powerful at the same time.

5. Conclusions

The consideration of knowledge aspects leads to a new viewpoint in man-machine communication. The problem of constructing understandable user-interfaces can be reduced to the question of an external knowledge representation adapted to the user's point of view. Our answer to this question is the idea of a two-dimensional representation of knowledge by graphic objects on a high-resolution screen, being subject to direct manipulation with a pointing device.

In this context, an integrated object-oriented software architecture which includes both the user-interface and the system kernel turns out to be very advantageous. An object-oriented user-interface allows the use of interaction objects which appear to the user as mouse-sensitive graphic objects on the screen of a computer terminal. But within the system they are active data objects communicating with the internal objects of the knowledge base. If the system kernel is driven by an object-oriented knowledge base every interaction object finds a unique internal counterpart and this guarantees a close connection between the internal and the external representation of knowledge.

The object as a fundamental concept of programming and representing knowledge makes it possible to construct metasystems for visualizing and modifying the facts and the concepts of an application system. Together with advanced techniques of man-machine communication, the object-oriented knowledge-based approach makes it easy to construct application systems which are more transparent than traditional programs and can be adapted by the user in many parts. Therefore this approach contributes a lot to the development of user-centered software environments.

References

[1] D.G. Bobrow, M. Stefik: *"The LOOPS Manual"*. Technical Report KB-VLSI-81-83, Knowledge Systems Area, Xerox Palo Alto Research Center (PARC), 1981.

[2] Brachmann. R. et al.: *"KL–ONE Reference Manual"*. BBN-Report 3848, BBN, July, 1978.

[3] B.G. Buchanan, E.H. Shortliffe: *The Addison–Wesley Series in Artificial Intelligence*: *"Rule–Based Expert Systems: The MYCIN Experiments of the Stanford Heuristic Programming Project"*. Addison-Wesley, Reading, Ma., 1984.

[4] R. Davis, D.B. Lenat: *Advanced Computer Science Series*: *"Knowledge Based Systems in Artificial Intelligence"*. McGraw-Hill, New York, 1982.

[5] F. Fabian Jr., A. C. Lemke: *"Wlisp Manual"*. Technical Report CU-CS-302-85, University of Colorado, Boulder, February, 1985. Translated by V. Patten and C. Morel.

[6] G. Fischer, M. Schneider: *"Knowledge–based Communication Processes in Software Engineering"*. In *Proceedings of the 7th International Conference on Software Engineering*, pp 358-368. Orlando, Florida, March, 1984.

[7] J.K. Foderaro, K.L. Sklower: *"The FranzLisp Manual"*. Technical Report, University of California, Berkeley, 1982.

[8] A. Goldberg: *"SMALLTALK–80, The Interactive Programming Environment"*. Addison-Wesley, Reading, Ma., 1984.

[9] M. Herczeg: *"INFORM–Manual: Icons"*. Institut für Informatik, Universität Stuttgart, 1985.

[10] C. Hewitt: *"Viewing Control Structures as Patterns of Passing Messages"*. *Artificial Intelligence Journal* 8, pp 323-364, 1977.

[11] E.L. Hutchins, J.D. Hollan, D.A. Norman: *"Direct Manipulation Interfaces"*. In D.A. Norman, S. Draper (editors), *User Centered System Design: New Perspectives on Human–Computer Interaction*. Lawrence Erlbaum Associates Ltd., 1986.

[12] M. Minsky: *"A Framework for Representing Knowledge"*. In P.H. Winston (editor), *The Psychology of Computer Vision*, pp 211-277. McGraw Hill, New York, 1975.

[13] C. Rathke: *"ObjTalk Primer"*. Translated Version by A.C. Lemke, V.M. Patten, C.P. Morel, Dept. of Computer Science, University of Colorado, Boulder - Technical Report CU-CS-290-85 -, INFORM, Institut für Informatik, Universität Stuttgart, 1985.

[14] C. Rathke: *"ObjTalk. Repräsentation von Wissen in einer objektorientierten Sprache"*. Dissertation, Fakultät Mathematik und Informatik der Universität Stuttgart, Oktober, 1986.

[15] W.-F. Riekert: *"Der graphische Wissenseditor ZOO – ein Metasystem zur Visualisierung und Manipulation von Wissensbasen"*. WISDOM-Forschungsbericht FB-INF-86-9, Institut für Informatik, Universität Stuttgart, 1986.

[16] B. Shneiderman: *"Direct Manipulation: A Step Beyond Programming Languages"*. *IEEE Computer* 16(8), pp 57-69, August, 1983.

[17] D.C. Smith, Ch. Irby, R. Kimball, B. Verplank: *"Designing the Star User Interface"*. BYTE, April, 1982.

The Filter Browser
Defining Interfaces Graphically

Raimund K. Ege[†], David Maier[†] and Alan Borning[‡]

Abstract

We describe a new approach to constructing user interfaces by declaratively specifying the relationships between objects via filters. A filter is a package of constraints dynamically enforced between a source object and a view object. For example, the relationship between an employee object in a database and a bitmap object represented on a display screen can be modelled as a filter. The object in the database can then be modified by manipulating the object on the screen, and changes made to the employee object by other programs are instantly reflected on the screen.

This paper describes a specification language for filters, an implementation of filters with the aid of a constraint-satisfaction system, and a graphical interface for designing filters. We illustrate the power and flexibility of the filter paradigm with an interface example and show that it stimulates and supports the re-use of existing components and gives a design methodology for constructing interfaces.

1 Introduction

This paper presents a new approach to building user interfaces in an object-oriented environment. In such an environment, all entities of interest are represented as objects, so all aspects of user interfaces are modelled as objects. In the Smalltalk model-view-controller (MVC) Paradigm [9], for example, the interface consists of model, view and controller objects. The model and view are basically two different representations of the same conceptual entity [6]. In Smalltalk's MVC paradigm, the model and view have procedural components that allow the controller to manage the interface correctly.

The Filter Paradigm : Our approach is to abandon procedural specification of user interfaces and relate the model (*source*) and *view* with a declarative interface specification. The idea is to use constraints to specify the conceptual relation between the *source* and *view* objects. For example, the relationship between an employee object and a bitmap object on a screen can be represented by constraints. The constraints state that the bitmap object always displays a certain rendering of the employee object. The constraints hide the procedurality of the interface. If the bitmap object on the screen is changed, then constraint satisfaction will ensure that the employee object is changed accordingly. If the employee object changes, then that change is reflected on the screen.

A *filter* is an object that describes and maintains these special constraints between objects in an interface. For example, consider an interface between two binary trees. The binary trees store an integer number at each node. The interface should be constructed in a way that one tree is the

---

Authors' addresses:
[†] Dept. of Comp. Science & Eng.   [‡] Dept. of Comp. Science, FR-35
Oregon Graduate Center   University of Washington
Beaverton, OR 97006-1999   Seattle, WA 98195
USA   USA

Research was supported by NSF grants IRI-8604923 and IRI-8604977.

reversal of the other tree, i.e., the interface can be viewed as the constraint that one tree is the mirror image of the other. This constraint can be represented as a filter between a binary tree as source and a binary tree as view object. Filters are constructed from subfilters on subparts of a source and view object. Figure 1 illustrates this tree reversal for two binary trees of height one constructed from three equality subfilters. The equality subfilters ensure that the integer numbers, stored in corresponding nodes, are kept equal. If a number is changed then the corresponding number on the other side of the filter is changed by the constraint-satisfaction system. If a subnode is added to a node on one side then a subnode is added by the constraint-satisfaction system on the other side of the filter and an equality subfilter is established between them. If a subnode is deleted from a node then the corresponding subnode is deleted from the other side of the filter and the equality subfilter is removed.

The definition of what types of the source and view objects are allowed for the filter and how the subfilters are connected to them is given by the *filter type*. Filter types specify how filters are built from atomic filters using set, iteration and condition constructors. Atomic filters are given by the implementation. The filter and object types are described by a filter specification language (*FiSpeL*) [8]. *FiSpeL* is currently a theoretical tool for composing filters; a compiler and optimizer for it are planned. The *Filter Browser* is a tool for constructing filters graphically. The *Filter Browser* lets the interface designer create filters by defining and manipulating filter types. Subfilters are added interactively by connecting them with the various constructors to the object types that are displayed in the browser. The *Filter Browser* also allows the designer to instantiate a filter from its filter type definition with sample objects to test the constructed interface.

Related Work : Our approach was guided by experience with the Smalltalk MVC paradigm [9]. Programming experience has shown that this paradigm is hard to follow. The Smalltalk Interaction Generator (SIG) tried to add a declarative interface on top of the MVC mechanism [12, 15]. One conclusion of SIG is that display procedures need type information about the objects they display and that Smalltalk does not provide this kind of typing. The Incense system [14] uses type information supplied by a compiler to display objects. The user can influence the display format but cannot update through this system. Editing can be used as an abstraction of user interaction [16] by separating the view from the source of data and defining a protocol for update. The Impulse-86 system [17] provides abstractions for objects as well as for interactions. Other approaches using algebraic techniques to specify user interfaces axiomatically [4] seem manageable only for small theoretical examples.

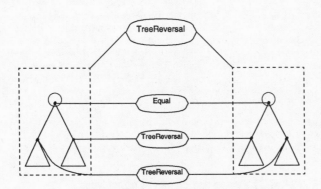

Figure 1: **Tree Reversal Filter.**

Constraints are used to specify relations and dependencies in Morgenstern's *active* database interface system [13]. Other systems use constraints as their major construct, such as ThingLab [1,2], which allows constraints to be expressed in a graphical manner. The Animus system [3,7] extends ThingLab with constraints that involve time. An early system that employed constraints to express graphical relations was Sketchpad [18]. The language Ideal [19], used in typesetting graphical pictures, is based on constraints and demonstrates their power and usefulness. Bertrand [11] is a term rewriting language that can specify constraint satisfaction systems. In its current implementation, however, it is not interactive and therefore not well suited for our problem. Constraints have also been used in the layout mechanism of a window management system [5].

Section 2 of this paper summarizes the filter specification language *FiSpeL*. Section 3 introduces the *Filter Browser* and elaborates an example session to generate an interface interactively. Section 4 gives details of how the objects, filters, constraints, and the *Filter Browser* are implemented in Smalltalk-80[1], and how the constraint satisfaction is performed by ThingLab [1]. The complete object and filter type definitions for the employee interface example from Sections 2 and 3 are listed in the appendix.

2 Objects and Filters

This section summarizes *FiSpeL*, a filter specification language for defining object and filter types. If we want to compose filters from subfilters, connecting objects of different kinds, it is necessary to type the objects to ensure that compositions of filters are well-defined. All entities in our filter paradigm are ultimately implemented by objects, so we put much effort in providing a comprehensive type system for the object model.

Object Types : The object type system supports the notions of aggregation and specialization. With aggregation we can build structured objects from components. Specialization allows us to refine existing objects via a hierarchy of object types and inheritance. We view object types as records. A record is a collection of typed fields. The fields have names called *addresses*. There are constant fields, which are constant for all instances of a type, and there are data fields, which are local to an instance of an object. Fields can be iterated by specifying an iteration factor; fields can be conditional by specifying a condition that must be true for the field to exist; and a field can specify its type

```
Object Type Person                      Object Type Employee
      lastName → String                       inherit from Person
      firstName → String                      salary → Integer
      socSecNum → Integer                     subNumber → Integer
      address → String                        supervises[subNumber] → Employee
end                                           supervisor → Employee
                                              jobDescription → String
                                        end
Object Type DisplayEmployee
      icon → PersonIcon
      name → String
      subNumber → Integer
      subordinates[subNumber] → DisplayEmployee
end
```

Figure 2: Person and Employee object types.

---

[1] Smalltalk-80 is a trademark of Xerox Corporation.

recursively. In addition, an object type can inherit fields from other object types and can place constraints on all fields.

Figure 2 shows the two object types, Person and Employee. Person includes the fields that are common to a person. Employee is a specialization of Person and defines additional fields, such as salary and jobDescription. The field supervises is an iterated address, i.e., an employee may supervise a number of subordinates. The number of subordinates is specified by the field subNumber.

Object types are used in the filter type definition to describe source, view and variables that are needed to connect subfilters. A field of an object is accessed by traversing a path of field names. We distinguish direct and delayed access to an object via a path. In direct access, the structure of the object is traversed according to the path and the correct field is returned. In delayed access, we store the object identity together with the path to allow access on need at a later time. Delayed access is needed because it is possible that an object does not comply with the given path at the time when the path is defined (conditional fields), or the object at an end of a path may change before it is used.

Filter Types : The filter type system defines the structure of filters. Filters represent constraints between two objects. The filter type defines the types of the source and view objects it relates. The filter type also declares the subfilters that compose the filter. In addition, the filter type can define variables to be used as intermediate objects when subfilters are combined. A filter that is not further decomposed is called a *filter atom* and is directly supported by the implementation. For example, filter atoms are used for low-level input/output, data conversion, or error handling. A filter that has subfilters is called a *filter pack*. The subfilter constructors are: sequence, iteration and condition. The sequence constructor (set of) declares several subfilters of possibly different types; the iteration constructor (iteration p times i) declares a certain number of filters of the same type; the condition constructor (condition) declares a subfilter only if a given condition is true. It is possible to declare another instance of the same filter type as a subfilter of the one being defined, much like a recursive procedure call in a conventional programming language.

Figure 2 shows the object type definition for DisplayEmployee that contains displayable information for an employee. In order to define an interface that will display an object of type Employee we have to extract the displayable information. Figure 3 shows the filter type definition EmployeeDisplay. It decomposes the constraint into subconstraints. The subconstraints specify that the name, the number of subordinates and the subordinates are the same in the source object of type Employee and in the view object of type DisplayEmployee. The example uses the sequence and iteration filter constructors. The iteration names the same filter type for each of the subordinates recursively. The iteration depends on the value that is stored in source.subNumber. Whenever that value changes, the number of subfilters that are instantiated for the subordinates is changed. When including a subfilter, the filter type associates source and view paths with it. For example, the subfilter StringEquality has source.firstName as its source object. When this filter type is instantiated, the filter instance will check whether the address firstName in fact refers to an object of type String. It is at this point that the path to the field is traversed to retrieve it. The newly

```
Filter Type EmployeeDisplay ( source : Employee, view : DisplayEmployee )
       make set of
              StringEquality (source.firstName, view.name)
              IntegerEquality (source.subNumber, view.subNumber)
              iteration source.subNumber times i
                     EmployeeDisplay(source.supervises[i],view.subordinates[i])
       end
```

Figure 3: EmployeeDisplay filter type.

defined filter type `EmployeeDisplay` can now be used as subfilter in other filter type definitions. The appendix contains the complete filter and object type definitions for a sample `EmployeeManipulation` interface.

3 The Filter Browser

The filter specification language is one way to define a user interface by defining filter types, but the goal here is to provide a graphical tool to build interfaces. Therefore, a tool similar to the Smalltalk [10], ThingLab [1] or Animus [7] browser, the *Filter Browser*, is used to define, manipulate and test filter types graphically. In defining filter types, we distinguish the external and internal parts of the definition. Externally, the filter type is identified by its name and the types of its source and view object. Internally the filter type specifies subfilters and variables. These details are encapsulated inside the filter type. A session with the filter browser has three different phases. In phase one, the name of the filter type and the type of source and view objects are given. In phase two, the variables and subfilters that participate in filter constructors, such as sequence, iteration and condition are specified. Phase one represents the external, phase two the internal definition. In phase three, a constructed filter type is instantiated. Figures 4, 5 and 6 show examples of the filter browser in each of the phases as we define the filter type `EmployeeManipulation`.

Phase one (Figure 4) : The filter browser is divided into several panes. In this phase only the upper left, lower left and lower right panes are used. The upper left pane shows a list of all filter types that are known to the system. The user can add a new filter type. The current subject of the filter type definition, i.e., the filter type that will be modified or newly defined, is emphasized. The filter browser displays two lists of all object types that are available for source and view types in the two panes below. The user can inspect all object types and select one for source and view. The object type also provides a sample instance (prototype) that can be used to instantiate the filter in phase three. The `EmployeeManipulation` filter type is defined on source objects of type `Company` and on view objects of type `FilterDevice` (these object types are emphasized).

Phase two (Figure 5) : The upper left pane displays a list of known filter types with the current selection, `EmployeeManipulation`, emphasized. To the right there are four panes to select the action that is to be performed on the current filter type. The user can *insert* subfilters, add

Filter Browser (Version 2.0)			
EmployeeDisplay	insert	delete	Example (Rectangle, FilterDevice)
EmployeeManipul			FaConstantDistance (Point, Point)
EmployeeRender	move	variable	FaConstantLength (Number, LineSeg

source	sequence	iteration	condition	view

------------------	FaConstantLength
CenteredText	FaMasterSlave
Company	FaPointEquality
DisplayEmployee	FaPointSensor
Employee	FaRender
EmployeeDisplay	FaTextEquality
EmployeeManipulation	FilterAtomThing
EmployeeRender	FilterBitmap
Example	**FilterDevice**
FaConstantDistance	FilterDisplayObject
FaConstantLength	FilterMergeObject
FaMasterSlave	FilterMouse
FaPointEquality	FilterPackThing
FaPointSensor	FilterRenderAtom

Figure 4: Filter Browser Phase One.

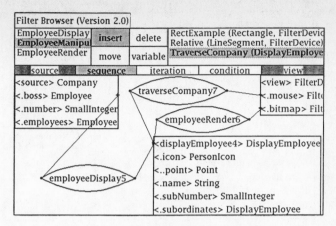

Figure 5: Filter Browser Phase Two.

variables, *move* or *delete* subfilters or variables in the picture pane below. The picture pane substitutes the two object lists from phase one. If the *insert* action is selected then the upper right pane shows a list of all filter types and the types of their source and view objects. This list also contains the currently defined filter type to allow the recursive specification of a filter type. The selected element in this list represents the object of the action that is performed, i.e., it names the filter type to be inserted as subfilter in the filter type. If the *variable* action is selected then the upper right pane shows a list of all available object types, from which the user may select. The type of filter constructor (sequence, iteration, condition) is selected with one of the three panes in the middle of the filter browser.

The picture pane is used to display the subfilters, variables and their connections. A variable is placed in the picture pane by selecting the *variable* action. The variable appears as a box that shows its name and type and the paths to its fields with their types. The user selects a location and places the variable. The variable is then inserted into the current filter type definition. A subfilter is placed in the picture pane by selecting the *insert* action and a subfilter from the upper right pane. The added subfilter is then connected (linked) to paths in either the source, view or variable objects by pointing at their location on the screen. For iteration or condition constructors, an iteration or condition object has to be selected by pointing to a path that represents the iteration factor or the condition. After the subfilter is placed in the picture pane it is inserted into the current filter type definition.

Figure 5 shows the filter browser as the user inserts the `TraverseCompany` subfilter into the `EmployeeManipulation` filter type. A variable of type `DisplayEmployee` has already been defined and connected to an `EmployeeRender` and `EmployeeDisplay` (see Section 2) subfilter. The `EmployeeRender` filter renders an object of type `DisplayEmployee` on the display bitmap. The `TraverseCompany` filter allows the selection of an employee within a company using a pop-up menu. These filters are already defined. After the *insert* action has been selected and the user moves the mouse cursor into the picture pane a lozenge for the `TraverseCompany` filter appears. The source link is connected to the `displayEmployee4` variable and the view link is connected to the `bitmap` address of the view object.

The picture pane represents the network of subfilters. The absolute position of the subfilters in the picture pane is not important, but it will be stored to redraw the subfilter network in the same way as it was defined. An important issue in connecting subfilters is typing. The external definition of a subfilter specifies the object type for its source and view object. Thus, when a source or view link of a subfilter is connected to addresses of source, view or variable objects of the currently defined filter

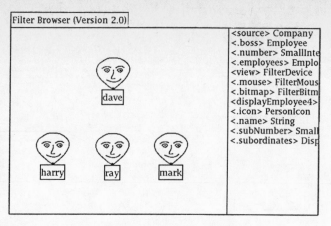

Figure 6: Filter Browser Phase Three.

type, it is necessary to check the corresponding types. These source and view links can be connected to object types that are of the same type as, or are subtypes of, their specified object types. For example, the source of the `TraverseCompany` filter has to be of type `DisplayEmployee` or one of its subtypes.

Phase three (Figure 6) : Instantiating a filter type means creating a Smalltalk object representing a filter. When instantiating, source, view and variable object instances of the correct object types have to be supplied. This instantiation operation is accessible from a pop-up menu in the upper left pane of the browser, where the filter type has been selected. The right pane of the filter browser simulates the display bitmap for the filters and all input is controlled by the filter browser, so it is possible to switch back to the previous phases. The right pane of the filter browser shows the participating instantiated objects. They can be selected, inspected and changed. Any change to participating objects will immediately change the display in the left pane. Figure 6 shows the instantiated `EmployeeManipulation` filter type for a prototype `Company`. The `FilterDevice` is simulated by the filter browser. The pane on the left displays the company's employees. We can traverse the tree of employees and make changes to the employees as they are stored for the company. The appendix lists the complete filter and object type definitions.

In phase three the user can test the filter type by observing its behavior and changing values of variables. The filter type can be changed incrementally. The user can switch back and forth between phases two and three, adding and deleting subfilters and variables or changing values of participating objects. All filter types are constructed from existing filters in a bottom-up fashion. The filter browser lists all existing filters together with their source and view type information. Filter types can only be constructed if the subfilters and variables are connected correctly and the filter can be instantiated while it is being developed to test its behavior. Thus the filter paradigm stimulates and supports the re-use of existing components and gives a design methodology for constructing interfaces.

4 Implementation

The *Filter Browser* is implemented on a Tektronix 4400 Series machine in Smalltalk-80[2]. ThingLab [1], an extension to Smalltalk, is used to do the constraint satisfaction. Filter and object

---

[2] Smalltalk-80 is a trademark of Xerox Corporation.

types in *FiSpeL* are represented as classes in Smalltalk. ThingLab extends the Smalltalk class definition with constraints, types for instance variables and dynamic access.

Object Types : Object types are modelled as Smalltalk classes. The fields of an object are instance variables, where the instance variable name is the address of the field. Iterated fields are represented as a set of fields, while conditional fields hold the value "nil" if the condition is not true. Fields can be inherited from superclasses. Field access is done through an access path that stores the field names that have to be traversed. Smalltalk does not keep information on the type of instance variables, so ThingLab augments the class definition to hold the type (reference to another object type class) for each instance variable[3]. Constraints that are defined within the object type are also stored in the class definition. An instance of an object type refers back to its class definition, so the constraint-satisfaction mechanism can retrieve the defined constraints.

Filter Types : Filter types are represented as subclasses of the object type classes. Fields are defined for the source and view objects, as well as for the variables. The subfilters are held in instance variables that can be conditional or iterated. The subfilters have source and view object information associated with them, i.e., what fields are used as source and view object for the subfilter. This information is modelled as equality constraints[4] from the field within the source, view or variable object to the appropriate source or view object of the subfilter. For example, consider the Employ-eeDisplay filter type in Figure 3. The StringEquality subfilter is held by a sequence filter constructor; its source is associated with the source.firstName field of the filter type. This association is modelled by an equality constraint defined for the EmployeeDisplay filter type class.

ThingLab : As mentioned earlier, the filter browser is implemented as an extension to ThingLab. Path access using addresses (field names) and the constraint satisfaction is handled by ThingLab. The field description within ThingLab was augmented to incorporate iterated and conditional fields. Filter atoms are directly implemented as ThingLab constraints. ThingLab's prototypes of things are reduced in their importance in that they are used to hold the graphical information used to display the filter network in phase two and to provide sample values for the instantiation in phase three of the filter browser, but they no longer are used to infer the type of an instance variable.

Not all objects will be defined within ThingLab. Objects outside ThingLab are the display bitmap, the keyboard, specialized input devices (mice), or existing complex objects in an application. These object can be incorporated by either providing a special object in ThingLab that holds the outside object and controls all accesses to it (object holder), or by providing special filters that link existing objects within ThingLab to those external objects (implementation filter atoms). Graphical primitives, such as line rendering or input sensing [8], are examples for filter atoms to incorporate I/O-objects.

5 Summary and Conclusion

The filter paradigm represents a new approach to interfaces in an object-oriented environment. Constraints are used as the basic building block for interfaces. Constructors are provided to allow building of structured interfaces in a declarative way. The feasibility of the filter paradigm is shown by providing a working interface generation tool. In addition, the object type system represents another approach to bring typing into Smalltalk.

Acknowledgements

This research has been funded by the National Science Foundation under Grants No. IRI-8604923 and IRI-8604977. Thanks also to Casey S. Bahr for many discussions that helped to refine the ideas for the implementation of the filter browser.

---

[3] Thus, at present, our typing mechanism does not allow an instance of a subtype to be stored in a typed instance variable. This is clearly an undesirable limitation, which we plan to remove. Removing it is not trivial, however, since depending on how the instance variable is used, we may need to ensure that the constraints on a subtype are not more restrictive than those on the specified type.

[4] Note that we do not distinguish between unification and equality constraint.

Bibliography

[1] Borning, Alan, *ThingLab - A Constraint-Oriented Simulation Laboratory*, PhD Thesis, Stanford University, 1979.

[2] Borning, Alan, The Programming Language Aspects of ThingLab, a Constraint-Oriented Simulation Laboratory, *ACM Trans. Prog. Lang. and Systems 3*, **4** (October 1981), 353-387.

[3] Borning, Alan and Robert A. Duisberg, Constraint-Based Tools for Building User Interfaces, *accepted for ACM Transactions on Graphics 5*, **4** (October 1986), .

[4] Chi, Uli, Formal Specification of User Interfaces: a Comparison and Evaluation of four axiomatic Methods, *IEEE Trans. on Software Eng. SE-11:8* (August 1985), 671-685.

[5] Cohen, Ellis S., Edward T. Smith and Lee A. Iverson, Constraint-Based Tiled Windows, *IEEE Computer Graphics and Applications*, May 1986.

[6] Deutsch, L. Peter, Panel: User Interface Frameworks, *OOPSLA'86 Conf. Proc.*, Portland, OR, September 1986.

[7] Duisberg, Robert A., *Constraint-Based Animation: The Implementation of Temporal Constraints in the Animus System*, Ph.D. Thesis, Department of Computer Science, University of Washington, 1986.

[8] Ege, Raimund K., The Filter - A Paradigm for Interfaces, Technical Report No. CSE-86-011, Oregon Graduate Center, Beaverton, OR, September 1986.

[9] Goldberg, Adele and D. Robson, *Smalltalk-80: The Language and its Implementation*, Addison Wesley, Reading, Mass., 1983.

[10] Goldberg, Adele, *Smalltalk-80: The Interactive Programming Environment*, Addison Wesley, Reading, MA, 1984.

[11] Leler, Wm, *Specification and Generation of Constraint Satisfaction Systems using Augmented Term Rewriting*, PhD Thesis, The University of North Carolina at Chapel Hill, 1986.

[12] Maier, David, Peter Nordquist and Mark Grossman, Displaying Database Objects, *Proc. First Int. Conf. on Expert Database Systems*, Charleston, South Carolina, April 1986.

[13] Morgenstern, M., Active Databases as a Paradigm for Enhanced Computing Environments, *Proc. 9th Int. Conf. on Very Large Data Bases*, Florence, Italy, October 1983.

[14] Myers, B., INCENSE: A System for Displaying Data Structures, *Computer Graphics 17(3)* (July 1983), 115-125.

[15] Nordquist, Peter, Interactive Display Generation in Smalltalk, Master's thesis, Technical Report CS/E 85-009, Oregon Graduate Center, March 1985.

[16] Scofield, J., *Editing as a Paradigm for User Interaction*, PhD thesis, University of Washington, Computer Science Department Technical Report 85-08-10, August 1985.

[17] Smith, Reid G., Rick Dinitz and Paul Bart, Impulse-86: A Substrate for Object-Oriented Interface Design, *OOPSLA'86 Conf. Proc.*, Portland, OR, September 1986.

[18] Sutherland, I., *Sketchpad: A Man-Machine Graphical Communication System*, PhD Thesis, MIT, 1963.

[19] Van Wyk, C., IDEAL User's Manual, Computing Science Technical Report No. 103, Bell Laboratories, Murray Hill, 1981.

Appendix

Section 2 and 3 described object and filter types as examples. The object and filter types given here incorporate those into an interface example that allows the manipulation of a sample employee database. Object or filter types from Figure 1 and 2 are not repeated here. The types `Integer`, `InputSensor`, `Interval`, `String`, `FormRender`, `StringRender`, `IntegerEquality`, `IntegerMultiply`, `IntegerDivide`, `BitStreamEquality`, `StringConversion`, `StringConcat`, `StringSensor` and `PopUpMenu` are atomic and given by the implementation.

```
Object Type Form                              Object Type Company
      width → Integer                               boss → Employee
      height → Integer                              number → Integer
      count → Integer                               employees[number] → Employee
      bits[count] → Bit                       end
      constraint IntegerMultiply((width,height), count)
end


Object Type PersonIcon                                    Object Type Device
      inherit from Form                                         display → Form
      constraint IntegerEquality (width, 30)                    sensor → InputSensor
      constraint IntegerEquality (height, 45)            end
      constraint BitStreamEquality ((bits,(O@O), '00001000010000100001...')
end


Filter Type ExtractHorizontal (source: (Form, Interval), view: Form)
      var
            ratio → Integer
            from → Point
      make set of
            IntegerEquality(source.width, view.width)
            IntegerMinus((source.second.high, source.second.low), ratio)
            IntegerMultiply((source.first.height,ratio), view.height)
            IntegerEquality(O, from.x)
            IntegerMultiply((source.first.height,source.second.low), from.y)
            BitStreamEquality((source.first.bits,from), view.bits)
end


Filter Type ExtractVertical (source: (Form, Interval), view: Form)
      var
            ratio → Integer
            from → Point
      make set of
            IntegerEquality(source.height, view.height)
            IntegerMinus((source.second.high, source.second.low), ratio)
            IntegerMultiply((source.first.width,ratio), view.width)
            IntegerEquality(O, from.y)
            IntegerMultiply((source.first.width,source.second.low), from.x)
            BitStreamEquality((source.first.bits,from), view.bits)
end


Filter Type EmployeeRender (source: DisplayEmployee, view: Form)
      var
            topForm, middleForm, bottomForm → Form
            verticalForms [source.subNumber] → Form
            formInterval [source.subNumber] → Interval
      make set of
            ExtractHorizontal ((view,(O,0.25)), topForm)
            ExtractHorizontal ((view,(0.25,0.3)), middleForm)
            ExtractHorizontal ((view,(0.3,1)), bottomForm)
            FormRender (source.icon, topForm)
            StringRender (source.name, middleForm)
            iteration source.subNumber times i
                  IntegerDivide ((i-1, source.subNumber), formInterval[i].low)
                  IntegerDivide ((i, source.subNumber), formInterval[i].high)
                  ExtractVertical ((bottomForm, formInterval[i])), verticalForms[i])
                  EmployeeRender (source.subordinates[i], verticalForms[i])
end


Filter Type EmployeeManipulation ( source : Company, view : Device )
      var
            bossDisplay → DisplayEmployee
      make set of
            EmployeeDisplay (source.boss, bossDisplay)
            EmployeeRender (bossDisplay, view.display)
            TraverseCompany (bossDisplay, view.sensor)
end
```

```
Filter Type TraverseCompany ( source : DisplayEmployee, view : InputSensor )
      var
            selection → Integer
            numberString, menuString → String
      make set of
            condition (source ≠ nil)
                  StringConversion(source.subNumber, numberString)
                  StringConcat(('name', numberString), menuString)
                  PopUpMenu ((selection, menuString), view)
                  condition (selection = 1)
                        StringSensor(source.name, view)
                  condition (selection ≠ 1)
                        TraverseCompany (source.subordinates[selection-1], view)
      end
```

The Common Lisp Object System: An Overview

by

Linda G. DeMichiel and Richard P. Gabriel
Lucid, Inc.
Menlo Park, California

1. Abstract

The Common Lisp Object System is an object-oriented system that is based on the concepts of generic functions, multiple inheritance, and method combination. All objects in the Object System are instances of classes that form an extension to the Common Lisp type system. The Common Lisp Object System is based on a meta-object protocol that renders it possible to alter the fundamental structure of the Object System itself. The Common Lisp Object System has been proposed as a standard for ANSI Common Lisp and has been tentatively endorsed by X3J13.

2. History of the Common Lisp Object System

The Common Lisp Object System is an object-oriented programming paradigm designed for Common Lisp. The lack of a standardized object-oriented extension for Common Lisp has long been regarded as a shortcoming by the Common Lisp community. Two separate and independent groups began work on an object-oriented extension to Common Lisp several years ago. One group is Symbolics, Inc. with New Flavors, and the other is Xerox PARC with CommonLoops. During the summer of 1986, these two groups met to explore combining their designs for submission to X3J13, a technical working group charged with producing an ANSI standard for Common Lisp.

At the time of the exploratory meetings between Symbolics and Xerox, the authors of this paper became involved in the technical design work. The major participants in this effort were David Moon and Sonya Keene from Symbolics, Daniel Bobrow and Gregor Kiczales from Xerox, and Richard Gabriel and Linda DeMichiel from Lucid.

By March 1987 this three-way collaborative effort had produced a strong draft of a specification for the bulk of the Object System. X3J13 has voted an endorsement of that specification draft, stating that it would almost certainly be adopted as part of the standard and encouraging implementors to proceed with trial implementations. This paper is a report on the specification that was presented to X3J13.

3. The Common Lisp Object System View of Object-Oriented Programming

Several aspects of the Object System stand out upon inspection: a) it is a layered system designed for flexibility; b) it is based on the concept of generic functions rather than on message-passing; c) it is a multiple inheritance system; d) it provides a powerful method combination facility; e) the primary entities of the system are all first-class objects.

3.1 *The Layered Approach*

One of the design goals of the Object System is to provide a set of layers that separate different programming language concerns from one another.

The first level of the Object System provides a programmatic interface to object-oriented programming. This level is designed to meet the needs of most serious users and to provide a syntax that is crisp and understandable. The second level provides a functional interface into the heart of the Object System. This level is intended for the programmer who is writing very complex software or a programming environment. The first level is written in terms of this second level. The third level provides the tools for the programmer who is writing his own object-oriented language. It allows access to the primitive objects and operators of the Object System. It is this level on which the implementation of the Object System itself is based.

The layered design of the Object System is founded on the *meta-object protocol*, a protocol that is used to define the characteristics of an object-oriented system. By using the meta-object protocol, other functional or programmatic interfaces to the Object System, as well as other object systems, can be written.

3.2 *The Generic Function Approach*

The Common Lisp Object System is based on *generic functions* rather than on message-passing. This choice is made for two reasons: 1) there are some problems with message-passing in operations of more than one argument; 2) the concept of generic functions is a generalization of the concept of ordinary Lisp functions.

A key concept in object-oriented systems is that given an operation and a tuple of objects on which to apply the operation, the code that is most appropriate to perform the operation is selected based on the classes of the objects.

In most message-passing systems, operations are essentially properties of classes, and this selection is made by packaging a message that specifies the operation and the objects to which it applies and sending that message to a suitable object. That object then takes responsibility for selecting the appropriate piece of code. These pieces of code are called *methods*.

With unary operations, the choice of a suitable object is clear. With multiary operations, however, message-passing systems run into problems. There are three general approaches to the problem of selecting a suitable object to which to send a message: currying, delegation, and distribution of methods.

Currying is a technique for turning a multiary operation into series of unary operations. In message-passing systems, this is accomplished by having the objects in question send messages among themselves to gather the contributions of each object to the final result of the operation. For example, adding a sequence of numbers can be done by asking each number to add itself to some accumulated total and then to send a message to the next object for it to do the same. Every object must know how to start and end this process. Currying may result in a complicated message-passing structure.

Delegation is a technique whereby an object is defined to handle an operation on a number of other objects. For example, to sum a sequence of numbers, there can be an object that will accept a message containing the identities of the numbers and then perform the addition. Thus, every object that can be involved in a multiary operations must know how to further delegate operations.

Distribution of methods is a technique whereby every object that can be involved in a multiary operation can be outfitted with enough information to directly carry out the operation.

In the generic function approach, objects and functions are autonomous entities, and neither is a property of the other. Generic functions decouple objects and operations upon objects; they serve to separate operations and classes. In the case of multiary operations, the operation is a generic function, and a method is defined that performs the operation on the objects (and on objects that are instances of the same classes as those objects).

Generic functions provide not only a more elegant solution to the problem of multiary operations but also a clean generalization of the concept of functions in Common Lisp. Each of the methods of the generic function provides a definition of how to perform an operation on arguments that are instances of particular classes or of subclasses of those classes. The generic function packages those methods and selects the right method or methods to invoke.

Furthermore, in Common Lisp, arithmetic operators are already generic in a certain sense. The expression

```
(+ x y)
```

does not imply that x and y are of any particular type, nor does it imply that they are of the same type. For example, x might be an integer and y a complex number, and the + operation is required to perform the correct coercions and produce an appropriate result.

Because the Object System is a system for Common Lisp, it is important that generic functions be first-class objects and that the concept of generic functions be an extension and a generalization of the concept of Common Lisp functions. In this way, the Object System is a natural and smooth extension of Common Lisp.

A further problem with message-passing systems is that there must be some way within a method of naming the object to which a message was sent. Usually there is a pseudovariable named something like "self." With generic functions, parameters are named exactly the same way that Common Lisp parameters are named—there is conceptual simplicity in using the fewest constructs in a programming language.

Some message-passing systems use a functional notation in which there is a privileged argument position that contains the object to which a message is to be sent. For example

```
(display x window-1)
```

might send a message to x requesting that x display itself on the window window-1. This expression might be paraphrased as

```
(send 'display x window-1)
```

With generic functions there are no such privileged argument positions.

In addition to these advantages over message-passing, there are three other fundamental strengths of generic functions:

1. It is possible to abstract the definition of a generic function into parts that are conceptually independent. This is accomplished by splitting the definition of a generic function into separate parts where each part is the partial function definition for a particular set of classes. This leads to a new modularization technique.

2. It is possible to spread the definition of a generic function among the places where the partial definitions make the most sense. This is accomplished by placing the appropriate **defmethod** forms where the relevant classes are defined.

3. It is possible to separate the inheritance of behavior from the placement of code. Generic functions select methods based on the structure of the class graph, but the generic functions are not constrained to be stored within that graph.

In a message-passing system, the class graph and the instances are truly central because the methods are associated with a particular class or instance. It makes sense in this setting to think of the methods as part of the structure of a class or an instance.

In a generic-function system, the generic functions provide a very different view of methods. Generic functions become the focus of abstraction; they are rarely associated unambiguously with a single class or instance; they sit above a substrate of the class graph, and the class graph provides control information for the generic functions.

Despite the advantages of generic functions, there may at times be reasons for preferring a message-passing style; such a style can be implemented by means of generic functions or by means of the Common Lisp Object System Meta-Object Protocol.

3.3 *The Multiple Inheritance Approach*

Another key concept in object-oriented programming is the definition of structure and behavior on the basis of the *class* of an object. Classes thus impose a type system—the code that is used to execute operations on objects depends on the classes of the objects. The subclass mechanism allows classes to be defined that share the structure and the behavior of other classes. This subclassing is a tool for modularization of programs.

The Common Lisp Object System is a multiple-inheritance system, that is, it allows a class to directly inherit the structure and behavior of two or more otherwise unrelated classes. In a single inheritance system, if class C_3 inherits from classes C_1 and C_2, then either C_1 is a subclass of C_2 or C_2 is a subclass of C_1; in a multiple inheritance system, if C_3 inherits from C_1 and C_2, then C_1 and C_2 might be unrelated.

If no structure is duplicated and no operations are multiply-defined in the several superclasses of a class, multiple inheritance is straightforward. If a class inherits two different operation definitions or structure definitions, it is necessary to provide some means of selecting which ones to use or how to combine them. The Object System uses a linearized *class precedence list* for determining how structure and behavior are inherited among classes.

3.4 *The Method Combination Approach*

The Common Lisp Object System supports a mechanism for method combination that is both more powerful than that provided by CommonLoops and simpler than that provided by Flavors.

Method combination is used to define how the methods that are applicable to a set of arguments can be combined to provide the values of a generic function. In many object-oriented systems, the most specific applicable method is invoked, and that method may invoke other, less specific methods. When this happens there is often a combination strategy at work, but that strategy is distributed throughout the methods as local control structure. Method combination brings the notion of a combination strategy to the surface and provides a mechanism for expressing that strategy.

A simple example of method combination is the common need to surround the activities of a method's invocation with a prologue and an epilogue: the prologue might cache some values in an accessible place for the method, and the epilogue will write back the changed values.

The Object System provides a default method combination type, *standard method combination*, that is designed to be simple, convenient, and powerful for most applications. Other types of method combination can easily be defined by using the **define-method-combination** macro.

3.5 *First-Class Objects*

In the Common Lisp Object System, generic functions and classes are first-class objects with no intrinsic names. It is possible and useful to create and manipulate anonymous generic functions and classes.

The concept of "first-class" is important in Lisp-like languages. A first-class object is one that can be explicitly made and manipulated; it can be stored anywhere that can hold general objects.

Generic functions are first-class objects in the Object System. They can be used in the same ways that ordinary functions can be used in Common Lisp. A generic function is a true function that can be passed as an argument, used as the first argument to **funcall** and **apply**, and stored in the function cell of a symbol. Ordinary functions and generic functions are called with identical syntax.

3.6 *What the Common Lisp Object System Is Not*

The Object System does not attempt to solve problems of encapsulation or protection. The inherited structure of a class depends on the names of internal parts of the classes from which it inherits. The Object System does not support subtractive inheritance. Within Common Lisp there is a primitive module system that can be used to help create separate internal namespaces.

4. Classes

A *class* is an object that determines the structure and behavior of a set of other objects, which are called its *instances*. It is not necessary for a class to have any instances, but all objects are instances of some class. The class system defined by the Object System and the Common Lisp type system are tightly integrated, so that one effect of the Object System is to define a first-class type system within Common Lisp. The class of an object determines the set of operations that can be performed on that object.

There are two fundamental sorts of relationships involving objects and classes: the subclass relationship and the instance relationship.

A class can inherit structure and behavior from other classes. A class whose definition refers to other classes for the purpose of inheriting from them is said to be a *subclass* of each of those classes. The classes that are designated for purposes of inheritance are said to be *superclasses* of the inheriting class. The inheritance relationship is transitive.

A typical situation is that one class, C_1, represents a possibly infinite set of objects, and a second class, C_2, represents a subset of that set; in this case C_2 is a subclass of C_1.

An object is an instance of a class if it is an example of a member of that class. If the class represents a set, then an instance is a member of that set.

Classes are organized into a *directed acyclic graph*. There is a distinguished class named t. The class t is a superclass of every other class.

Classes themselves are objects and are therefore instances of classes. The class of a class is called a **metaclass**. The existence of metaclasses indicates that the structure and behavior of the class system itself is controlled by classes. Generic functions are also objects and therefore also instances of classes.

The Object System maps the Common Lisp type space into the space of classes. Many but not all of the predefined Common Lisp type specifiers have a class associated with them that has the same name as the type. For example, an array is of type **array** and of class **array**. Every class has a corresponding type with the same name as the class.

A class that corresponds to a predefined Common Lisp type is called a *standard type class*. Each standard type class has the class **standard-type-class** as a metaclass. Users can write methods that discriminate on any primitive Common Lisp type that has a corresponding class. However, it is not allowed to make an instance of a standard type class with **make-instance** or to include a standard type class as a superclass of a class.

All programmer-defined classes are instances of the class named **standard-class**, which is an instance of the class named **class**; the class named **class** is an instance of itself, which is the fundamental circularity in the Object System.

Instances whose metaclass is **standard-class** are like Common Lisp structures: they have named slots, which contain values. When we say that the structure of an instance is determined by its class and that that class is an instance of **standard-class**, we mean that the number and names of the slots are determined by the class, and we also mean that the means of accessing and altering the contents of those slots are controlled by the class.

4.1 *Defining Classes*

The macro **defclass** is used to define a new class.

The definition of a class consists of the following: its name, a list of its direct superclasses, a set of slot specifiers, and a set of class options.

The direct superclasses of a class are those classes from which the new class inherits structure and behavior. When a class is defined, the order in which its direct superclasses are mentioned in the **defclass** form defines a *local precedence order* on the class and those superclasses. The local precedence order is represented as a list consisting of the class followed by its direct superclasses in the order mentioned in the **defclass** form.

A slot specifier includes the name of the slot and zero or more slot options that pertain to that particular slot. The name of a slot is a symbol that could be used as a Common Lisp variable name. The slot options of the **defclass** form allow for the following: providing a default initial value form for the slot; requesting that methods for appropriately named generic functions be automatically generated for reading or writing the slot; controlling whether one copy of a given slot is shared by all instances or whether each instance is to have its own copy of that slot; and specifying the type of the slot contents.

There are two kinds of slots: slots that are local to an individual instance and slots that are shared by all instances of the given class. The **:allocation** slot option to **defclass** controls the kind of slot that is defined.

In general, slots are inherited by subclasses. That is, a slot defined by a class is also a slot implicitly defined by any subclass of that class unless the subclass explicitly shadows the slot definition. A class can also shadow some of the slot options declared in the **defclass** form of one of its superclasses by providing its own description for that slot.

Slots can be accessed in two ways: by use of generic functions defined by the **defclass** form and by use of the primitive function **slot-value**.

The syntax of **defclass** provides several means for generating methods to read and write slots. Methods can be requested for all slots or for particular slots only. Methods can be requested to read and write slots or to read slots only. If a slot *accessor* is requested, a method is automatically generated for reading the value of the slot, and a **setf** method is also generated to write the value of the slot. If a slot *reader* is requested, a method is automatically generated for reading the value of the slot, but no **setf** method for it is generated. Readers and accessors can be requested for individual slots or for all slots. Reader and accessor methods are added to the appropriate generic functions. It is possible to modify the behavior of these generic functions by writing methods for them.

The function **slot-value** can be used with any of the slot names specified in the **defclass** form to access a specific slot in an object of the given class. Readers and accessors are implemented by using **slot-value**.

Sometimes it is convenient to access slots from within the body of a method or a function. The macro **with-slots** is provided for use in setting up a lexical environment in which certain slots are lexically available as variables. It is also possible to specify whether the macro **with-slots** is to use the accessors or the function **slot-value** to access slots.

A class option pertains to the class as a whole. The available class options allow for the following: requesting that methods for appropriately named generic functions be automatically generated for reading or writing all slots defined by the new class; requesting that a constructor function be automatically generated for making instances of the class; and specifying that the instances of the class are to have a metaclass other than the default.

For example, the following two classes define a representation of a point in space. The class **x-y-position** is a subclass of the class **position**:

```
(defclass position () ())

(defclass x-y-position (position)
    ((x :initform 0)
     (y :initform 0))
  (:accessor-prefix position-))
```

The class **position** is useful if we want to create other sorts of representations for spatial positions. The x- and y-coordinates are initialized to 0 in all instances unless explicit values are supplied for them. To refer to the x-coordinate of an instance of the class **x-y-position**, **position**, one writes

```
(position-x position)
```

To alter the x-coordinate of that instance, one writes

```
(setf (position-x position) new-x)
```

The macro **defclass** is part of the Object System programmatic interface and, as such, is on the first of the three levels of the Object System. When applied to an appropriate metaclass, the function **make-instance** provides the same functionality on the second level.

4.2 *Class Precedence*

Each class has a *class precedence list*. The class precedence list is a total ordering on the set of the given class and its superclasses for purposes of inheritance. The total ordering is expressed as a list ordered from most specific to least specific.

The class precedence list is used in several ways. In general, more specific classes can *shadow*, or override, features that would otherwise be inherited from less specific classes. The method selection and combination process uses the class precedence list to order methods from most specific to least specific.

The class precedence list is always consistent with the local precedence order of each class in the list. The classes in each local precedence order appear within the class precedence list in the same order. If the local precedence orders are inconsistent with each other, no class precedence list can be constructed, and an error will be signaled.

5. Generic Functions

The class-specific operations of the Common Lisp Object System are provided by generic functions and methods.

A *generic function* is a function whose behavior depends on the classes or identities of the arguments supplied to it. The *methods* associated with the generic function define the class-specific operations of the generic function.

Like an ordinary Lisp function, a generic function takes arguments, performs a series of operations, and returns values. An ordinary function has a single body of code that is always executed when the function is called. A generic function is able to perform different series of operations and to combine the results of the operations in different ways, depending on the class or identity of one or more of its arguments.

The operations of a generic function are defined by its methods. Thus, generic functions are objects that can be *specialized* by the definition of methods to provide class-specific operations.

The behavior of the generic function results from which methods are selected for execution, the order in which the selected methods are called, and how their values are combined to produce the value or values of the generic function.

Thus, unlike an ordinary function, a generic function has a distributed definition corresponding to the definition of its methods. The definition of a generic function is found in a set of **defmethod** forms, possibly along with a **defgeneric-options** form that provides information about the properties of the generic function as a whole. Evaluating these forms produces a generic function object.

In addition to a set of methods, a generic function object comprises a lambda-list, a method combination type, and other information. In Common Lisp a lambda-list is a specification of the parameters that will be passed to a function. The syntax of Common Lisp lambda-lists is complex, and the Object System extends it further.

The lambda-list specifies the arguments to the generic function. It is an ordinary function lambda-list with these exceptions: no &aux variables are allowed and optional and keyword arguments may not have default initial value forms nor use supplied-p parameters. The generic function passes to its methods all the argument values passed to it, and only these; default values are not supported.

The method combination type determines the form of method combination that is used with the generic function. The *method combination* facility controls the selection of methods, the order in which they are run, and the values that are returned by the generic function. The Object System offers a default method combination type that is appropriate for most user programs. The Object System also provides a facility for declaring new types of method combination for programs that require them.

The generic function object also contains information about the argument precedence order (the order in which arguments to the generic function are tested for specificity when selecting executable methods), the class of the generic function, and the class of the methods of the generic function. While the Object System provides default classes for all generic function, method, and class objects, the programmer may choose to implement any or all of these by using classes of his own definition.

Generic functions in the Object System are nearly indistinguishable from ordinary functions: they can be applied, stored, and manipulated exactly as ordinary functions are. In this way, the Object System is smoothly integrated into the Common Lisp framework, and there is no sense in which Common Lisp programs are partitionable into the functional parts and the object-oriented parts.

5.1 *Defining Generic Functions*

Generic functions are defined by means of the **defgeneric-options** and **defmethod** macros.

The **defgeneric-options** macro is designed to allow for the specification of properties that pertain to the generic function as a whole, and not just to individual methods.

If a **defgeneric-options** form is evaluated and a generic function of the given name does not already exist, a new generic function object is created. This generic function object is a generic function with no methods. The **defgeneric-options** macro may be used to specify properties of the generic function as a whole—this is sometimes referred to as the "contract" of the generic function. These properties include the following: the lambda-list of the generic function; a specification of the order in which the required arguments in a call to the generic function are to be tested for specificity when selecting a particular method; declarations that pertain to the generic function as a whole; the class of the generic function; the class of all the methods of the generic function; and the method combination type to be used with this generic function. The Object System provides a set of default values for these properties, so that use of the **defgeneric-options** macro is not essential.

When a new **defgeneric-options** form is evaluated and a generic function of the given name already exists, the existing generic function object is modified. This does not modify any of the methods associated with the generic function.

The **defmethod** form is used to define a method. If there is no generic function of the given name, however, it automatically creates a generic function with default values for the argument precedence order (left-to-right, as defined by the lambda-list), the generic function class (the class **standard-generic-function**), the method class (the class **standard-method**), and the method combination type (standard method combination). The lambda-list of the generic function is congruent with the lambda-list of the new method. In general, two lambda-lists are congruent if they have the same number of required parameters, the same number of optional parameters, and the same treatment of **&allow-other-keys**.

When a **defmethod** form is evaluated and a generic function of the given name already exists, the existing generic function object is modified to contain the new method. The lambda-list of the new method must be congruent with the lambda-list of the generic function.

6. Methods

The class-specific operations provided by generic functions are themselves defined and implemented by *methods*. The class or identity of each argument to the generic function indicates which method or methods are eligible to be invoked.

A method object contains a *method function*, an ordered set of *parameter specializers* that specify when the given method is applicable, and an ordered set of *qualifiers* that are used by the method combination facility to distinguish among methods.

Each required formal parameter of each method has an associated parameter specializer, and the method is expected to be invoked only on arguments that satisfy its parameter specializers. A parameter specializer is either a class or a list of the form (quote *object*).

A method can be selected for a set of arguments when each required argument satisfies its corresponding parameter specializer. An argument satisfies a parameter specializer if either of the following conditions holds:

1. The parameter specializer is a class, and the argument is an instance of that class or an instance of any subclass of that class.

2. The parameter specializer is (quote *object*) and the argument is eql to *object*.

A method all of whose parameter specializers are t is a *default method*; it is always part of the generic function but often shadowed by a more specific method.

Method qualifiers give the method combination procedure a further means of distinguishing between methods. A method that has one or more qualifiers is called a *qualified* method. A method with no qualifiers is called an *unqualified method*.

In standard method combination, unqualified methods are also termed *primary* methods, and qualified methods have a single qualifier that is either :around, :before, or :after.

6.1 *Defining Methods*

The macro **defmethod** is used to create a method object. A **defmethod** form contains the code that is to be run when the arguments to the generic function cause the method that it defines to be selected. If a **defmethod** form is evaluated and a method object corresponding to the given generic function name, parameter specializers, and qualifiers already exists, the new definition replaces the old.

Each method definition contains a *specialized lambda-list*, which specifies when that method can be selected. A specialized lambda-list is like an ordinary lambda-list except that a *parameter specifier* may occur instead of the name of a parameter. A parameter specifier is a list consisting of a variable name and a parameter specializer name. Every parameter specializer name is a Common Lisp type specifier, but the only Common Lisp type specifiers that are parameter specializers names are type specifier symbols with corresponding classes and type specifier lists of the form (quote *object*). The form (quote *object*) is equivalent to the type specifier (member *object*).

Only required parameters can be specialized, and each required parameter must be a parameter specifier. For notational simplicity, if some required parameter in a specialized lambda-list is simply a variable name, the corresponding parameter specifier is taken to be (*variable-name* t).

A future extension to the Object System might allow optional and keyword parameters to be specialized.

A method definition may optionally specify one or more method qualifiers. A method qualifier is a non-**nil** atom that is used to identify the role of the method to the method combination type used by the generic function of which it is part. By convention, qualifiers are usually keyword symbols.

Generic functions can be used to implement a layer of abstraction on top of a set of classes. For example, the class **x-y-position** can be viewed as containing information in polar coordinates.

Two methods are defined, called **position-rho** and **position-theta**, that calculate the ρ and θ coordinates given an instance of the class **x-y-position**.

```
(defmethod position-rho ((pos x-y-position))
   (let ((x (position-x pos))
         (y (position-y pos)))
     (sqrt (+ (* x x) (* y y)))))

(defmethod position-theta ((pos x-y-position))
   (atan (position-y pos) (position-x pos)))
```

It is also possible to write methods that update the 'virtual slots' **position-rho** and **position-theta**:

```
(defmethod-setf position-rho ((pos x-y-position)) (rho)
   (let* ((r (position-rho pos))
          (ratio (/ rho r)))
     (setf (position-x pos) (* ratio (position-x pos)))
     (setf (position-y pos) (* ratio (position-y pos)))))

(defmethod-setf position-theta ((pos x-y-position)) (theta)
   (let ((rho (position-rho pos)))
     (setf (position-x pos) (* rho (cos theta)))
     (setf (position-y pos) (* rho (sin theta)))))
```

To update the ρ-coordinate one writes

```
(setf (position-rho pos) new-rho)
```

This is precisely the same syntax that would be used if the positions were explicitly stored as polar coordinates.

7. Class Redefinition

The Common Lisp Object System provides a powerful class-redefinition facility.

When a **defclass** form is evaluated and a class with the given name already exists, the existing class is redefined. Redefining a class modifies the existing class object to reflect the new class definition.

When a class is redefined, changes are propagated to instances of it and to instances of any of its subclasses. The updating of an instance whose class has been redefined (or that has a superclass that has been redefined) occurs at an implementation-dependent time; this will usually be upon the next access to that instance or the next time that a generic function is applied to that instance. Updating an instance does not change its identity. The updating process may change the slots of that particular instance, but it does not create a new instance.

Users may define methods on the generic function **class-changed** to control the class redefinition process. The generic function **class-changed** is invoked automatically by the system after **defclass** has been used to redefine an existing class.

For example, suppose it becomes apparent that the application that requires representing positions uses polar coordinates more than it uses rectangular coordinates. It might make sense to define a subclass of **position** that uses polar coordinates:

```
(defclass rho-theta-position (position)
   ((rho :initform 0)
    (theta :initform 0))
 (:accessor-prefix position-))
```

The instances of **x-y-position** can be automatically updated by defining a **class-changed** method:

```
(defmethod class-changed ((old x-y-position)
                          (new rho-theta-position))
 ;; Copy the position information from old to new to make new
 ;; be a rho-theta-position at the same position as old.
 (let ((x (position-x old))
       (y (position-y old)))
   (setf (position-rho new) (sqrt (+ (* x x) (* y y)))
         (position-theta new) (atan y x))))
```

At this point we can change an instance of the class **x-y-position**, **p1**, to be an instance of **rho-theta-position** by using **change-class**:

```
(change-class p1 'rho-theta-position)
```

8. Inheritance

Inheritance is the key to program modularity within the Object System. A typical object-oriented program consists of several classes, each of which defines some aspect of behavior. New classes are defined by including the appropriate classes as superclasses, thus gathering desired aspects of behavior into one class.

8.1 *Inheritance of Slots and Slot Description*

In general, slot descriptions are inherited by subclasses. That is, slots defined by a class are usually slots implicitly defined by any subclass of that class unless the subclass explicitly shadows the slot definition. A class can also shadow some of the slot options declared in the **defclass** form of one of its superclasses by providing its own description for that slot.

In the simplest case, only one class in the class precedence list provides a slot description with a given slot name. If it is a local slot, then each instance of the class and all of its subclasses allocate storage for it. If it is a shared slot, the storage for the slot is allocated by the class that provided the slot description, and the single slot is accessible in instances of that class and all of its subclasses.

More than one class in the class precedence list can provide a slot description with a given slot name. In such cases, at most one slot with a given name is accessible in any instance, and the characteristics of that slot involve some combination of the several slot descriptions.

Methods that access slots know only the name of the slot and the type of the slot's value. Suppose a superclass provides a method that expects to access a shared slot of a given name, and a subclass provides a local description of a local slot with the same name. If the method provided by the superclass is used on an instance of the subclass, the method accesses the local slot.

8.2 *Inheritance of Methods*

A subclass inherits methods in the sense that any method applicable to an instance of a class is also applicable to instances of any subclass of that class (all other arguments to the method being the same).

The inheritance of methods acts the same way regardless of whether the method was created by using **defmethod** or by using one of the **defclass** options that cause methods to be generated automatically.

9. Class Precedence List

The class precedence list is a linearization of the subgraph consisting of a class, C, and its superclasses. The **defclass** form for a class provides a total ordering on that class and its direct superclasses. This ordering is called the *local precedence order*. It is an ordered list of the class and its direct superclasses. A class precedes its direct superclasses, and a direct superclass precedes all other direct superclasses specified to its right in the superclasses list of the **defclass** form. For every class in the set of C and its superclasses, we can gather the specific relations of this form into a set, called R.

R may or may not generate a partial ordering, depending on whether the relations are consistent; we assume they are consistent and that R generates a partial ordering. This partial ordering is the transitive closure of R.

To compute the class precedence list at C, we topologically sort C and its superclasses with respect to the partial ordering generated by R. When the topological sort algorithm must select a class from a set of two or more classes, none of which is preceded by other classes with respect to R, the class selected is chosen deterministically. The rule that was chosen for this selection process is designed to keep chains of superclasses together in the class precedence list. That is, if C_1 is the unique superclass of C_2, C_2 will immediately precede C_1 in the class precedence list.

It is required that an implementation of the Object System signal an error if R is inconsistent, that is, if the class precedence list cannot be computed.

10. Method Combination

When a generic function is called with particular arguments, it must determine what code to execute. This code is termed the *effective method* for those arguments. The effective method can be one of the methods of the generic function or a combination of several of them.

Choosing the effective method involves the following decisions: which method or methods to call; the order in which to call these methods; which method to call when **call-next-method** is invoked; what value or values to return.

The effective method is determined by the following steps: 1) selecting the set of applicable methods; 2) sorting the applicable methods by precedence order, putting the most specific method first; 3) applying method combination to the sorted list of applicable methods, producing the effective method.

When the effective method has been determined, it is called with the same arguments that were passed to the generic function. Whatever values it returns are returned as the values of the generic function.

The Object System provides a default method combination type, *standard method combination.* The programmer can define other forms of method combination by using the **define-method-combination** macro.

10.1 *Standard Method Combination*

Standard method combination is the default method combination type. Standard method combination recognizes four roles for methods, as determined by method qualifiers.

Primary methods define the main action of the effective method; *auxiliary methods* modify that action in one of three ways. A primary method has no method qualifiers. The auxiliary methods are :**before**, :**after**, and :**around** methods.

The semantics of standard method combination are given as follows:

If there are any :**around** methods, the most specific :**around** method is called. Inside the body of an :**around** method, **call-next-method** can be used to immediately call the next method. When the next method returns, the :**around** method can execute more code. By convention, :**around** methods almost always use **call-next-method**.

If an :**around** method invokes **call-next-method**, the next most specific :**around** method is called, if one is applicable. If there are no :**around** methods or if **call-next-method** is called by the least specific :**around** method, the other methods are called as follows:

1. All the :**before** methods are called, in most specific first order. Their values are ignored.

2. The most specific primary method is called. Inside the body of a primary method, **call-next-method** may be used to pass control to the next most specific primary method. When that method returns, the first primary method can execute more code. If **call-next-method** is not used, only the most specific primary method is called.

3. All the **:after** methods are called in most specific last order. Their values are ignored.

If no **:around** methods were invoked, the most specific primary method supplies the value or values returned by the generic function. Otherwise, the value or values returned by the most specific primary method are those returned by the invocation of **call-next-method** in the least specific **:around** method.

If only primary methods are used, standard method combination behaves like Common-Loops. If **call-next-method** is not used, only the most specific method is invoked, that is, more general methods are shadowed by more specific ones. If **call-next-method** is used, the effect is the same as **run-super** in CommonLoops.

If **call-next-method** is not used, standard method combination behaves like **:daemon** method combination of New Flavors, with **:around** methods playing the role of whoppers, except that the ability to reverse the order of the primary methods has been removed.

The use of method combination can be illustrated by the following example. Suppose we have a class called **general-window**, which is made up of a bitmap and a set of viewports:

```
(defclass general-window ()
   ((initialized :initform nil)
    (bitmap :type bitmap)
    (viewports :type list))
   (:accessor-prefix general-window-))
```

The viewports are stored as a list. We presume that it is desirable to make instances of general windows but not to create their bitmaps until they are actually needed. Thus there is a flag, called **initialized**, that states whether the bitmap has been created. The **bitmap** and **viewport** slots are not initialized by default.

We now wish to create an announcement window to be used for messages that must be brought to the user's attention. When a message is to be announced to the user, the announcement window is exposed, the message is moved into the bitmap for the announcement window, and finally the viewports are redisplayed:

```
(defclass announcement-window (general-window)
   ((contents :initform "" :type string))
   (:accessor-prefix announcement-window-))

(defmethod display :around (message (w general-window))
   (unless (general-window-initialized w)
    (setf (general-window-bitmap w) (make-bitmap))
    (setf (general-window-viewports w)
          (list (make-viewport (general-window-bitmap w))))
    (setf (general-window-initialized w) t))
   (call-next-method))
```

```
(defmethod display :before (message (w announcement-window))
   (expose-window w))

(defmethod display :after (message (w announcement-window))
   (redisplay-viewports w))

(defmethod display ((message string) (w announcement-window))
   (move-string-to-window message w))
```

To make an announcement, the generic function **display** is invoked on a string and an annoucement window. The **:around** method is always run first; if the bitmap has not been set up, this method takes care of it. The primary method for **display** simply moves the string (the announcement) to the window, the **:before method** exposes the window, and the **:after** method redisplays the viewports. When the window's bitmap is initialized, the sole viewport is made to be the entire bitmap. The order in which these methods are invoked is the following: 1) the **:around** method, 2) the **:before** method, 3) the primary method, and 4) the **:after** method.

11. Meta-Object Protocol

The Common Lisp Object System is implemented in terms of a set of objects that correspond to predefined classes of the system. These objects are termed *meta-objects*. Because meta-objects underlie the rest of the object system, they may be used to define other objects, other ways of manipulating objects, and hence other object-oriented systems. The use of meta-objects is specified by in the Common Lisp Object System meta-object protocol.

The meta-object protocol is designed for use by implementors who need to tailor the Object System for particular applications and by researchers who wish to use the Object System as a prototyping tool and delivery environment for other object-oriented paradigms. It is also designed for the implementation of the Object System itself.

The Object System provides the predefined meta-objects **standard-class**, **standard-method**, and **standard-generic-function**.

The class **standard-class** is the default class of classes defined by **defclass**.

The class **standard-method** is the default class of methods defined by **defmethod**.

The class **standard-generic-function** is the default class of generic functions defined by **defmethod** and **defgeneric-options**.

There are also other, more general classes from which these metaclasses inherit.

The classes **class**, **standard-class**, **slot-description**, **standard-slot-description**, **method**, **standard-method**, **generic-function**, and **standard-generic-function** are all *instances* of the class **standard-class**.

These classes represent a minimal structure and functionality on which the implementation of all other classes in the system is based. Implementations may choose to add additional slots for these classes.

12. Evaluation of the Design Goals for the Common Lisp Object System

Even when designers start with a clean slate, it is difficult to achieve the design goals of a language, but the task of satisfying those goals is very much more difficult when two different languages with existing user communities are being merged. The final design of a language—its shape and clarity—depends on the ancestor languages. If the ancestor languages do not have a clean design, the designers must weigh the desirability of a clean design against the impact of changes on their existing user communities.

In this case there were two such ancestor languages, each with a young but growing user community. CommonLoops has a relatively clean design. Its experimental implementation, "Portable CommonLoops," is freely distributed to a small user community. New Flavors is the second generation of a basic system called "Flavors." Flavors is an older, commercially supported message-passing system. New Flavors is a generic-function-based descendant of Flavors, but a descendant that supports compatibility with its ancestor. The design of New Flavors is not as clean as that of CommonLoops, but its user community is larger and is accustomed to commercially motivated stability.

With these facts in mind, let us examine the design goals for the Common Lisp Object System.

1. Use a set of levels to separate programming language concerns from each other.

This goal was achieved quite well. The layering is well defined and has been shown to be useful both in terms of implementing the Object System as well as in terms of implementing another object-oriented system (Hewlett-Packard's CommonObjects). CommonLoops already has a layered design.

2. Make as many things as possible within the Object System first-class.

This goal was also achieved quite well. Both classes and generic functions are first-class objects. Generic functions were not first-class objects in either CommonLoops or New Flavors, but fortunately the user-community disruption is minimal for these changes.

3. Provide a unified language and syntax.

It is tempting when designing a programming language to invent additional languages within the primary programming language, where each additional language is suitable for some particular aspect of the overall language. In Common Lisp, for example, the **format** function defines a language for displaying text, but this language is not Lisp nor is it like Lisp.

There are two additional languages in the Object System: the language of method combination keywords and a pattern language for selecting methods, which is used when defining new method combination types. Method combination was considered important enough to tolerate these additional languages.

CommonLoops has no additional languages. New Flavors has a rich method combination facility with more complex versions of the two additional languages just mentioned; these two languages were simplified for inclusion in the Object System.

4. Be willing to trade off complex behavior for conceptual and expository simplicity.

This was largely achieved, although it required a considerable amount of additional technical work. For example, the class precedence list algorithm was altered from its original form largely because the original was not easily explainable.

5. Make the specification of the language as precise as possible.

The specification of Common Lisp is fairly ambiguous because it represents a technical compromise between several existing Lisp dialects. The ground rules of the compromise were explicitly established so that with a small effort each of the existing Lisp dialects could be made into a Common Lisp.

The Object System design group was in a similar position to the Common Lisp design group, but on a smaller scale. The language of the specification is considerably more precise than the language of the Common Lisp specification.

13. Conclusion

The Common Lisp Object System is an object-oriented paradigm with several novel features; these features allow it to be smoothly integrated into Common Lisp.

14. References

Daniel G. Bobrow, Linda G. DeMichiel, Richard P. Gabriel, Sonya Keene, Gregor Kiczales, and David A. Moon, *Common Lisp Object System Specification*, X3J13 Document 87-002.

Daniel G. Bobrow, Kenneth Kahn, Gregor Kiczales, Larry Masinter, Mark Stefik, and Frank Zdybel, "CommonLoops: Merging Lisp and Object-Oriented Programming," ACM OOPSLA Conference, 1986.

Adelle Goldberg and David Robson, *Smalltalk-80: The Language and its Implementation*, Addison-Wesley, Reading, Massachusetts, 1983.

Guy L. Steele Jr., *Common Lisp: The Language*, Digital Press, 1984.

Reference Guide to Symbolics Common Lisp: Language Concepts, Symbolics Release 7 Document Set, 1986.

Concurrency Features for the Trellis/Owl Language

J. Eliot B. Moss – Department of Computer and Information Science
Walter H. Kohler – Department of Electrical and Computer Engineering
University of Massachusetts, Amherst, MA 01003

Abstract. Trellis/Owl is an object oriented programming language being developed as part of the Trellis programming environment by the Object Based Systems group within Corporate Research and Architecture at Digital Equipment Corporation's Hudson, MA facility. Trellis/Owl incorporates support for concurrency. Here we describe the high level language features designed, the rationale for that design, the implementation techniques used, the principles behind them, and experience with the resulting system to date. We show how the object oriented nature of Trellis/Owl influenced the design, and how it affected the implementation.

1. Introduction

Trellis/Owl (simply Owl in this paper) is an object oriented programming language being developed as part of the Trellis[1] programming environment. Unlike Smalltalk-80[2], Owl is strongly typed and offers inheritance from multiple supertypes. Owl is targeted to slightly different uses as well: development and maintenance of moderate to large programs. Owl's different objectives strongly affected its design, but actually had little direct impact on the concurrency features or their implementation. For further information on Owl and Trellis see [Schaffert et al. 85, O'Brien 85].

The concurrency features were designed to support moderate to large grain parallelism: an arbitrary operation invocation may be run as a separate activity. No attempt was made to support finer grained concurrency, say at the expression level as for a dataflow architecture, or for vector or array processing. We assumed that the primary source of concurrency would be the logically concurrent tasks requested by the user when interacting with the system. That is, we believed that the applications of most interest to us (programming environments and tools) would not exhibit high concurrency by themselves. This position might have to be reconsidered if the project were one focusing more on concurrency rather than object oriented computing.

We assumed that, in an object oriented environment with large grain parallelism, concurrency is expressed through the interaction of multiple activities on shared objects. This is in sharp contrast to, for example, Hoare's communicating sequential processes [Hoare 85], which organize concurrency around the activities and messages passed between them. Object oriented computing emphasizes modularity of design more in terms of data (objects), with type definitions defining access control and synchronization, rather rather than giving processes the primary role. We feel this approach is more consistent with the overall thrust of Owl, and object-oriented languages in general. However, message passing (e.g.,

via a user defined message queue data type) is certainly possible within our design, and could be tailored to meet the needs of the application. Since most objects will likely not be shared, we placed the burden of managing access to shared objects on the user. On the other hand, we provided facilities for mutual exclusion and scheduling which allow rather sophisticated concurrency control to be implemented in a modular fashion.

We chose not to incorporate transaction-oriented concurrency in this design. The primary reason for that decision was to allow us to attack and solve an easier problem, so as to offer a working base for building the programming environment. We also wanted to see how well a less ambitious design could meet our needs, and to get a better idea of exactly which additional features should be investigated. However, we tried not to include anything in our design that would interfere with a transaction concurrency mechanism. Rather, we believe the features provided will integrate well and assist in implementing transaction support.

Below we review the high level features of the design and further discuss our rationale for choosing them. The design is influenced less by object orientedness *per se* than by data abstraction. There is considerable similarity between the Owl features and ones proposed in [Weihl and Liskov 85] for use with Argus [Liskov and Scheifler 83]. However, there are substantial differences, which we will review later.

We then present the implementation, which has two major aspects. The first is the representation of the specific data types and the algorithms for manipulating them. This aspect is relatively straightforward, so we concentrate mainly on how some novel features are implemented and on how the implementation is tuned to the expected patterns of usage. The second aspect of the implementation is how we achieved appropriate atomicity of execution of various actions in the system. Unlike most interpreter based systems (including the Smalltalk systems of which we are aware), we take a permissive approach to interrupt handling: we allow interrupts and task switches everywhere except in critical sections. Other systems generally check for interrupts in the main interpreter loop, or improve on that in various reasonably simple ways (see, e.g., [Deutsch and Schiffman 84]). We used a number of methods to solve a variety of problems. Other implementers of heap based languages may find our descriptions of these problems and solutions useful.

We conclude with a brief discussion of experience to date with the concurrency features and their implementation.

2. Language Features

Our choice of concurrency features for Owl was based on two major assumptions. First, that activities (threads of control) will be used primarily to model conceptually independent tasks. Second, the activity

---

[1] Trellis, VAX, VMS, VAXStation, and MicroVAX are trademarks of Digital Equipment Corporation.

[2] Smalltalk-80 is a trademark of Xerox Corporation.

mechanism should be cheap enough that a new activity can be forked whenever a new thread of control would better reflect the task structure of the application. Two implications of the first assumption are that a forking activity may not need to wait for the results of a forked activity, since the two activities are logically independent, and it is unlikely that frequent conflicts over shared data will occur. Activities are not intended to be the principle units of functionality or modularity in Owl; those roles are taken by operations and type definitions (respectively).

The language features we have added to Owl to support concurrency include mechanisms for forking an activity and for awaiting termination of one. We have also provided concurrency control mechanisms to serialize and schedule concurrent access to shared objects by multiple activities.

2.1 The Activity Type

In Owl, we represent activities by objects of type Activity. New activities are forked by the create operation. For example, if example_act is a variable of type Activity,

```
example_act :=
  create (Activity, "FOO", {a1, a2, ...});
```

forks a new activity to perform operation FOO, providing arguments a1, a2, etc. The activity object example_act identifies the new thread of control, and provides means for monitoring its status, as well as a handle for debugging. Any operation can be forked as a separate activity.

An activity terminates only by completing the operation it was forked to perform, whether that completion be normal (via a return) or exceptional (via a signal).[3] It cannot be aborted by another activity, not even its parent, since this might leave the objects it was manipulating in an inconsistent state.[4] However, a collection of activities can be designed to coordinate their termination by explicitly setting and checking the state of a shared object.

Generally we do not expect parent activities to want to wait until a child activity completes, but we do think there will be cases when one activity will want to monitor another activity and handle exceptions that arise, or use the results returned by the forked invocation. To support this type of coordination we provide two operations on activity objects: await and await_with_timeout.

Assume that A and B are activities. If A does await(B), A is blocked until activity B terminates. If A invokes await_with_timeout(B), A is blocked until B terminates or the wait times out. Timeout is indicated by having the call to await_with_timeout signal the exception timeout rather than returning normally.

Since an activity may want to start a number of new activities and then wait until some or all of them complete, we also provide an iterator[5] on objects of type Activity_Set. An Activity_Set is

a set of activities, with some special operations for monitoring completion. We may insert new activities into an Activity_Set, close it (to indicate no more activities will ever be added), and process its members, as they terminate, with the await_next iterator. This iterator finishes only when all activities in the Activity_Set have both terminated and been provided by the iterator for processing, and the set has been closed. Note that Activity_Set has just the operations necessary for handling termination of each member of a dynamically defined set of activities, and no more. It is sufficiently special that it is not really useful to define it as a subtype of Set[Activity].

2.2 Concurrency Control

Since we have assumed that activities interact primarily through the use of shared objects, we provide mechanisms for the implementers of a data type to serialize and schedule operations on shared objects by concurrent activities. The synchronization primitives we provided for Owl are quite basic, but they can be used to implement sophisticated synchronization policies in a modular fashion.

Synchronization in Owl is supported by two complementary mechanisms: *locks* for mutual exclusion, and *wait queues* for waiting and signaling. Locking with waiting and signaling is also the basis for the monitor approach to synchronization [Andrews and Schneider 83], but we did not include the automatic encapsulation provided by monitors, feeling it to be too rigid.

Mutual Exclusion Locks

Our locking mechanism uses a mutual exclusion Lock type with three basic operations: create, acquire and release. In use, a lock object is generally included as a component of a shared object. Acquire and release operations on the lock can be used to guarantee exclusive access to the shared object. Usually, however, these operations would not be invoked directly by the application programmer. Instead, they are used by the system as part of a structured *lock block*, which will be discussed later.

The Lock operations act as follows. To create a new lock object, one uses create. Newly created locks start unlocked. An activity that invokes acquire (via a lock block) is granted the lock immediately if it is currently unlocked. If the lock is held by another activity, the requesting activity is suspended in a first-in, first-out queue associated with the lock. The release operation is used to unlock a lock that is currently held.

Since waiting activities may hold locks while waiting for a new lock, there is potential for deadlock. If lock deadlock occurs, it is detected by the system[6] and one or more waiting activities are chosen as deadlock victims. Each deadlock victim's acquire operation will raise the deadlock exception. It is up to the programmer to determine how to handle the deadlock, but a deadlock victim should release some locks to enable other activities to obtain the locks and proceed. However, an activity that has raised a deadlock exception is not forced to release its other

---

[3]Owl's exception handling is similar to that of CLU (see [Liskov, et al. 1981]) or Ada. Ada is a registered trademark of the U.S. Government (Ada Joint Program Office).

[4]The implementation supports more powerful manipulation of activities, intended for use by a debugger utility only.

[5]An *iterator* is an operation that provides members of some collection of objects one by one to a loop body for processing.

See also [Liskov, et al. 1977, Liskov, et al. 1981].

[6]Deadlock detection and resolution has been designed but has not yet been implemented.

locks, and it is not prohibited from requesting additional locks. If it requests additional locks, the system will test for deadlock again and this may raise another deadlock exception. After a lock is released, the first activity in the lock's first-in, first-out queue will be allowed to acquire the lock and proceed.

Lock deadlock is not the only potential cause of unbounded waiting. As we will see later, activities can also be waiting for a wakeup signal from another activity that will never occur. The potential for this type of wait/signal infinite wait is a common feature of concurrent programming. No satisfactory solution is known. Consequently, the Owl system does not attempt to detect the situation automatically. A timeout mechanism is provided that can be used to assist in detecting and handling unbounded waits.

Lock Blocks

The *lock block* structure solves the problem of how to unlock automatically at every exit point from a block of code protected by a lock. Lock blocks are similar to critical regions. For example, code that is to be executed only while a lock is held is written within the body of a block of the form:

```
lock l do
    ... protected code ...
end lock;
```

Entry to the lock block will cause the invocation of the acquire operation on lock l before the body is executed. At the end lock, or at any other exit from the scope of the lock block (such as an exception being signaled), release is executed on lock l. If the acquire signals deadlock, the body will not be executed and the deadlock exception will be caught by the nearest exception handler enclosing the lock block. Exceptions raised within the body of a lock block are handled in the normal way by exception handlers within the block. Multiple locks can be acquired sequentially by nesting lock blocks.

There is an optional else clause allowed in lock blocks. If the else is present, an acquire_nowait lock operation is invoked rather than acquire. The effect of the no wait variant is that if the lock can be acquired immediately without queueing the request, then the normal body of the lock block is executed; otherwise the else body is executed. The no wait form of the lock block is:

```
lock l do
    normal body: executed if lock is granted
else
    alternate body: executed if lock is not granted
end lock;
```

While the structured lock block form for setting and releasing locks presented here should help the programmer avoid some common errors, such as forgetting to release a lock, it must be used cautiously. For example, if an unexpected signal arises in a lock block, the lock will be released automatically when the signal is passed outside the block. If the signal arises because the resource protected by the lock is broken, it is the type implementers responsibility to catch the exception and take action to fix or remove the resource.

Wait Queues

Often an activity cannot continue until some condition is satisfied by another cooperating activity. In order for the cooperating activity to establish the condition, it may be necessary for the waiting activity to release temporarily some of the locks it holds so that the other activity can access the required data. Once the cooperating activity has established the necessary state condition, it needs a way to notify the waiting activity. We provide for this type of waiting and signaling by using a data type called a Wait_Queue.

The type Wait_Queue has four major operations: create, wait, wakeup, and empty. A wait queue would commonly be a component of a shared object that is used by cooperating activities. Wait queues allow an activity to:

• indivisibly: release locks, enqueue on the wait queue, and suspend execution; and
• wakeup, reacquire the released locks, dequeue from the wait queue and resume execution.

Let qid be a variable of type Wait_Queue that has been assigned a newly created wait queue:

```
qid := create (Wait_Queue);
```

The operation wait(qid) has the following effect. The invoking activity indivisibly performs the following three actions:

• enqueues itself on the qid wait queue;
• releases all locks acquired within the current operation (note that there is exactly one lock per lexcially enclosing lock block); and
• suspends execution.

At a later time, some other activity's execution of wakeup(qid) restarts the waiter. However, before the waiter is released from the wait queue, the previously released locks are reacquired. There may be a delay while reacquiring locks; the details of lock reacquisition are discussed below. After lock reacquisition, the waiter continues immediately after the wait(qid) statement (with the locks it held before the wait).

The effect of wakeup(qid) is to awaken the activity at the front of the first-in, first-out suspended activity list for qid. That activity will proceed to reacquire locks, etc. If there are no activities waiting on qid, the wakeup is ignored. The wakeup is also ignored if there is already an activity in the process of waking up (i.e., reacquiring locks). In these cases we say the wakeup is *lost*. The rationale for losing wakeups is discussed below.

Since it is useful in implementing some scheduling policies (e.g., readers/writers access to a shared variable), we provide the operation empty(qid), for testing whether there are any waiters on wait queue qid. To help detect infinite waits, we provide a timeout mechanism. If the activity that invokes wait(qid) has set the per-activity parameter wait_timeout_interval, and the activity is not awakened via a wakeup(qid) within that amount of time, the wait will terminate with the exception wait_timeout rather than returning normally.

In sum, wait provides a "hole" in the lock block, and a Wait_Queue is similar to a condition variable used with monitors. Our lock block is similar to the seize statement of [Weihl and Liskov 85], and our wait statement is analogous to their pause. However, pause results in busy waiting, while we block a waiting activity and explicitly send wakeups later. Busy waiting was perhaps reasonable in their case, since the conditions they are considering are transaction commit and abort, which are relatively asynchronous and independent of the seize code. However, we expect lock blocks with wait statements to be used for synchronization and scheduling code: the scheduling state variables are protected by a mutual exclusion lock, and accessed only in lock blocks. In this case blocking and wakeups are reasonable, since we are doing scheduling, not asynchronous notification.

Since we wish to support scheduling of access to shared resources, it is a good idea to help insure that the condition indicated by a wakeup is still true when the awakened activity resumes execution. There are two steps we took towards that goal. First, we give reacquirers priority over normal acquirers of the same lock. This prevents new activities from disrupting the condition established by a wakeup. Second, we discard wakeups presented while an activity is reacquiring locks. If we did not discard such wakeups, the first awakened activity might invalidate the condition expected by the second one. Thus, in our design each activity must send wakeups to the appropriate wait queues. This design reflects our bias towards using the synchronization mechanism for scheduling rather than communication. Also because of this bias, we feel that activities should always block when executing a wait statement. Hence, we discard wakeups sent to empty queues.

While the design decisions just described improve the chances that the condition leading to a wakeup remains true until acted upon, care must still be taken to insure that the condition is not negated between the wakeup and when the lock is released by the activity doing the wakeup. In the design process we considered a number of examples from the literature, and found it easy and natural to achieve this in practice. The next section includes an example of wait and wakeup.

Since waiting involves releasing and then reacquiring locks, the wait statement raises the issue of deadlock. Giving reacquirers priority over new acquirers helps prevent deadlock, but we went a step further: reacquirers are ordered according to when they are awakened. This ordering prevents deadlock between reacquirers needing the same lock (or the same set of locks). However, deadlocks can occur between reacquirers if they still hold some locks from a containing scope. The reacquire ordering also provide fairness, which is usually preferred in scheduling problems. For a discussion of some alternative concurrency designs, see [Andrews and Schneider 83].

An Example

The fragment of Owl code for Shared_Char_Buffer shown below demonstrates how the lock block and wait queue mechanisms can be used to synchronize access to a character buffer shared by producers who insert characters and consumers who remove them. The shared type is constructed from an unsynchronized type Char_Queue, by adding a lock component for mutual exclusion, and a wait queue for empty synchronization. A Char_Queue is assumed to be an extensible data structure that never overflows (this is readily implemented in Owl).

Note that in the remove operation it is not necessary to check for empty again after the wait. A wakeup is done only when the buffer is not empty, and the non-emptiness condition cannot be negated before the first waiter gets the lock and proceeds to remove the newly added item. Furthermore, because reacquirers have priority over acquirers, it is not possible for multiple inserts to occur before a waiting remover gets the first inserted item. This prevents situations where the first waiting remover is successful, but later wakeups are lost so that other waiting removers do not wakeup, even though the buffer is non-empty.

```
type_module Shared_Char_Buffer

component me.mutex    : Lock;
component me.nonempty : Wait_Queue;
component me.buffer   : Char_Queue;

operation create (Mytype) returns (Mytype)
  is allocate
  begin
    me.mutex    := create (Lock);
    me.nonempty := create (Wait_Queue);
    me.buffer   := create (Char_Queue);
  end;

operation insert (me, x: Char)
  is begin
    lock me.mutex do
      insert (me.buffer, x);
      wakeup (me.nonempty);
    end lock;
  end;

operation remove (me) returns (Char)
  is begin
    lock me.mutex do
      if empty (me.buffer) then
        wait (me.nonempty)
      end if;
      return remove (me.buffer);
    end lock;
  end;

end type_module;
```

3. Implementation Data Structures

There are four major data types that must be implemented to support the features discussed above: *activities*, *activity sets*, *locks*, and *wait queues*. Implementation of most operations on these objects is obvious. However, the wait statement implementation is more interesting, as is the timeout mechanism, so we describe them after a brief discussion of the data types.

3.1 Activities

For expedience, we implemented activities in two parts: a "permanent", Owl part called an *activity object*, and a "temporary", low level *stack part*.

• An Owl activity object resides in the heap (dynamic storage area). It may be relocated by garbage collection (gc) and exists as long as there are references to it, even if the activity has terminated execution. Activity objects support many of the Owl (i.e., high level) operations on activities, and each contains a reference to its stack part.

• A stack part is similar to a process state block in a multiprogrammed operating system, but is tailored to Owl. It is allocated by requesting space from the operating system, and cannot be moved or reclaimed by gc, though it can be *recycled* and used for another activity later. It consists mainly of the obvious things: a register save area, a subroutine call stack[7], and so on. Stack parts "exist" only until the corresponding activity is terminated.

It is not necessary to implement activities in two, but it is useful because it separates high and low level implementation concerns, and because it allows easier re-use of the bulk of the storage consumed by an activity.

Every stack part has two sets of threading pointers. One thread simply chains together all active stack parts, so the debugger and other tools can find all "live" activities easily. The other thread chains together activities having the same execution state (ready, running, etc.). Here are the execution state lists maintained in our implementation:

• *Ready lists*: There are 32, to support that many priority levels.
• *Running list*: Contains exactly the currently running activity.
• *Lock acquisition list*: One rooted in each lock; holds the activities requesting that lock, in request order.
• *Wait queue list*: One rooted in each wait queue; holds the activities waiting on that wait queue, in wait order.
• *Frozen list*: Contains activities marked by the debugger as currently ineligible for execution (*frozen*), but otherwise ready.
• *Free list*: Contains allocated but currently unused stack parts, for recycling.
• *Reacquire list*: Contains all activities in the process of reacquiring locks after receiving a wakeup in a wait statement, in the order in which they were awakened. This list is discussed in more detail later.

In addition, all non-terminated activity stack parts are chained onto a global *active list*, so that the debugger and other tools can find all "live" activities easily.

3.2 Activity Sets

Activity sets are implemented entirely in Owl, using the rest of the concurrency features. The members of a set are stored as elements of an array, and the array is "grown" (replaced with a larger one and the elements copied over) if it fills up. Linear search is used for membership testing, etc. This is deemed adequate for typical activity sets, which are expected to be small. However, it would be very easy to substitute a different implementation for this abstraction in the future.

---

[7]For simplicity, the call stacks are of a single fixed size, which limits overall recursion depth. This is not as bad as it might seem, since most Owl data is in the heap, not in the stacks.

3.3 Locks

Mutual exclusion locks consist of:

• The current holder of the lock; a null pointer if the lock is free.
• The lock acquisition list: as mentioned previously.
• The earliest awakened activity desiring to reacquire this lock; a null pointer if none.
• A count of the number of activities waiting to reacquire this lock.

The rationale for the last two items is postponed to the discussion of the implementation of the wait statement.

3.4 Wait Queues

Wait queues are similar to counting semaphores, but the desired high level semantics requires additional features in the implementation. Recall that Owl wait queues lose wakeups when there is no activity waiting, and when an activity is in the process of waking up (reacquiring locks). For communication with external devices and the operating system, interrupts may be turned into wakeups. However, the Owl wakeup semantics is not always appropriate for these uses. Therefore, the implementation makes losing of wakeups optional. In fact, three separate boolean flags provide a total of eight different wait modes in the implementation, of which perhaps four or five are useful. These flags are:

• Lose wakeups when no activity is waiting: if requested, when an activity is about to wait on a wait queue, any pending wakeups are first discarded, thus guaranteeing that the activity will block. This option is in effect for normal Owl waits.
• Lose wakeups while reacquiring locks: if requested, when an activity is finished reacquiring locks after being awakened, discard any pending wakeups. This option is also in effect for normal Owl waits.
• Wakeup the next activity: if requested, as its last action before continuing after being awakened and reacquiring locks, an activity will perform a wakeup on the wait queue, so as to awaken the next activity in the queue. This is not used in normal Owl waits.

Various combinations of the above options support the normal Owl wait, counting semaphores, events that happen once and thereafter do not cause a wait, and other potentially useful semantics. These features can be made available to the Owl programmer in at least two ways.

• We can add new operations the Wait_Queue type, for waiting in different modes; or
• we can provide a separate *type* for each kind of waiting. These types might be presented as subtypes of the Owl Wait_Queue type, all of which share the same low level representation, differing only the parameters passed to the implementation when a wait operation is invoked at the Owl level.

The first alternative requires the user to insure that each activity that waits on a given queue requests the same wait mode, if consistent, predictable behavior is to be expected. Hence the second alternative is better because it is safer.

To support the above functionality, wait queues consist of: a wakeup count, a first-in, first-out queue of waiting activities, and a reference to the currently waking up activity (a null pointer if there is none).

3.5 The Wait Statement

The Owl wait statement requires that locks be granted to reacquiring activities in preference to other requesters, and in wakeup order. To support the preference, each lock has a count of the number of activities needing to reacquire that lock. To support the wakeup order requirement, reacquisitions are granted according to the order of activities in the one, global, reacquire list, which is maintained in wakeup order. To speed lock granting, each lock refers to its next reacquirer. The lock reacquisition count allows us to see if the lock has additional reacquirers. If it does not, then the search for the next highest priority reacquirer can be avoided. We expect that in typical use there will never be more than one reacquirer for a given lock at a time, so we will in practice avoid searching the reacquire list at all. This is a case where we have tuned to expected use, though we support the full semantics as designed.

To support automatic freeing and reacquisition of locks at a wait statement, the activity stack part has a separate lock stack. The lock stack has an entry for each lock named in a (dynamically) enclosing lock statement (i.e., all locks the activity held just before the wait statement). In addition, each entry indicates the Owl stack frame for that lock. Thus wait releases and reacquires exactly those locks associated with the current frame (the frame is identified by another slot in the activity stack part). The lock stack also supports debugging, provides consistency checks, and allows automatic deadlock detection. The lock statement does lock pushes and pops on the lock stack. At a later date equivalent information may be stored directly in the activity's execution stack, removing the current fixed depth limitation on the lock stack. However, the fixed depth has never been a problem.

3.6 Efficient Timeouts

Since most operations that can timeout probably will not do so in practice, the implementers is challenged to avoid excessive overhead in setting up and removing timeouts. We use the time slice ticks to drive the timeout mechanism, so we avoid extra operating system overhead. However, we still need a data structure that indicates the next activity to timeout. Further, as activities are entered and removed, the data structure has to be maintained efficiently.

We chose to use a balanced binary tree, threaded directly in the activity stack parts, to hold the timeouts. In this tree each node has a sooner timeout than any of its descendant nodes, so the root is the first to time out. Suppose we number the nodes in the tree so that the root is numbered 1, and the children of the node numbered i are numbered $2i$ and $2i + 1$. If we have n nodes in the data structure, the next item is added at position $n + 1$, and then iteratively propagated upwards (by swapping with its parent) until its parent has a sooner timeout (or the next item becomes the root). This arrangement of data and insertion procedure is patterned after the heapsort sorting algorithm. It turns out that upward links are not needed in the tree, since a node's number tells you how to find it from the root. The resulting data structure supports finding the soonest

timeout in constant time, and insertion and deletion take $O(\log n)$.

4. Additional Implementation Features

A number of features were added to the implementation that were not required in the design for the high level language programmer. The main motivation was to provide convenient support for system functions, a debugger, performance monitor, and other tools. However, some provision was made for possible language extensions (e.g., the addition of a variety of wait modes for wait queues). A number of operations were added to allow the low level state of the objects (activities, locks, and wait queues) as well as the scheduler to be examined. Support for a variety of breakpoints was added. Means for responding to interrupts were provided, including pre-emptive priority scheduling in addition to round robin time slicing of activities having the same priority. Time slicing can be turned off, and its rate adjusted. We have already mentioned that activities can be frozen for debugging. Once frozen they can be examined, and their frames manipulated, though not in as general a way as Smalltalk. Slots for variables, arguments, and temporaries may be examined and updated, and returns or exceptions may be forced. Activities may be identified as being members of zero or more of a moderate number of groups of activities (identified by bit flags in the activity), and such groups may be examined, reorganized, and collectively frozen and thawed.

5. Providing Atomicity

Owl takes a permissive approach to interrupt handling and context swapping: interrupts and swaps are allowed except in critical sections. Note that it is not immediately clear exactly what constitutes a critical section. That is, what should be atomic depends on what model and capabilities are offered by the system. We clarify our model and goals below.

Our permissive approach to interrupts and swapping avoids the overhead and additional latency of explicit checks, but requires a more intricate design. We first describe our model and the atomicity problems that must be solved, and then discuss the techniques we used to achieve atomicity.

5.1 Atomicity Problems

The basic requirement is: when an activity is suspended the debugger and gc must be able to act upon it. Both the debugger and gc require the stack to be interpretable. Gc must also be able to find and adjust all pointers, even those in an activity's registers. The requirement that suspended activities be interpretable raises the following problems:

• Frames in the stack must be whole and recognizable. Guaranteeing this requires frame construction and destruction to be atomic.
• An activity stack must not contain uninitialized data, which might confuse the garbage collector or debugger. Hence, local variables must be set to some legal value as frames are built. We chose to use a value recognizable an uninitialized, in order to support detection of uses of uninitialized variables. Con-

veniently enough, a value of all 0's serves this purpose.

• An activity's saved registers must be interpretable by gc. In particular, gc must be able to distinguish pointers from non-pointers.

The last item has several implications. First, support routines, since they are written in another language where we do not have control over register usage, must be atomic. How we make them so will be discussed in detail below. If we did allow suspension in the middle of a support routine, we likely could not interpret the register contents reliably. The few routines that allow suspension in the middle (e.g., those implementing concurrency control) are specially coded to avoid problems. This is done by copying any Owl pointers that are in local variables to a special place before blocking, and reloading those pointers into local variables upon waking up.

Routines that may suspend in the middle are also vulnerable to being caught there by the debugger. Therefore, we made provision for debugger commands that would break out of the suspension as cleanly as possible. A further consideration is that since most routines are guaranteed to be executed atomically, they do not need to take special care to leave registers in an easy to find location in the stack. Blocking routines do a little extra work to make it possible for gc and the debugger to find registers, and for the debugger to change them effectively (including cutting back the stack, and so forth).

Communication to large external packages where activity switching in the middle may be desirable must be done without giving those packages direct access (pointers) to Owl objects. One approach is to have an array of object pointers and let external packages refer to Owl objects through routines that are given only the index of an object on the table rather than an Owl pointer. To pass information from Owl to external routines, the information is either copied, or Owl objects are created in a noncompacted area (so that they will not move out from under the external package). Reclamation from such an area might be prohibited, or left under user control (an explicit free operator). External packages also imply stack areas that do not obey the Owl rules. We have designed and built a simple mechanism for external packages, but it has not yet been fully tested or evaluated.

5.2 Techniques for Achieving Atomicity

Let us briefly review the atomicity requirements that must be met:

• Stack frame creation and destruction, and some other short, frequently occurring, instruction sequences must be atomic.
• Some reasonably short code sequences that are logically inline, but are implemented as assembly language subroutines to save space, must be atomic. (These routines do not follow the usual Owl calling conventions.)
• Most calls to the runtime system must be atomic. Those routines that may suspend in the middle must be specially coded.
• As in any system, there are some critical sections that must execute without the possibility of another activity gaining the processor in the middle.
• Each "global variable" (called a *fixed name* in Owl)

has associated initialization code, which is run upon first access to that variable[8]. We must make sure that the initialization code is atomic, to the extent that the initialization is not done twice. (If a second activity requests the value while the first is calculating it, the second is to wait for the first.)

Each of the above problems is solved in a slightly different way. This has partly to do with feasibility of different methods in different situations, but is also related to performance. In particular, building stack frames takes only a few instructions. Adding two or three instructions to the normal case code just to achieve atomicity would be unacceptable. On the other hand, two or three instructions of normal case overhead on a thirty instruction subroutine that is not executed all that frequently may be all right. We describe the methods we used to solve each problem after first giving an overview of the structure of interrupt handling and scheduling in our design.

Overview of Interrupt Servicing and Scheduling

Fielding and responding to interrupts in Owl consists of several stages: *registering*, *handling*, *delivering*, and *responding*, each described in detail below. The overall goal is to gain a *response* from an activity. This is done by *delivering* a wakeup to an appropriate Wait_Queue. *Registering* is the initial recording of interrupt information, and *handling* is the process of deciding when to act on that information.

When the operating system[9] delivers an asynchronous system trap (AST), by forcing a call of a previously designated trap handling subroutine, the AST handler will call a routine we provide, which will *register* the interrupt. Registration stores an identification of the Wait_Queue to wakeup and the activity that was running when the interrupt occurred. A few system defined interrupts are delivered to a special Wait_Queue, for debugger use; each user defined interrupt can be delivered to any desired Wait_Queue. The interrupt information is saved in a ring buffer. Registration acts as a producer, storing into the buffer, and delivery acts as a consumer, reading out of the buffer and posting to Wait_Queue objects. Ring buffer access is synchronized with appropriately atomic instruction sequences.

In addition to storing information in the ring buffer, registration must insure that the next step, *handling*, will take place. This is done in different ways depending on the current status of the system. As will be explained in more detail later, there is a flag indicating whether we are currently in interruptible code. If we are interruptible, then the program counter is saved and the interrupt handler's return point modified so that handling will take place immediately. If we are executing non-interruptible code, we need only set a flag indicating that an interrupt has occurred; the non-interruptible code will check this flag later. If the Owl system was completely idle (pending input/output, for example), then a special signal is made to the operating system, to break out of the idle wait after dismissing the interrupt.

---

[8]Owl requires a fixed name to be initialized some time before the first use. The current implementation executes the initialization code upon the first attempt to use the fixed name.

[9]The implementation we describe runs under VMS. However, the techniques and almost all of the code are operating system independent.

As mentioned previously, interrupts are handled either immediately, or when non-interruptible code is finished. The handling code either immediately calls a routine to *deliver* all pending interrupts, or uses one of the atomicity mechanisms to defer handling to a later time. This is discussed more fully when the mechanisms are described.

Delivering interrupts is reasonably simple: each item in the ring buffer is consumed and the appropriate Wait_Queue is given a wakeup. This may cause some activities to become ready. Interrupt delivery is itself atomic, but when it is finished a new activity may be chosen for execution. The activity awakened by a delivered wakeup, when run, will then *respond* to the interrupt. Activity priorities can be adjusted to give response appropriate to the interrupt. This is similar to the technique described in [Goldberg and Robson 83].

Here is a brief summary of the interrupt servicing stages:

- *Registering:* The fact that an interrupt has occurred is recorded.
- *Handling:* The system decides when to act upon the information (immediately, if possible; otherwise at the end of the current critical section).
- *Delivering:* The appropriate Wait_Queue is given a wakeup, thus notifying the Owl code of the event.
- *Servicing:* The system or application Owl code responds to event as desired.

We now consider the atomicity mechanisms.

Very Short Atomic Sequences: Emulation

The problem in making short instruction sequences atomic is achieving acceptably low overhead. In particular, even if we could protect these sequences with one instruction at each end, the overhead would still be substantial, especially since operation call and return (stack frame creation and destruction) is so common. Our solution to this problem is to have the interrupt handling code detect when we are in one of these sequences and effectively delay handling until the sequence is complete. The sequences are recognized by the occurrence of particular opcodes; the "delay" is achieved by emulating these instructions on the saved state. (Actually, very little of the state is saved, and in many cases the instructions can be directly executed.) Emulation continues until we are out of the sequence, and then handling begins.

Since we are matching based on opcodes (plus the registers and addressing modes used), it is possible that we occasionally emulate instructions unnecessarily. However, because all the sequences are short, we will not waste much time with such unneeded emulation. A more subtle problem is insuring that emulation terminates. We do this by checking for each opcode to be emulated in the same order they occur in the atomic sequences, and after emulating one instruction we continue by performing the *next* check on the next opcode, rather than going back to the start of the emulation tests.

Emulation involves overhead when handling interrupts (we have to check for instructions to emulate whenever we are about to handle interrupts), and is somewhat slower than executing the emulated instruction directly. However, it occurs rarely enough that the cost does not substantially impact overall performance. We chose not to use the single-step

trap on the VAX for emulation. Rather, since almost all the registers are intact, once we recognize an instruction requiring emulation, it is usually easy to execute a corresponding instruction (or a few instructions) to update the registers. The program counter has been saved, so branches are emulated by updating the saved value, etc.

Almost Inline Routines: Location and Restart

The subroutines that are too long to be inline are grouped into a particular area of memory, and current execution of one of them is detected by examining the saved program counter value to see if it falls in that region. These routines are carefully coded to be restartable, so the handler just backs them up to the point of call (a legitimate location in Owl code), and delivers interrupts at that point.

Non-Restartable Routines: The Interrupt Flag

For non-restartable routines, as well as low level critical sections, a flag is set to indicate when we are executing non-interruptible code. This flag is actually a counter, incremented upon entering a critical section, and decremented and tested on exit. Using a counter allows critical sections to be nested, though we have not used this flexibility in the system. A special coding of the interrupt flag simplifies matters here. The second most significant bit of the counter is normally set, and is cleared when an interrupt is registered. The counter value is thus always ≥ 0, and equals 0 only when an interrupt has been registered and we are not in a critical section. Thus, when the counter is decremented to zero, we have just finished a critical section in which an interrupt occurred.

Decrementing, testing, and conditionally branching to the interrupt handler takes more than one instruction, so emulation is used to insure atomicity of the critical section exit sequence. Emulation could also be used to make the critical section entry code atomic, if it were more than one instruction long.

Non-Owl Support Code: Return Traps

This method is a bit more specific to our circumstances, but might still be useful in more general situations. For speed, since it does not require all the features of the VAX calling convention, Owl uses a simplified calling convention. This is part of why the stack frame manipulation is not atomic. Non-Owl code is called using the VAX convention, which modifies a particular register: fp - the VAX frame pointer register. By checking to see if the contents of this register is different from the initial fp value (saved when an Owl activity is created), we can immediately tell if we are executing Owl code (or almost inline code), or external support code.

If we are in external support code, the handler should defer handling until the external subroutine completes. This is done by tracing up the stack and changing the return address of the frame that would return to Owl. The new return address causes a branch to an entry of the interrupt handler; the old address has been saved in a particular place. We call this technique a *return trap*. Return traps make support routines atomic without any entry/exit sequence. Should an activity block with a pending return trap, the trap is removed, and handling is attempted on the newly scheduled activity (which may result in the placement of a new return trap).

High Level Code: Swap Deferral

To separate low level code, of which there is not much, but which is carefully crafted assembly language and C, from high level Owl code, the interrupt flag mechanism is not used for high level critical sections. This allows us to guarantee, for example, that an activity will not block in the middle of non-interruptible code. It also gives us some bound on the time between interrupt registration and delivery, and thus control over whether or not the interrupt ring buffer might overflow.

For high level critical sections, we provide a *swap deferral flag*, which prevents pre-emption of the current activity, unless it explicitly blocks itself. One place this is used is in the activity termination code: swaps are deferred while all the activities that are in an `await` on the terminating activity are made ready, one by one.

Swap deferral does not delay interrupt registration, handling, or delivery. However, it does delay actual scheduling of activities awakened by interrupts, and hence holds off interrupt response. Similar to the interrupt flag, the swap deferral flag is a count. However, it is maintained separately for each activity. Thus, if an activity has a non-zero swap defer count, it indicates exactly those places where it is all right to be interrupted by other activities by blocking or explicitly calling a routine that performs a rescheduling.

Initialization of Globals: Double Check

Initialization of globals is made atomic by using an additional slot associated with each variable. This slot gives the identity of the activity initializing the variable. The variable is a candidate for initialization only if its value is a code that means *uninitialized*, namely zero. In that case, a critical section is entered, and a determination is made between the following courses of action:

- The variable has acquired a value between the time we first looked at it and the time we entered the critical section. In this case, just return that value.
- The variable is still uninitialized, but another activity is initializing it. Go to sleep on a special `Wait_Queue`. When awakened, check the variable's status again.
- The variable is still undefined, and no activity is initializing it. Indicate that the current activity is initializing it, and do so. When done, wakeup all waiters in the special `Wait_Queue`.

This method causes extra context switches if conflict on initialization is common and the conflict occurs on more than one variable, since a single `Wait_Queue` is used for all initialization waits. However, we have no reason to expect conflicts to be common.

Of more significance is that we check the value of a variable twice: once outside the critical section, and again inside it. The first check totally avoids the overhead of critical sections and immediately provides the value when the variable is already initialized. The code sequence is short enough that it is done inline. If the variable appears to need initialization, a subroutine is called, which then enters the critical sections and takes action as described above.

5.3 Applicability of Techniques

We feel that the techniques we have described are broadly applicable to language runtime systems that must deal with concurrency.

- Emulation is appropriate for short, stylized code sequences, such as those produced by compiler code generators. It also compensates for any lack of convenient non-interruptible instructions.
- The interrupt flag mechanism is an obvious technique, quite similar to hardware interrupt enable flags. However, it can be used when access to the hardware is impossible, and use of operating system features is too expensive. It works on general sequences of code, but has a few instructions of overhead, in time and space.
- Restartability also bears some similarity to hardware features. It is much less applicable than the previous mechanisms, and requires extreme care in writing the code. Its applicability is further reduced by the difficulty of distinguishing restartable code from non-restartable code, a problem we solved by putting all restartable routines in a special region of memory.
- Return traps are very nice for making subroutines atomic. Their use depends on efficient recognition of the routines that are to be protected that way, on ready interpretation of the stack, and on guarantees that the routines will not bypass the return trap in some fashion. We recognize routines according to calling convention, but location in memory would also work very well. Our routines can bypass the return trap, but only by calling some particular entries, which we fixed to take care of the potential problem.

5.4 Conclusions about Atomicity

The design and implementation of atomicity mechanisms was strongly affected by the presence of garbage collection. It is essential that gc be able to locate all pointers, and to fix the ones to objects moved during compaction. Eliminating compaction does not substantially reduce the problem. In this sense the object oriented nature of Owl had great impact on the implementation. However, features such as inheritance and compile-time type checking did not have much influence on low level implementation; neither did the operating system. We hope that Owl can be ported to other operating systems available for the VAX. Porting to other architectures would require substantially more effort. In our experience this is true of most garbage collected languages: for reasonable performance they require considerable tuning to the specific architecture. However, as we indicated above, the general approach and many of the specific techniques should carry over well.

6. Experience

Since the Trellis environment is still under construction and has few users outside the development team, there is little experience with our concurrency mechanism. However, it does appear adequate for building the system, and its collection of tools. Specifically:

- The mechanisms are working dependably.
- They are not too slow. For example, the debugger forks a new activity to process each user command, with no noticeable pause.
- The features are sufficient for a multiprogrammed debugger, for the window system and browser, etc.

The concurrency features are in fact more than just sufficient. Having multiple threads of control available actually simplifies implementation and improves functionality of the system. The debugger is a good example of these effects. Running an interactive debugger as a different activity from the code being debugged has the strong advantage of separating the stacks and thus simplifying the manipulations the debugger must perform on the debugged activity. We can even have multiple debuggers in existence simultaneously, each dedicated to debugging a particular activity. The debugger has also been used effectively in debugging parts of itself. In short, our experience is overwhelmingly positive, though limited.

7. Performance

The performance of our implementation is quite good; it is certainly at least adequate for the uses intended. A few preliminary benchmark tests are quoted below. They were performed on a VAX 11/785 and on a VAXStation II (MicroVAX), both running VMS. Each test was run a large number of times, with and without the code to be tested, so that the difference provides the cost of the code being measured. The times given consist of user mode processor time only. None of the operations (except the first activity creation, to allocate a stack part) involves operating system calls. The 785 time is stated first, with the MicroVAX time in parentheses. The numbers are averages of five runs, each with many repetitions of the operation measured, and are accurate to about two decimal places. Most of the support code is written in C; some small parts (e.g., low level task switching) are written in assembly language.

- Task switch: 170 μsec (260 μsec).
- Lock acquire/release pair, as in lock block, when the lock is available: 130 μsec (230 μsec).
- Synchronized data exchange (via a type similar to Shared_Char_Buffer): 0.93 msec (1.9 msec) per exchange (two messages, one in each direction, between a pair of activities).[10]
- Activity creation/destruction overhead: 2.5 msec (4.0 msec) (given stack parts available for recycling). The total cost to create and wind down an activity is somewhat higher, since it includes finding the code to execute given the string name of the operation and the arguments. This additional cost will be reduced by planned changes to string handling and by integration of multiple activities with the compiler.

Acknowledgements. The design of concurrency features for Owl was performed by a group of researchers led by Toby Bloom. The group included Craig Schaffert (Digital), Bill Weihl (MIT), and Bar- bara Liskov (MIT), in addition to the authors. The entire Trellis group reviewed the design. We implemented it, with assistance and guidance from Craig Schaffert and others. All support was provided by Digital Equipment Corporation. The group manager is Ken King.

References

[Andrews and Schneider 83] Gregory R. Andrews and Fred B. Schneider, "Concepts and Notations for Concurrent Programming", *Computing Surveys*, Volume 15, Number 1, March 1983, pp. 3-43.

[Deutsch and Schiffman 84] L. Peter Deutsch and Allan M. Schiffman, "Efficient Implementation of the Smalltalk-80 System", *Conference Record of the Eleventh Annual ACM Symposium on Principles of Programming Languages*, January 1984, pp. 297-302.

[Goldberg and Robson 83] Adele Goldberg and David Robson, *Smalltalk-80: The Language and its Implementation*, Addison-Wesley, 1983.

[Hoare 85] C. A. R. Hoare, *Communicating Sequential Processes*, Prentice-Hall International, 1985.

[Liskov, et al. 1977] Barbara Liskov, Alan Snyder, Russell Atkinson, and Craig Schaffert, "Abstraction Mechanisms in CLU", *Communications of the ACM*, Volume 20, Number 8, August 1977, pp. 564-576.

[Liskov, et al. 1981] B. Liskov, R. Atkinson, T. Bloom, E. Moss, J. C. Schaffert, R. Scheifler, A. Snyder, *CLU Reference Manual*, Springer-Verlag, 1981.

[Liskov and Scheifler 83] B. Liskov and R. Scheifler, "Guardians and Actions: Linguistic Support for Robust Distributed Programs", *ACM Transactions on Programming Languages and Systems*, Volume 5, Number 3, July 1983, pp. 381-404.

[O'Brien 85] Patrick O'Brien, "Trellis Object-Based Environment: Language Tutorial", Version 1.1, Eastern Research Laboratory, Digital Equipment Corporation, Technical Report 373, November 1985.

[Schaffert et al. 85] Craig Schaffert, Topher Cooper, Carrie Wilpolt, "Trellis Object-Based Environment: Language Reference Manual", Version 1.1, Eastern Research Laboratory, Digital Equipment Corporation, Technical Report 372, November 1985.

[Weihl and Liskov 85] William Weihl and Barbara Liskov, "Implementation of Resilient, Atomic Data Types", *ACM Transactions on Programming Languages and Systems*, Volume 7, Number 2, April 1985, pp. 244-269.

---

[10]Note that this includes two acquire/release pairs which block, two waits, two wakeups, and two task switches.

OBJECTS AS COMMUNICATING PROLOG UNITS[*]

Paola Mello, Antonio Natali

DEIS - Facolta' di Ingegneria
University of Bologna-ITALY

ABSTRACT

The aim of this paper is to present a set of extensions to the
Prolog language in order to insert in it concepts typical of parallel, distributed
object-oriented systems. A program is a collection of objects (P-Units) that represent chunks of knowledge expressed as separate Prolog programs. P-units interact by
asking for the demonstration of goals conceived as requests for operations. P-units
can perform operations in parallel. Policies of interaction between objects, the
creation of parallel activities, inheritance and delegation mechanisms are not
frozen in the basic interpreter, but can be explicitly expressed in particular P-
units that act as meta-objects. This approach enhances both the flexibility and reusability of the resulting object-oriented system.

1.INTRODUCTION

The object-oriented programming paradigm has shown itself to be very useful in a
number of applications because of its protection and flexibility features. Systems
based on the object model are intrinsically modular, easy to use and potentially
open towards new multi-processor and distributed architectures.
On the other hand, logic programming languages [1], in spite of their very attractive declarative style and their expressive power, seem to be lacking in precisely
the object-oriented characteristics mentioned above. In particular, in the most
widely used language of this type, Prolog [2], it is difficult to express concepts
such as modularity, protection and information hiding. Besides that, Prolog is a
sequential language which does not allow programmers to exploit the advantages of
multi-processor and distributed architectures, and, again, it is also very hard in
logic to deal with problems which need the concept of state, such as the control of
physical devices. Problems of this type have been solved in Prolog by introducing
built-in, non-logical predicates.
The lack of object-oriented features could prevent Prolog from being used to develop large, complex software systems, even if its declarative style and efficient
implementation [3] make it very attractive for several applications.
The main aim of the proposal presented in this paper (called CPU - Communicating
Prolog Units - [13]) is to explore the usefulness and the synergetic advantages of

----

[*]This work has been supported by CEE Esprit Project p973, ENIDATA S.p.A. and Italian
National Research Council (CNR)

the combination of logic- and object- oriented programming to overcome the limitations mentioned above.

The integration of logic and object-oriented programming has already been the subject of research. Perhaps the most interesting and complete proposals are based, at the current state of the art, on Concurrent Prolog [6], [7], a language that is intrinsically parallel and not compatible with Prolog.
Moreover, the concept of 'multiple worlds', providing a way to group together assertions about a concept and the possibility to describe inheritance of properties between concepts, has already been adopted in several proposals of extension to Prolog such as Prolog/KR [8] , ESP [9], MULTILOG [26], SPOOL [10], and [11]. However, in these proposals there is no possibility to express explicit parallel objects.
Instead, the aim of CPU is to fully subsume Prolog and allow parallel activities to be explicitly expressed. Besides, it exploits meta-programming [19] in order to enhance software flexibility and re-usability and make it easier to experiment with different object-oriented organizations, according to rapid prototyping techniques.
In summary, CPU introduces the following concepts:
a) the compact Prolog database (facts and rules) is split into a collection of separate Prolog programs called P_UNITs, assimilable to CLASSES. P-units are the basic construct for modularity, information hiding and knowledge structuring, but no pre-defined policy is introduced for these topics;
b) the behavior of a single P-unit is modelled as a set of parallel demonstration activities, each owning a local state (INSTANCES);
c) interactions between different P-units are expressed as requests of goal demonstration (MESSAGES);
d) explicit communication policies between different P-units and instances are expressed in terms of "meta-rules" written in "meta-P-units" associated to "object-P-units". Static and dynamic INHERITANCE mechanisms, frozen at the implementation layer in traditional object-oriented systems (e.g Smalltalk [4] and Flavors [5]), can be explicitly stated in meta-P-units.

The impact of these concepts on the design and implementation of large software applications is currently investigated with reference to a programming environment for Prolog in the context of the ALPES Esprit project [12].
The paper is organized as follows. Section 2 introduces CPU classes, instances and basic communication mechanisms. Section 3 discusses other forms of communication between object instances. In section 4 the CPU approach to knowledge sharing between different objects is discussed.

2. THE CPU MODEL

2.1 CLASSES

In the CPU model [13] (see figure 1) a program is conceived as a collection of separate (and - if needed - distributed) objects, each one representing a chunk of knowledge on a particular domain. Each object (called P-unit) is expressed as a Prolog database [2]. A Prolog database is a collection of Horn clauses, i.e. logical implications of the form $A_0:-A_1,A_2,....A_n$ where A_i (i=1,..,n) is an atomic formula and n $>=0$. Variables occurring in atomic formulas are denoted by constants beginning with an upper-case letter, and are universally quantified.
Prolog clauses -that can be read declaratively as logical assertions- can also be interpreted procedurally: e.g. "to solve a goal (or to execute an operation suc-

cessfully) matching A_0, solve (execute successfully) the subgoals (operations) $A_1 \ldots, A_n$ in sequence". Backtracking can be activated to find the right solution if

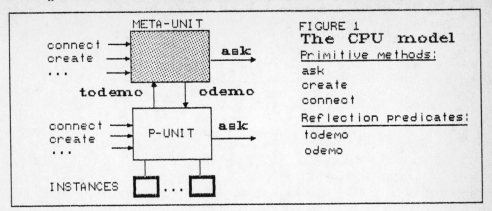

FIGURE 1
The CPU model
Primitive methods:
ask
create
connect
Reflection predicates:
todemo
odemo

more than one definition for the same operation exists.

Thus, in CPU, operations (methods) are simply represented by Prolog clauses. In the following example the P-unit 'list' containing methods to manipulate lists is presented. It defines the methods: 'append', 'insert' and 'notempty'.

```
unit(list).
append(...):-     ...
notempty(LIST):-  ...
insert([],ELEM,[ELEM]).
insert([FIRST¦REST],ELEM,[FIRST¦R1]):- isless(FIRST,ELEM),insert(REST,ELEM,R1 ),!.
insert([FIRST¦REST],ELEM,[ELEM,FIRST¦REST]).
isless(FIRST,ELEM):-...
```

P-units can communicate by sending messages; a message sent to a particular object can be conceived as a request to demonstrate a goal using a particular database. The primitive predicate ask(Dest, Goal, Res) embeds a synchronous message passing. It asks a P-unit 'Dest' to demonstrate 'Goal' with result 'Res'.

'ask' acts as a (remote) procedure call [17] where the caller waits until the invoked operation is terminated. 'Res' is bound to 'true' if the demonstration of 'Goal' into 'Dest' ends with success. In this case some of the variables within 'Goal' may have been bound to terms. In the case of failure, 'Res' is bound to any constant different from 'true'. The default value for a failure is 'unknown' and not 'false' because P-units are open-worlds [14]: the close world assumption of Prolog (which usually justifies a concept of falsity) must be established, if needed, in an explicit way.

If the method (goal) invoked is local to the current P-unit, the 'ask' primitive can be omitted. In the following example 'list' invokes the P-unit 'integer' to demonstrate the external goal 'isless'.

```
unit(list).
append(...):- ...
insert([],ELEM,[ELEM]).
insert([FIRST¦REST],ELEM,[FIRST¦R1]):- ask(integers,isless(FIRST,ELEM),true),
                                insert( REST,ELEM,R1 ),!.
insert([FIRST¦REST],ELEM,[ELEM,FIRST¦REST]).
```

Expressing methods as Horn clauses and method invocations as goals to demonstrate, leads to a set of important features:
1) knowledge is expressed in a declarative style. This helps in building knowledge-based systems;
2) the use of goal arguments as either input- or output-parameters of operations is determined by the context at the execution-time thanks to unification [15];
3) the same method can have multiple definitions (see 'insert' in 'list'). In this case, the right solution is automatically searched via backtracking;
4) the system is not necessarily uniform: unification can be profitably applied to logical terms which are not represented as object instances.

2.2 INSTANCES

P-units can activate different and, if needed, parallel demonstration processes to solve goals (i.e. to perform requested operations). Thus, P-units can be considered as TYPE or CLASS objects whose instances are agents performing operations on behalf of an external sender object (MASTER) and sharing the knowledge base represented by the clauses of the class. The Basic Machine supporting a P-unit is conceptually a multi-processor system with shared memory and a finite but not limited number of processors.

In the P-unit 'list' presented before, a demostration process is implicitly activated every time a 'list' method invocation is received and the caller is suspended until such a process has produced an answer. List demonstration processes, like unserialized actors [16], have no private state. Thus, it is not necessary for the programmer to name them explicitly. Demonstration processes are only passive servers of external requests and can be completely transparent to the user.

However, although logic programming does not permit multiple assignments of values to logic variables, the instances of an object-oriented system normally have a private state that can be changed by the execution of methods. For this reason, CPU associates to each P-unit the primitive method 'create' in order to explicitly create parallel, independent INSTANCES with a private state.
When a P-unit 'ul' receives a request for the method: create(Iname, Goal), it creates an instance with name 'Iname' to perform the demonstration of 'Goal' using the Prolog data-base of 'ul'.
The 'create' method terminates with success just after the activation of 'Iname'. Thus, the instance 'Iname' performs the operation 'Goal' in parallel with its creator (the caller of 'create'). The names of explicit instances are represented as Prolog lists as follows: [unit_name, <unique-identifier>]. The state of an explicit instance is represented by the refutation-tree related to the goal to be demonstrated and by the local bindings of logical variables. As in object-oriented systems based on Concurrent Prolog, instance variables are represented by logical variables. CPU instances do not change their state by using assignment but by recursively calling themselves with different argument values, according to a side-effect-free style of programming. Prolog predicates such as 'assert' and 'retract' should not be used to obtain state change because they usually do not produce a modification on a specific instance, but a change in the whole Prolog database (Class) shared among all instances.

Let us consider the following example. A Class named 'Point' is defined whose instances represent points in a two-dimensional coordinate system. Each instance of this class has an instance variable, X, that represents its horizontal coordinate, and an instance variable, Y, that represents its vertical coordinate. Each instance can assign different values to X and Y ('set-new'), show its current position ('show') or delete the point ('delete').

```
unit(point).
erase(X,Y):-     <on screen operations>.
move(X,Y,Z,W):- <on screen operations>.
display(X,Y):- <on screen operations>.
/* this part of Point represents the methods 'erase', 'move' and 'display'*/

point(X,Y) :- serve(set-new(Z,W)),!,move(X,Y,Z,W),point(Z,W).
point(X,Y) :- serve(show(X,Y)),display(X,Y),!,point(X,Y).
point(X,Y) :- serve(delete),!,erase(X,Y).
/* this part of point represents the definition of its main loop; the arguments
of point predicate (X and Y) represent the instance variables. The 'serve'
predicate will be explained in more detail in the following */

new(X,Y):-   repeat,point(X,Y).
/* the 'new' method is called to create a new point with initial state repre-
sented by X and Y actual values */
```

The main loop 'point(_,_)' is a specification of the behavior of a point: "A point with coordinates X and Y can serve a 'set-new' message and become a point on the screen with new coordinates Z and W; it can serve a 'show' message and maintain its old state; it can receive a 'delete' message and cancel itself".
When an object O1 wants to create a new point 'p1' with X=3 and Y=5 the following message has to be sent to the class 'Point':

$$ask(point,create(p1,new(3,5)),Res).$$

Once the new point has been created, the object O1 continues its computation without waiting for demonstration of the goal new(3,5).
An instance terminates when the refutation process fails or when it ends with success. In the example the latter situation occurs when a 'delete' message is served.

2.3. META-PROGRAMMING TO SPECIFY OBJECT BEHAVIOR

A main concept in CPU is that the specification of object interactions can be considered a typical domain of meta-programming [19]. To support this concept, the model introduces a clear distinction between objects and meta-objects and a mechanism to define precise relationships between them.
A meta-unit, 'mu' can be associated with an object-unit 'u' by executing the following primitive method with success in 'u': connect(mu).
Since 'mu' is a P-unit, it can be connected to another 'meta-meta-P-unit' and so on: for this reason meta-levels can grow indefinitely. When a unit is associated to a meta-unit, each instance of the object-unit performs a DEFAULT COMMUNICATION with its meta_unit for each (sub)goal to be demonstrated. This consists in asking the meta-unit for demonstration of the following goal :

$$todemo(Master, Instance, Current-U, Goal, Result)$$

where 'Instance' is bound to the name of the object-level instance that has to demonstrate 'Goal'; 'Master' is bound to the name of the unit for which the demonstration is executed (in general the name of the calling P-unit), and 'Current-U' is bound to the name of the object-level unit involved in the goal demonstration. 'Result' represents the result of the 'Goal' demonstration.

For example, let us assume that the explicit instance [point,p1] executes:
ask(integers,isless(3,5),true). The following invocation is then automatically
generated in the meta-unit -if it exists- associated with 'integers':

todemo(point, [point,p1] , integers, isless(3,5), true).

Successful execution of the method 'isless' is strictly related to the successful
execution of 'todemo' with the specified arguments.

Transition from the object-level to the meta-level is only half of the communication pattern which allows the sharing of results between these two levels according
to the reflection principle [18]. Transition from the meta-level to the object level
occurs when a meta-unit sends to its object-unit the goal

odemo(Master,Instance,Unit,Goal,R)

which forces the demonstration process 'Instance' to solve 'Goal' (with result 'R')
into the object-unit 'Unit' with the specified 'Master'.
In the following example the P-unit 'list' has been associated with the meta-unit
'meta-list'. 'List' has been modified in order to enclose interconnection policies
in its meta-unit only, to enhance system modularity and flexibility.
A list of characters can now be implemented without changing the 'list' class code:
it is only necessary to connect it with another meta-unit. "Generic" [20] classes
can be easily defined in this way.

```
unit( meta-list ).
todemo(Caller,I,U,isless(A,B),Res):- ask( integers, isless( A,B ),Res ).
todemo( Caller,I,U,G, R ):-              odemo(Caller,I,U,G,R ).
```

```
       todemo |          odemo
unit(list).
insert([],ELEM,[ELEM]).
insert([FIRST¦REST],ELEM,[FIRST¦R1]):- isless(FIRST,ELEM),insert(REST,ELEM,R1),!.
insert([FIRST¦REST],ELEM,[ELEM,FIRST¦REST]).
```

Let us note that meta-P-units are different from meta-classes of object-oriented
languages such as Smalltalk [4]. In fact, while the main task of meta-classes in
Smalltalk is the general description of Classes, the main task of meta-P-units in
this example is that of specifying relationships between objects. More generally,
specification of a P-unit can be confirmed, modified, or completed by the associated
meta-P-unit. According to this interpretation, the behavior of the instances of a
Class 'c' is determined not only by the object P-unit 'c', but also by its
associated meta-P-unit.

There are several reasons for investigating an object-oriented model in which
each object communicates with its meta-level before doing any operation. In particular, even if Classes are represented as collections of methods, the use of meta-
level allows the definition of a single method [21] to answer all messages that an
object receives. This feature could be useful to trace or record all messages sent
to an object in a history-list, to debug its behaviour or to redirect messages.
Moreover, concepts and mechanisms usually frozen in language notations (e.g. scope
rules, exception mechanisms, synchronization and communication protocols) can be
expressed by meta-rules.
Further examples of meta-level applications will be discussed in the following. In
particular section 4 will be devoted to discussing the impact of meta-programming in
the implementation of inheritance mechanisms.

3. DEFINING COMMUNICATIONS BETWEEN OBJECT INSTANCES

The 'ask' primitive is used to send goals to P-Units that behave like Classes. P-Units (and their associated meta-P-units) activate processes in order to perform goal demonstrations. However, as happens in traditional object models, the need to send messages to specific instances with an explicit name and a local state, is present. For example, to move the particular point [point,p1], an explicit message must be sent to it and not to its generic class.

Since CPU is intended for distributed programming, the CPU model does not allow the sharing of logical variables between different instances (even if they belong to the same class). For this reason, the interaction between instances is not expressed in terms of streams and annotated variables, as in object models based on Concurrent Prolog [6]. There is no need for explicit 'merge' operators, so an incremental style of programming is encouraged. In particular, low-level communication between instances can be performed by calling the methods of predefined 'queue' P_units. Producer instances can insert messages in a queue using an 'out' method while consumer instances can remove them by calling an 'in' method. Queues are objects with an internal state represented by the messages received and not yet removed. Because queues are here conceived as the building blocks of instance communication, they cannot be represented as explicit instances. Therefore, their state cannot be represented by logical variables. In CPU, queues of messages are simply represented by ordered collections of Prolog facts; 'in' and 'out' operations are implemented through side-effects using Prolog pre-defined predicates 'assert' and 'retract'. Inspection and manipulation of messages is performed in a very simple and expressive way, thanks to unification.

In order to make queues able to share methods but not their local state, queue methods can be defined in a 'meta-queue' unit. In this case object-units can be assimilated to instances and the shared meta-unit to their class.

Thus, each P-unit can behave as a queue if it is connected to a meta-unit including the following meta-rules:

todemo(Caller,Inst,U,out(Message),Res):-odemo(Caller,Inst,U,assert(Message),true).
/* a message is inserted in the object queue */
todemo(Caller,Inst,U,in(Message),Res):- odemo(Caller,Inst,U,retract(Message),true).
/* if it exists, a message is removed from the object queue */

Concurrent accesses to the database of a P-unit using assert and retract predicates are assumed to be disciplined through built-in synchronization protocols so that modification to the database is performed in a consistent way.

3.1 AN EXAMPLE: ASYNCHRONOUS COMMUNICATION

Let us consider the point example of section 2. An asynchronous communication between 'screen' instances, to display, change or delete points, and 'point' instances, can be established by writing the following meta-P-units:

```
unit(request-server).
todemo(Caller,Instance,U,serve(Goal),Res):-
                    !,ask(queue1,in(message(Source,Instance,Goal)),Res).
/* to serve an external request for a particular 'Instance', a request message
for such an 'Instance' must be removed from the queue. If no message exists, the
'Instance' backtracks. */
todemo(C,I,U,G,R):-odemo(C,I,U,G,R).   /* other goals are solved locally */
```

```
unit(request-sender).
todemo(Caller,Instance,U,send(Dest,Goal),Res):-
          !,ask(queue1,out(message(Instance,Dest,Goal)),Res)
  /* to send a request to a particular 'Instance' a message for such an Instance is
  inserted in 'queue1' */
todemo(Caller,Instance,U,Goal,Res):-odemo(Caller,Goal,Res).
```

If we connect 'point' to 'request-server' meta-unit, 'screen' to 'request-sender' meta-unit, and 'queue1' to 'meta-queue' (figure 2), then the instances of 'screen' and 'point' classes communicate in an asynchronous way.

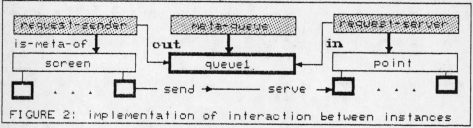

FIGURE 2: implementation of interaction between instances

When a point instance calls the 'serve' method with a 'set-new(X,Y)' argument, a request for the 'set-new' method is searched in 'queue1'. If this message exists it is extracted from the queue and executed; otherwise backtracking is induced in the 'point' instance and messages 'show' and 'delete' are sequentially searched for. If none of these messages is present in the queue the main loop is repeated and the 'serve' operations retried. Thus, 'point' instances perform a busy form of waiting for requests, using the backtracking mechanism of Prolog. Of course, if instances share the same processor this mechanism can be replaced by rescheduling policies.

Let us note the expressive power achieved through the unification mechanism for message-handling operations, when instance names are normal Prolog structures:

a) if 'Source' within the 'in' goal is not bound, a message can be received from any instance;

b) if 'Source' is partially specified (e.g. it has the form: [screen,X]), only messages sent by 'screen' instances can be received.

c) if 'Dest' is only partially specified within the 'out' goal, (e.g. it has the form [point,Any]) then the message is served by the first 'point' instance that executes a 'serve' predicate;

d) depending on the form of the requested operation ('Goal'):

　　　1) the first message in the queue is extracted;

　　　2) only a particular message is looked for.

The previous policies are examples of low-level process interaction mechanisms upon which different, higher level interaction policies (e.g. synchronous message passing) can be defined at meta-level. In [13] we have introduced a high form of interaction between instances called "synchronization clauses", based on the rendez-vous [20] model, similar to generalized clauses presented in [22]. Their implementation in terms of meta-rules is reported in [27].

3.2 CONTINUATIONS

When an instance terminates, it could send a last message with its final results to a 'continuation' [23] process, specified at its creation. For example, when each point instance terminates, it could send a special message to a particular 'garbage collector' process. This policy can be easily implemented without any modification

in the 'point' code, by simply writing the following meta-rule:
```
todemo(Master,Instance,U,new(Continuation,X,Y),R):-
    odemo(Master,Instance,U,new(X,Y),R),
    ask(queue1,out(Instance,Continuation,end(Instance,R)),true).
```

4. BUILDING INHERITANCE MECHANISMS

Very different mechanisms have been introduced in object-oriented languages for the purpose of sharing knowledge. In Smalltalk [4] simple inheritance is introduced; Flavors [5] supports multiple inheritance and combination; in Actors systems, delegation [21] is used. Since universal agreement seems impossible [24], the approach of CPU is to allow programmers to explicitly express rules to share knowledge between different objects. Experiments on different models of knowledge structuring and sharing can be performed in a rapid and flexible way since inheritance rules can be well expressed by meta-rules. Let us consider the following example. A 'special-point' class could be defined with the same behavior as 'point' (e.g. the same state representation, main loop, and sheduling policy) except a different 'move(X,Y,W,Z)' method. 'Special' point could be defined as a subclass of 'point' that only defines a new method for 'move'. Implementation of the required inheritance between these two classes can be expressed by an 'inheritance' shared meta-unit (figure 3).

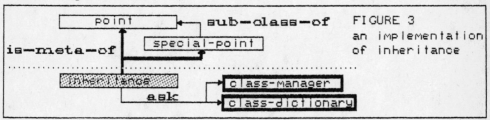

FIGURE 3
an implementation
of inheritance

If we suppose that the 'class-dictionary' unit specifies the methods defined in every class and the 'class-manager' states that 'super(special-point,point)', then meta-rules implementing inheritance can be written (in the order of their leading numbers) as follows.

A request for execution of a method 'G' by an 'Instance' of a 'Class' is accepted if 'G' is defined in it (rule 4); otherwise the execution of 'G' is delegated to the superclass 'SuperC' of 'Class' (if it exists) (rule 5).
```
4) todemo( C,Instance,Class,G,R):- ask(class-dictionary,def-method(Class,G),true),
                                   !,odemo( C,Instance,Class,G,R ).
5) todemo(C,Instance,Class,G,R):-  ask(class_manager,super(Class,SuperC),true),
                                   todemo(C,Instance,SuperC,delegate(Class,G),R).
```

A request for execution in 'SuperC' of an inherited method 'G' is directly executed if 'G' is defined in 'SuperC' (rule 2); otherwise the execution of 'G' is delegated (with the same, initial subclass 'SubC') to the superclass 'SU' of 'SuperC', if it exists (rule 3).
Let us note that when a method is executed for a subclass, the Master is named in a special way (i.e. subclass(SubC)) to allow the selection of rule 1.

```
2) todemo(C,I,SuperC,delegate(SubC,G),R):-
                         ask(class-dictionary,def-method(SuperC,G),true),
                         !,odemo(subclass(C,SubC),I,SuperC,G,R ).
```

```
3) todemo(C,I,SuperC,delegate(SubC,G), R ):-
                          !,ask(class_manager,super(SuperC,SU),true),
                          todemo(C,I,SU,delegate(SubC,G),R ).
```

When a method invoked in a subclass 'SubC' is executed in a superclass 'SuperC', a local methods have to be solved by searching for the corresponding code in the inheritance tree, starting from 'SubC' (rule1). For example if, during execution of the 'point' main loop, the 'move' method is invoked, the corresponding code in the 'special-point' subclass must be executed. Let us note that a similar rule referring to instances is embedded at the implementation layer in traditional object-oriented systems like Smalltalk, and obtained by using the 'Client' variable [24] in delegation-based systems.

```
1) todemo(subclass(C,SubC),I,SuperC,G,R):- !,todemo(C,I,SubC,G,R).
```

If all the conditions previously mentioned are not verified, the result of the method invocation is the constant 'not-def' that can be interpreted as exception by the caller (rule 6).

```
6) todemo(C,I,U,G,not-def).
```

If a class has more than one super-class (e.g. when a new relation such as super(special-point,graphic) is written in the 'class-manager' unit) a multiple inheritance mechanism is automatically implemented: the inheritance tree is searched depth-first using the backtracking mechanism of the standard Prolog interpreter.
Using the same methodology more sophisticated inheritance mechanisms could easily be obtained. For instance, different dynamically-determined policies of knowledge sharing could be obtained depending on the method arguments or on the involved instances. We are still investigating the possibility of building delegation policies [21] using the basic CPU mechanisms introduced in the paper.

FINAL REMARKS

In this proposal, concepts typical of object-oriented models have been introduced in a logic programming framework based on the Prolog language. The use of meta-programming, typical of logic-based systems, allows programmers to build concepts and mechanisms usually frozen in specific language notations, e.g. communication and inheritance policies, in terms of meta-rules. The CPU model even though somewhat lacking in linguistic support, seems to be promising for defining highly dynamically reconfigurable systems and, in particular, flexible programming environments for rapid system prototyping. One of the objectives we will pursue in the Esprit ALPES project is to build a CPU working prototype and an environment kernel in which tools have a satisfactory degree of re-usability and flexibility in order to support rapid development of new abstractions in process interaction, deeply integrated with those related to knowledge representation. The first CPU implementation on a SUN machine showed the usefulness of combining object-oriented and logic programming models even if it still lacks in good performances, for the overhead due to the automatic transition to meta-level.
In order to enhance performances, we are going to investigate, among other things, the application of partial evaluation techniques [25] typical of logic programming languages.

REFERENCES:

[1] R.Kowalski: "Predicate Logic as Programming   Language",   Proc. IFIP-74

Congress. North Holland, pp. 569-574, 1974.

[2] W.F. Clocksin, C.S. Mellish : " Programming in Prolog ", Springer-Verlag, New-York, 1981.

[3] D.Warren et alii: "Prolog - The Language and its implementation compared with Lisp", SIGART Newsletter 64, pp. 109-115, 1977.

[4] A.Goldberg, D. Robson: Smalltalk-80, The Language and its Implementation. Addison Wesley, 1983.

[5] D.Moon et alii: "LISP Machine Manual", MIT-Books, AI Laboratory, 1983.

[6] K.Kahn: "Objects in Concurrent Logic Programming Languages", Proc. OOPSALA-86, Portland, Oregon, September 1986.

[7] K.Furukawa et alii: "Mandala: A Logic Based Knowledge Programming System", in International Conference on Fifth Generation Computer Systems, 1984.

[8] K.Nakashima "Knowledge Representation in Prolog/KR", International Symposium on Logic Programming, Atlantic City, February 1984.

[9] T.Chikayama: "ESP Reference Manual", ICOT Report, Feb. 1984.

[10] K.Fukunaga: "An experience with a Prolog-based Object-Oriented Language", Proc. OOPSALA-86, Portland, Oregon, September 1986.

[11] C.Zaniolo: "Object Oriented Programming in Prolog", International Symposium on Logic Programming, Atlantic City, February 1984.

[12] ALPES Esprit Project P973. Technical Annex 1985.

[13] P.Mello, A.Natali: "Programs as Collections of Communicating Prolog Units" In: ESOP, Saarbrucken, March 1986, Lecture Notes in Computer Science n.213, Springer-Verlag.

[14] C.Hewitt, P.De Jong :"Open Systems", Tech. Rep. MIT-AIM 691 December 1981.

[15] J.A.Robinson: "A machine-oriented logic-based on the Resolution Principle", Journal of ACM, 12, 23-41, 1965.

[16] D.G. Theriault: "Issues on the Design and Implementation of ACT2", Tech. Rep. MIT AI-TR 728, June 1983.

[17] B.J.Nelson: Remote Procedure Call. Dept. of Computer Science, Carnagie-Mellon Univ. , Ph.D. Thesis, Rep. CMU-CS-81-119, May 1981.

[18] K.Bowen, R.Kowalski :"Amalgamating language and metalanguage in logic programming", in Logic Programming , Academic Press, 1982.

[19] L.Aiello, G.Levi:" The uses of meta-knowledge in AI Systems", ECAI-84, Pisa, September 1984.

[20] "Reference manual for the Ada programming language ", U.S.Departement of Defense, ANSI/MIL-std 1815-a, Jan.1983.

[21] H.Lieberman: "Delegation and Inheritance: Two Mechanisms for Sharing Knowledge in Object-Oriented Systems", in J.Bezivin, P.Cointe (editors), 3eme Journees d'Etide language Oriente Objets, AFCET, Paris, 1986.

[22] M.Falaschi, G.Levi, C.Palamidessi: "A Synchronization Logic: Axiomatics and Formal Semantics of Generalized Horn Clauses." Information and Control, Academic Press, Jan.1984.

[23] R.E. Filman, D.P. Friedman: "Actors", in 'Coordinated Computing ', Prentice-Hall, 1984.

[24] H.Lieberman: "Using Prototypical Objects to Implement Shared Behavior in Object Oriented Systems", Proc. OOPSALA-86, Portland, Oregon, September 1986.

[25] R.Venken: "A Prolog Meta-Interpreter for Partial Evaluation and its Application to Source to Source Transformation and Query-Optimization", in Proc. of ECAI-84, North Holland, 1984.

[26] H. Kauffman, A. Grumback: "MULTILOG: MULTIple worlds in LOGic programming", ECAI-86.

[27] P.Mello, A.Natali: "Configuration of Software Systems: A Domain for Meta-Programming", Technical Report DEIS, September 1986.

AN OBJECT MODELING TECHNIQUE FOR CONCEPTUAL DESIGN

M.E.S. Loomis, A.V. Shah, J.E. Rumbaugh

GE/Calma Company   General Electric CR&D
9805 Scranton Rd.   P.O. Box 8, Bldg. K-1
San Diego, CA 92121   Schenectady, NY 12301

Abstract

Our Object Modeling Technique is a software engineering technique for collecting and representing information about requirements and designs. It enforces the object–oriented notions of modularity, separation of implementation details from external behavior, and abstract data types. We have successfully applied the Object Modeling Technique to support conceptual design, followed by implementation using both conventional programming languages and an object–oriented language.

Introduction

The term "object–oriented" has become a buzzword that means different things to different people. It has been used synonymously with such terms as modularity, information hiding, encapsulation, and abstract data types. "Object–oriented" also refers to a system design philosophy, that makes objects active components of a system, responsible for manipulating their own internal states. By contrast, a procedure–oriented design philosophy makes data passive and manipulated by active procedures, whose definition is external to the data.

The Object Modeling Technique discussed here is a software engineering technique that we have developed for collecting and representing information about requirements and specifications. We have applied the technique to establish the scope of problem areas, to communicate precisely system specifications, to show clearly the dependencies between subsystems, to help in planning and scheduling projects, to structure databases, and to drive the coding and testing of software.

The object–oriented approach can permeate a system to various degrees. We have used the Object Modeling Technique in Calma product architecture work for communicating high–level interfaces and functionality. We have used it to specify applications that will be implemented using conventional programming languages (FORTRAN, C). These languages, however, implicitly encourage a procedure–oriented design philosophy. We have also used the Object Modeling Technique in conjunction with an object–oriented programming language.

The benefits of taking an object–oriented approach stem primarily from the modularity of the resultant specifications and codes. This modularity provides for well–specified interfaces, and encapsulates the data structure and operations of the objects that make up a system. As a result, the objects become potentially reusable code modules. Each object is responsible for its own actions; side-effects are not invisibly strewn throughout the system.

An object model is a model diagram, method descriptions, and a glossary of class definitions. We refer to an object model diagram constructed using our Object Modeling Technique as an OMT diagram. This paper discusses the major concepts and representation of object classes, attributes, methods, and relationships, and outlines a modeling procedure.

Object Classes

An *object class* describes a set of things (physical or abstract) that have the same behavior and characteristics. Every object class has a name, a set of attributes, and a set of methods. The attributes of an object class are also known as its fields or variables; the methods are also known as operators. Object classes are commonly referred to simply as classes, and we now begin using that term.

For example, "Chair" is the name of a class; the "chair in the corner of the room" is one object in the class Chair, the "chair in the center of the room" is another.

An *object instance* has specific values for each of the attributes defined in its object class. For example, the attribute SeatingMaterial of the class Chair may have the value "cane" for a specific chair object.

One object instance can be associated with other object instances through relationships defined for their classes. For example, a Chair object may be "next to" a Wall object, and may be "contained in" a Room object.

Note that the term "object" is often used in the literature and common discussion to refer to both an object class and to a specific object instance, the reader having to derive the distinction from context. The same confusion between "entity class," "entity" and "entity instance" plagues other data modeling techniques. Here we will consistently use the term "class" to mean object class, and "object" to mean an instance of a class.

A class is indicated in an OMT diagram by a box containing three sections, separated by horizontal lines (Fig. 1). The first section contains the class name; the second section contains a list of the class attributes; the third section contains a list of the class methods. The attribute and method sections can be omitted during early development or if it is unimportant to show them for a particular purpose.

An important characteristic of an object-based system is separation of external and internal specifications. Internals should be hidden from users so that implementation considerations do not influence the logical use of a system. For example, the developer of a graphics class Circle has to be concerned about data structures to store information about circles in a database and about algorithms to scale and move circles. But a user of the class Circle need only know about the attributes and behavior of the class.

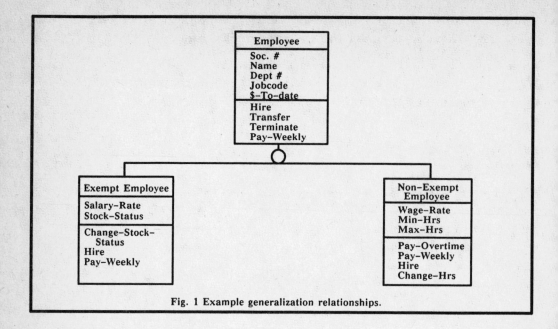

Fig. 1 Example generalization relationships.

The Object Modeling Technique is used first for defining the class' external specifications, which are visible to users of the objects, then for defining internal representations. Algorithms are specified with other techniques that show flow, timing, and so forth. Successive refinement of the data definition and structure can drive all the way to code.

Attributes

A class has a set of attribute specifications. Every attribute has a name and an optional type and annotation. A class cannot have more than one attribute with the same name. An attribute is indicated in an OMT diagram by listing its name in the second section of the appropriate class box.

The attribute name is followed by a type, which is the name of the class that determines the valid set of values for the attribute. The type can be of any class, including a user-defined class. The familiar types include character, integer, float, double, short, and so forth, e.g., Color:character, X:float, BirthDate:date. The type is optional in an object model reflecting a conceptual design. However, it must be specified when the model is used to reflect a detailed design.

Methods

A class has a set of methods, each with a name and behavior. A class cannot have two methods with the same name. A method is indicated in an OMT diagram by listing the name of the method in the third section of the class box.

A method's external effects are its behavior. The method's behavior is described in text that accompanies the OMT diagram. This behavioral description specifies the method's input and output parameters, effects on the attributes of the classes involved, the names of other methods to be invoked by this method, and the sequence of their invocation.

For example, consider the class Array, with its method Append. Append's behavior can be specified as follows:

Append (Array, Object) -> Array
> *Inputs are an Array and another object.*
> *Increments the Size of the Array by 1.*
> *Copies the object into the Array.*

The algorithm for the method is not detailed in the conceptual object model, but rather would appear elsewhere in the internals specification.

Another example is the method NewVersion in the class Design:

NewVersion (Design, Time, Date) -> NewDesign
> *Inputs are a Design object, the current Time and Date.*
> *Increments the Design's VersionNumber by 1;*
> *records Time and Date in the VersionTime and*
> *VersionDate attributes respectively.*
> *Makes this Design object the current Design.*

The algorithm for versioning is not detailed in the conceptual object model. Forward differences, backward differences, or complete copies may be saved, but this is internal detail that is hidden from the user and is not external to the class.

Methods to simply set, retrieve, or change attribute values typically are not shown in a conceptual object model, but are assumed.

Relationships: General Classification

A relationship is a logical association between classes. Our Object Modeling Technique requires that relationships be between two classes. A relationship is shown in an OMT diagram by a line connecting the pair of classes. Each relationship is defined by a pair of class names and a relationship type.

There are three types of relationships, each of which has its own distinct semantics: generalization, aggregation, and association. It is in this area of relationships that our Object Modeling Technique differs most from the conventional object–oriented paradigm of Smalltalk80 [1], which directly supports only the relationship notions of generalization. We need to represent aggregation and association, especially in developing CAD systems. Others (e.g. [2,3]) include some of these notions in their object–oriented languages, but without sufficient details of semantics or representation.

A notion that pertains to several types of relationships is cardinality, which indicates the number of objects of one class that are related to objects of the other class. The cardinality of a class in a relationship is shown in an OMT diagram by an annotation on the line at the point where it meets a class box. Although the Object Modeling Technique supports more precise specification, in practice the most important distinction is between a case of finite cardinality, usually {0,1} or {1}, and one of infinite cardinality, usually {0+}. These cases are so common that they are denoted by special shapes on the relationship line: {0,1} is a small open circle, {1} is a simple line, and {0+} is a small solid circle.

Generalization Relationships

Generalization is used to show families of similar objects. Generalizations are also called "a kind of" or "is a" or "category" or "specialization" relationships. The notion of generalization appears in the database world in semantic data models [e.g., 4,5], but is not well supported by commercial database management systems [6]. By contrast, generalization is the primary type of relationship that is supported directly by object–oriented programming languages such as C++ [7], Objective–C [8], and Smalltalk80 [1].

In a generalization, one class has the role of \fIsuperclass\fP and the other has the role of *subclass*. The subclass is a specific case of the superclass. For example, the superclass Student could have subclass GraduateStudent. It might also have a specialization with subclass UndergraduateStudent.

Subclasses are shown in an OMT diagram as connected to the superclass by a line ending in a large circle, on top of a line which sprouts one line for each of its subclasses (Fig. 1). A generalization can be read:
> *<subclass> is a kind of <superclass>.*
> *<superclass> can be a <subclass1> or a <subclass2> ...*
For example, in Fig. 1,
> *ExemptEmployee is a kind of Employee.*
> *NonExemptEmployee is a kind of Employee.*
> *Employee can be an ExemptEmployee or a NonExemptEmployee.*

If all the pertinent subclasses of the superclass are not shown, then a "floating" sprout is drawn (Fig. 2). A Student can be a GraduateStudent or an UndergraduateStudent or neither. UnclassifiedStudent is not shown as a class because it has neither its own attributes nor methods in this example.

The attributes, methods and relationships of the superclass are inherited by its subclass through the generalization. That is, whatever semantics apply to the superclass automatically apply to the subclass as well. For example, in Fig. 1, each ExemptEmployee has attributes SalaryRate, StockStatus, and those inherited from Employee: Soc#, Name, Dept#, JobCode, and $toDate. Its methods are ChangeStockStatus, Hire, PayWeekly, and two inherited from Employee: Transfer and Terminate. Inheritance leads to reusability of superclass attribute, method and relationship specifications and implementations.

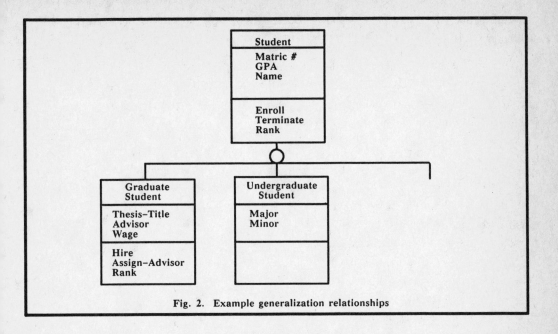

Fig. 2. Example generalization relationships

The search for a subclass' attribute or method proceeds from the subclass "up to" its superclass. When the desired name is found, the value or method there is used. For example, the JobCode value for a particular NonExemptEmployee object would be implicitly found in its superclass Employee object. Inheritance can proceed up any number of levels of generalization.

A subclass can specialize the actions of an inherited method by including the name of that method in the subclass definition.   Two forms of method specialization are *override* and *augmentation*. With override, the subclass' method is found first and executed instead of the superclass' method. With augmentation, the subclass' method is found and executed first, then the same-named method in the superclass is executed. The distinction between override and augmentation is specified in the behavioral descriptions of the methods.

Aggregation Relationships

Aggregations are also called "a part of" relationships, and are used to show groupings of objects. They appear in the database world in a restricted way as bill-of-material structures, which are conveniently represented by network data models, and are less obvious in hierarchic and relational databases.   Aggregation is ignored by the popular object-oriented programming languages, e.g., [1,7,8].

In an aggregation, one class has the role of assembly and the other has the role of *component*. Each assembly instance is composed of a set of component instances. For example, the assembly Car could have a component Door. Car might also have an aggregation with component class Hood.

The number of objects of the component class that are allowable for an assembly object may be any valid cardinality, depending on the real world being modeled. For example, the aggregation between assembly Car and component Door has cardinality 1-to-many; the aggregation between assembly Car and component Hood is 1-to-1.

Aggregations are shown in an OMT diagram by a line, terminated at the assembly class box by an arrow and at the component class box by the appropriate cardinality annotation. Several examples are shown in Fig. 3. An aggregation can be read:

> *<component> is part of <assembly>.*

Going from the assembly to the components:

> *<assembly> contains <cardinality1> <component1>*
> *and <cardinality2> <component2> ...*

For example in Fig. 3, the relationships are:

> *Door is part of Car.*
> *Hood is part of Car.*
> *Car contains many Doors and a Hood.*
> *Bicycle contains two Wheels and a Frame.*
> *Shipment contains many Cars and many Trucks.*

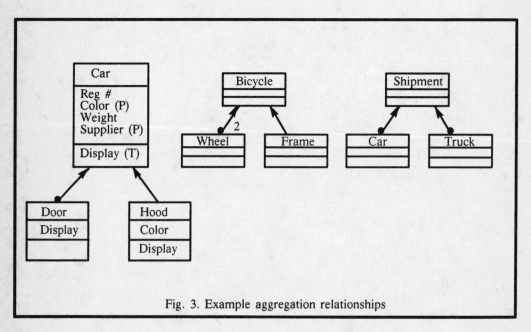

Fig. 3. Example aggregation relationships

The attribute values of an assembly class can be selectively propagated to each of its component classes. In contrast to inheritance, which applies to all the attributes of the superclass, propagation is done on an attribute by attribute basis. There are two kinds of attributes: transitive and intransitive. Transitive attributes (e.g., Color, Material, Supplier) apply to the entire assembly and all its components. Intransitive attributes (e.g., Weight, Cost, Length, Strength) apply only to the assembly as a whole.

An attribute to be propagated to component classes is shown on an OMT diagram by appending (P) to the attribute name in the assembly class. The search for a component object's attribute value ends in the component object if the desired attribute is found with a non-null value, or proceeds "up" any number of levels of aggregation, stopping when the target (P)-annotated attribute is found with a non-null value. For example (Fig. 3), the Supplier value propagates to both Door and Hood. Neither Reg# nor Weight is marked for propagation. Color always propagates to Door, but propagates to Hood only if the value for Color in Hood is null.

The methods of a component class can be triggered selectively by invoking the methods of its assembly class. A triggering method is shown on an OMT diagram by appending (T) to the method name in the assembly. The triggering method iterates over the members of the assembly, invoking the same-named methods in its component objects, according to a specified sequence. For example, invoking the Display(T) method of the assembly Car object invokes the Display method of each of its component objects.

Association Relationships

Associations are user-defined relationships. The relationship has a specific, user-defined role relative to each of the associated classes. For example, in an association between Person and Car, the relationship could have the role Owner relative to Person and the role Asset relative to Car.

Associations appear in the database world as inter-record relationships (i.e., set types in CODASYL databases, parent-child relationships in hierarchic databases, and foreign-key relationships in relational databases [6]). By contrast, associations are not directly supported by the popular object-oriented programming languages (e.g., [1,7,8]).

An association is shown in an OMT diagram by a solid line connecting two class boxes. The role of the association relative to a class is named on the line near the class box (Fig. 4). Appropriate cardinality annotations or symbols are affixed to the ends of the line. An association can be read:

> *<role1> of <class1> is <cardinality1> <class2>.*

For example, in Fig. 4, the associations are:

> *Responsibility of Employee is many Projects.*
> *Manager of Project is one Employee.*
> *Input of Machine is many Materials.*
> *Output of Machine is many Materials.*
> *Consumer of Material is a Machine.*
> *Producer of Material is a Machine.*

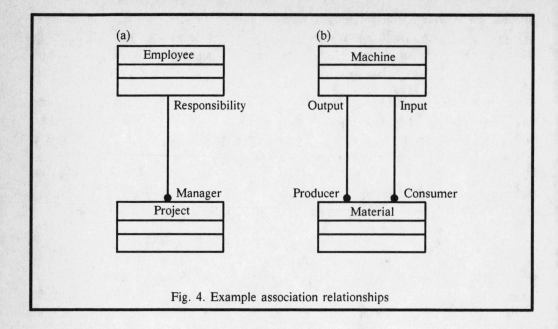

Fig. 4. Example association relationships

There is direct interchangeability between associations and attributes. This allows programming languages, that do not support associations directly, to support them indirectly. For example,Project in Fig. 4a could be implemented as a class with attribute Manager, whose type is the Employee class. The Employee class could have an attribute Responsibility, whose type is a set of keys for the Project class. Similarly, Machine in Fig. 4b could be implemented as a class with attributes Input and Output, each with its type the Material class. The Material class could have attributes Consumer and Producer, each with its type a set of Machine objects.

The role name of an association defaults to the pertinent class name if a role name is not specified explicitly. When default role names are used, an association may be given a verb name to help explain its meaning. For example, the association between Person and Car could be given the verb name "owns / is owned by". The relationship would be read:

> *Person owns Car; Car is owned by Person.*

Qualified Relationships

Qualified relationships are special cases of associations, in which an object selection mechanism is added.

In Fig. 5a there is a 1–to–many association between classes Company and Person, with the role of Emp relative to Company. Fig. 5b further specifies this association. The small box appended to Company's class box contains Emp#. The combination of a Company object and an Emp# value uniquely identifies a Person object. The qualifier, Emp#, is relative to the Company class;

in itself it is not necessarily a unique identifier in the sense of a primary key in a relational database.

The class Person may have different identifiers in the context of various usages. For example, Fig. 5b adds to Fig. 5a a qualified relationship to further specify the Airline – Person association. The combination of an Airline object and a FrequentFlyer# identifies a Person object.

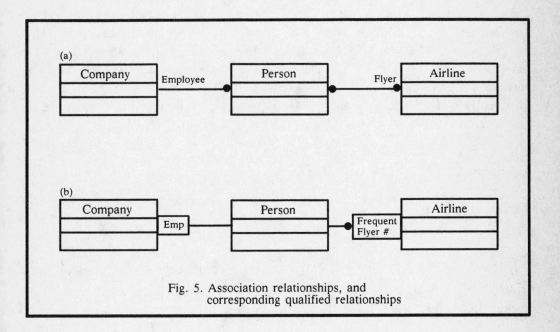

Fig. 5. Association relationships, and
corresponding qualified relationships

Modeling Procedure

The fundamental steps to using the Object Modeling Technique to prepare a conceptual design include the following:

1. Talk to experts in the subject area to be modeled and write a statement of the scope of the effort.
2. Create an initial list of classes, whose names are commonly the nouns in a description of the area being modeled. Write a definition for each class.
3. Find the relationships between the classes and begin using the OMT notation. Typically relationships are most easily found in the following order: associations, generalizations, aggregations, qualified relationships.
4. Annotate the aggregations and associations with their correct cardinalities. These often change later when the problem is better analyzed.
5. Review the model with additional subject–area experts.
6. List the methods for each class.

7. Trace the path in the model needed to evaluate each method. If paths or classes are missing, add them. If a path is ambiguous, add information to make it unambiguous.

8. List the attributes of each class.

9. Collapse relationships where possible.

10. Review the model with additional subject–area experts.

There is a great deal of feedback and iteration among these steps, especially steps 3 through 9. The process of identifying methods may cause the modeler to introduce additional generalizations, or the process of identifying attributes may cause the modeler to combine classes. The increased level of semantic knowledge captured at each step may cause a modification of the structure already developed. Each iteration of model development makes the specification increasingly explicit. The hard parts are performing the correct abstractions to simplify things.

References

[1] Goldberg, A. and D. Robson. Smalltalk–80: The Language and its Implementation, (Addison–Wesley, 1983).

[2] Atwood, T.M. "An Object Oriented DBMS for Design Support Applications," CompInt 85 Computer Aided Technologies, IEEE, Montreal, (Sept. 8–12, 1985), pp. 299–307.

[3] Woelk, D., W. Kim and W. Luther. "An object–oriented approach to multimedia databases," Proc. SIGMOD '86, ACM, 1986, pp. 311–325.

[4] Smith, J. and D.C.P. Smith. "Database abstractions: aggregation and generalization," ACM Transactions on Database Systems, Vol. 2, No. 2., 1977, pp. 103–133.

[5] Elmasri, R.A., J. Weeldreyer, and A. Hevner. "The category concept: An extension to the entity–relationship model," in Data & Knowledge–Engineering, (North–Holland, 1985), pp. 75–116.

[6] Loomis, M.E.S. The Database Book, (New York NY: Macmillan Publ. Co., 1987).

[7] Stroustrup, B. The C++ Programming Language, (Reading MA: Addison–Wesley Publ. Co., 1986).

[8] Cox, B.J. Object Oriented Programming: An Evolutionary Approach, (Reading MA: Addison–Wesley Publ. Co., 1986).

A Modeller's Workbench: Experiments in Object-Oriented Simulation Programming

Dr. *Wolfgang Kreutzer;* Computer Science Dptm. University Of Canterbury, New Zealand

UUCP: {watmath, mcvax, munnari} ! cantuar ! wolfgang

Abstract:

The research reported in this paper is part of an ongoing effort to explore potential benefits of using new software technologies for various classes of system simulation. Queueing network scenarios have been chosen as the first area of application. Our experiences in the use of two object-oriented simulators are described, using a simple example.

Pose is a Scheme based queueing network simulator. It demonstrates the suitability of symbolic languages and exploratory programming for system simulation. Some characteristics of window-based and graphical programming environments are then briefly discussed, with reference to a Smalltalk-based simulation tool.

The final chapter suggests that object-oriented simulation languages embedded in interactive modelling environments hosted on powerful workstations may well offer major breakthroughs in terms of user acceptance. The bandwidth of user/tool interfaces should be as wide as possible, drawing on modern techniques for graphical interaction and multi-process systems supporting the 'desktop' metaphor. Use of Smalltalk permits quick and easy exploration of design alternatives through rapid prototyping. Embedding such tools in Scheme preserves their functionality while making them more accessible to a wider community. Computational efficiency, while a lesser concern to 'modelling for insight', remains unsatisfactory in simulation for quantitative predictions. This problem may hopefully be overcome through future advances in software and hardware technologies.

1. Tools & Techniques of Simulation Programming

The term **"simulation"** is used for a wide variety of methods for computational animation of a descriptive model. Any exploration of states and patterns of behaviour under a chosen experimental frame is a simulation experiment in this sense.

A "good" **model** is always the simplest one which may still be justified. Analytical models are extremely useful as long as questions are simple and models can be properly validated. There are, however, a great number of more complex situations for which simulation is the only applicable method of analysis. Often no other techniques exist to explore strongly interconnected and irregular systems. Also, direct experimentation with a real system may not be possible; i.e. it may be non-existent, unobtainable, too dangerous or costly.

One of the most important motivations of model building is rooted in a desire to predict a system's likely response, so that appropriate actions can be taken to fulfill a given objective. Depending on the required degree of accuracy this leads to the use of models; either to aid in selection between a range of a priori alternatives, or as vehicles for thought experiments. In the first case there is an emphasis on generating sufficiently precise quantitative information. This is the classical style of modelling, as use, for instance, in operations research. Its successful application is critically dependent on acceptable model validations and skillful variation of policy parameters. This will always remain an expensive tool, because each simulation run yields only a single point on a model's response surface and, if stochastic components are involved, has to be replicated a large number of times to establish statistical credibility. "Modelling for insight" as an alternative approach, strives less for numerical solutions, but for an improved understanding of complex systems. It supports a more exploratory, speculative style of model analysis and may reap the full benefits of new technological developments. Under this approach relatively little need to be known about a system. A well defined problem may not even exist. We are using modelling at a proto-theoretical stage, striving for a better intuition about a system's behaviour, essential aspects, sensitivities ... which we may gain in the process.

AI-miniworlds are simulations in this sense. Many people believe that such a computational exploration of symbol structures will soon overshadow the traditional use of simulation as an aid to decision making.

One important facet of the simulation method is the fact that it is an experimental technique, comprising aspects of model calibration and data collection as well as experimental designs and output analysis. This is often considered the "scientific" aspect of simulation methodology. Statistical methods can answer questions on how to start and stop simulation runs, and how to analyze their results ([Fishman 1978], [Bratley et. al. 1983]). A complementary aspect of computer-aided simulation revolves around the activities of model and program design, implementation and verification. At the center of this is the art of **simulation programming**. In this area a number of prototypical modelling frameworks have evolved over a period of almost fourty years (see **figure 1**), with a multitude of tools to support them [Kreutzer 1986].

The programming tools discussed in this paper are restricted to queueing network scenarios, although we believe that basic principles and conclusions hold true for other kinds of modelling activity. **Queueing network scenarios** model systems of capacity-constrained resources and the effects of different allocation and scheduling strategies on performance measures such as utilization, throughputs, and time delays. This class of models has a long history, including job shop simulations and, more recently, computer system performance analysis. Basic data types perceived in this domain include resources and transactions (often called machines and materials), data collection devices and distributions. Entities for process

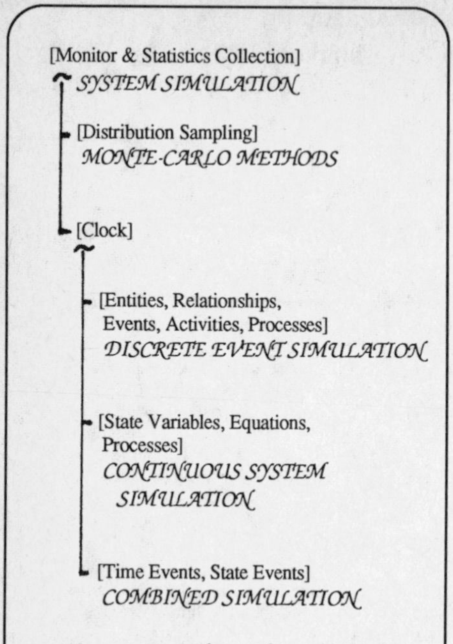

[Monitor & Statistics Collection]
SYSTEM SIMULATION

[Distribution Sampling]
MONTE-CARLO METHODS

[Clock]

[Entities, Relationships,
Events, Activities, Processes]
DISCRETE EVENT SIMULATION

[State Variables, Equations,
Processes]
*CONTINUOUS SYSTEM
SIMULATION*

[Time Events, State Events]
COMBINED SIMULATION

Figure 1: Four Classes of System Simulation

synchronization (i.e. queues) are also required. A great number of different programming languages have been developed to support their design and implementation. Traditionally a distinction is drawn between event, activity and process oriented world views, with the merits of process orientation becoming almost universally accepted.

Tools and notations are not independent of the model building methodologies by which they are employed; one serves to shape the perception of the other. Simulation programming's main concern has always focussed on structuring complexity. The better of theses tools strive for control of complexity through conceptual closure and "familiarity" to the task domain, in order to reduce the conceptual distance between perceptions of "relevant" parts of a system and their implementation in a program. *GPSS* and *DEMOS* are two of the most popular languages for modelling queueing network scenarios. Well designed scenario languages can graft concepts and terminology of specific application areas onto effective and user-friendly modelling frameworks, although it should be stressed that any specialized tool can also be misapplied.

GPSS (General Purpose System Simulator) [Bobillier et. al. 1976] is a good example. It is a very convenient tool for representation of material-oriented queueing networks; i.e. models in which material objects ("transactions") are the only "active" class of entities, from whose perspective all changes of state are defined. It does, however, lack the flexibility to cope with other, more complicated scenarios.

Demos (Discrete Event Modelling on Simula) [Birtwistle 1979] is a much more flexible simulator, embedded in a general purpose programming language (Simula), extending iit through specialized data types and operations carrying

the main concepts of queueing network scenarios. Demos offers distribution sampling, automatic statistics collection and report generation, a process-oriented framework for modelling system dynamics and predefined templates for different classes of entities (i.e. queues and resources). When prefixed accordingly (**Demos** BEGIN ... END;) any Simula programs can use these features, which may also be modified if the need arises. Demos encourages the use of **life cycle diagrams** [Hutchinson 1975] as a graphical structuring device.

2. "The Garden Party" - a Simple Queueing Model

Suppose that we are interested in the likely degree of contention expected during a Queen's garden party. Relevant objects may therefore include a number of loyal royal subjects wishing to shake a royal hand and, of course, a Queen providing this service.

Figure 2 shows a life cycle description of a simple model of such an event. Flows between states and activities define life cycles for classes of entities. This scenario depicts an "open" (i.e.loyal subjects are temporary entities, entering through a "source" and leaving through a "sink") and material-oriented approach (i.e. temporary entites (loyal subjects) are active in seeking the Queen's favours, while she (passively !) only allows her hand to be grabbed and released). Let us further assume that the Queen's handshake be uniform with a duration of 0.5 to 1.5 minutes, while royalist's arrivals are negative exponentially distributed at a rate of 0.5 per minute. Once they have been shaken, 70 % of all subjects leave immediately, while 30% long to repeat the experience. The only relevant statistics is a tally of "time spent in garden" across all royal subjects.

Program 1 shows a corresponding Demos model, in which 3 classes of objects are defined. In the program body these are instantiated with appropriate values and bound to previously declared identifiers. A *Source* called *ArrivalProcess* is used to generate a steady stream of subjects, sampling their interarrival-time from the relevant distribution. Royal subjects themselves are created as images of the *RoyalSubject* process class definition, defining all actions of the life cycle shown in figure 2. Their last statement activates *Sink* object *ThatsAllItTook*, which performs appropriate updates on flowtime statistics. These are gathered throughy a *Tally*, a device for collecting non-weighted information about time series. *Hold* statements model the passage of model time, with *Schedule* commands used to activate or reactivate concurrent object (class instances).

Measures of queue length and server utilization are part of a standard report, shown in **figure 3** for a simulation of 100 time units (minutes). From this we deduce that we can expect a typical subject to spend about 1.5 minutes in the garden.

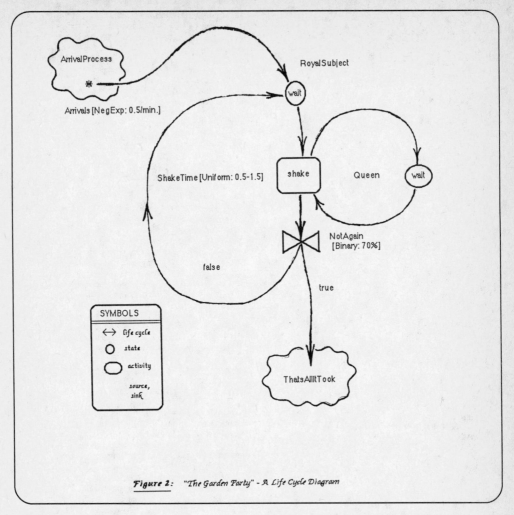

Figure 2: "The Garden Party" - A Life Cycle Diagram

3. Two Experiments in Object-Oriented System Simulation.

In the author's opinion, process oriented scenarios embedded in some flexible general purpose base language currently offer the most useful modelling tools within the framework of traditional programming methodology. Large sectors of different simulation communities have now finally accepted process orientation as the most convenient modelling world view. The benefits of closure and strong modularization, as offered by abstract data types or Simula's class concept, still have to gain sufficiently strong footholds, although the resultant ease of mapping all relevant structural and behavioural aspects of real world objects into conceptual entities can hardly be disputed.

The main drawbacks of a tool like Demos lie in the fact that it is rooted in traditional programming methodology and therefore only ill suited to more interactive and exploratory styles of systems analysis. The belief that one should always start from precise specifications, using formal deduction to arrive at a working program has long dominated "main stream" computer science. From this viewpoint programming is similar to theorem proving; "*program development and proof should go hand in hand*". The merits of this approach are convincingly demonstrated in [Wulf et. al. 1984], and Dijkstra, Hoare and Gries are some of its most vocal proponents. It works well for problems whose properties are well understood and for which rigorous specifications can be derived prior to the coding stage. In keeping with mathematical tradition it is predominantly concerned with justifying the correctness of implementations and gives little guidance to the process of discovery. "Traditional" methodology advises us to avoid applications with ill defined specifications, thereby excluding many "interesting" problems from our range. We should first gain a sufficiently precise understanding of a system before we may try to program it. But how can such understanding be obtained ? Traditional methodology is silent on this issue.

This framework has proven too restrictive for many modelling applications, which are experimental and exploratory in nature. System identification, problem specification, model implementation, verification and

```
BEGIN

EXTERNAL CLASS demos;

demos BEGIN
 REF (Source) ArrivalProcess;
 REF (Res   ) Queen;
 REF (Sink  ) ThatsAllItTook;
 REF (Rdist ) ShakeTime;
 REF (Bdist ) NotAgain;

Entity CLASS Source;
BEGIN
 REF (Rdist ) Arrivals;
 Arrivals :- NEW NegExp ("Arrivals",0.5);
 WHILE TRUE DO
 BEGIN
 NEW RoyalSubject("Hilda"). Schedule (Now );
 Hold (Arrivals.Sample );
 END while;
END;

Entity CLASS RoyalSubject;
BEGIN
 BOOLEAN hooked;
 REAL   timeOfEntry;
 hooked   := TRUE;
 timeOfEntry := Time ;
 WHILE hooked DO
 BEGIN
 Queen.Acquire (1);
 Hold (ShakeTime.Sample );
 Queen.Release (1);
 hooked := NOT (NotAgain.Sample );
 END while;
 ThatsAllItTook.quitter :- THIS RoyalSubject;
 ThatsAllItTook.Schedule (Now );
END;

Entity CLASS Sink;
BEGIN
 REF (Tally      ) flowTime;
 REF (RoyalSubject) quitter ;
 flowTime :- NEW Tally ("ItTook");
 WHILE TRUE DO
 BEGIN
 flowTime.Update (Time - quitter.timeOfEntry);
 Cancel ;
 END while;
END;

COMMENT: Body of MAIN program;

OutF :- NEW OUTFILE ("GardenParty.out");
OutF .OPEN (BLANKS (80));

Queen        :- NEW Res     ("Queen",1);
ShakeTime    :- NEW Uniform ("Shakes",0.5,1.0);
NotAgain     :- NEW Draw    ("NotAgain",0.7);
ArrivalProcess :- NEW Source ("Source");
ThatsAllItTook :- NEW Sink   ("Sink");
ArrivalProcess.SCHEDULE (NOW);

Hold (100); COMMENT: Simulate for 100 time units!;

END of Demos context;
END;
```

Program 1:   _Garden party in DEMOS_

validation are closely intertwined. Initially, precise specifications are unknown. Simulation model building must therefore be an inductive, not a deductive process. It is more closely related to experimentation than to theorem proving. A different programming methodology, which views computers as tools for heuristic exploration of complex symbol systems, is therefore required. It must be possible to quickly build, test and modify prototypes and gain an improved understanding in the process. Since control of program complexity has become one of the main hurdles for many modelling applications, we need good tools to utilize the computer's potential to reduce a programmer's memory load by freeing her from any essentially "mechanical" chores. It must always be possible to change our minds without undue penalty in intellectual complexity. Recent advances in hardware technology have made machine efficiencies comparatively less relevant. The programmer needs all the help she can get; never mind the expense.

These convictions have prompted us to explore the potential of using exploratory programming tools and environments for system simulation, focussing on queueing network scenarios as a first paradigmatic class of applications {see [Astroem/Kreutzer 1986] for a parallel approach to control systems analysis}. Software tools to support this style of man/computer interaction have been built and refined by the Artificial Intelligence community since the early sixties. They are typically hosted in sophisticated interactive programming environments and emphasize ease of representation and manipulation of dynamic symbol structures. Intelligent browsers, editors, interpreters, compilers, debuggers, optimizers, tools for program instrumentation and project management aid in the manipulation of textual and graphical information. Multiple concurrent processes and some variant of the "desktop" metaphorare usually also supported.

There are various reasons why **exploratory programming** and its associated software tools are now attracting wider attention. Firstly, the advent of sufficiently powerful, self-contained workstations makes truly interactive programming styles possible and tempers much of the traditional concerns with machine efficiencies. Secondly, many of the "easy" computer applications have already been implemented. Since ambition always seems to expand to tax the limit of current technology there is a need for better support of the programming process itself, to enable us to cope with higher levels of complexity in a more reliable fashion.

Although user communities, methodologies and terminology have traditionally been almost completely independent from one another, many programming aspects of artificial intelligence and simulation model building are closely related. This is particularly obvious in some "rediscoveries"; i.e. the similarity between the activity scanning approach and production system interpreters. The importation of sophisticated tools and programming environments to the field of system simulation, grafted on an object oriented approach to program development, seems a particularly promising way to lighten the programmer's burden to remain in control of complex models' evolution.

The "_Modeller's workbench_" project at the University of Canterbury seeks to pursue this objective. In a number of experiments we will study the benefits of using

```
                        CLOCK TIME = 100.00

                ************************************
                *                                  *
                *              REPORT               *
                *                                  *
                ************************************


                          DISTRIBUTIONS
                          *************

        TITLE    /  (RE)SET /  OBS  / TYPE   / A    / B    /   SEED
        Shakes      0.000       76    UNIFORM  0.500  1.000    33427485
        Notagain    0.000       75    DRAW     0.700           22276755
        Arrivals    0.000       56    NEGEXP   0.500           46487980


                            TALLIES
                            *******

        TITLE    /  (RE)SET /  OBS  / AVERAGE /EST.ST.DV/ MINIMUM / MAXIMUM
        ItTook      1.295       53     1.507    0.926      0.500     4.561


                           RESOURCES
                           *********


        TITLE    /  (RE)SET /  OBS  /LIM/MIN/NOW/ %USAGE /AV.WAIT/ QMAX
        Queen       0.000       75    1   0   0   55.296   0.343    3
```

Figure 3: The Garden Party - Results

symbolic, interactive programming languages embedded in multi-window, reactive programming environments for various paradigms of system simulation [Kreutzer 1986]. A second phase will then apply these experiences to tools and techniques for model design by visual interaction, and aid in their analysis through animated symbolic scenarios.

This approach is predicated on the assumptions that object oriented programming and exploratory programming styles offer extremely appropriate metaphors for system simulation. The first achieves a close correspondence between model and reality as well as potential increases in model reliability through strong localization of information. Property inheritance, furthermore, allows the cognitive economy of "differential" system description; specifying new objects by enumerating how they differ from those which are already known. The second belief hinges on a desire to shorten the cycle of definition, testing, exploration, validation and modification of prototype models. This permits us to gain sufficiently "deep" understanding of representations and experiments appropriate for "relevant" aspects of some problem situation. The following two prototype systems were built to gather empirical evidence for this theory.

Pose [Stairmand 1987] is an object oriented queueing network simulator built on top of Scheme [Abelson et. al. 1985]; a member of the Lisp family. In the author's opinion **Scheme** is a small and compact, but also an extremely expressive and elegant language. This elegance stems from a small core of simple, orthogonal and very flexible features. Scheme supports lexical scoping, explicit declaration of all objects, closures with persistent local variables, and makes it easy to experiment with new control structures. Lambda expressions are "first class objects", which means that they can be assigned, passed or returned as parameters. Using these features, object orientation, message passing, property inheritance and coroutines can quickly be grafted onto the language kernel.

Scheme is an interactive language, supporting an exploratory programming style. Structure editors and sophisticated debugging tools are often provided as part of the programming environments in which it is embedded. Structure editors can go a long way to remove the drawbacks of its sparse syntax.They ease program design and debugging, in spite of Lisp's proverbial jungle of parentheses.

A stylistically good Scheme program should be built in levels, as demonstrated by Allen (1978) and Abelson et. al. (1985). This methodology draws on sound engineering principles and can equally easily be used to structure the process of model identification, definition and implementation. By encapsulating and localizing information as tightly as possible, object orientation carries this idea one step further. After identifying relevant levels, all primitives of a given level (objects and operations; state variables and transformations; entities and actions) should be defined. These are then implemented through functions to construct instances, select components, modify representations, evaluate predicates and display objects.

Pose provides features for modelling queueing network scenarios which are very similar to those of Demos. Chez Scheme [Dybvig 1986] is used as a base. Although this is transparent to a naive user of the system, it is built on top of a flavours package implemented with a Smalltalk-like class system to support object oriented programming. **Program 2** shows our garden party example.

(*DefMonitor* **GardenParty**)

(*Define-Process* **RoyalSubject**
  ((hooked #!TRUE)) GardenParty
  (WHILE hooked
      (Queen '*Acquire* 1)
      (*Self* '*Hold* (ShakeTime '*Sample*))
      (Queen '*Release* 1)
      (WHEN (NotAgain '*Sample*)
          (SET! hooked #!FALSE)))
  (ThatsAllItTook '*Swallow*))

(*DefBinary* **NotAgain**   0.7 12345)
(*DefNegExp* **Arrivals**   0.5 67891)
(*DefUniform* **ShakeTime** 0.5 1.5 23457)

(*DefRes* **Queen**   1 GardenParty)
(*DefSink* **ThatsAllItTook** GardenParty)
(*DefSource* **ArrivalProcess**
  RoyalSubject Arrivals '#!TRUE GardenParty)

; simulate this scenario for 100 time units
(GardenParty 'DURATION 100)

Program 2: *Garden Party in POSE*

The concepts of Monitor, Entity and Process form the top of a hierarchy of object classes. Distributions, Sources, Resources, Bins, WaitQs, CondQs and Sinks are currently implemented as subclasses. Statistics collection and reporting is automatic, although special data collection objects (i.e. Tally, Accumulate, Histogram) may easily be implemented.
Monitor objects are used to control simulation experiments. Normally there is only one monitor, responsible for model execution. This is, however, not a necessary restriction. The notion of simulation monitors is a recursive one and multiple layers of monitors (i.e. for controlling experiments across a number (or instatiations) of models, models containing models as subcomponents, ...) can also be accomodated. Among other relevant information each monitor owns a counter (sampler or clock), an agenda of scheduled tasks, a list of lists of model entities of various classes, and a reference to the currently active process. Instances are created by the *DefMonitor* macro. They may then respond to a number of predefined messages.
  Distributions use a multiplicative congruential simulator [Knuth 1969] to obtain samples from a 0 to 1 uniform random number distribution , with appropriate transformations to other distributions delegated to subclasses. All of these respond to appropriate *Sample* messages. **Uniform**, **NegExp**, **Normal** and **Binary** distributions are currently implemented as subclasses. Note that distributions are conceived as global objects and are independent of any specific monitor.
  Res is a subclass of **entity**, modelling capacity-constrained resources. Its instances respond to *acquire*, *release* and *report* messages. **Bins**, **WaitQs** and **CondQs** are also patterned after the corresponding Demos concepts. **Sinks** will report flowtime statistics of processes. For this purpose each process is automatically time-stamped at the time it is created by a source and should be swallowed by a sink just before it leaves the model.
  Processes contain basic mechanisms (implemented via the Scheme function "*call/cc* ") for detaching, resuming and scheduling. They respond to *monitor*, *startTime*, *timeStamp!*, *hold* and *schedule* messages. *hold* is predominantly used by a process to delay its own progress (i.e. self 'hold 10), while *schedule* is used to influence other processes' evolution. A monitor is responsible for coordinating execution of all processes it is associatd with. **Sources** are a special subclass of processes. They have a predefined body of actions, which causes them to generate a new process of the appropriate type in intervals sampled from the associated distribution, until a simulation terminates or its attached condition evaluates to false.

Pose is still in an experimental stage. Preliminary explorations of various simple examples have shown it to be conceptually just as powerful as Demos, with important advantages regarding flexibility. The interactive environment permits a significant speedup in model development time. Execution efficiency remains a problem. While incremental definition and modification of models is fast, they are slow to execute. The reason for this lies in the multiple levels of interpretation imposed by the methodology of layered design and in the fact that Chez Scheme, while generally a remarkably fast and compact implementation, can currently not compete with good optimising compilers for "classical" programming languages. Currently this certainly impedes the use of Pose for quantitative decision making. Future advances in implementation techniques and hardware technology will hopefully make this a less relevant concern. As a first step towards this goal, an "intelligent" back-end compiler could be employed to automatically transform a model into a fast executable representation once its design has stabilized.

Our second experiment has focussed on the synergistic benefits of using object oriented programming styles in a more sophisticated modelling environment.
We should be free to specify, design, implement and experiment with a model, alternating between different activities at will and, if convenient, leaving processes in some intermediate stage of execution. This is typical for the style most people use when working at their desks. Several tasks may be relevant to particular projects and may need to be interleaved if the creative process is not to be inhibited. Modelling environments predicated on this idea may improve both productivity and quality of the model building process by an order of magnitude.

The *Smalltalk* system [Goldberg & Robson 1983] seemed the most appropriate vehicle to testthe suitability of this metaphor for system simulation. There are two aspects to Smalltalk, its programming paradigm and its programming environment. Smalltalk's programming paradigm centers on the concepts of classes, inheritance hierarchies and message passing, while its programming environment features a multi-process implementation of the "desktop metaphor" with windows, mouse-driven user interaction and browsers. It has sometimes been claimed that the merits of Smalltalk's programming paradigm and programming environment are two orthogonal and largely unrelated issues. Our experiences do not confirm this conjecture. It rather seems that the full benefits of object oriented systems can only be obtained in an appropriate environment containing source code inspection, debugging, analysis and project management tools. The reasons for this may be found in the fact that object oriented programming systems are large, with many predefined objects available for reuse and modification. It may be claimed that its typical programming style shifts emphasis from creation of new to skillful modification of existing pieces of code. Object oriented programs also tend to contain many small method definitions. Appropriate tools for navigation, inspection and modification of information are therefore vital; even more so than in conventional programming projects. Such tools must be tightly integrated into the editing and execution process. Smalltalk's concepts of browsers, debuggers and inspectors cater for these requirements.

We have used the simulator described in chapter 3 of the "blue book" [Goldberg & Robson 1983] as our initial point of departure. This system has been implemented in **PS-Smalltalk** on a Sun-3 workstation and augmented with various data collection devices [Irwin 1986]. In its current form it comes again very close to the Demos system, containing a multitude of classes of probability distributions, a simulation monitor, consumable and non-consumable resources, process synchronization and statistics collection entities.

Simulation subclass: #MeetTheQueen
instanceVariableNames: **'arrivals thatsAllitTook'**
classVariableNames: "
poolDictionaries: "
category: *'Simulation Applications'*

MeetTheQueen methodsFor: 'initialization'

defineArrivalSchedule
  self *scheduleArrivalOf:* RoyalSubject
    accordingTo: arrivals.
  self *schedule:* [self *finishUp*] at: 100

defineResources
  self *produce:* 1 *of:* 'Queen'

initialize
  super *initialize*.
  arrivals ← **Exponential** *named:* 'Arrivals'
    mean: 0.5.
  thatsAllitTook ← **Tally** *named:* 'ItTook'

MeetTheQueen methodsFor: 'recording'

recordExperience: aNumber
  thatsAllitTook *update:* aNumber

MeetTheQueen methodsFor: 'reporting '

printStatisticsOn: aStream
  (self *provideResourceFor:* 'Queen')
    printStatisticsOn: aStream.
  thatsAllItTook *printStatisticsOn:* aStream

SimulationObject subclass #RoyalSubject

instanceVariableNames: **'birthTime'**
classVariableNames: "
poolDictionaries: "
category: *'Simulation Applications'*

RoyalSubject methodsFor: 'accessing'

timeStamp: aTimeValue
  birthTime ← aTimeValue

birthTime
  ↑ birthTime

flowTime
  ↑ (**Simulation** *active now*) - self birthTime

RoyalSubject methodsFor: 'simulation control'

tasks
  |shake notAgain hooked myQueen|
  self timeStamp: *now* .
  shake ← **Uniform** *named:* 'Shake' *min:* 0.5
                max: 1.5.
  notAgain ← **Binomial** *named:* 'NotAgain'
                prob: 0.7.
  hooked ← 'True'.
  hooked whileTrue:
    [myQueen ← self *acquire:* 1 *ofResource:* 'Queen'.
    self *holdFor:* shake *next* .
    self *release:* myQueen.
    hooked ← (notAgain *next*) not].
  (**Simulation** *active*) recordExperience: flowTime

Program 3: Garden Party in SMALLTALK

Program 3 shows the Smalltalk implementation of our garden party. A monitor called *GardenParty* is created as a subclass of *Simulation*, with object arrivals and resources defined by *initialize*, *defineArrivalSchedule* and *defineResources* methods. Since we choose a material oriented approach, active processes of class *RoyalSubject* drive the simulation; implemented as subclasses of *SimulationObject*. **Figure 4** shows a typical Smalltalk screen.

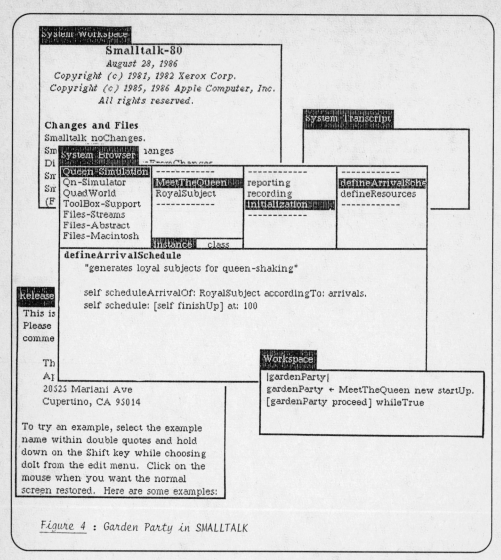

Figure 4 : *Garden Party in SMALLTALK*

It is very difficult to convey any taste of programming in Smalltalk without reference to practical experience. Browsing, construction, modification, execution and debugging of classes and methods is a highly interactive process with frequent switches among contexts. Smalltalk offers an extremely powerful environment for system developoment, but it must be stressed that it is predominantly a tool for the professional programmer.

4. Future Research & Developments

Self-contained **workstations with integrated system development environments** will make a large impact on the shape of programming in the 90s. Exploratory prototyping of complex systems, an acceptance of the inevitability of change in system specifications, and a shift in emphasis from writing new to modifying existing programs will further increase the attraction of late binding, object orientation and powerful program management tools for browsing, design, testing, modification, instrumentation and optimization of code.

Interactive programming environments for simulation have received relatively little attention in the past. Nelson (1979) showed how such a capability can be built into a simulation language (Simula) and greatly enhances its quality. The recent shift in price-performance ratios for personal workstations makes such tools conceptually attractive and economically viable. First steps in this direction have already been taken. **Stella** [Richmond 1985] offers interactive construction and analysis of graphical System Dynamics scenarios on the Apple MacIntosh. **SimLab** is a Simscript implementation in a relatively simple interactive environment for the IBM PC. Goldberg and Robson (1979) report on an experiment linking queueing network simulation and graphical animation in Smalltalk. [Birtwistle 1984]. [Sheppard 1984], [Birtwistle 1984], [Vaucher 1984], [Birtwistel et al. 1982, 1984], [Unger et al. 1984], [Birtwistle & Luker 1984], [Sol 1984] and [Stanridge et al. 1984] argue convincingly for the merits of augmenting computer-based **simulation laboratories** with graphical animation. Such simulation workstations should integrate collections of general purpose and simulation specific tools, accessed through a uniform and friendly interface. In implementing such systems, methodologies and tools will be needed from the field of Artificial Intelligence. Some research in this area promises interesting results; see, for example, [SCS 1985], [Birtwistle 1985], [Lavery 1985], [O'Keefe 1985, 1986], and [Kerkhoffs & Vansteenkiste 1986].

Any notation has its particular strengths and weaknesses. None of them is equally well suited to all purposes. **Object orientation** seems a particularly appropriate metaphor for simulation model building. It has many advantages over traditional methodologies, particularly for the representation of complex systems; but most importantly it results in a change of perception. The key concepts of object-oriented programming systems are the notions of closure, message passing, concept inheritance and the idea of programming as simulation of some miniworld. The economy of differential system description and a close correspondence of formal representation and real life manifestation of segments of reality enhances our understanding and communication with application experts.
There is empirical evidence for this within the Simula community. Strongly modular object encapsulation also encourages more reliable and modifyable programs.
Negative attributes of object-oriented knowledge representations are rooted mainly in their resource requirements. The idea of message passing as the sole means of communication typically results in long chains of indirect references and many transient data structures, particularly in the case of frequently interacting objects.

Our experience with the **Pose** system has caused us to believe that object orientation is indeed an appropriate style for simulation programming. This corresponds well with experiences gained in writing Artificial Intelligence applications. Since managing complexity is at the heart of both simulation and AI programming, we should not be surprised by a convergence of concerns; even though this may be well hidden by different traditions and terminologies.

The question of **what language** would be most appropriate to host simulation laboratories is difficult to answer, since there are now a number of programming systems which claim to support both object oriented and exploratory programming. The cost of subscribing to new programming paradigms is not insignificant. New concepts and programming idioms must be learned and machine efficiencies may drop considerably. The overall advantages in shortening development cycles, increased program reliability and ease of change, however, should easily outweigh this investment.
Flexible and powerful programming environments are well established in the Lisp family of languages. It is very likely that Lisp will remain the most important language for symbolic programming for quite some time, although Prolog continues to rise in popularity as a tool for education and prototyping. This trend may accelerate as more intelligent compilers become available and hardware efficiencies become relatively less important (i.e. by exploiting parallelism). Smalltalk will probably remain primarily in the research domain, but the merits of its pioneering combination of an object oriented approach with window based

programming environments are already well established. Evidence for this trend is clearly visible in many modern expert system development tools.

Good modelling environments must offer high resolution graphics and provide meaningful and extensible symbol sets. There should be some pointing device, such as a mouse, for feature selection. It should also be possible to view different processes in different stages of execution (i.e. a graphical model specification, a view of the model's state, various statistical measures, ...). The mouse may be used to select and activate processes, with more detailed control provided by menu selection. Options may include starting a simulation, resetting it to a previous state, editing models, tracing an object's states, obtaining cross references, performing statistical analyses, ...
If we ignore speed of execution as a main criterion, **Smalltalk** would be an almost ideal environment to host simulation workbenches. Our project views it as a tool for rapid prototyping in order to experiment with appropriate modelling interfaces for a number of simulation styles (i.e. queueing networks, system dynamics, monte carlo simulations, ...). This will hopefully be particularly productive during stage 2, where graphical scenarios are involved. It seems currently still unrealistic to assume availability of such systems on a large scale. The use of **Scheme** is a reasonable compromise for making some of the workbenches available on more widely accessible systems. One of our next projects will therefore, for instance, graft a simple menu-based environment onto Pose implemented on an Apple MacIntosh.

Pose will also serve as a stepping stone to explore the application of **expert systems** as intelligent advisors during different phases of the simulation modelling cycle.
There will be a gradual **convergence** or at least an interchange of experiences (tools and methods) between **artificial intelligence** and **simulation programming**, caused by a common concern with the intellectual complexity of the systems we must cope with. The technique of object orientation originated in simulation programming (Simula) and has been exported to and popularized in AI (Smalltalk, actor languages, Expert Systems). Modern expert system development tools (i.e. KEE, KnowledgeCraft, ART) already provide some simulation capability. There is also a trend towards integration of model based reasoning in knowledge based systems.
It may be hoped that the field of system simulation will now, in return, reap the benefits of a more mature technology grafted onto user friendly environments which cater for interactive and experimental styles of model design and exploration.

4. References

Abelson,H./ Sussman,J./ Sussman,J.
Structure and Interpretation of Computer Programs
Cambridge, MA 1985

Allen, J.R. *Anatomy of Lisp* New York 1978

Astroem, K.J./ Kreutzer, W.
System Representation Proceedings of
"3rd Symposium on Computer Aided Control System Design" IEEE 1986

Birtwistle, G.M. *Discrete Event Modelling on SIMULA* London / Basingstoke 1979

Birtwistle, G.M. *Future Directions in Simulation Software* in: [SCS 1984] 120,121

Birtwistle, G.M. (ed.)
Proceedings of 'AI, Graphics & Simulation' SCS 1985

Birtwistle,G./Liblong,B./Unger,B./ Witten, I. *Simulation Environments*
Proceedings of *"Simulation: a Research Focus"* Rutgers University 1982

Birtwistle,G./Lomov,G./Unger,B./ Luker, P. *Process Style Packages for Discrete Event Modelling: Data Structures and Packages in SIMULA*
Transactions of the SCS 1(1), 61-82

Birtwistle, G./ Luker, P.
Dialogs for Simulation in: [SCS 1984], 90 - 97

Bobillier,P.A./Kahan,P.C./ Probst, A.R. *Simulation with GPSS and GPSS V*
Englewood Cliffs 1976

Bratley,P./Fox,D.C./ Schrage,L.E.
A Guide to Simulation Heidelberg/New York 1983

Carnegie Group Inc. *Knowledge Craft - Overview*
Pittsburgh 1986

Dybvig,K./Smith,B.
Chez Scheme Reference Manual Bloomington,Indiana,
Cadence Inc. 1985

Fishman,G.S. *Principles of Discrete Event Simulation*
London / New York / Sydney 1978

Goldberg,A. *SMALLTALK-80 - The Interactive Programming Environment* Reading, MA 1984

Goldberg,A./ Robson,D.
A Metaphor for User Interface Desig Proceedings of *12th Hawaii International Conference on System Sciences* 1979; 148 - 157

Goldberg,A./ Robson,D.
SMALLTALK-80 - The Language and its Implementation
Reading, MA 1983

Hutchinson,G.K. *Introduction to the Use of Activity Cycles as a Basis for Systems Decomposition and Simulation*
SIMULETTER 7(1) 1975, 15 - 23

Irvin, W. *A Smalltalk Queueing Network Simulator*
Honours Project, Dptm. of Computer Science, University of Canterbury 1986

IntelliCorp *The Knowledge Engineering Environment*
Menlo Park 1984

Kerkhoffs,E.J.H./Vansteenkiste,G.
The Impact of Advanced Information Processing on Simulation - An Illustrative Review SIMULATION 46(1) 1986, 17 - 26

Kreutzer,W. *System Simulation - Programming Styles and Languages* Sydney/Wokingham/Reading 1986

Lavery,R.G. (ed.) *Modelling and Simulation on Microcomputers* SCS 1985

Nelson,S.S. *CONSIM: A Study of Control Issues in Conversational Simulation*
The Computer Journal 22(2) 1979, 119-126

O'Keefe,R.M. *Expert Systems and Operational Research - Mutual Benefits* Journal Opl.Res.Society 36(2) 1985, 125-129

O'Keefe,R.M. *Simulation and Expert Systems - A Taxonomy and some Examples*
SIMULATION 46(1) 1986, 10-16

Richmond,B. *A Users' Guide to Stella*
High Performance Systems Inc, Lyme, N.H. 1985

SCS (Simulation Council Inc.)
Proceedings of an SCS Conference on Simulation with Strongly Typed Languages La Jolla 1984

SCS (Simulation Council Inc.)
Proceedings of an SCS Conference on Artificial Intelligence and Simulation San Diego 1985

Sheppard,S.S. *Simulation Workstations of the Future - Panel Discussion* in: [SCS 1984], 119

Sol,H. *A SIMULA Problem Solving Environment*
in: [SCS 1984], 99 - 104

Stairmand,M. *Expert Advice for Queueing Network Simulations* MSc thesis - Dptm. of Computer Science, University of Canterbury 1987

Stanridge,C.R./Pritsker,A.A.B./ O'Reilly,J. *Integrated Simualtion Support Systems. Concepts and Examples* Proceedings of the 1984 Ann. Simulation Symp.IEEE 1984, 141-151
Unger,B./Birtwistle,G./Cleary,J./ Hill,D./Lomov,G./Neale,R./ Peterson,M./ Witten,I./Wyvill, B. *JADE: a Simulation and Software Prototyping Environment*
in: [SCS 1984], 77-83

Vaucher,J. *Future Directions in Simulation Software - Panel Discussion* in: [SCS 1984], 122

Wulf,W.A./Shaw,M./Hilfinger,P.N./ Flon,L. *Fundamental Structures of Computer Science*
Reading 1981

Behavioral Simulation Based on Knowledge Objects

Takeo Maruichi, Tetsuya Uchiki, and Mario Tokoro
Department of Electrical Engineering
Keio University
3-14-1 Hiyoshi, Yokohama 223
JAPAN
+81 44 63 1926
maruichi%keio.junet@japan.cs.net
mario%keio.junet@japan.cs.net

Abstract

The purpose of behavioral simulation is to simulate the behavior of the characters having behavior rules in the surrounding environment. This kind of simulation, which differs from the traditional simulation based on a statistical model of the world, provides us with a more precise simulation with regard to individuals. Because of the nature of behavioral simulation, characters, the environment in which the characters exist, and messages which are passed among characters, are the main elements that should be considered. The notion of object-orientation is one of the most attractive computational models for providing the basis of behavioral simulation. Specifically, we employ the notion of knowledge objects which are objects having knowledge contained within themselves. We first establish a behavioral simulation model based on the notion of knowledge objects, then design and implement a behavioral simulation system PARADISE. To demonstrate the capability and effectiveness of this simulation model, *barracuda and herring school* is used as an example of this simulation system.

1 Introduction

Most simulations have traditionally been based on statistic or mathematic models about the world. However, the real world is actually made up of individuals. Therefore, if we need to simulate the world in a more precise way, simulation cannot be based on the statistics of a group's behavior, but on the rules of an individual's behavior. The goal of this research is to establish a method to build a simulated world based on the rules of the behavior of individuals. In this paper, we choose an animal's behavioral simulation as an example.

In behavioral simulation, the behavior of characters, having their behavioral rules, are simulated taking into account the surrounding environment. One good example of behavioral simulation is found in simulated motion animation such as the *barracuda and herring school* model [Partridge 1982] [Reynolds 1985], which is illustrated in Fig.1. Such kind of simulation is effective not only for animation without scripts, but also a wide variety of simulations for education and experiments, including robotic behavior, traffic control, cognition, and psychological behavior.

In order to realize behavioral simulation, we have to consider the model of a behavioral character. The notion of a knowledge object [Tokoro 1984] [Ishikawa 1987] is an attractive computational model to represent a character in behavioral simulation. A knowledge object is a concurrent object consisting of local variables, methods, and knowledge (or a set of rules). It is possible to represent a character, which decides its action based on its local state and knowledge, using the knowledge object. In order to realize behavioral simulation more exactly, the following issues should be discussed in addition:

- Representation of behavioral rules for the character

  Each character has not only actions, but also their behavior rules, which are knowledge concerning its local state and environment. A means for easily representing behavioral rules for a character must be defined.

- A simple execution mechanism for a behavioral simulation

  Basic components including a character in a simulated world should be defined in a single unified way. A simple computational model is also important.

- A programming and debugging environment for behavioral simulation

  In behavioral simulation, each character simultaneously sends/receives information (messages) to/from the environment and changes its state. A visual programming and debugging environment for such concurrent characters is inevitable.

In this paper, we investigate behavioral simulation and discuss components of a simulated world, then describe the implementation of a behavioral simulation system PARADISE. A programming example is also described.

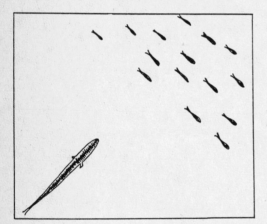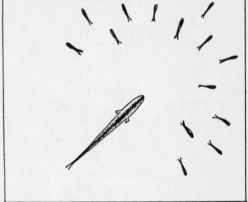

Fig.1 Barracuda and herring school

2 A Behavioral Simulation Model

In behavioral simulation, characters behave in the simulated world. We first noticed that each character is influenced by the surrounding environment. For instance, if it rains, a character's behavior differs from that in fine weather. Also, a character is a part of the environment for another character. In addition, a character might communicate with other characters. This information exchange among characters is achieved in terms of a message. In behavioral simulation, such a message is sometimes influenced by the environment. Smell is a good example. Smell actually moves with the wind. Therefore, for one character, all the other characters and messages are a part of the environment. In order to realize such a simulation world, characters, messages, and the environment are defined as follows:

2.1 Character Model

For example, a human being collects information by means of sight, sound, or smell from the environment through his sense organs, then decides its next action and behaves. A character such as a human being is an abstract model of an active entity to be simulated. This character basically behaves like a process, and collects messages voluntarily.

According to the above discussions, a character has the following functions:

1. Internal Status

   The character has its local status. This is defined by the instance variables of an object.

2. Sensor

   The sensor is similar to the eyes or ears of an animal. Each character receives information (messages) through its sensors. A sensor has its accessible area, or scope, and can receive information (messages) existing in that area of the environment.

3. Behavioral Rules

   Behavioral rules define the behavioral pattern of the character taking into account the conditions of both the character's local status and information (messages) from the environment. These rules would properly be represented by production-rules.

4. Behavioral Methods

   After defining the behavioral pattern of the character, its behavioral methods are executed, and the state of the character is changed. These methods are normally treated as local procedures.

2.2 Message Model

Many kinds of messages are used for communication in the real world, such as sight, sound, or smell. Such a message can move and change its state. Thus, a message in our simulation model is different from that in object-oriented languages. It is more natural to represent a message as an object.

A Message has the following functions:

1. Transmissive Area

   A message has its transmissive area. For example, loud sounds are transmitted far way while a quiet sound is not. This area is related to a sensor's accessible area described above.

2. Life Span

   Messages such as sounds exist only for a moment, but message such as a smell do not disappear immediately. Therefore each message has its own life span.

3. Action

   Some messages change their state. For example, a message such as a smell moves with the wind. To represent a change in state, a message has information about its location, velocity, direction, etc.

2.3 Environment Model

The environment is the world or field where characters exist. The environment contains and manages the characters and the messages. It has the following functions:

1. Management of Space

   The environment manages the distance between characters and messages. Concretely, this distance is between the accessible area of a character's sensor and the transmissive area of a message.

2. Management of Time

   All characters and messages are executed within a certain unit of time in order to maintain consistency. The environment manages synchronization among all such characters as processes. Therefore, it can be considered to have a role as the process scheduler.

3. Graphic Output

The environment has a window to show the animation (or sequence of frames) produced by simulation. The area shown in the environment can be changed.

3 A Behavioral Simulation System : PARADISE

3.1 Simulation Mechanism

As mentioned above, each character is an active object which voluntarily searches for messages to take in from the environment. This mechanism for selecting messages is called **message searching**. Therefore, each character communicates with one other indirectly by sending and receiving messages to/from the environment. The behavioral simulation model proposed by us is illustrated in Fig.2.

A character accepts only messages, and the environment manages messages. During simulation, PARADISE's scheduler manages to calculate all the characters' behavior within one simulation unit of time, and then updates the state of the environment for the execution within the next time unit. This is repeatedly performed. The synchronization among concurrent objects is automatically performed by the PARADISE scheduler.

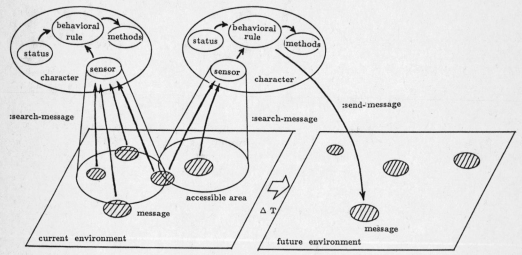

Fig.2 A behavioral simulation model

3.2 Message Management and Message Detection

The environment consists of two parts, the current message pool and future message pool. During the execution of a time unit, each character searches for messages from the current message pool and places messages into a future message pool. The procedures for accessing these two message pools are provided by the environment and sensors of a character. After all characters have finished their execution in the time unit, the environment collects all messages in the future and current message pools. The environment possesses a lifetime counter for each message and puts those into the current message pool. If its lifetime counter expires, the environment removes the message.

The sensor of a character selects messages in the environment depending on the specified ability of the sensor and the property of the messages. Though various situations for message detection can be considered, in the current implementation, only messages within the accessible area of the sensor are provided, which are shown in Fig.3.

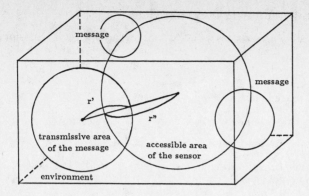

Fig.3 Message detection

3.3 Implementation

The behavioral simulation system PARADISE is implemented using PANDORA [Maruichi 1987]. PANDORA is an experimental multiparadigm programming language/environment based on object-orientation and programmed in KCL (Kyoto Common Lisp) [Yuasa 1985] running on a VAX-11 and a Sony NEWS workstation. PANDORA uses LOOPS' syntax [Bobrow 1983] and has a production system class, which is an extended OPS5 [Forgy 1981], and a process class for concurrent execution.

Characters, messages, and the environment are all designed as classes. The character class has two superclasses, one includes the production-system class and the other includes the process class. Because each character has its own production-system and executes like a process, PARADISE can be said to be a distributed production-system. Users can define their characters and messages by defining subclasses of the character and message classes, respectively.

4 Programming

The behavioral simulation of the *barracuda and herring school* model is used to exemplify how we write programs for behavioral simulation. The characters, which represent barracudas and herrings, are assumed to recognize other characters by sight messages. Therefore only sight messages are passed to/from the environment, and two kinds of characters exist in the environment.

4.1 Definition of Characters

The barracuda and herring classes are defined as characters. An example definition for herrings is shown in Fig.4. The environment, the sensor, and other variables are declared in this definition. The *environment* is an object named **sea** which is an instance of class **environment**, and has a scheduler and message pools. The **sensor** is a class name. When an instance of herring class is created, an instance of sensor class is also created. The variables, *position*, *direction*, and *velocity* represent the state of a herring. The variable *status* will be described in the next section. In this example, several instances of the herring class form a school and some instances of barracuda attack a school of herrings.

Each such instance is treated as a process and supervised by the PARADISE scheduler.

4.2 Behavioral Rules and Behavioral Methods

Both the barracuda and herring classes need their knowledge, or a set of behavior rules, to decide actions based on their internal status and messages collected from the environment. Such a set of rules of a character usually contains many rules, and thus programming becomes complex.

To avoid this complexity, rules should be categorized by the situation of the character. For instance, a herring has the following three situations:

1. A herring is normally swimming forward when there is nothing around it.

2. A herring schools with other herrings when there is no barracuda near it.

3. A herring escapes from any barracudas when any are near it. In this case, a herring ignores other herrings because of panic.

These three conditions are named **alone**, **schooling**, and **escaping**, respectively, as shown in the state transition diagram in Fig.5. Each arrow between states is equivalent to a production rule. Each circle, which indicates a situation is equivalent to a behavioral method. Each arrow is then translated by a programmer into a production rule, shown in Fig.6.

Collected messages and a character's status are stored in the working memory of the character, and behavior rules are invoked. After behavioral rules are selected and executed, behavioral methods are invoked by message passing on the right hand side of each production rule. Behavioral methods which appeared in Fig.6 are described in Fig.7.

Then, the characters change their screened information, send new messages to the environment, and a new frame for motion animation is created.

However, in the case of more complex behavioral simulation, such as a simulation of strategies in vollyball game, it is not easy to make the state transition diagram. The effort is similar to building expert systems. This is done by understanding the actions of characters and is deeply related to behavioral psychology.

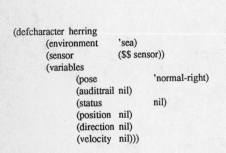

```
(defcharacter herring
        (environment    'sea)
        (sensor         ($$ sensor))
        (variables
            (pose       'normal-right)
            (audittrail nil)
            (status     nil)
            (position nil)
            (direction nil)
            (velocity nil)))
```

Fig.4   The definition of a character

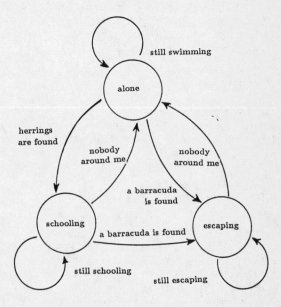

Fig.5   State transition of a herring

```
(start-production-rules herring
   (class-in-working-memory
        herring figure-message msg-list))

(p alone-swimming
        (herring ^status alone)
        (msg-list ^number-of-messages 0)
   -->
        (<- self :swimming) (halt))

(p alone-with-barracuda
        (herring ^status alone)
        (figure-message ^type barracuda)
        (msg-list ^number-of-messages <> 0)
   -->
        (<- self :@status 'escape)
        (<- self :escaping
             (<- (@wm 3) :get-character 'barracuda))
        (halt))

                    .
                    .
                    .

(p escape-still-barracuda
        (herring ^status escape)
        (figure-message ^type barracuda)
        (msg-list ^number-of-messages <> 0)
   -->
        (<- self :escaping
             (<- (@wm 3) :get-character 'barracuda))
        (halt))

(p escape-to-alone
        (herring ^status escape)
      - (figure-message ^type barracuda)
   -->
        (<- self :@status 'alone)
        (<- self :swimming) (halt))

(end-production-rules herring)
```

Fig.6 Behavioral rules of a herring

```
(defmethod swimming ((self herring))
   (prog (x y z)
        (multiple-value-setq (x y z) (<- (@ position) :get))
        (<- (@ position) :put
             (+ x (round (* (@ velocity) (cos-table (@ direction)))))
             (- y (round (* (@ velocity) (sin-table (@ direction)))))
             z)
        (multiple-value-setq (x y z) (<- (@ position) :get))
        (<- (@ sensor) :put x y z)
        (return self)))

                    .
                    .
                    .

(defmethod escaping ((self herring) barracuda)
   (prog (x y z x1 y1 z1 message r)
        (setq message (car barracuda))
        (multiple-value-setq (x y z) (<- (@ position) :get))
        (multiple-value-setq (x1 y1 z1)
                    (<- (@ (@ message sender) position) :get))
        (setq r
             (round (natural (- (* 180 (/ (atan (- y y1) (- x1 x)) pi)) 180))))
        (setf (@ direction)

             (round (natural
                    (if (and (> r (- (@ direction) 10))
                             (< r (+ (@ direction) 10)))
                    (then
                      (if (< r (@ direction))
                          (+ (@ direction) 70)
                          (- (@ direction) 70)))
                      (+ r (if (< r (@ direction)) 30 -30))))))
        (<- self :swimming)
        (return self)))
```

Fig.7 Behavioral methods of a herring

```
(defmessage        figure-message
        (direction        0)
        (type             nil))
```

Fig.8 The definition of a message

4.3 Message Passing and Message Searching

A character collects messages through its sensor(s) from the environment. All the messages are kept in the environment. For instance, the figure of the barracuda is defined as a message as shown in Fig.8. This message contains its lifetime, location and direction of the character, the effective area in which the message is transmitted, and the character who sends this message.

The environment selects messages which a sensor of a character needs and returns those message to the sensor. A character has the following methods:

- (<- self :search-message) for searching the messages from the environment by its sensor(s).

- (<- self :send-message a-message) for sending a message to the environment.

4.4 Programming Environment

The *barracuda and herring school* behavioral simulation program is executed as shown in Fig.9. In this picture, one barracuda and several herrings swim in the sea. There are two windows which show the messages in the current and future pool of the environment. Additionally, there are some buttons named **event**, **sensor**, **message**, **environment**, etc to monitor the characters, messages and environment. In this case, the sensor button is pressed, and the accessible areas of the sensors are displayed as circles.

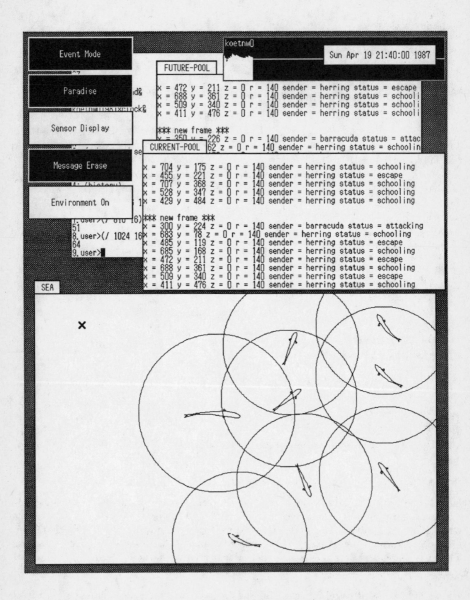

Fig.9   Simulated behavior of a school of herrings attached by a barracuda

5 Discussion

An object in Smalltalk-80 [Goldberg 1983] is an integrated entity composed of a data structure and methods. When an object receives a message, the object invokes a method associated with the message. This object model is considered to be a passive object model, because an object cannot be active unless it receives a message.

Rehearsal [Gould 1984] is a visual programming environment implemented in Smalltalk-80. An educator who is not a programmer can develop educational software using performers on a stage in a metaphor called theater. A performer (object) is a process which is active while it receives a cue (message). Process switching is done in an event-driven order. In Rehearsal, programming is making a script using a mouse and objects which appear on the screen as performers.

Director [Kahn 1978] and ASAS [Reynolds 1982] use the actor model [Hewitt 1977]. An actor is an asynchronous, concurrent entity and is considered to be a passive object model. However, the object model used in Director and ASAS can be called an active object model. Because an actor is invoked in every time unit, while it keeps messages from other actors on the stack in FIFO order. This is different from an actor which cannot receive any messages unless other actors send messages. Let us call this object model a dependent active object model. The purpose of ASAS is computer animation. ASAS has rich 3D graphical functions with which to operate an actor in a 3D world. Everything needed to make a movie such as camera, audio, light, are represented by actors. Programming is considered to be writing an operation sequence in a formal script. ASAS interpreter interprets scripts and sends messages to actors. Each actor behaves under the control of the scripts.

In PARADISE, the characters have behavioral patterns as its knowledge. Such a character can be considered to be another active object model. The character is also controlled in time-slice order. A character object does not receive any messages directly, but voluntarily searches and collects messages. Thus, message passing is indirect, using the environment. Lets us call this object model an independent active object model. The mechanism by which a character object voluntarily searches for messages is similar to that in which a process selects information from a black board in [Hayes-Roth 1979]. In Director and PARADISE, there are no scripts. Programming is representing an object's behavioral pattern as its knowledge.

The most interesting point of PARADISE, compared with the other systems, is that a message in PARADISE is an object, so that it is not related to a message selector. A method to be executed is decided by the matched behavioral rule according to the message objects and current state. The comparison of the object model, script, scheduling, instruction for communication, and the purposes of Rehearsal, ASAS, and PARADISE are shown in Table 1.

Table 1: Comparison of Rehearsal, ASAS, and PARADISE

	kind of object	script	scheduling	instructions for communication	purpose
performer in Rehearsal	passive object	YES	event-driven	direct send	education, visual programming
actor in ASAS	dependent active object	YES	time-slice	direct send, direct send all	computer animation
character in PARADISE	independent active object	NO	time-slice	indirect send, search	behavioral simulation, experiment

6   Conclusion

We have proposed a behavioral simulation model and implemented a behavioral simulation system called PARADISE. Some applications are running and being implemented, such as traffic simulations, a car driver's psychological simulations, and panic evacuation simulations.

The authors would like to express their sincere gratitude to Mr. Michio Isoda of Keio University for his reliable advice. The authors are also grateful to Mr. Hirohisa Ishino and Mr. Junichi Nagahama for implementing the animation display part of the PARADISE system.

References

[Partridge 1982] Partridge, B., *The Structure and Function of Fish Schools*, Scientific American 246(6), 1982.

[Reynolds 1985] Reynolds, C., *Description and Control of Time and Dynamics in Computer Animation*, notes for the SIGGRAPH'85, Symbolics Graphics Division, 1985.

[Tokoro 1984] Tokoro, M. and Ishikawa, Y., *An object-oriented approach to knowledge systems*, Proc of Int'l Conf. on Fifth Generation Computer Systems, ICOT, 1984.

[Ishikawa 1987] Ishikawa, Y., and Tokoro, M., *Orient84/K : An Object-Oriented Concurrent Programming Language for Knowledge Systems*, in Object Oriented Concurrent Programming, A.Yonezawa and M.Tokoro, eds, MIT Press, 1987.

[Maruichi 1987] Maruichi, T. and Tokoro, M., *PANDORA : A Multiparadigm Programming Language/Environment (in Japanese)*, Department of Electrical Engineering, Keio University, 1987.

[Yuasa 1985] Yuasa, T. and Hagiya, M., *Kyoto Common Lisp Report*, Research Institute for Mathematical Sciences, Kyoto University, 1985.

[Bobrow 1983] Bobrow, D., and Stefik, M., *The LOOPS Manual*, Xerox Palo Alto Research Center, KB-VLSI-81-13, 1983.

[Forgy 1981] Forgy, C., *OPS5 User's Manual*, CMU-CS-81-135, Carnegie Mellon University, 1981.

[Goldberg 1983] Goldberg, A. and Robson, D., *Smalltalk-80 - The language and its implementation*, Addison-Wesley, 1983.

[Gould 1984] Gould, L. and Finzer, W., *Programming by Rehearsal*, Xerox Palo Alto Research Center, SCL-84-1, 1984.

[Kahn 1978] Kahn, K. and Hewitt, C., *Dynamic Graphics using Quasi Parallelism*, SIGGRAPH'78 Conference Proceedings, published as Computer Graphics 12(3), 1978.

[Reynolds 1982] Reynolds, C., *Computer Animation with Scripts and Actors*, SIGGRAPH'82 Conference Proceedings, published as Computer Graphics 16(3), 1982.

[Hewitt 1977] Hewitt, C., *Viewing Control Structures as Patterns of Passing Messages*, Artificial Intelligence 8, North-Holland, 1977.

[Hayes-Roth 1979] Hayes-Roth, B. and et.al, *Modeling Planning as an incremental, opportunistic process*, IJCAI'79 Conference Proceedings, 1979.

Conformance, Genericity, Inheritance and Enhancement

Chris Horn

Distributed Systems Group, Department of Computer Science,
Trinity College Dublin, IRL–Dublin 2   (horn@tcdcs.uucp)

A recent paper by Meyer compared the usefulness of Genericity and Inheritance as a basis for static type checking in object oriented systems. Conformance is also being considered by some researchers, and Meyer's paper is re-examined here using Conformance. Some problems result related to the conformance of formal and actual parameters of operations. Additional rules for conformance are introduced to overcome these problems and these lead naturally to the concept of Enhancement as a union of the techniques of Conformance, Genericity and Inheritance.

This work has been partially sponsored under the ESPRIT programme, in project 834 Comandos - Construction and Management of Distributed Office Systems.

Object-orientation is gaining acceptance as a powerful philosophy for software production. A number of researchers are currently investigating the use of static typing to improve the performance of object-oriented programming languages on conventional hardware architectures, as well as providing early notification of programming errors. In the recent OOPSLA conference, Meyer [Meyer86] informally analysed genericity and inheritance as two techniques to improve the extendibility, re-useablility and compatibility of software subsystems. In particular he noted how genericity could be simulated in a programming language offering only inheritance, but not vice-versa. Nevertheless he concluded that genericity is more elegant than inheritance when the genericity is unconstrained: that is when the actual type parameters substituted for a generic formal type parameter need not support any particular operations. Constrained genericity (in which there is such a requirement on the actual type parameters) can be implemented using inheritance and abstract superclasses.

In addition to genericity and inheritance, conformance and subtyping are being considered by some as the basis for a flexibly typed object based system: for example the Emerald project[Black87], Trellis/Owl [Schaffert86], Galileo [Albano85], as well as [Cardelli85]. Basically, conformance can allow one object (of a particular type) to be used *as if* it were another (of another type). In a system supporting inheritance, (an instance of) a subtype can always be used as if it were (an instance of) any of its supertypes. However conformance may allow a more general relationship between types than that implied by inheritance (whether multiple or single) alone. Whereas inheritance allows one type to extend or redefine the representation of another, one type may conform to another without necessarily obtaining executable code (methods) or data (instance variables) from it. Essentially, an abstract type S conforms to another type T (written $S \leq T$), if [Black86]:

1. S provides at least the operations of T (S may have more operations).
2. For each operation in T, S has the same number of arguments and results.
3. The abstract types of the results of S's operations conform to the abstract types of the results of T's operations.
4. The abstract types of the arguments of T's operations conform to the abstract types of the arguments of S's operations (ie arguments must conform in the *opposite* direction).

Then if $T_1 \leq T_2$:

a. An expression of type T_1 can be assigned to an object of type T_2
b. An actual argument of type T_1 can be assigned to a formal argument of type T_2 in an operation invocation
c. An actual result of type T_2 can be used to receive a formal result of type T_1

Conformance and subtyping are considered more precisely in [Cardelli85]. The chief potentials are the ability to partially order abstract types as well as concrete types [Albano85]; and extensibility and a uniform object model in a distributed environment, by permitting different implementations of the same abstract type [Black87].

In view of the interest in conformance, it is interesting to reconsider Meyer's OOPSLA paper, and determine how the notion of conformance can be successfully integrated with those of genericity and inheritance. In section 1 therefore, Meyer's Swap utility is considered using conformance alone. Problems occur due to the conformance rule 4 above, and in section 2, before continuing to investigate the other problems which Meyer studies, instead an abstract type having multiple implementations is considered, an application for which conformance is reputedly well suited. It consequently becomes apparent that the conformity rules as stated above may be too restrictive, and it is suggested that it is sometimes beneficial to allow one type S to conform to another type T without S necessarily implementing all of T's operations. This introduces the concept of *enhancement*, and in this case we shall say that type S can be *enhanced* to type T. In section 3, nesting of enhanced types is considered. It may sometimes be useful to obtain a new abstract type which is a limited "view" of another - having a subset of the operations - and in section 4 the concept of restriction is introduced as a suitable mechanism, together with the ability to rename operations for convenience. In section 5 Meyer's remaining problems are re-examined using enhancement. Section 6 briefly considers the implications of enhancement on data modelling. Finally in Section 7, we draw some conclusions.

A syntax reminiscent of Modula-2 and Ada is used throughout the following examples, rather than any particular existing object oriented language: the reader is free to alter the syntax where desired.

1 Meyer's swap problem

We start by considering Meyer's first problem, in which an operation is required to swap two instances of some arbitrary type T. Assume there is some type TOP to which all types conform. Using *only* conformity, a utility to swap such instances might be outlined as follows:

```
ABSTRACT TYPE Swapper IS                                      /1/
    Swap(x,y : IN OUT TOP);          (* x and y are both arguments and results *)
END Swapper;

CONCRETE TYPE SwapperImplementation IS    (* should conform to the Abstract Type *)
    Swap(x,y : IN OUT TOP) IS
        LOCAL t : TOP;
        t := x;  x := y;  y := t;
    END Swap;
END SwapperImplementation;

VAR a,b      : INTEGER;            (* Let's try swapping two integers....*)
    DoSwap   : SwapperImplementation;
    ....
    DoSwop.Swap(a,b);              (* this is actually incorrectly typed !!!!! *)
```

Here it is intended that since DoSwop expects a pair of objects conformant to TOP, DoSwop should thus be a polymorphic utility for exchanging any two arbitrarily typed objects. However although the actual arguments a and b of DoSwap.Swap(a,b) conform to the stipulated type of the formal arguments (rule b), the type of the formal results does not conform to that of the actual results (rule c). Hence DoSwop.Swap(a,b) is incorrectly typed. In fact the only objects which can be swapped using DoSwop are those of type TOP! This might have been anticipated, since it might undesireable to swap two objects of *differing* types (eg an INTEGER with a BOOLEAN) as the above example might have permitted. In effect, there is a loss of type information when receiving the DoSwop result parameters.

It would perhaps be more in the spirit of object orientation if the Swap operation were relative to the "current" object: ie that one parameter to Swap is made implicit as the current object. We might anticipate that this does not resolve the problem either:

```
ABSTRACT TYPE Swapper IS                                                    /2/
    Swap(Other : IN TOP) : TOP;                 (* Function returning a result of type TOP *)
END Swapper;

CONCRETE TYPE Swappable IS
    Me : TOP;
    Swap(Other : IN TOP) : TOP IS
        LOCAL t : TOP;
        t := Me;  Me := Other;  RETURN t;       (* Result returned by function is t *)
    END Swap;
END Swappable;

VAR a,b     : Swappable;
    x       : INTEGER;
    ...
    b := a.Swap(b);                             (* Type checks OK - but not very useful *)
    x := a.Swap(x);                             (* Typing error for function result ! *)
```

Instances of type Swappable can indeed be swapped - but that is the only operation they support! More interesting is to try and swap, for example, INTEGERs: however although INTEGER conforms to type TOP, it does not conform to type Swappable - hence we cannot use Swap on INTEGERs.

A concrete type SwappableInteger might be envisaged instead, which would provide a Swap operation for INTEGERs. However if this type had additional operations for INTEGERs - eg a "+" operation - then it would not conform to the abstract type Swappable due to conformance rule 4 above. In any case, it would defeat our original intention to have one implementation of Swap for all types! Meyer notes a similar problem in his paper when using inheritance alone, and introduces his technique of *declaration by association* as a solution.

The conclusion is that genericity, as Meyer advocates, is the most elegant solution to the Swap problem. Although here we have considered just conformance alone (as a possible alternative to genericity), the Emerald and Trellis/Owl projects which do use conformance, are both also including support for genericity.

2 The Sequence

Before considering Meyer's remaining problems, in view of the difficulties encountered above with the Swap problem, let us investigate instead a problem for which conformance is reputedly well suited - that of multiple implementations of some abstract type. A sequence is chosen as a representative problem, to which items can be appended and removed at either the front or tail of the sequence, together with an operation to append two sequences. We first consider only sequences of INTEGERs, and later in section 3 extend to generic sequences:

```
ABSTRACT TYPE IntSequence IS                                                /3/
    Empty                       : BOOLEAN;
    AddFront(i : INTEGER)       : IntSequence;
    RemoveFront                 : INTEGER;
    AddLast(i : INTEGER)        : IntSequence;
    RemoveLast                  : INTEGER;
    Append(s : IntSequence)     : IntSequence;
END IntSequence;
```

Now a supposed implementation which should conform with IntSequence, and which uses an ARRAY:

```
CONCRETE TYPE IntArraySequence IS                                           /4/
    d : ARRAY[1..100] OF INTEGER;
    front,back : CARDINAL INITIALLY 0;

    Empty : BOOLEAN                         ...Implementation of Empty;
    AddFront(i : INTEGER) : IntArraySequence ...Implementation of AddFront;
    RemoveFront : INTEGER                   ...Implementation of RemoveFront;
    AddLast(i : INTEGER) : IntArraySequence ...Implementation of AddLast;
    RemoveLast : INTEGER                    ...Implementation of RemoveLast;
```

```
     MaxLengthOfSequence : INTEGER            ...Implementation of MaxLengthOfSequence
  Append(s : IntArraySequence) IS
     LOCAL i : INTEGER;
     i := s.front;
     WHILE i <> s.back
        DO back := (back+1) MOD 100;  d[back] := s.d[i];   i := (i+1) MOD 100;  END;
     s.front := s.back;                                          (* s now empty *)
     RETURN SELF;
  END Append;
END IntArraySequence;
```

For Append, it has been assumed that the representation of another instance of IntArraySequence can be accessed directly. In C++ [Stroustrup 84], this is indeed legitimate; in Smalltalk-80 it is not and one can never directly access the representation of any object other than the current object.

If IntArraySequence is to be an implementation of the abstract type IntSequence, then IntArraySequence must conform to IntSequence. This is it does if IntSequence in turn conforms to IntArraySequence (by virtue of the formal argument of Append, and conformance rule 4). Hence IntArraySequence and IntSequence must be mutually conformant. This is unfortunate since IntArraySequence may have additional operations to IntSequence - such as MaxLengthOfSequence.

To solve this paradox, let us redefine Append in IntArraySequence (/4/) to use the abstract type rather than the concrete type as the formal parameter. However then Append must be coded so that it can append any implementation of IntSequence to an instance of IntArraySequence - that is we cannot directly access the representation of the formal parameter "s" and must use operations upon it (as would be done in Smalltalk-80):

```
     Append(s : IntSequence) IS                                              /5/
        WHILE NOT s.Empty DO
           SELF.AddLast(s.RemoveFront); END;
        RETURN SELF;
     END Append;
```

IntArraySequence now conforms to IntSequence and the requirement for mutual conformance is relaxed.   Naturally now a second and alternative implementation of IntSequence could be given, which would conform to IntSequence and which would use a different representation than IntArraySequence - for example a linked list in a concrete type IntLinkedListSequence. An Append operation in either concrete type would be able to append two instances having different representations - for example a sequence implemented using a linked list could successfully be appended to a sequence using an array. Exactly the same implementation of Append would however appear in both concrete types! This would be unexpected, unusual and undesireable in the object approach, in which code is normally shared and reused as much as possible.

Our conclusion is that those operations which require formal parameters of the abstract type itself could sometimes be implemented in conjunction with the abstract type. Using a slightly different syntax:

```
     TYPE IntSequence(R AS IntBasicSequence) IS                              /6/

        <R>;                                            (* An IntSequence has as representation any
                                                           type which conforms to IntBasicSequence *)
        Append(s : R) : R IS
           WHILE NOT s.Empty
              DO SELF.AddLast(s.RemoveFront); END;
           RETURN SELF;
        END Append;
     END IntSequence;

     TYPE IntBasicSequence IS                           (* An Abstract Type *)
        Empty                    : BOOLEAN;
        AddFront(i : INTEGER)    : IntBasicSequence;
        RemoveFront              : INTEGER;
        AddLast(i : INTEGER)     : IntBasicSequence;
        RemoveLast               : INTEGER;
     END IntBasicSequence;
```

The AS clause specifies that IntSequence is an *enhancive type* - it enhances any type which is conformant with IntBasicSequence. The Append operation takes an instance of the same type as is used for the representation of SELF. An implementation of IntBasicSequence could be:

```
TYPE IntArraySequence IS                                          /7/
    d : ARRAY[1..100] OF INTEGER;
    front,back  : CARDINAL INITIALLY 0;

    Empty : BOOLEAN                    ...Implementation of Empty;
    AddFront(i : INTEGER) : IntArraySequence   ...Implementation of AddFront;
    RemoveFront : INTEGER              ...Implementation of RemoveFront;
    AddLast(i : INTEGER) : IntArraySequence    ...Implementation of AddLast;
    RemoveLast : INTEGER              ...Implementation of RemoveLast;
    MaxLengthOfSequence : INTEGER    ...Implementation of MaxLengthOfSequence;
END IntArraySequence;
```

IntArraySequence is a concrete type. Since IntArraySequence conforms to IntBasicSequence, IntArraySequence can be used as an actual type parameter for the formal type R in /6/. Naturally IntLinkedListSequence could be similarly defined.

As a result, neither of the concrete types IntArraySequence or IntLinkedListSequence need implement Append, and yet can still conform to IntSequence if they implement Empty, AddFront, RemoveFront, AddLast and RemoveLast. So a type T_1 which is to conform to another type T_2 need *cnly conform to certain* operations of T_2 and if it does, will be *enhanced* by further operations. This contrasts with the (conventional) conformance rules 1-4 given earlier.

In a sense we have provided a mechanism similar to abstract superclasses in Smalltalk-80. However the mechanism here is more powerful as a result of using conformance rather than (single) inheritance. It is possible that a given type T may conform to many different types $T_1..T_n$, and using our mechanism, gain access to additional operations in each of these types $T_1..T_n$ which T itself does not implement. Hence the mechanism is akin to inheritance from multiple abstract superclasses, rather than just one. Further, instances of superclasses cannot be created in Smalltalk-80, and finally, the precise "abstract superclasses" in the mechanism here need not be explicitly enumerated at the time the "subclass" is defined. Continuing, an example of usage would be:

```
VAR a : IntSequence;                                             /8/
    b, c : IntArraySequence;
    i : INTEGER;
    ...
    a := b;                    (* IntArraySequence does conform to IntSequence *)
    a.PutFront(i);
    a.Append(c);               (* Appends two Array sequences *)
```

(note we allow the result of a function to be ignored if desired) Here "b" as an IntArraySequence is enhanced to an IntSequence, and as a consequence gains an additional operation Append not originally defined for IntArraySequences.

Before examining instantiation of these types the four conformity rules given earlier should first be extended with rules for enhancement, and for expansion of enhancive types.

2.1 Expansion and Enhancement rules

An enhancive type T with n formal type parameters can be *expanded* as follows:

5.   If $T(t_1 \text{ AS } T_1, t_2 \text{ AS } T_2,...t_n \text{ AS } T_n)$ and if $p_i \leq T_i$ for all i:1..n then:

5.1 $T = T(T_1,T_2,...T_n)$ ie if T is unqualified it can be treated as $T(T_1,T_2,...T_n)$

5.2 $T(p_1,p_2,...p_r) = T(p_1,p_2,...p_r,T_{r+1},...T_n)$ where $r \leq n$

Secondly, the rules for enhancement:

6. If $T(t_1 \text{ AS } T_1, t_2 \text{ AS } T_2,...t_n \text{ AS } T_n)$ has representation t_i, where $1 \le i \le n$ - ie

TYPE $T(t_1 \text{ AS } T_1, t_2 \text{ AS } T_2,...t_n \text{ AS } T_n)$ IS
   <t_i>;
   .....
END T

and if $p \le T_1$, then $p \dashrightarrow T(p)$ (p can be enhanced to T(p))

Enhancement can then be used as follows:

d. **Static usage:** If $p \dashrightarrow T(p)$, then an instance of T(p) can be declared.

e. **Dynamic usage:** If $p \dashrightarrow T(p)$, then an expression of type p can be assigned to an object of type T, or passed as an actual argument in an operation invocation for a formal argument of type T, or returned as a result for an operation invocation where the actual result parameter is of type T.

f. **Temporary usage:** If $p \dashrightarrow T(p)$, then an instance x of type p can be temporarily enhanced to be of type T(p) for a single operation invocation x.T(p)~a, where a is the name of an operation in the signature of T.

g. **Protracted usage:** If $p \dashrightarrow T(p)$, then an instance x of type p can be enhanced protractedly to be of type T(p) using: WITH x AS T(p) DO ... END;

The usage of IntSequence (as defined in /6/), IntBasicSequence (/6/), IntArraySequence (/7/) and IntLinkedListSequence can now be considered. (In fact, we only consider here enhancive types having a single formal type parameter, for simplicity. Multiple formal type parameters requires further rules to resolve possible name clashes) First, assume the following declarations:

```
VAR IntSeq         : IntSequence;                                                      /9/
    IntSeqASeq     : IntSequence(IntArraySequence);
    IntASeq        : IntArraySequence;
    IntLLSeq       : IntLinkedListSequence;        (* NOT conformant with IntArraySeq *)
    i              : INTEGER;
```

(note that we also assume IntArraySequence and IntLinkedListSequence are **not** mutually conformant). As indicated in rules d to g above, there are four possible different enhancement methods. The first is *Static:* instances of an enhancive type such as IntSequence statically define their representation.   When an instance of an enhancive type is declared, actual type parameters can be supplied (for at least some of) the formal types specified in the AS clause of the enhancive type - examples are IntSeq and IntSeqASeq above. Example usage might be:

```
IntSeq.AddFront(45);                    (* 5.2, 4 and b *)            /10/
i := IntSeq.RemoveLast;                 (* 5.2, 3 and c *)
IntSeq.Append(IntLLSeq);                (* 5.2, 1-4 and b *)
IntSeqASeq.Append(IntLLSeq);            (* Type error!!! 1-4 and b *)
```

Since the declaration of IntSeq did not define an actual type parameter for its formal parameter in the AS clause, any type conformant with IntBasicSequence can be used subsequently for the parameter. However the same is not true for IntSeqASeq, and the parameter to an Append operation on it must conform to IntArraySequence.

The second method is *Dynamic:* an instance of an enhancive type may change its representation at execution time:

```
IntSeq := IntASeq;                      (* IntSeq is now represented by an array: 5.1, 1-4, 6 and e *)  /11/
IntSeq.Append(IntLLSeq);               (* 5.1, 6 and b *)
IntLLSeq := IntSeq.Append(IntLLSeq);   (* Type error!!! 5.1, 6 and c *)
IntSeq := IntLLSeq;                     (* Now change IntSeq's representation: 5.1, 1-4, 6 and e *)
IntSeq.Append(IntASeq);                (* 5.1, 6 and b *)
```

Dynamic usage may also be used for argument transmission and result reception in operation invocations.

The third method is *Temporary:* this allows a concrete type such as IntArraySequence to be enhanced for a single operation invocation:

IntASeq.IntSequence(IntArraySequence)~Append((IntLLSeq);   (* 5.2, 6, h and b *)   /12/

This is useful to allow a type to temporarily gain access to additional operations which were not originally defined for itself.

The final method is *Protracted:* a concrete type may be enhanced over several statements:

```
WITH IntASeq AS IntSequence(IntArraySequence)                    (* 5.2, 6 and i *)      /13/
    DO   ....
        IntASeq. Append(IntLLSeq);                               (* b *)
    ....
END;
```

3 The Generic Sequence

IntSequence (/6/), IntBasicSequence (/6/) and IntArraySequence (/7/) can now be changed to handle sequences of arbitrary type:

```
TYPE Sequence(R, AS BasicSequence) IS                                                   /14/
    <R>;

    Append(s : R) : R IS
        WHILE NOT s.Empty
            DO SELF.AddLast(s.RemoveFront); END;
        RETURN SELF;
    END Append;

END Sequence;

TYPE BasicSequence(T as TOP) IS
    Empty                   : BOOLEAN;
    AddFront(i : T)         : BasicSequence;
    RemoveFront                             : T;
    AddLast(i : T)          : BasicSequence;
    RemoveLast              : T;
END BasicSequence;

TYPE ArraySequence(T AS TOP) IS
    d : ARRAY[1..100] OF T;
    front, back  : CARDINAL INITIALLY 0;

    Empty : BOOLEAN                  ...Implementation of Empty;
    AddFront(i : T) : BasicSequence  ...Implementation of AddFront;
    RemoveFront : T                  ...Implementation of RemoveFront;
    AddLast(i : T) : BasicSequence   ...Implementation of AddLast;
    RemoveLast : T                   ...Implementation of RemoveLast;
    MaxLengthOfSequence : INTEGER    ...Implementation of MaxLengthOfSequence;
END ArraySequence;
```

Depending on how instances of these types are declared, homomorphic sequences can be created (in which all items in the sequence have the same type), as well as polymorphic sequences (in which items of differing types can simultaneously be stored in the same sequence). However only instances of TOP can be retrieved from a polymorphic sequence if static type checking is used.

Further rules are required to allow nested enhancive types: those whose formal parameters are instantiated by further enhancive types. For example Sequence has a formal type parameter BasicSequence, which in turn has a formal type parameter TOP.

3.1 Further enhancement and expansion rules for Enhancive Types

7.   If $T(t_1 \text{ AS } T_1)$, and $p(t \text{ AS } T_2) \leq T_1(t_2 \text{ AS } T_2)$ and $q \leq T_2$ then:

7.1 $p \dashrightarrow T(p)$

7.2 $p(q) \dashrightarrow T(p(q))$

7.3 $p(q) \to T(T_1(q))$

7.4 $p(q) \to T(T_1(T_2))$

Rule 7 generalises to an arbitrary degree of nesting and arbitrary number of parameters. For expansion of nested enhancive types:

     8.   If $T(t_1 \text{ AS } T_1)$, $T_1(t_2 \text{ AS } T_2)$, and $p \leq T_1$, $q \leq T_2$ then:

8.1 $T = T(T_1(T_2))$

8.2 $T(p) = T(p(T_2))$

Rule 8 likewise generalises.

3.2   Usage of the generic sequence

Examples of the application of rules 7 and 8 are now given:

```
VAR SqASq      : Sequence(ArraySequence);                              /15/
    SqASqInt   : Sequence(ArraySequence(INTEGER));
    SqBSqInt   : Sequence(BasicSequence(INTEGER));
    ASq        : ArraySequence;
    ASqInt     : ArraySequence(INTEGER);
    LnkSq      : LinkedListSequence;
    Sq         : Sequence;
    i          : INTEGER;
    t          : TOP;
    ....
    SqASq.AddFront(i);                         (* 8.2, 5.1 and b *)
    i := SqASq.RemoveFront;                     (* Type error !!  8.2, 5.1 and c *)
    t := SqASq.RemoveFront;                     (* 8.2, 5.1 and c *)
    SqASqInt.AddFront(i);                       (* b *)
    SqASq.Append(LnkSq);                        (* Type error!!  8.2, 5.1 and b *)
    SqBSqInt := ASqInt;                         (* 7.3 and e *)
    Sq := ASqInt;                               (* 8.1, 5.1, 7.4 and e *)
    SqBSqInt.Append(LnkSq);                     (* Type error!!  5.1 and b *)
    Sq.Append(LnkSq);                           (* 8.1 and 5.1 *)
    ASq := Sq.Append(LnkSq);                    (* Type error! ASq NOT ≤ BSq, & rule c fails *)
    ASq.Sequence(ArraySequence)~Append(LnkSq);  (* 7.1, 5.1 and f *)
    WITH ASq, LnkSq AS Sequence                 (* 5.1 and g *)
        DO ASq.AddFront(3);                     (* b *)
            t := LnkSq.RemoveFront;             (* c *)
            ASq.Append(LnkSq);                  (* b *)
END;
```

4   Restriction and Renaming

Any implementation of the BasicSequence in /14/ could be used to implement abstractions other than that of a Sequence, for example a Stack. An abstract type similar to Sequence in /14/ could be defined for a Stack, but not all the operations applicable to BasicSequence should be allowable on a Stack. Hence although the representation of a Stack could be a BasicSequence, the set of operations made available must be restricted, as follows:

```
TYPE Stack(R AS BasicSequence({AddFront, RemoveFront, Empty}) IS        /16/
    <R>;
END Stack;
```

where the {..} notation denotes a set of operation names. Any type conformant with BasicSequence may be used for Stack, but only the AddFront, RemoveFront and Empty operations will be invokable on instances of Stack. This obviates the need to introduce an additional type definition explicitly: instead a new type is implicitly introduced having a "hidden" type name and only the specified operations.

It would actually be preferable if the operations on a Stack could be given more meaningful names, and of course, there might also be additional operations on a Stack which are not available on BasicSequences (as there was the operation Append for Sequence), as follows:

```
TYPE Stack(R AS BasicSequence({Push <= AddFront, Pop <= RemoveFront, IsEmpty <= Empty}) IS          /17/
    <R>;

    Empty IS     (* Collapse entire Stack *)
        LOCAL t : TOP;
        WHILE NOT SELF.IsEmpty
            DO t := SELF.Pop; END;
    End Empty;

END Stack;
```

Here AddFront is renamed as Push, and RemoveFront as Pop, to "users" of a Stack. The renaming implies the first conformance rule (rule 1) must take account of explicit name changes to operations.

As a second example, BasicSequence could be used to implement a FIFO queue:

```
TYPE FIFOQueue(R, R1 AS BasicSequence({Put <= AddFront, Get <= RemoveLast, Empty}) IS          /18/
    <R>;
END FIFOQueue;
```

Note that now we can treat the *same* instance of an ArraySequence (/14/) as a Sequence (/14/), or as a Stack (/17/), or as a FIFOQueue (/18/)!

```
VAR a1,a2 : ArraySequence;                                                          /19/
    b    : Sequence;
    c    : Stack;
    d    : FIFOQueue;
    ...
    b := a1;                        (* Treat a1 as a Sequence *)
    b.Append(a2);                   (* a1 can use the "inherited" Append  *)
    c := a1;                        (* Now treat a1 as a Stack *)
    c.Empty;                        (* a1 can be flushed *)
    d := a1;                        (* Finally treat a1 as a FIFOQueue *)
    d.Put(90);                      (* a1 supports Put as a synonym for AddFront *)
```


4.1 Restriction and Enhancive Types

Although BasicSequence does conform with BasicSequence({AddFront, RemoveFront, Empty}) as in /17/, in general a type T does not necessarily conform with a restriction of itself. T shall be called the *base* type of the restriction. For example, INTEGER does not conform to INTEGER({"+"}), because of conformance rule 4 and because the arguments to "+" for the restricted type will themselves be of type INTEGER({"+"}). With restricted types, we can introduce a further rule:

9. If an enhancive type is given an actual type parameter which is a restricted type, then any actual arguments or results of operations, whose formal types are the restricted type, can be any subtype of the base of the restricted type.

Examples of the use of this rule are given below when constrained genericity is considered.

5 Constrained Genericity

Having considered how to extend the conventional conformance rules, let us now return to Meyer's problems. Using the additional rules 5 to 8 given above, it is straight forward to describe solutions to both the Swap utility and the Stack which Meyer considers: this is left as an exercise for the interested reader. His examples of constrained genericity require both the additional rules and the restriction and renaming mechanism introduced in section 4, as follows.

Meyer's first example of constrained genericity is a utility to find the minimum to two values of the same arbitrary type: however their type must obviously support a comparison operation. Rule 9 above allows a solution since an INTEGER can be passed as an actual parameter for a formal parameter of type INTEGER({le <= "+"}), even though INTEGER does not of itself conform to the restriction. It is also left as an exercise to the reader.

The second of Meyer's examples of constrained genericity is a matrix package, which allows matrices whose elements are of the same type to be added and multiplied: this type must support add and multiply operations itself (on the elements) as well as a zero and unity value. Such a type is a Ring:

```
TYPE Matrix(R AS TwoDimensionalArray(RingType)) IS                          /20/
    <R>;                                              (* a 2-D array of RingType *)

    Plus(Other : R) : R IS                 ...Implementation of Plus;
    Multipy(m : R) : R IS                  ...Implementation of Multiply;

END Matrix;

TYPE RingType IS
    Zero      : RingType;
    Unity     : RingType;
    Plus(Other : RingType) : RingType;
    Multiply(Other : RingType) : RingType;
END RingType;
```

and a possible usage:

```
VAR m1,m2 : Matrix(TwoDimensionalArray(INTEGER({Zero <= 0,Unity <= 1, Plus <= "+", Multiply <= "*"})));    /21/
    ...
    m1.Plus(m2);
```

6 Data Modelling

So far an approach based on abstract data types has been used in the discussion and examples. This resulted from our consideration of conformance in Emerald, and Meyer's particular examples. However conformance between one type and another can also be based on data valued attributes: for example, a record (or tuple) type R_1 would conform to another record type R_2 if R_1 had at least the fields of R_2, and the types of those fields conform. [Albano85] and [Cardelli85] consider subtyping and conformance in greater detail.

The examples have shown how a type could be enhanced by additional operations not originally defined upon it. In the same way, a record type may in principle be augmented by additional fields, and thus enhanced using static, dynamic, temporary or protracted enhancement. Dynamic enhancement appears particularly useful since it allows an object to gain additional attributes, and adopt many different roles, as its "life" progresses, as in /19/. Exactly what these additional attributes are need not be decided when the object is first created, but can be added subsequently. It appears possible to enhance the object and modify its behaviour throughout its lifetime, yet without abandoning static type checking.

Note also that given N enhancive types, 2^N combinations of types can be created. This mechanism is a solution to the addition of *mix-ins* to object instances, as discussed by Hendler [Hendler86].

7 Conclusions

We have observed that it may be useful to extend the usual rules for conformance so that a type can be enhanced to gain additional operations or data attributes, and yet still be statically type checked. In a sense the extension is similar to multiple abstract superclassing. However the major difference from languages which do support multiple inheritance is that using enhancement, the "inheritance" need not be statically determined, but can be achieved at execution time.

In retrospect, the concept of enhancement given here is similar to the *descriptive classes* of Sandberg [Sandberg86], although enhancement is derived from considering conformance, and descriptive classes from abstract superclassing. The chief difference appears that when an instance of a descriptive class is created, actual class parameters must be supplied for all the formal class parameters. As a result such an instance cannot augment its representation at run-time, and for example, much of example /15/ given here might not be possible using descriptive classes.

The concept of enhancement is now being considered as a modelling and implementation tool for the infrastructure for Office Systems, and other application environments, in the context of the ESPRIT Comandos project.

8 Acknowledgements

I am indebted to my colleagues on the Comandos project at Trinity for their constructutive criticisms: V. Cahill, A. Donnelly, E. Finn, N. Harris and I. White. I would also thank my colleagues in the other institutions participating in Comandos, and in particular R. Balter, E. Bertino, R. Gagliardi, L. Martino, G. Mueller and A-K Proefrock.

9 References

[Albano85]   "Galileo: A Strongly-Typed, Interactive Conceptual Language", A. Albano, L. Cardelli and R. Orsini, ACM Transactions on Database Systems, Vol. 10, No. 2, June 1985

[Black86]   "Object Structure in the Emerald System", A. Black, N. Hutchinson, E. Jul and H. Levy, Technical Report 86-04-03, Department of Computer Science, University of Washington, April 1986.

[Black87]   "Distribution and Abstract Types in Emerald", A. Black, N. Hutchinson, E. Jul, H. Levy and L. Carter, IEEE Transactions on Software Engineering, Vol SE-13, No 1, January 1987.

[Cardelli85]   "On understanding Types, Data Abstraction, and Polymorphism", L. Cardelli and P. Wegner, ACM Computing Surveys, Vol 17, No 4, Dec 85.

[Goldberg83]   "SmallTalk-80: The Language and Its Implementation", A. Goldberg and D. Robson, Addison-Wesley, 1983

[Hendler86]   "Enhancement for multiple-inheritance", J. Hendler, ACM Sigplan Notices, Vol 21, No 10, October 1986.

[Meyer86]   "Genericity versus Inheritance", B. Meyer, 1986 Proc. of Object-Oriented Programming Systems, Languages and Applications (OOPSLA) (also in ACM SIGPLAN Notices, Vol 21, No 11, November 1986)

[Sandberg86]   "An Alternative to Subclassing", D. Sandberg, 1986 Proc. of Object-Oriented Programming Systems, Languages and Applications (OOPSLA), (also in ACM SIGPLAN Notices, Vol 21, No 11, November 1986).

[Schaffert86]   "An introduction to Trellis/Owl", C. Schaffert et al, 1986 Proc. of Object- Oriented Programming Systems, Languages and Applications (OOPSLA) (also in ACM SIGPLAN Notices, Vol 21, No 11, November 1986).

[Stroustrup84]   "The C++ Programming Language - Reference Manual", B. Stroustrup, AT&T Bell Labs Computing Science Technical Report No 108, January 1984.

Inheritance and Subtyping in a Parallel Object-Oriented Language

Pierre America

Philips Research Laboratories

Eindhoven, the Netherlands

Abstract

We have investigated the concepts of inheritance and subtyping in order to integrate them in a parallel object-oriented language. In doing so, we have concluded that inheritance and subtyping are two *different* concepts, which should not be confused in any object-oriented language (be it parallel or sequential). Inheritance takes place on the implementation level of classes, and it is a convenient mechanism for code sharing. It can be supported, for example, by introducing inheritance packages into a programming language. Subtyping deals with the message interface of objects, and it leads to a conceptual hierarchy based on behavioural specialization. Subtyping should take place on the basis of specifications of the external behaviour of objects, and as much as possible of these specifications should be formal. Some specific problems with introducing these two concepts into a *parallel* language are also discussed.

1 Introduction

ESPRIT project 415 aims at the development of new architectures and languages to speed up applications in the area of artificial intelligence by the use of large-scale parallelism. Subproject A of this large project is mainly carried out at Philips Research Laboratories in Eindhoven, the Netherlands. Here object-oriented programming has been chosen as the approach to follow towards this goal. A parallel architecture, called DOOM (Decentralized Object-Oriented Machine), is being developed [14], and a language, POOL (Parallel Object-Oriented Language), is being designed to program this machine. For more details on the language than can be given here, we refer to [2].

This paper is motivated by the wish to enrich the language POOL with a mechanism commonly called *inheritance*. Inheritance is regarded by many people as the hallmark of object-orientedness in programming languages [7]. We do not agree with this view, and argue that the essence of object-oriented programming lies somewhere else (see section 2.1). Nevertheless, inheritance is a very important concept and a useful mechanism to structure large systems. Therefore it would be advantageous for any object-oriented language to have a nicely integrated form of inheritance.

In section 2 we introduce the language POOL, together with the concepts on which it is based. This serves as a reference point for the rest of our discussion. The concept of inheritance and a related concept, subtyping, are introduced in section 3, where we also show that the distinction between the two is too important to confuse them, as is done in most existing object-oriented languages. For both concepts we shall indicate ways of dealing with them in an object-oriented language. Then, in section 4 we discuss the specific problems and possibilities of integrating these concepts in a parallel language like POOL.

This work is carried out in the context of ESPRIT project 415: "Parallel Architectures and Languages for Advanced Information Processing — a VLSI-directed approach".

2 The language POOL

In this section we present an overview of the language POOL, in order to introduce the concepts on which it is based, and to indicate the objectives that directed its design.

2.1 Object-oriented programming

The basic notion in object-oriented programming is of course the notion of an *object*. An object is an entity that contains some internal data, and has several procedures associated with it (these are called *methods*, following the object-oriented jargon). In general, objects are very dynamic entities: They can be created dynamically and their local data can change during their lifetime.

The important point is that the data in an object cannot be accessed directly by the outside world (i.e., by other objects): the only way of interacting with an object is sending it a *message*. A message is a request for the receiver to execute one of its methods, and such a method *can* access the local data of the object it belongs to. The fact that an object can only be manipulated through this fixed and controlled interface provided by its methods gives rise to a very powerful protection mechanism, which protects the local data of each object against uncontrolled access from every other one. This mechanism also provides a separation between the *implementation* of an object (its set of variables and the code of the methods) and its external behaviour (the way it responds to message). In this way the programming technique of abstract data types can be used in object-oriented programming.

In our opinion this protection mechanism based on objects is the basic and essential principle of object-oriented programming (cf. the locality laws of [12]). In POOL, care has been taken not to diminish the power of this protection mechanism in any way: there are no exceptions or detours around it.

In POOL, like in most object-oriented languages, objects are grouped into *classes*. All the objects in one class (the *instances* of the class) have the same structure of their internal data (the instance variables) and they have the same methods. Classes also have the task to create new instances of themselves. In many object-oriented languages (e.g., Smalltalk-80 [11]) this is modelled by viewing classes again as objects, so that the creation of new instances can be done in class methods (methods of the class object). In POOL, a different approach is chosen: A class provides its users with so-called *routines*. A routine is another kind of procedure, which can be called by any object in the system, and which is associated with a class rather than with a specific object. Routines are a suitable abstraction mechanism to encapsulate, among others, the creation and initialization of new objects.

2.2 Parallelism

There are several ways to introduce parallelism in an object-oriented language (see [18]). In POOL, this is done by giving objects a local activity of their own. Each object has a so-called *body*, a local process which starts executing as soon as the object is created. In an object's body it is indicated explicitly when the object sends a message and when it is willing to accept one. All the objects in one class execute the same body. Parallelism arises because, in principle, the bodies of all the objects can execute in parallel. There is no parallelism within one object.

Message passing is done in a way like the Ada rendez-vous [1]: The sender and the receiver wait for each other until both are ready to exchange the message, then the receiver executes the specified method, it returns the result (an object) to the sender, and after that both pursue their own activities in parallel again. When sending a message, the sender specifies the destination object, the method to be executed, and possibly some parameters (again objects). In order to accept a message, an object executes an answer-statement, specifying a set of methods. The first incoming message that specifies one of these methods is accepted. A select-statement, allowing conditional message acceptance, is also present in the language.

2.3 Typing

In contrast to many other object-oriented languages, POOL is not principally meant for rapid prototyping. Rather, it aims at the systematic construction of reliable and maintainable software (in this respect it resembles Trellis/Owl [15]). For this reason, we want the compiler to be able to detect as many errors as possible in a program statically, i.e., before the program is executed. Therefore POOL is a statically typed language.

Let us precisely define some terms: A *type* is a collection of objects that share some properties, notably the operations that can be performed on them (see also [8]). In object-oriented languages, the only operation that can be applied to an object is sending it a message, so the relevant information here is the set of methods that an object has available. Therefore, at this point (we shall refine this later) a type coincides naturally with a class.

Now we call a language *statically typed* if for any expression in a program, it is possible to determine statically, i.e., from the program text alone, the type of the objects this expression will represent during program execution. In POOL, like in many other statically typed languages, this is done by indicating the type of each variable, each parameter and result of a method or routine, and each constant. The type of every expression can then be determined starting from the types of its ingredients (by analysis of the program text), in such a way that it is guaranteed that whenever the expression is evaluated, the value will be an instance of this type.

In many other object-oriented languages (e.g., Smalltalk-80 [11]), this concept of type does not occur in the language; they are not statically typed. However, in most cases, the concept plays a role in the mind of the programmer, because he will make assumptions about the properties of the objects he is dealing with. Therefore, even when using such languages, it is useful to have a good understanding of the concept of typing.

3 Inheritance versus subtyping

3.1 Basic principles

The concept of inheritance was already present in the first object-oriented languages, like Simula [10] and Smalltalk-80 [11]. The basic idea is that in defining a new class it is often very convenient to start with all the variables and methods of an existing class and to add some more in order to get the desired new class. The new class (let us call it B) is said to *inherit* the variables and methods of the old one (which we shall call A). This inheritance mechanism constitutes a very successful way of incorporating facilities for *code sharing* in a programming language.

But there is more to this mechanism: It is clear that in the situation described above class B has all the variables and methods of class A. Therefore, in a way, we can consider every object of class B equally well as an object of class A: At any point where we expect an object of class A, an object of class B will satisfy our needs, because it will accept all the messages an object of class A would accept. The objects in class B can be considered as *specialized* versions of the ones in class A. To express this, class B is called a *subclass* of A, and conversely A is called a *superclass* of B.

If we compare this with the concept of typing, as introduced in section 2.3, we could see the type associated with class B as a *subtype* of the type associated with class A. More precisely, we could take a type τ comprising all the instances of class B, and a type σ which contains all the instances of the classes A and B *together*. Now τ is a subtype of σ in the sense that every element of τ is also an element of σ. (Note that, in order to avoid confusion, we shall *not* say that an instance of class B is also an instance of class A.) In this way, we can establish a one-to-one correspondence between the concepts of inheritance and subtyping.

Conceptually, if we consider objects in a program as representations of entities in the real world (for example in a database or simulation system), this makes good sense, especially if we concentrate on the variables, which contain the local data of the object. For example, if we have defined a class Vehicle with variables to store the owner and the maximum speed, it is convenient to define the class Car as a subclass of Vehicle so that we only have to add a variable to store the license number. An instance of class Car is then automatically considered as an element of the type associated with class Vehicle.

Of course, this procedure can be repeated several times. For instance, we can define a class Truck as a subclass of Car, with an extra variable to store the load capacity, we can define Bus as another subclass of the class Car, with a variable for the number of seats, and we can define Bike to be a subclass of Vehicle, adding a variable containing the number of speeds. In this way we can get a whole hierarchy of classes, which has the form of a tree:

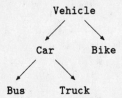

Moreover, it is possible to allow a new class to inherit from more than one existing class. This mechanism is called *multiple inheritance*, in contrast to *linear* inheritance. For example, a horse can be considered as an animal (having, for example, a father and a mother) and as a vehicle, and therefore the class Horse can be defined conveniently as a subclass of both Animal and Vehicle. In the case of multiple inheritance, the class hierarchy is not a tree any more; it becomes an acyclic directed graph:

The mechanism we have described above constitutes the basis of inheritance/subtyping as it is incorporated in most existing object-oriented languages. It has proved to be a very powerful mechanism to structure large software systems, and its presence has determined the success of object-oriented languages for a large part. This is not very surprising, because such a structuring mechanism is very useful in the development of large software systems, and while (as we have argued in section 2.1) inheritance is *not* essential for object-oriented languages, the object-orientedness *is* essential for inheritance: Only in languages where we in fact consider the internal details of only one object at a time, it is possible to replace one object by a more specialized one, which offers the same functionality as the old one, but possibly some more.

3.2 Problems with inheritance and subtyping

However useful the above mechanism is, it has some problems associated with it. One of the most evident problems is what to do when a new class wants to inherit from two existing classes that both have a variable or method with the same name. Should one of the two be chosen, and if so, which one? Or otherwise, if both are included in some way in the new class, how are they named and accessed? A symptom for the fact that the inheritance mechanism is problematic is the large variety of ways in which the basic mechanism is augmented in languages like Smalltalk-80 [11,6], LOOPS [5], Flavors [17], etcetera.

The origin of many of these problems lies in the fact that the inheritance structure, used for code sharing, and the conceptual subtyping hierarchy, originating from specialization, are *not* the same thing. They lie on different levels of abstraction in the system: inheritance is concerned with the *implementation* of the classes, while the subtyping hierarchy is based on the *behaviour* of the instances (as seen from the outside, by other objects).

For simple, record-like objects whose main function is to store data the practical difference between these two points of view are not very large. But for more complicated objects the distinction between the interface with the outside world and the internal implementation is much more important, and therefore the discrepancy between inheritance and subtyping is clear.

It may well be that in many cases the hierarchical relationships induced by inheritance and by subtyping coincide, but this is certainly not always the case: On the one hand it is very well possible in many cases to define a class that really specializes the behaviour of another class, but employing a totally different structure of variables and having different code even for methods with the same name (so we have subtyping without inheritance). On the other hand, it is also possible that, by simply adding some methods to an existing class, the behaviour even of the old methods is changed in an essential way (the new methods might assign to the variables of the object in such a way that an invariant, on which the old methods rely, is violated). In the latter case the new class cannot be said to give rise to a subtype of the old one, so we have inheritance without subtyping.

Therefore we argue that the concepts of inheritance and subtyping should be decoupled and that each should be considered on its own right (of course, the commonalities between the two should not be forgotten). This observation is not totally new (for example, it was already presented in [16]), but in exploring this line of thought further, we shall encounter some new consequences.

3.3 Inheritance

Let us first concentrate on inheritance. Now that we consider inheritance *only* as a mechanism for code sharing, we can see more clearly what it should look like. First of all, because inheritance is not the same as subtyping, it is not necessary that inheriting from a class means inheriting *everything* from that class: Since the new class is not necessarily associated with a subtype of the old one, it does not have to have all the old methods. It should be possible to inherit only a subset of the variables and methods of a given class. Of course, if a method is inherited that acts on a certain variable, that variable should also be present in the new class. A way to ensure this would be to inherit such a variable automatically with the method.

Generalizing this a little, it is reasonable to say that a new class should inherit a *consistent subset* of the variables and methods of an old one. This leads to the idea of an *inheritance package* of variables and methods, which can be inherited in one piece. Such an inheritance package could be accompanied by an *inheritance interface*, listing the variables and methods that can be used freely by the inheriting class. It would be possible to include variables and methods in the package that are not in the inheritance interface. These can be used by the methods in the inheritance interface but they remain hidden from the definer of the inheriting class. In this way a certain amount of abstraction and encapsulation can be built into the inheritance mechanism. (It is even possible to completely detach inheritance packages from classes, so that inheritance packages exist independently and can be used and shared by classes.)

In fact, we get *two* interfaces for each class: the message interface (dealing with the messages accepted by instances of the class), and the inheritance interface (dealing with the inheritance packages, the code that can be inherited by other classes). This phenomenon was also observed in [16], but there inheritance meant inheriting everything from an existing class (which is, of course, an important special case of our more general mechanism).

Considering multiple inheritance, it is clearly very useful to allow a class to inherit more than one inheritance package from possibly different existing classes. However, these packages should not have conflicting methods or variables. Every method and variable should of course be present only once in the resulting class. A simple renaming mechanism would allow the combination of inheritance packages that are conflicting originally (note that with subtyping renaming is impossible because it destroys the subtype property). The variables and methods in the inheritance package that are not in the inheritance interface are assumed to be renamed in such a way that they can never cause any name conflict.

Different ways of combining methods (like in Flavors [17]) can also be used together with this mechanism. The question is only whether the additional complexity of the language is justified by the ease of programming resulting from such extensions.

3.4 Subtyping

We have seen (in section 2.3) that a type is a collection of objects sharing some properties. In section 3.1 we encountered the concept of subtyping. It is clear that for σ to be a subtype of τ, it is necessary that all elements of σ have the properties required by τ. This brings us to the issue of what information at all should be associated with a type. Let us remember that we want to use types to base our conceptual specialization hierarchy on, or more precisely that we want this hierarchy to consist of types ordered with the subtype relation. Then it is clear that a type should give us information about the *behaviour* of the objects that belong to it. This means that a type should consist of a *specification* of the behaviour of these objects. Ideally, this should be a formal specification of all the aspects of this behaviour that we are interested in. In general this will include the messages that can be sent to such an object (the methods it has available), the order in which these messages may be sent, the conditions on the values of the parameters, the value of the result, possibly also the messages the object will send itself, and perhaps even the time the object needs to perform all these actions.

Let us suppose that for each type we have a formal specification of the behaviour of its elements, in the form of a formula in some kind of logic. For example, let the type σ be specified by the formula $\phi(x)$, meaning that for every element β of σ we have $\phi(\beta)$. Now it is easy to formulate the condition that must be satisfied in order to be able to regard one type as a subtype of another type. If the type σ has the specification $\phi(x)$ associated with it and τ has the specification $\psi(x)$, then τ can be considered as a subtype of σ precisely if, for all x, $\psi(x)$ implies $\phi(x)$. This means that every object α that is a member of τ so that we have $\psi(\alpha)$, will automatically satisfy $\phi(\alpha)$ and can thus be considered as an element of σ.

Unfortunately, formal specification technology is not yet in a position that formal specifications of this kind can be included in a practical programming language. One could even say that especially for object-oriented languages there has been surprisingly little research on the formal description of program behaviour (see for example [4]). In regard of the fact that formal specification theory can contribute substantially to the understanding of mechanisms like subtyping in object-oriented programming, it certainly deserves more attention. However, even with (partly) informal specifications, it is useful to keep the above characterization of subtyping in mind. Therefore, lacking a suitable formalism to express the behaviour of objects in a type, we should at least associate with each type an informal description of this behaviour.

One aspect of this behaviour that can and should be described formally for each type, is the set of available methods, together with the types of their parameters and results. For this aspect the above subtype condition reduces to the following: In order for a type τ to be a possible subtype of σ, the following should hold: For each method m listed for σ, with parameter types $\alpha_1, \ldots, \alpha_n$ and result type β, the type τ should have a method with the same name m, with parameter types $\gamma_1, \ldots, \gamma_n$ and result type δ, in such a way that, for every i between 1 and n, α_i is a subtype of γ_i, and δ is a subtype of β.

If this condition is fulfilled, we know that every object in τ will behave like an element of σ (at least with respect to the messages it accepts): It will accept each message that specifies such a method name m, listed with σ, it will be able to handle parameters from the types $\alpha_1, \ldots, \alpha_n$, like σ says it should, (it can even handle parameters from the larger types $\gamma_1, \ldots, \gamma_n$), and it will return a result of the type β, complying with σ's wishes (the result will even be a member of the smaller type δ). This is the well-known "contravariant" parameter rule described in [7] and used for example in the language Trellis/Owl [15].

However, let us remember very well that there is more to types than this condition: a type represents a constraint on the behaviour of its elements, and only a part of this behaviour is captured by the above rule. For example, a type Stack, with the methods put and get (having the obvious meaning), is not distinguished by the above rule from the type Queue, with the same methods. Yet their behaviour is clearly different and none of them should be considered as a subtype of the other. Nevertheless, both are subtypes of the type Bag, again with the methods put and get, where get is supposed to return an *arbitrary* element that was previously inserted by put.

In statically typed languages, the contravariant parameter condition can be checked by the compiler, and one can be sure that during the execution of a program it will never happen that an object is sent a message for which it has no method. But as we have seen, the behaviour of objects cannot yet be formalized in all its aspects, so the compiler cannot check completely that one type is a subtype of another one. This is the reason why the subtype relation should *not* be assumed *automatically* whenever the contravariant parameter condition is satisfied. To ensure that a subtype really specializes its supertype with respect to its behaviour, a certain discipline is required from the programmer: To the formal description of the available methods and their parameter and result types, an informal description of the behaviour of the elements of the type should be added, and whenever the programmer asserts a subtype relationship between two types, he should check the condition on the associated behaviour descriptions himself. The situation is like in traditional statically typed languages: the compiler can ascertain the absence of certain errors, but not of all errors.

Let us finally note that in this setting, *multiple* subtyping is a naturally occurring phenomenon: it is often the case that a type is a subtype of several, mutually unrelated types. Conflicts, like we saw above with inheritance, do not arise.

4 Integrating it in POOL

In the last section we have investigated the essential properties of inheritance and subtyping, which are valid for sequential as well as parallel object-oriented languages. In this section we shall look at the specific issues arising when we try to integrate these concepts into a POOL-like language. Now that we have seen that inheritance and subtyping are two different concepts, we can deal with each of them in turn.

Let us first talk about inheritance. It is clear that inheritance of methods and variables does not present any additional problem in a parallel language. The same scheme using inheritance packages can be used, as we described it in section 3.3. Inheriting routines (cf. section 2.1) does not make much sense, because routines can anyway be called from everywhere in the system.

The most difficult question is how to do something suitable with inheritance in the definition of the *body* (the local process of an object). There are several theoretically appealing options, like putting inherited bodies in parallel, or one after the other, or even nesting them. None of these possibilities seems very useful in practice, and it seems best not to allow inheritance of bodies. Nevertheless, there is one promising option: In general, the first part of a body will be concerned with the initialization of the variables. It seems very useful to include this part of the body in the inheritance package to which the variables belong. Then these statements will be prefixed to the body of any class that uses this inheritance package. In this way it is also ensured that the hidden variables in this package are initialized correctly.

However, as the bodies of objects become a more important part of their code, inheritance becomes a less useful mechanism for code sharing. Therefore it might well be that for parallel systems the importance of inheritance (at least in the above form) is not so great as for sequential systems.

For the integration of subtyping within a parallel object-oriented language the same kind of problems apply as in sequential languages. Of course, the formal description of the behaviour of *parallel* objects is probably even more difficult than in the sequential case. Nevertheless, there is some more work going on in this field (see for example [3,9,13]). As this work has not yet resulted in a practical way of formally specifying object behaviour (it is not even sure that it ever will), we shall have to help ourselves with informal descriptions, complemented with a formal specification of the available methods and their parameter and result types, just like in the sequential case. Let us realize that here the formal part of the description captures an even smaller fraction of the relevant object behaviour: For example, the order in which messages can be accepted and sent is much more important than in a sequential system. Failing to take these things into account can lead to nasty problems like deadlock. In this situation, where there is a greater need for formal specification, the prospects for it are worse.

Like inheritance, it may well turn out that subtyping will play a relatively less important role in parallel than in sequential languages: As there are more aspects of object behaviour that can make a difference (e.g., the order in which messages are sent or received), it is less likely that one type is really a specialization of the other.

5 Conclusion

As we have seen in section 3, inheritance and subtyping are two different, though related, concepts, and they should not be confused. We have also developed some ideas on how to integrate them in object-oriented languages in general. In section 4 we have shown some possibilities to introduce these concepts into a parallel language like POOL. We have also observed that in a parallel language it is questionable whether the importance of inheritance and subtyping will be as great as in sequential languages.

As to the status of our own work: At the moment of this writing we have not yet completed a language design along the lines sketched above. We are certainly planning to experiment with inheritance and subtyping in the near future. However, at the moment we give a higher priority to the design of a language without these features, in which reliable programs can be written in a reasonably easy way, and which can be efficiently implemented on a parallel, decentralized machine.

References

[1] *The Programming Language Ada Reference Manual.* ANSI/MIL-STD-1815A-1983, published in: Lecture Notes in Computer Science, Vol. 155, Springer-Verlag, 1983.

[2] Pierre America: Definition of the programming language POOL-T. ESPRIT project 415A. Doc. No. 0091, Philips Research Laboratories, Eindhoven, the Netherlands, September 1985.

[3] Pierre America, Jaco de Bakker, Joost N. Kok, Jan Rutten: Operational semantics of a parallel object-oriented language. *Conference Record of the 13th Symposium on Principles of Programming Languages*, St. Petersburg, Florida, January 13–15, 1986, pp. 194–208.

[4] Pierre America: Object-oriented programming: a theoretician's introduction. *Bulletin of the European Association for Theoretical Computer Science*, No. 29, June 1986, pp. 69–84.

[5] Daniel G. Bobrow, Mark Stefik: The LOOPS Manual. Technical Report KB-VLSI-81-13, Xerox Palo Alto Research Center, Palo Alto, California, 1981.

[6] Alan H. Borning, Daniel H.H. Ingalls: Multiple Inheritance in Smalltalk-80. *Proceedings of the AAAI Conference*, Pittsburgh, August 1982, pp. 234–237.

[7] Luca Cardelli: A semantics of multiple inheritance. In: G. Kahn, D.B. MacQueen, G. Plotkin (eds.): *Semantics of Data Types*. Springer-Verlag, Lecture Notes in Computer Science, Vol. 173, 1984, pp. 51–67.

[8] Luca Cardelli, Peter Wegner: On understanding types, data abstraction, and polymorphism. *ACM Computing Surveys*, Vol. 17, No. 4, December 1985, pp. 471–522.

[9] William D. Clinger: Foundations of actor semantics. Technical report 633 (Ph. D. Thesis), Massachusetts Institute of Technology, Artificial Intelligence Laboratory, May 1981.

[10] Ole-Johan Dahl, Kristen Nygaard: Simula — an ALGOL-based simulation language. *Communications of the ACM*, Vol. 9, No. 9, September 1966, pp. 671–678.

[11] Adele Goldberg, David Robson: *Smalltalk-80, The Language and its Implementation*. Addison-Wesley, 1983.

[12] Carl Hewitt, Henry Baker: Laws for communicating parallel processes. In: *Proceedings of IFIP-77*, Toronto, Canada, August 1977, pp. 987–992.

[13] Van Nguyen, Alan Demers, David Gries, Susan Owicki: A model and temporal proof system for networks of processes. *Distributed Computing*, Vol. 1, 1986, pp. 7–25.

[14] Eddy Odijk: The Philips Object-Oriented Parallel Computer. In: J.V. Woods (ed.): *Fifth Generation Computer Architecture (IFIP TC-10)*. North-Holland, 1985.

[15] Craig Schaffert, Topher Cooper, Bruce Bullis, Mike Kilian, Carrie Wilpolt: An introduction to Trellis/Owl, *Proceedings of the ACM Conference on Object-Oriented Programming, Systems, Languages and Applications*, Oregon, September 1986, pp. 9–16.

[16] Alan Snyder: Encapsulation and inheritance in object-oriented programming languages. In: *Proceedings of the ACM Conference on Object-Oriented Programming, Systems, Languages and Applications*, Oregon, September 1986, pp. 38–45.

[17] Daniel Weinreb, David Moon: Flavors: Message passing in the Lisp machine. AI Memo 602, November 1980, Massachusetts Institute of Technology, Artificial Intelligence Laboratory.

[18] Akinori Yonezawa, Mario Tokoro (eds.): *Object-Oriented Concurrent Systems*. MIT Press, 1987.

ON SOME ALGORITHMS FOR MULTIPLE
INHERITANCE IN OBJECT
ORIENTED PROGRAMMING

R. DUCOURNAU[*], M. HABIB[**]*

[*]SEMA-METRA
16-18 rue Barbès,
92126 Montrouge cédex.

[**]LIB (Laboratoire commun ENST Br et UBO)
Département Informatique et Réseaux,
Ecole Nationale Supérieure des Télécommunications de Bretagne,
ZI de Kernevent, BP 832,
29285 Brest cédex.

ABSTRACT

We study here some problems yielded by multiple inheritance in object-oriented languages. We give an interpretation and a formalism of heritance mechanisms within the framework of partially ordered sets theory. An inheritance mechanism can be regarded as a traversing algorithm of the inheritance graph, and we prove that those which yields linear extension (total order) play a central role.

We discuss some operational semantic aspects of multiple inheritance, with the introduction of a concept named by *multiplicity*. After a presentation of some well-known inheritance algorithms we propose two new algorithms based upon depth-first search techniques and some particular classes of linear extensions, recently studied.

We end by applying these results in the case of inheritance with exceptions and by setting a few problems. All these results are implemented in the frame-based language YAFOOL[1].

Keywords : *Object oriented language, multiple inheritance, partial ordered sets, linear extensions, depth-first-search, inheritance with exceptions.*

---

[1]   *Yet Another Frame-based Object Oriented Language.* YAFOOL was developped by SEMA-METRA, with the participation of INRIA, under contract with the "Centre de Programmation de la Marine", and is the basis of Y3[®], the expert systems toolbox of SEMA-METRA.

I INTRODUCTION

Nowadays the paradigms of object-oriented programming are very fruitful and popular in software engineering for prototyping (see GOLDBERG and ROBSON [1983] or BEZIVIN [1986]) or even in classical languages (namely ADA or EIFFEL (see MEYER [1986])) and also in artificial intelligence for representing real-world knowledge (see for example the notion of semantic networks in FAHLMAN [1979]). Among these paradigms, inheritance is a way of sharing knowledge between objects : namely values, attributes, methods and reflexes or deamons can be inherited.

We can distinguish three main aspects in an inheritance mechanism :

1. An interpretation.

2. An operational semantic. (How it works).

3. An inheritance algorithm. (How the inheritance is computed).

There exist many interpretations of inheritance, see BRACHMAN [1983] for a survey, and LIEBERMAN [1986] for a discussion between inheritance and delegation, and BRIOT [1985] for a discussion on the relationships between instanciation and inheritance. We were mainly concerned with the second and third aspects of inheritance. When inheritance is allowed it is quite natural to enlarge it to multiple inheritance. Although with simple inheritance (where the hierarchy of an object is simply a path and the inheritance graph only a tree), the inheritance algorithms are very simple and well defined, it is not so clear when multiple inheritance is allowed.

In this paper we shortly present our results about multiple inheritance algorithms, in the framework of partially ordered sets theory.

I.1 SOME USEFUL GRAPHS AND ORDERED SETS NOTATIONS.

Let X be a finite set and R a binary relation on X, we shall denote by
G = (X,R) the graph of this relation. Elements of X are called *vertices* and those of R, denoted by (x,y) are called *arcs*. Furthermore x and y are respectively the origin and extremity of this arc, y is also called a *successor* of x and R(x) denotes the set of all successors of x in G.
A *path* $[x_1,...,x_k]$, of length k>1, is an ordered sequence of vertices such that
$\forall$ i$\in$ [1,k-1], $(x_i,x_{i+1}) \in$ R. This path is a *cycle* if $x_k = x_1$.
An (x,y) $\in$ R is a *transitivity* arc if there exists at least one path of length strictly greater than one going from x to y in G. Such an arc is also called *redundant*.

When G is *acyclic* (without cycle) then its transitive and reflexive closure yields a partial order (*poset* for short) denoted by $\leq_R$.
For Y $\subseteq$ X, R/Y denotes the restriction of R to Y, and G/Y = (Y,R/Y) the induced subgraph. Finally, R^d the *dual* of R, satisfies (x,y) $\in$ R iff (y,x) $\in$ R^d.

II   MULTIPLE INHERITANCE SYSTEMS AND POSETS.

From all the interpretations of inheritance systems (logical systems, set theory, ...) we can assume that an inheritance systems yields a partially ordered relation on the set of objects. More precisely, we can define :

DEFINITION 1 : An inheritance graph is a directed acyclic graph $G = (X,H,\omega)$ where X is the universe of objects, H the inheritance relation which transitive closure is a partially ordered set and ω which is the unique anti-root (or root in the inheritance terminology) of H.

In object oriented systems terminology, ω is called the universe root, and if $(x,y) \in H$ (resp. $x \leq_H y$), y is called a *father* (resp. an *ancestor*), and x, in both cases, is called a *descendant* of y.

In our applications we are only concerned by the following central problem : *For a given object, determine its inheritance.*

DEFINITION 2 : For an object $a \in X$, its inheritance graph (also called its *hierarchy*) is $G(a) = (X_a, H/X_a)$, where $X_a = \{x \in X, a \leq_H x \}$, the set of its ancestors (including a itself). In partial order terminology X_a is the upper ideal of a.

Now we can state our first inheritance principle :

PRINCIPLE 1 : An inheritance mechanism must follow the inheritance partial order.

In particular, the root ω is always the last vertex to be considered.

DEFINITION 3 : An inheritance search is a total order $\wp_a$ on X_a.

An object a inherits of a property P, with respect to an inheritance search $\wp_a$, in the following way :

1. P(a) is the first value encountered following $\wp_a$, in a vertex of X_a that admits this property, if there exists any.

2. If there is no such vertex, then a has not the property P. *(This is our closed world assumption).*

This definition yields *hidding effects*, i.e. if x and y admits a property P, and $x \leq_H y$, then P(y) is hidden by P(x). This can be also understood in terms of default, each property P of an object is a default value for all its descendants in the inheritance graph, which admits this property.

DEFINITION 4 : The inheritance mechanism is a mapping $: \wp : a \in X \rightarrow \wp_a$.

In the following, in order to build such mapping, we have to precise the operational semantic of inheritance we play with.

PROPERTY 1 : The inheritance searches must be stable under redondancy.

We notice that the above property is not essential, we could as well have chosen the opposite and so used the redundancy arcs as a programming control tool.

PRINCIPLE 2 : (uniformity) The inheritance is an uniform mechanism, and its searches apply identically for all object properties.

II.1 MULTIPLICITY.

If an object $a \in X$ has two fathers b *and then* c in the inheritance graph, it is natural to interpret this order as a priority : *a inherits more from b than from c.*

DEFINITION 6 : We define by $\mu(a)$ *the multiplicity relative to a* the total order relation in H(a), the set of fathers of a, and the *multiplicity*, the mapping : $\mu : a \in X \rightarrow \mu(a)$.

This notion is implicit in every graph or poset representation in machine, and moreover is used in every graph traversing algorithm, so we propose to use it as another operational programming control tool (in some way there is an analogy with the implicit ordering of the litterals of a PROLOG clause). Thus an inheritance graph is $G=(X,H,\omega,\mu)$, and moreover we denote by M_a the union of all transitive closures of the $\mu(x)$ for x in X_a and by $M = (X_a,M_a)$ the resulting graph.

PRINCIPLE 3 : (inheritance versus multiplicity) In any case the inheritance relation excels the multiplicity.

For an object a, we say that the multiplicity contradicts the inheritance when the graph $G(a) \cup M=(X_a,H/X_a \cup M_a)$ has a cycle. This may happen in many cases as can be seen in figure 1.

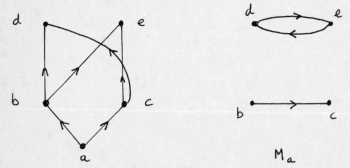

Fig. 1 : Contradictions between multiplicity and inheritance.
Remark : In all the figures, the decreasing multiplicity is drawn from left to right.

PRINCIPLE 4 : When there is no contradiction between multiplicity and inheritance the inheritance search must follow the partial order $H \cup M_a$ yielded by the graph $G(a) \cup M=(X_a,H/X_a \cup M_a)$.

The above principle only generalizes the first principle to multiplicity. But it is still not enough to completely determine the operational semantic of inheritance, we may add a further constraint such as :

PROPERTY 2 : For every object a ∈ X, if b and c are two fathers of a, with (b,c)∈M_a, then a must inherit from X_b-X_c before X_c-X_b, with no condition on $X_b∩X_c$.

As well as property 1, this second property is also arbitrary and can be understood as a depth-first-search choice. We shall examine in detail this property in the following section.

III   LINEAR ALGORITHMS.

III.1 SOME KNOWN INHERITANCE SEARCHES.

Most object oriented languages, which allow multiple inheritance, such as for example Common Loops (BOBROW et al. [1986]), or Flavors (MOON [1986]), or Le_Lisp, (CHAILLOUX et al. [1986]), use a depth-first search of the inheritance graph as inheritance search. These traversing graph algorithms are well known since the work of TARJAN [1972]. Some others use a breadth-first search technique like MERING (FERBER [1983]) and even some use some composition of these two searches.

III.1.1 Depth-first search according to multiplicity.

Such a technique always violates our principle 1, since the root ω is not considered last, as can be seen in figure 2.

III.1.2 Breadth-first search according to multiplicity.

Similarly in the right graph of figure 2, by adding a new vertex d, we obtain a counter-example for this search.

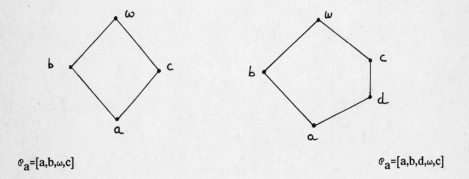

$\wp_a$=[a,b,ω,c] $\wp_a$=[a,b,d,ω,c]

Fig. 2 : contradictions of "naive" searches.

III.2 LINEAR EXTENSIONS.

Following TOURETZKY [1986] and AIT-KACI and NASR [1985] we think that it is worth to dig inside partially ordered theory in order to analyze inheritance problems. It is not the only possible approach that can be done, see DUGERDIL [1986] for a completely different point of view.

Let us now, to this aim, introduce a few algorithmic concepts in posets.

DEFINITION 8 : Let $P=(\leq p, X)$ be a poset :

1. A total order τ on X, is a *linear extension* of P, if $x \leq_p y \Rightarrow x \leq_\tau y$.

2. A linear extension τ of P is *greedy* (resp. *depth-first greedy (dfgreedy for short))* if it can be obtained by application of the following rules :

   a) Choose for x_1 any minimal element of P.

   b) If $x_1,...,x_i$ is greedy (resp. dfgreedy), then choose for x_{i+1} any minimal element of $P_i = P - \{x_1,...,x_i\}$ covering x_i, (resp. covering x_k where $k \leq i$ is the greatest subscript possible), if there exists one, otherwise choose any minimal element of P_i.

In other words the rule *"take a minimal element and climb as high as you can"* yields the greedy linear extensions. These linear extensions were introduced by COGIS and HABIB [1979], and have now been very well studied (mostly for scheduling problems). Dfgreedy linear extensions were recently introduced by PRETZEL [1985], and BOUCHITTE et al. [1985] have studied some of their algorithmic properties. Figure 3 gives some examples of such linear extensions.

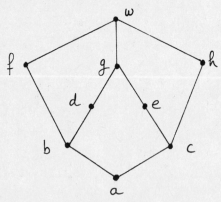

[a,b,c,h,e,g,ω,f,d] is not a linear extension.
[a,b,c,d,e,f,g,h,ω] is a linear extension but not greedy.
[a,b,f,c,h,e,d,g,ω] is a greedy linear extension but not dfgreedy.
[a,b,f,d,,c,h,e,g,ω] is a dfgreedy linear extension.

fig. 3 : greedy and dfgreedy linear extensions.

Let us now formulate our inheritance problem in this framework :

Principle 1 : $\wp_a$ is a linear extension of H/X_a.

Principle 4 : $\wp_a$ is a linear extension of $H/X_a \cup M_a$.

Property 2 : $\wp_a$ is a dfgreedy linear extension of H/X_a according to multiplicity.

Furthermore the algorithms we are looking for, in order to build those linear extensions, must be of good algorithmic complexity (if possible linear-time algorithms).

III.3 TWO INHERITANCE ALGORITHMS.

DEFINITION 9 : A depth-first in a graph $G = (X,U)$ yields two total orderings of the vertices, namely : *dfi(G)* (resp. *dfo(G))* which is, for every vertex $x \in X$, defined by dfi(x) = i (resp. dfo(x)= i) if x enters (resp. quits) the stack of the depth-first search at the ith rank.

The following theorem relates depth-first search and dfgreedy linear extensions.

THEOREM : BOUCHITTE et al. [1986]. Let P be a poset with a unique minimal element a, and G(a) be the diagram of P (i.e. the graph of the relation P with no transitivity arcs) then there is an isomorphism between the set of dfgreedy linear extensions of P and the set of dfo^d orders yielded by depth-first searches on G(a) starting from the vertex a.

This immediately yields our first inheritance algorithm.

ALGORITHM 1 :

1. Perform a depth-first search of G(a), according to μ^d, starting from the vertex a.

2. $\wp^1_a$ = dfo^d(G(a));

(i.e. in the depth-first search that gives dfo(G(a)) in each vertex b its successors are explored following the decreasing values of the total ordering $\mu(b)$, from right to left in our figures).

PROPOSITION 1 : $\wp^1$ satisfies principle 1 and when G(a) has no transitivity arcs it also satisfies property 2. Furthermore its complexity is in O(n+m) with n = $|X_a|$ and m = $|H/X_a|$.

Proof : From TARJAN [1972], we know that dfo^d((G(a)) is a linear extension of H/X_a, and from theorem 1, we know its a dfgreediness. This algorithm is obviously linear, since we only use a depth-first search in the inheritance graph.

Unfortunately, $\wp^1$ does not satisfy principle 4, as can be seen in figure 4.

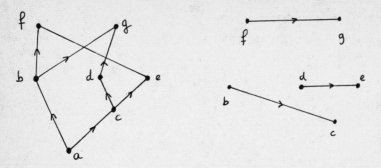

$\wp^1{}_a$ gives [a,b,c,d,g,e,f] and the unique linear extension of $H/X_a \cup M_a$ is [a,b,c,d,e,f,g].

Fig. 4 : an example where $\wp^1$ contradicts principle 4.

In the case where multiplicity and inheritance do not contradict themselves, we can obtain a second algorithm using local modifications, which satisfies principle 4. More precisely let us call *contradiction arc* an arc $(x,y) \in M_a$ such that $dfo^d(y) < dfo^d(x)$. (For example (f,g) is a contradiction arc in figure 4).

When performing algorithm 1, we can detect such arcs and then change their status from M_a to H/X_a. Let us call this operation a *setting*. Then we obtain the following algorithm.

ALGORITHM 2 :

1. $CA \leftarrow M_a$; $M_0 \leftarrow M_a$;

2. While $CA \neq \emptyset$
   Perform a depth-first search on $G(a)$, according to μ^d, starting from a.
   $CA \leftarrow \{\text{contradiction arcs of this search}\} \cap M_0$;
   If $dfo^d(G(a))$ is a linear extension of $H/X_a \cup M_a$ we have finished;
   Else perform the setting of all contradictions arcs.
   $H/X_a \leftarrow H/X_a \cup CA$; Update also M_a;

3. $\wp^2{}_a = dfo^d(G(a))$;

PROPOSITION 2 : When there is no contradiction between multiplicity and inheritance, $\wp^2$ yields a dfgreedy linear extension of $H/X_a \cup M_a$. Its complexity is $O(k(n+m))$ where k denotes the number of iterations in the above procedure.

Hints for the proof : Clearly this algorithm gives a linear extension of $H/X_a \cup M_a$. The only problem is the on-line characterization of the contradiction arcs. Happily this can be done by noticing that the example of figure 4, is a characteristic one. This yields the annonced complexity.

Thus we finally have obtained an inheritance search that satisfies principles 1,4, and property 2. Furthermore, we can imagine an algorithm $\wp$ which first perform the poset $H/X_a \cup M_a$ and then apply on it the algorithm 1. But the resulting complexity is analogous to those of transitive closure algorithms. A discussion on this algorithm as well as a study of the contradiction between the multiplicity and inheritance is presented in DUCOURNAU and HABIB [1986].

IV   SOME CONCLUSIONS

These two algorithms presented has been implemented in the frame-based language YAFOOL (see DUCOURNAU and QUINQUETON [1985]). The first one is now the standard inheritance algorithm of this language. The second one is much more time consumer and will be only used for special applications that need it.

Furthermore since the great challenge for representing real-world knowledge is to be able to support various exceptions and commonsense reasoning (see CHOURAQUI et al. [1985] or KAYSER [1984]), we have also investigated the problems yielded by multidimensional inheritance as well as that of carrying exceptions in our inheritance algorithms (see DUCOURNAU and HABIB [1987] and DUCOURNAU [1987]). In our framework, we have obtained algorithmic results (generalizations of the algorithms $\wp^1$ and $\wp^2$) on exceptions problems very similar to those studied by ETHERINGTON and REITER [1983], FAHLMAN [1979], FAHLMAN et al. [1981], or TOURETZKY [1986].

In fact, a kind of multidimensional inheritance is used in Le_lisp (CHAILLOUX et al. [1986]), for the primitives SEND2 and GETFN2, and is also used in YAFLOG (DUCOURNAU [1986]) which is a PROLOG-like inference engine written in YAFOOL. So, we are convinced that we have only made the first observations about the following problem : *What are the linear extensions involved in inheritance systems, and how to compute them ?* Much work is still to be done, and it seems to be a very promising research area, for example to determine properties analogous to property 2, which found semantically inheritance and are easy to compute.

V   REFERENCES.

1. H. AIT-KACI, R. NASR, *"LOGIN : a logic programming language with built-in inheritance"*, The Journal of Logic Programming, n°3 (1985) 185-215.

2. J. BEZIVIN, *"Langages objets et prototypage"*, Rapport de Recherche N°86-9, Lab. Informatique de Brest, 1986.

3. D.G. BOBROW, K. KAHN, G. KICZALES, L. MASINTER, M. STEFIK, F. ZDYBEL, *"Common loops merging Lisp and object-oriented programming"*, OOPSLA Conf., ACM (1986) 17-29.

4. V. BOUCHITTE, M. HABIB, M. HAMROUN, R. JEGOU, *"Depth-first search and linear extensions"*, Rapport de Recherche N°86-5, Laboratoire Informatique de Brest, 1986.

5. R.J. BRACHMAN, *"What IS-A is and isn't : an analysis of taxonomic link in semantic network"*, Computer, Vol. 16, N°10 (1983) 30-36.

6. J.P. BRIOT, *"Instanciation et héritage dans les langages objets"*, Thèse de 3ème cycle, Paris 1985.

7. J. CHAILLOUX et al., *"Le_Lisp, version 15.2"*, INRIA 1986.

8. E. CHOURAQUI, H. FARRENY, D. KAYSER, H. PRADE, *"Modélisation du raisonnement et de la connaissance"*, TSI 4:4 (1985) 391-399.

9. O. COGIS, M. HABIB, *"Nombre de sauts et graphes série-parallèles"*, RAIRO, Informatique Théorique / Theoretical Informatics, vol. 13, n°1 (1979) 3-18.

10. R. DUCOURNAU, M. HABIB, *"De l'héritage multiple dans les langages orientés objet"*, Working Paper N° 87-1, Laboratoire Informatique de Brest, janvier 1987, submitted.

11. R. DUCOURNAU, J. QUINQUETON, *"YAFOOL, encore un langage objet à base de frames"*, Rapport Technique N°72, INRIA, août 1986.

12. R. DUCOURNAU, *"YAFLOG, une implémentation de PROLOG en YAFOOL"*, Rapport interne, SEMA-METRA, novembre 1986.

13. P. DUGERDIL, *"A propos des mécanismes d'héritage dans un langage orienté objet"*, CIIAM 86 Intelligence Artificielle, Marseille (1986) 67-77.

14. D.W. ETHERINGTON, R. REITER, *"On inheritance hierarchies with exceptions"*, Proc. AAAI (1983) 104-108.

15. S.E. FAHLMAN, *"NETL : a system for representing and using real-world knowledge"*, MIT Press, Cambridge, MA, 1979.

16. J. FERBER, *"MERING : un langage d'acteur pour la représentation et la manipulation des connaissances"*, Thèse de Docteur Ingénieur, Université Paris VI, 1983.

17. A. GOLDBERG, D. ROBSON, *"SMALLTALK : the language and its implementation*, Addison-Welsey, 1983.

18. D. KAYSER, *"Examen de diverses méthodes utilisées en représentation des connaissances"*, Actes RFIA 4, tome 2, Paris (1984) 115-144.

19. H. LIEBERMAN, *"Delegation and inheritance : two mechanisms for sharing knowledge in object-oriented systems"*, Journées Langages Orientés Objet, Bigre+Globule, N°48 (1986) 79-89.

20. B. MEYER, *"EIFFEL, user's manual"*, Software Engineering inc., Santa Barbara, 1986.

21. D.A. MOON, *"Object programming with FLAVORS"*, in Object Oriented Programming Languages Conference, OOPSLA Proceedings, ACM SIGPLAN Notices (1986) 1-8.

22. O. PRETZEL, Problem presented at Oberwolfach Conference on Ordered Sets (1985).

23. R.E. TARJAN, *"Depth-first search and linear graph algorithms"*, SIAM J. of Computing 1:2 (1972) 146-169.

24. D.S TOURETZKY, *"The mathematics of inheritance systems"*, Research Notes in Artifical Intelligence, Pitman 1986.

FORK: A System for Object- and Rule-Oriented Programming

C. Beckstein, G. Görz and M. Tielemann

University of Erlangen-Nürnberg

Zusammenfassung. Das Ziel des FORK-Projekts besteht in der Implementierung eines primär objekt-orientierten Wissensreprsentationssystems und seiner Anwendung auf den Entwurf und die Fehlerdiagnose technischer Systeme. Während der Kern des Repräsentationssystems FORK vollständig objekt-orientiert ist, soll das System als Ganzes eine Vielfalt von Programmierstilen unterstützen. Im folgenden beschreiben wir eine Erweiterung zur regel-orientierten Programmierung, die die sprachliche Ausdruckskraft von FORK über diejenige von LOOPS hinaushebt. Als eine Anwendung der regel-orientierten Komponente wurde eine Constraint-Sprache (relations-orienterter Programmierstil) implementiert, die ein wichtiges Werkzeug im Rahmen unseres Ansatzes zum Entwurf und zur Fehlerdiagnose technischer Systeme darstellt.

Der nächste Schritt im FORK-Projekt schließt die Entwicklung eines allgemeinen logischen Rahmensystems ein, wozu eine logische Rekonstruktion objekt-zentrierter Repräsentationen, Zugriff auf komplexe Beschreibungen mittels Unifikation und Deduktionen über strukturierte Objekte gehören. Das Problem der Nicht-Monotonität wird durch einen DeKleers ATMS ähnlichen Modul behandelt werden. Weiterhin erhoffen wir Fortschritte durch einen neuen allgemeinen Ansatz zur Darstellung zeitlicher Verhältnisse bei der Modellierung technischer Systeme, was u.E. eines der wichtigsten Themen in diesem Bereich ist.

Abstract. We describe progress made within the FORK project, whose goals are the implementation of a primarily object-oriented knowledge representation system and its application to the design and fault diagnosis of technical systems. Whereas the kernel of the FORK representation system is completely object-oriented, the system as a whole is supposed to integrate a variety of different programming styles. In the following, an extension for rule-oriented programming is described, which raises the descriptive power of the FORK system beyond that of LOOPS. As an application of the rule-oriented component, a constraint language has been implemented which plays an important rule in our approach to the design and fault diagnosis of technical systems.

The next steps in the FORK project will include the development of a general logical framework, comprising a logical reconstruction of object-centered representations, retrieval of complex descriptions by unification, and deductions on structured objects. The problem of non-monotonicity will be dealt with on the meta level by a module similar to DeKleer's ATMS. Further progress shall be achieved by concentrating on a general treatment of the problem of time in modelling technical systems which is to our opinion one of the most important issues.

1   FORK: A Flavor-Based Object-Oriented Knowledge Representation System

1.1   Knowledge Representation and Object-Oriented Programming

Knowledge-based systems differ from other software systems in that they contain an explicit encoding of the respective domain knowledge. There are at least two kinds of prerequisites for knowledge representation: methodological (i.e. epistemological and logical) and technical (in a sense linguistic) ones. In the following we concentrate on the second aspect in presenting a knowledge representation framework which is easy to use, extensible, and in particular suitable to represent the kinds of knowledge required for designing and diagnosing technical systems.

Under the technical aspect, representing knowledge in a computational system is nothing else than a special kind of programming. For programming seen as a linguistic activity, questions of expressiveness of the programming language and of adequacy and suitability of its means with respect to the field(s) of application are of immediate importance. Within the last twenty years, a broad variety of knowledge representation languages has been proposed ranging from more or less direct derivatives of first-order logic to schemata based on cognitive psychology or applied computer science like associative networks, production systems, or procedural languages. One of the most advanced approaches along this line were Minsky's [14] frames. Minsky tried to find a synthesis between declarative and procedural systems with an emphasis on object-centered representations. With a few exceptions, most of these systems were very experimental in character and could not achieve wide usage.

In the meantime in the field of programming languages a new programming "paradigm" emerged: the *object-oriented* style. The ideas of object-oriented programming were realized in various ways, either as programming languages in their own right, like Smalltalk-80, or as extensions to already existing languages.

Which are the salient features of the object-oriented programming style? Object-oriented systems offer an integrated view of the concepts of *abstract data types* and *generic functions* (see [17]). The underlying processing model is characterized as a system of communicating *objects* which *pass messages* among each other. Each object has a set of acquaintances, which are denotations of objects it "knows of", i.e. it can send messages to. Messages themselves are also objects; each message contains (a reference to) the addressee, (a denotation of) an operation, and — optionally — argument objects. Each object has a *protocol* which is a set of *methods;* these are the procedures or operations contained in messages it can process. The internal state of an object — a set of attributes — as well as its internal processing cannot be inspected from the outside. An object may be in an active or passive state, and its activities consist in sending, receiving, and processing of messages. Processing a message can cause the sending of other messages. Furthermore, most object- oriented systems offer means for structuring the object world through a *class system* by accumulating objects with the same protocol in one class. There are distinct class objects which generate instance objects as the result of processing a particular message ("instantiate"). Classes can usually be ordered in generalization hierarchies, along which inheritance relations with respect to their attributes — declarative or procedural, the latter being methods — hold.

So object-oriented systems offer a lot of features which are desirable for the purpose of knowledge representation. Even some features like the distinction between classes and instances and the inheritance mechanism are introduced in a methodologically cleaner and clearer way than in most knowledge representation systems. For these reasons, the FORK system [1] has been based on an object-oriented framework.

Primarily for its flexibility and extensibility LISP was chosen as the host language. Its essential advantage is that it does not enforce a particular programming style, but instead allows various programming styles based on different processing models, e.g. the imperative, functional and object-oriented styles. Because there is no fundamental distinction between program and data in LISP, the integration of object-oriented programming is facilitated by employing the dualism between "passive" data and "active" procedures.

One of the best known object-oriented extensions of LISP is the so called *Flavor* system [19], a portable reconstruction of which was the starting point for the FORK system. For the Flavor system, there are two kinds of objects: *Classes*, which are also called *"Flavors"*, and their *instances*. Classes represent generic objects; they describe instances by specifying sets of declarative (variables) and procedural (methods) attributes and inheritance relations:

- *local variables:* the so called *instance variables,*

- *class variables:* variables, which are owned by the class, but can be referred to by its instances; this is an extension to the original Flavor proposal,

- *component classes*, which themselves provide variables and methods through inheritance mechanisms,

- *methods:* procedures to process *messages:* the *protocol.*

In FORK classes as well as instances are able to process messages: Whereas classes can process messages immediately, instances pass messages to their class they have been instantiated from.

With classes, a *generalization hierarchy* can be built, which is also called the *flavor graph*. By referring to other classes ("superflavors") within the definition of a new class, attributes of the superclasses are inherited. The root of this — in general directed — graph is denoted by the most general class VANILLA which owns those methods which are valid for all classes. For the construction of the protocol of a new class, inherited methods can be combined in predefined ways (for "primary" methods and "before/after-demons"). So, starting from VANILLA successively more specialized object classes can be defined with the possibility of *multiple inheritance* of attributes.

The Portable Flavor system does not require — in contrast to the original — any modifications to the LISP interpreter. The only requirement to the underlying LISP system is full functionality of the closure mechanism. Presently versions for InterLISP and CommonLISP exist.

1.2 FORK as an Extension of Flavors for Knowledge Representation

Although there is a close resemblance between an object-oriented system like Flavors and object-centered knowledge representation languages like Frames, the latter ones provide a repertoire of specialized constructs which are particularly useful for knowledge representation. Therefore the Portable Flavor system has been extended with the following features to constitute the FORK kernel:

- A *type concept* has been introduced such that restricting ranges of values and the definition of modalities for attributes like optional or obligatory are possible.

- FORK automatically supervises *structural relations* (integrity constraints) over whole objects as defined by the user.

- *Set-valued variables* are supported such that besides type constraints for their elements also cardinality is checked automatically. Special methods to handle sets are provided.

- In addition to instance variables there are also *class variables*, as mentioned above.

- FORK has a versatile interface to the *inheritance mechanism* which allows different ways to control and influence inheritance. With respect to the descriptors of variables it is possible to differentiate inheritance according to specific roles, to refuse inherited attributes, or to transform inherited attributes (e.g. to rename variables).

- FORK allows the expression of *multiple perspectives*.

The following example, defining a class MOVING-OBJECT and a method SPEED for it, may illustrate some of these features:

```
(DEFFLAVOR MOVING-OBJECT
           (X-POS Y-POS X-SPEED Y-SPEED MASS)
           :gettable-instance-variables
           (:settable-instance-variables
              X-POS Y-POS X-SPEED Y-SPEED)
           (:initable-instance-variables MASS)

(DEFMETHOD (MOVING-OBJECT SPEED) ()
           (sqrt (+ (square X-SPEED)
                    (square Y-SPEED))))
```

Now we define a CAR as a particular MOVING-OBJECT:

```
(DEFFLAVOR CAR
           (FRAME-NUMBER
           (NO-WHEELS :MOD OBL
                      :DEFAULT 4)
```

```
(AGGREGATES :MOD OBL
              :DEFAULT 'OK)
(FUEL :MOD OPT
        :RESTR (ONE-OF EMPTY FULL)
        :DEFAULT 'FULL)
(OIL :DEFAULT 'MAX)
(BATTERY :RESTR (AN ACCU)
           :DEFAULT BAT-45AH)
(TYRE-PRESSURE :MODE OBL
                 :DEFAULT 'HIGH)
(DRIVER :RESTR (A PERSON)
          :DEFAULT DUMMY))
(MOVING-OBJECT)
(:settable-instance-variables NO-WHEELS AGGREGATES
    FUEL OIL BATTERY TYRE-PRESSURE DRIVER)
(:gettable-instance-variables FRAME-NUMBER)
(:initable-instance-variables FRAME-NUMBER)
(:required-flavors ACCU PERSON)
(:documentation The flavors ACCU and PERSON should
    also be defined at time of first instantiation))
```

The instance variable FUEL is restricted by ONE-OF to the values EMPTY and FULL, which is the default. The variable BATTERY does only accept instances of the class ACCU as values. Defining CAR as a subclass of MOVING-OBJECT enables access to MOVING-OBJECT's instance variables (with the aception of MASS) and methods, i.e., in addition to the instance variables defined in CAR, each instance of CAR has also the inherited instance variables X-POS, Y-POS, X-SPEED, Y-SPEED. Furthermore a class variable SELLING-COMPANY is defined, which participates with the instance variable OWNER (an instance of PERSON) in an integrity constraint.

Volkswagens are a brand of CARs:

```
(DEFFLAVOR VW      ; instance variables:
         ((CAR-TYPE :RESTR (ONE-OF PASSAT POLO GOLF)
          (OWNER :MOD OBL
                  :DEFAULT (SEND-SELF 'GET 'SELLING-COMPANY))
          (ID :MOD OBL))
         (CAR)   ; superclass
         (:class-variables (SELLING-COMPANY
                               :DEFAULT VOLKSWAGEN-AG
                               :RESTR (A COMPANY)))
         (:initable-instance-variables CAR-TYPE)
         (:settable-instance-variables OWNER ID)
         (:gettable-instance-variables CAR-TYPE OWNER ID))
```

Now we create an instance of the VW class:

```
(SETQ MY-CAR (SEND VW 'CREATE-INSTANCE
```

```
'(CAR-TYPE  POLO
  OWNER     BECKSTEIN
  DRIVER    TIELEMANN
  ID        ERH-E-536
  BATTERY   BAT-45AH)))
```

Of course, the implementation of FORK includes tools for debugging, editing, and handling objects (e.g. an interface to the file package).

2 Rule-Oriented Programming in FORK

2.1 Rulesets, Rules, and Rule Interpreters

The first extension to the kernel of the FORK system introduces a new kind of methods: Besides methods wrjitten in the traditional procedural or functional style, they can also be defined in the form of rule systems. To be precise, a method may be given as a forward-chaining, i.e. data-driven production system. In its present form, the rule-oriented component of FORK [18] is more powerful then that of LOOPS [4], because it offers additional means for *conflict resolution* and for processing *vague information*.

Each method written in the rule-oriented style is a *ruleset*, which consists of rules of the form

{rule-name} IF premise THEN action {! meta-info}

Each ruleset has its own rule-interpreter associated with it which executes the rules under a forward chaining control regime, which in turn may use different control structures varying among rulesets for the selection and processing of rules.

Because rulesets are ordinary methods of objects, they can be inherited (also as "before-" and "after-methods"), so that large rulesets can be structured according to an object hierarchy. As ordinary methods, rulesets are activated by message passing. Since the control structure (meta-knowledge) for processing rules is associated to a ruleset, a clear separation between control and domain knowledge can be achieved. Each rule interpreter has the following structure:

1. Preselection of a subset of rules within the ruleset through comparison of rule specific scores with a threshold value which is local with respect to the ruleset. This mechanism allows prescreening of the ruleset at runtime.

2. The preselected rules are checked for applicability and then one applicable rule is selected. For this phase three control strategies are possible:

   - FIRST or ALL: In this case the ruleset is assumed to be ordered and the check for applicability is performed in the given order. With FIRST the first applicable rule is selected, with ALL each applicable rule.

   - PRIO: The value calculated by the evaluation of the premise at runtime is used to rank the rules, and the one with the highest value is selected.

The FIRST and ALL modes correspond to DO1 and DOALL in LOOPS. With each control strategy, rulesets can also be processed iteratively by means of a WHILE option.

The following method CONTROL for CAR is defined as a ruleset of three rules:

```
(DEFRULESET (CAR CONTROL) ()        ; no local variables
             ((C-FUEL                ; rule set
                IF (EMPTY FUEL-LEVEL)
                     THEN (SIGNAL "no fuel"))
              (C-OIL
                 IF (EQ OIL-LEVEL 'MIN)
                     THEN (SIGNAL "no oil")
                          (SEND ME 'STOP-ENGINE)
                          (STOP! 'EMERGENCY-OFF))
              (C-BATTERY
                 IF (LESSP (SEND BATTERY 'VOLTAGE) 6)
                     THEN (SIGNAL "low voltage")
                          ! (:USAGE ONE-SHOT-BANG)) )
              (:DOC ruleset for controlling ...)
              (:CHECK-MODE ALL)
              (:WHILE (ON IGNITION))))
```

As soon as this method is activated, the rule C-BATTERY is checked for applicability only once (ONE-SHOT-BANG), and never checked again during eventually subsequent iterations, i.e. as long as the ignition is turned on.

In contrast to the FIRST and ALL modes, for PRIO no static order criterion holds. Instead the ordering of rules is determined dynamically by priorities which are determined by the rule premises. To achieve that, first of all a transition from qualities to quantities has to be made by which a measure of evidence (Certainty Factors CF) is determined from the values of premises:

```
(not NIL) & (not (NUMBERP X))  -->  CF := MAXCF
                      X = NIL   -->  CF := 0
              (NUMBERP X)       -->  CF := X
```

with $CF \in [0, MAXCF] \subset \mathbf{N}_0$.

Boolean combinations of premises are calculated by special methods ($AND, $OR, $NOT).

The priority calculated in this way is used to schedule the respective rule in a multilevel agenda, from which afterwards the first rule from the level with highest priority is selected.

3. After selection, the action part of the respective rule is executed by the rule interpreter. The working memory (context) within the execution is performed is the FORK object to which the ruleset method belongs.

It should be noted that using the PRIO control strategy MYCIN-like rules can be expressed imediately with FORK's rule formalism.

2.2 Implementation of the Rule-Oriented Component

For the implementation of rulesets and rules, the kernel language of FORK has been used as a metalanguage, i.e., the whole rule component of FORK itself is expressed by means provided by the FORK kernel. Rulesets as well as rules are represented as FORK objects with appropriate methods. Rulesets are instances of a class RULESET which includes parameters and local variables as static components (instance variables), methods with defaults for conflict resolution and control- and meta-information (the rule interpreter) as dynamic attributes and rules as component flavors. In the same way rules are instances of a class RULE with appropriate methods. The programming environment of FORK has been augmented for rule-oriented programming with methods for debugging, editing, and handling rulesets, and rules which interface to particular attributes of the RULESET and RULE classes.

2.3 A Rule-Based Implementation of a Constraint Language

To demonstrate the versatility of rule-oriented programming in FORK, it has been used to implement a constraint language (after [16]. Constraint languages are a tool for relation-oriented programming and, therefore, play an important role in our approach to the diagnosis problem (see section 3). What a constraint language has at least to offer are means to represent objects which express *elementary relations* ("constraints") and *connections* between these objects. So, e.g. a constraint representing an ADDER has two input connectors A and B and an output connector S such that the following relations hold: S = A + B, and, at the same time B = S - A and A = S - B. Connecting objects of this kind leads to the construction of *constraint networks* in which computations are performed by *propagation* of values. In constraint languages, the term propagation covers local computations satisfying local dependences (as expressed by the equations for ADDER) as well as spreading values through connectors within a network.[1] In general, there is no preferred direction for spreading values.

So a minimal constraint language has at least to provide constructs to express

- *definitions* of constraints,
- *construction* of constraint networks,
- *integration* of new constraints into an already existing network,
- *communication* with the network interface (input and output).

With FORK, there is a straightforward approach to implement that by expressing constraints and connectors as objects and networks as aggregates of those. The propagation of values, which is locally restricted, is specified by rules belonging to constraint objects. For the case of electronic circuits, there are prototypic building blocks, like ADDER, of which instances are generated, which in turn are then combined to descriptions of network by attaching their connectors with each other. As a benefit of the object-oriented representation, such a description of a complex network is nothing else than *one* object on a higher descriptive level.

The following piece of code defines an ADDER:

---

[1]Spreadsheet programs are a special kind of constraint systems.

```
(DEFCONSTRAINT ADDER (A1 A2 SUM)
                NIL                     ; local variables
                (A1-A2                  ; rule set
                  IF (ALL-KNOWN? A1 A2)
                     THEN  (SET-VALUE! SUM
                                  (PLUS (GET-VALUE! A1)
                                        (GET-VALUE! A2))
                            &ME))
                (A1-SUM
                  IF (ALL-KNOWN? A1 SUM)
                     THEN (SET-VALUE! A2
                                  (DIFFERENCE (GET-VALUE! SUM)
                                              (GET-VALUE! A1))
                            &ME))
                (A2-SUM
                  IF (ALL-KNOWN? A2 SUM)
                     THEN (SET-VALUE! A2
                                  (DIFFERENCE (GET-VALUE! SUM)
                                              (GET-VALUE! A2))
                            &ME)))
```

A constraint network then can easily be constructed in the following way:

```
(DE CONSTRAINT-NET ()
   ...
   (SETQ A (MAKE-CONNECTOR))     ; generate new instances of
   (SETQ B (MAKE-CONNECTOR))     ; CONNECTOR
   ...
   (LET ((X (MAKE-CONNECTOR))
        ...)                     ; now generate new instances of
        ...                      ; constraint ADDER
       (MAKE-CONSTRAINT 'ADDER 'A1 A 'A2 B 'SUM X)
       ... ))
```

3   Future Work

In parallel to the implementation of the FORK system, a first study in the field of diagnosis has been conducted, aiming at a clarification of the basic problems and representational needs (cf. [3,13,10]). After considering more traditional rule-based approaches to the diagnosis problem, we concentrated on an approach known as "based on *structure* and *behavior*" (cf. [6,9]). Starting with an algorithm to diagnose multiple failures in electronic circuits, considerable extensions had to be made for the more complicated case of electromechanical systems. The kernel of the resulting diagnosis system, DIAG-TECH, has been implemented in the object-oriented style. In fact, DIAGTECH is a hybrid system, because it also supports the rule-based style of diagnosis, for which our logic-based "expert system shell" DUCKITO [12] is used as a subsystem.

In DIAGTECH, the treatment of conflicts, or inconsistency, as well as particular diagnostic heuristics, were embedded into one algorithm. To guarantee the usefulness of the chosen approach in the long run, it has to be generalized in a way that the recording and processing of inconsistency is performed by a separate general module. Indeed, as DeKleer [7] points out, most problem solvers search; if otherwise, a direct algorithm would solve the task. Then, two important problems are to be solved, namely, how the spaces of alternatives can be searched efficiently, and how the problem solver should be organized in general. DeKleer's solution is convincing: On the one hand it is a consequent continuation of the "Truth Maintenance Systems" (TMS) line, which forces a clean division within a problem solver between a module solely concerned with rules of the domain and another module concerned with recording the current state of the search. While the first module draws inferences, the second, the TMS, records inferences ("justifications"). So, the TMS serves three roles:

1. It serves as a "cache memory" for all inferences in that inferences, once made, need not be repeated. Inconsistencies, once detected, are avoided in the future.

2. It allows the problem solver to draw non-monotonic inferences. If non-monotonic justifications are present, the TMS has to use a constraint satisfation procedure to determine what data are assumed to be valid.

3. It assures that the data base is contradiction-free. The procedure of *dependency-directed backtracking* identifies and adds justifications to remove inconsistencies.

DeKleer's ATMS (Assumption Based TMS) [7] is a very efficient TMS module. In particular from our experience with DIAGTECH, but also from general considerations about a logical extension to our object-oriented representation system, we decided to realize such a module within our framework as the next step of the FORK project. We believe this will be a mandatory prerequisite to address the perspective of logic programming, namely (predominantly descriptive) representation and processing of relations (constraints) and implications in the object domain, and, in particular, the representation and treatment of time in a more general way. The gap between a logical reconstruction of object-centered representations (cf. [15,11]) and logic-based representation systems with their inferential properties is still to be closed. Retrieval of complex descriptions requires a powerful extension to the well-known unifcation algorithms. The direction of this research is also influenced by our previous experience with DUCKITO, which contains a truth maintenance module and an explanation component on the basis of data dependences.

As far as the problem of representing time and temporal relations is concerned, we are currently investigating approaches which reach beyond the one used within DIAG-TECH. The latter one has been constructed in the spirit of Doyle's [8] JACK system. The main problem we encountered with it is not a lack of expressive power, but a fundamental discrepancy between constraint-based representations on the one hand and the directionality introduced by temporal expressions on the other. Constraint systems assume simultaneous propagation of values in all possible directions of a constraint network, i.e. non-directionality of components and multiple values. A temporal order does not allow to consider all "possible worlds" at once, but enforces an order on propagation. We hope to find a synthesis of the advantages of both by means of a modal logic approach.

References

[1] Beckstein, C.: *Integration objekt-orientierter Sprachmittel zur Wissensrepräsentation in LISP.* Diplomarbeit, IMMD und RRZE, Universität Erlangen-Nürnberg. RRZE-IAB-219, 1985.

[2] Beckstein C., Görz, G., Tielemann, M.: *FORK: Ein System zur objekt- und regelorientierten Programmierung.* In: Rollinger, C., Horn, W. (Hg.): GWAI-86. 10th German Workshop on Artificial Intelligence und 2. Österreichische Artificial Intelligence Tagung. Berlin: Springer IFB 124, 312-317, 1986.

[3] Beckstein C., Görz, G., Hernàndez, D., Tielemann, M.: *An Integration of Object-Oriented Knowledge Representation and Rule-Oriented Programming as a Basis for Design and Diagnosis of Technical Systems.* To appear in: Annals of Operations Research. Also: RRZE-IAB-248, Univ. Erlangen-Nürnberg, 1986.

[4] Bobrow, D., Stefik, M.: *LOOPS Manual & Rule Oriented Programming in LOOPS.* Xerox PARC Report, Palo Alto, 1983.

[5] Bobrow, D. (Ed.): *Qualitative Reasoning about Physical Systems.* Amsterdam: North-Holland, 1984.

[6] Davis, R.: *Diagnostic Reasoning Based on Structure and Behavior.* 1984, In: Bobrow 347–410, 1984.

[7] DeKleer, J.: *(a) An Assumption-Based TMS. (b) Extending the AMTS. (c) Problem Solving with the ATMS.* AI Journal 28, 127-163-197-224, 1986.

[8] Doyle, R.: *Hypothesizing and Refining Causal Models.* MIT-AI-Memo 811, Dec. 1984.

[9] Genesereth, M.: *The Use of Design Descriptions in Automated Diagnosis.* In: Bobrow (1984), 411–436, 1984.

[10] Görz, G., Hernández, D.: *Knowledge-Based Fault Diagnosis of Technical Systems.* In: This Conference Proceedings.

[11] Hayes, P.: *The Logic of Frames.* In: Metzing, D. (Ed.): *Frame Conceptions and Text Understanding.* Berlin: DeGruyter, 1980.

[12] Hernández, D.: *Modulare Softwarebausteine zur Wissensrepräsentation.* Studienarbeit, IMMD IV und RRZE, Universität Erlangen-Nürnberg, 1984.

[13] Hernández, D.: *Wissensbasierte Diagnose technischer Systeme.* Diplomarbeit, IMMD und RRZE, Universität Erlangen-Nürnberg. RRZE Mitteilungsblatt Nr. 44, 1986.

[14] Minsky, M.: *A Framework for Representing Knowledge.* In: Winston, P.H. (Ed.): *The Psychology of Computer Vision.* New York: McGraw Hill, 211–277, 1975.

[15] Nilsson, N.: *Principles of Artificial Intelligence.* Berlin: Springer, 1982.

[16] Steele, G.L.: *The Definition and Implementation of a Computer Language Based on CONSTRAINTS.* MIT-AI-TR-595, Aug. 1980.

[17] Stoyan, H., Görz, G.: *Was ist objekt-orientierte Programmierung?* In: Stoyan, H., Wedekind, H. (Hg.): *Objekt-Orientierte Software- und Hardware-Architekturen.* Stuttgart: Teubner, 1984.

[18] Tielemann, M.: *Eine regelorientierte Erweiterung des Repräsentationssystems FORK.* Diplomarbeit, IMMD und RRZE, Universität Erlangen-Nürnberg. RRZE-IAB-236, 1986.

[19] Weinreb, D., Moon, D.: *Flavors: Message-Passing in the LISP Machine.* MIT-AI-Memo, 1981.

C. Beckstein
University of Erlangen-Nürnberg, IMMD VI
Martensstr. 3, D-8520 Erlangen
Network: unido!fauern!faui70!beck

G. Görz
University of Erlangen-Nürnberg, RRZE
Martensstr. 1, D-8520 Erlangen
Network: Goerz@SUMEX.ARPA, GOERZ@DERRZE1.BITNET

M. Tielemann
University of Erlangen-Nürnberg, IMMD VI
Martensstr. 3, D-8520 Erlangen

Overview of a Parallel Object-Oriented Language CLIX

Jin H. Hur and Kilnam Chon

Department of Computer Science
Korea Advanced Institute of Science and Technology
P.O. Box 150 Chongryang, Seoul 131, Republic of Korea

UUCP: {mcvax,seismo}!kaist!jhhur
Internet: jhhur%sorak.kaist.ac.kr@relay.cs.net

ABSTRACT

CLIX is a parallel object oriented language that embodies communicating process model of object oriented programming. It incorporates the notion of objects with communications in distributed systems. The objects in CLIX are encapsulation of information and communication handlers that operate on the information in response to messages. The underlying communication system is modeled as a mail system. In addition to presenting an overview of CLIX, it is reviewed in terms of relevant issues in parallel object oriented programming.

1. Introduction

Objects in object oriented programming can be viewed in many ways. In Smalltalk [12], objects are the information containers interrelated by the hierarchy of metaclass-class-instance and superclass-subclass. Objects in the Actor model [13] are active entities that communicate: Communicating Parallel Processes [7]. Objects in [20] is regarded as first class citizens of typed data abstraction augmented with type inheritance.

Objects can be viewed as self-contained active information processing agents that interact with their environment only through well-defined communication interfaces: the communicating process model [17]. A computation in the model is represented as a communication pattern over a network of objects [13]. Each object has the independent control thread of the execution; A network of objects has multiple, independent control threads. The objects thus may be units in concurrent computation. In sum, the object oriented system viewed as communicating processes renders itself for concurrent computation in distributed systems[1][2].

CLIX (Concurrent Language In EXperiment) is a parallel object oriented programming language that embodies the communicating process model of object oriented programming [14]. It is designed for programming in message passing architectures. CLIX incorporates the notion of objects with communications in distributed systems. In this sense, the objects in CLIX are equivalent to actors in the Actor model for the concurrent computation in distributed systems[1, 2]. CLIX also incorporates other issues of distributed computation like parallelism, and features of object oriented programming like class/instance relationship and inheritance mechanism by delegation[16].

In the subsequent section, an overview of the language CLIX is presented. In Section 3, the communication system, the central part of the model for CLIX, is described with an informal semantic description. Section 4 reviews CLIX in terms of relevant issues in parallel object oriented programming. Finally in Section 5 comes the current development status of CLIX.

2. Overview of CLIX

---

[1] The term 'distributed systems' in this context is to be interpreted in a broad sense including computer networks and message passing architecture such as multiprocessor systems without common store among processors.

2.1. Process Model for Objects in CLIX

Basic elements in CLIX are objects and communications. The objects in CLIX are similar to processes in distributed systems. The objects form a community executing asynchronously and communicating through message passing. In addition, the objects encapsulate information in themselves and provide well-defined communication interfaces to their environment. Encapsulation and communication handling are the two major functionalities of objects.

Objects in CLIX provide for the encapsulation of information in themselves with a communication interface invariant over their life time. The communication interface abstracts the detailed chores in accessing the internal data structure. Each object acts as a communication handler for the messages defined by the communication interface, and is activated only upon the receipt of a message.

CLIX basically provides for asynchronous communications in the underlying mail system; An object need not wait for the termination of the computation of the message receipient after message sending. In addition to the asynchronous communications, it provides for synchronous communications to deal with the case where the result is required for further processing. Thus, the programmer can have the full control over the communication system.

2.2. Objects

Objects in CLIX are encapsulation of local state information and communication handlers that operate on the local state. The definition of objects with common behavior is embodied in a class definition.

An object is composed of three parts: the object-id, the local state, and methods for acceptable incoming messages. The *object-id* is a system-wide unique mail address assigned to an object to which other objects - possibly itself - can send messages. The *object-id* is assigned to each object when the object is created. It may form a part of the local state of other objects, and may be passed around among objects. The *local state* is a collection of mail addresses to which messages can be sent, and is named by variables. The object may manipulate the local state by sending messages to the objects referenced by the local state variables. The *methods* are the actions the object takes in response to the corresponding incoming messages.

An object upon creation and appropriate initialization is ready to process incoming messages. Upon the receipt of a message, it executes the corresponding method and waits for the next message. The incoming messages are processed one by one in sequential manner unlike the pipelined processing of messages in the Actor system[1, 2]. It is due to the nature of sequential execution behavior internal to an object pertaining to our model. A class is defined as follows in the EBNF form:

```
(define <id> [ (with <pattern>) ]
  [ (constant {<constant definition>} ) ]
  [ (state   {<local state variable declaration>}) ]
  [ (initially <action>) ]
  (method   {<method definition>} ))
```

2.3. Primitives

In response to the incoming messages, an object performs a sequence of three kinds of primitive actions in the method:

(1)   Local state change: The object may change the value of the local state variables, hence incurring a side-effect in processing subsequent messages to the object. The action is expressed in **setq**-command.

```
(setq X [X + 10])
```

(2)   Communications: The object may issue communications to objects - possibly itself - to transfer information. The communication may be a reply to the incoming message or may be requests to some objects to perform some actions. There are four primitives for handling the communications:

```
(send next add: aVal)
(ask aFactorial eval: 3)
(forward next tally: currentSum)
(reply [t1 * t2])
```

(3) Creation of a new object: The object may create a new object. The network of objects may grow as the computation proceeds by creating new objects in response to messages. The action is expressed in **new-expression**.

(new Window (with X: 0 Y: 0 width: 10 height: 10))

(4) Control structure commands: In addition to those primitives above, directives to control the sequence of the actions are provided. They are **conditional**-command, **loop**-command, **select**-command, and **let**-command. The **conditional**-command and the **loop**-command have the conventional meaning: for conditional branch and for iteration, respectively. The **select**-command introduces the choice nondeterminism in the form of the Dijkstra's guarded command. The expressions in the guard arms are evaluated concurrently, and one guard whose expression is evaluated as TRUE is selected nondeterministically. The **let**-command introduces a form of lexical scope for transient variables by binding values to identifiers to set up the execution environment of the body. The expressions whose values are to be bound to the variables are evaluated concurrently. The two commands above are the only source of the concurrent execution in one command.

An object has communication handlers called methods constructed out of the above primitives. A method is defined as follows:

```
('[' <pattern> ']' [ where <expression> ]
  [ (using <id list>) ]
  <command > {<command>} )
```

A method is identified by its message pattern that is composed of a message selector and variables that are to be bound to incoming arguments. The format of message patterns is similar to that of Smalltalk:a single keyword or a sequence of 'keyword argument' pairs. The method is invoked only when the incoming message of the given pattern satisfies the accompanying expression to be TRUE. Otherwise, the next message is tried, and the current message is tried again after the next message. If there is no next message, the object is blocked until there arrives another message. In addition to local state variables, there are temporary variables that constitute the execution environment of the method. They are distinguished from the local state variables in that they are not regarded as a part of the local state. For example, they are not stored when the object is stored into the secondary storage as a persistent object. The remaining part is the commands to execute.

A program in CLIX is a set of class definitions and a sequence of commands to act upon the class definitions.

```
(program <id>
  { <import directive> | <class definition> }
  [ (var <id list>) ]
  <command> { <command> } )
```

A class definition may be included directly in the program or may be imported from the previously defined classes. When a program is executed, a special object called *root object* is created. The root object behaves just like other objects except that it doesn't have any communication handler. It may create some objects, issue communications, and change its own local state. These actions are the same as the regular objects. Unlike regular objects, however, it terminates its execution when it reaches the end of its body.

3. Communication System

The computation model of CLIX largely depends upon the semantics of communication primitives. This section presents the model and the primitives for the communication system.

3.1. Characterization

The communication system is characterized as follows:

- Point-to-point
  An object, S, can send a message to another object, R, only when S knows of the mail address of R. S gets to know R by either creating R or receiving the address of R in incoming messages. The communication pattern hence is point-to-point between objects, and does not imply direct broadcasting nor stream.

- Guarantee of delivery
  Once a message sending request is issued, the message is guaranteed to be delivered to the destination object. It's the underlying communication system's responsibility to make sure of the delivery.

- Preservation of message ordering
  When an object, S, sends two or more messages to an object, T, the temporal ordering of the message receipt by T is the same as the temporal ordering of the message sending by S. This characteristics gives yet simpler semantics for the computation than the Actor system [2, 21].

The communication system of CLIX is modeled as a mail system where the message sending is asynchronous.

A message is composed of two parts: mail header and message body. The mail header carries the relevant information concerning the communication itself. The mail header consists of four parts: to, from, reply-to, and message-id. *To* identifies the message receipient, and *from* identifies the sender. *Reply-to* designates the continuation point to which a reply, if any, is sent to. *Message-id* is a system-wide unique tag that identifies a transaction requested by an object. It differs from the tag in the Actor system[2] in that the former uniquely identifies a higher level sequence of actions in a transaction while the latter identifies the message itself uniquely. We can preserve the continuation point in a sequence of communications by means of *reply-to* and *message-id*; they in combimation can realize the inheritance mechanism by delegation[16, 22]. In executing a method for a message, the object can access the values of the message header throught a set of leterals like '@from'. They are not a part of the local state, but form a part of the execution environment for the method the object executing at the time.

The message body is the information transferred between objects. It consists of a message selector and arguments for an appropriate method. The format of the message body is similar to that of Smalltalk: a single keyword or a sequence of pairs of keyword and argument. The keywords form the message selector for the corresponding method.

3.2. Primitives

There are four primitives in our communication system.

> (**send** <destination> <message pattern>)
>
> (**ask** <destination> <message pattern>)[2]
> (**forward** <destination> <message pattern>)
> (**reply** <expression>)

When an object issues *send* command, the sender resumes its execution right after the message is sent regardless of the response of the receiver. The message is appended to the message queue of the message receipient to be handled later. This form of asynchronous communication is the canonical form of requesting an object an action.

When the sender object requires the result of the method execution by the receipient object returned back, the *ask* primitive is issued. The *ask* primitive is used as a part of expressions in CLIX programs. When the *ask* is issued, a system-wide unique tag is generated and is included in the request message as *message-id*. The sender then waits for a reply message with the same *message-id*.

When an object receives an *ask* request, it may not be able to reply by itself, but need to delegate the job to another object. The *forward* primitive is provided for that purpose. It has the same semantics as *send* except that the values of *reply-to* and *message-id* field of the mail header are preserved in the

---

[2] (ask <destination> <message pattern>) can be abbreviated as [<destination> <message pattern>] as syntactic sugaring.

forwarded message so that the message receiver can reply to the original sender directly. The object issuing the *forward* primitive can then proceed for its own work.

The primitive, *reply*, is provided to express the reply action to the *ask* request, and returns the object representing the result of the method execution. The *ask-reply* pair can express the conventional call/return style method call[2].

3.3. Typical Scenario

The followings are an informal description of the semantics of typical communications.

(1) When an object, S, issues a communication request to an object, R, it packs an appropriate message according to the request type. Variations according to the request type of either send, ask, or forward come from the handling of the mail header. See Appendix for how the mail header is set up.

(2) If the message is acceptable by R, namely there is a method with the same message pattern, it is appended to the message queue of R^3. Otherwise, an error state occurs. The sender enters the *wait* state for the reply in case it has issued an *ask* request, or proceeds its own computation in other cases.

(3) When R is ready to process another message, it picks up the first message in the queue that satisfies the expression of the corresponding method as TRUE, and dequeues the message.

(4) R sets up the execution environment, and executes the corresponding method. The execution environment includes the initialized temporary variables and the mail header values in addition to the local state variables. When a *reply* command is executed in the method, R retrieves the value of mail headers *reply-to* and *message-id* from its execution environment, packs a message with those values, and sends the message to S. S then resumes the execution from *wait* state. In this case, the queued messages at S, if any, are preempted by the reply message.

(5) S and R proceed their own execution in parallel.

(6) When R finishes the execution of the method, it gets ready for another message.

4. Issues in Parallel Object Oriented Programming

4.1. Object-oriented-ness

The computation model in CLIX adopts the uniform object oriented metaphor from small objects like integers to large objects like databases as in Smalltalk. Conceptually, all request even to integers are made in the form of communications like

(ask 1 + 1)

It provides a programmer a uniform view on the computation solely in terms of communications. It allows the programmer to break down a problem into subproblems and map the subproblems into objects, and to break down each subproblem into subproblems further, and so on. It comes in line with the concept of object oriented programming where objects are the realization of real world problems [12].

4.2. Inheritance

Inheritance mechanisms in many object oriented languages are expressed as the structural relationship among classes, and assume copy semantics; viz, a part of the code of superclasses is copied into the body of objects in the subclass[4]. Usually, the inheritance hierarchy matches the type hierarchy where a class is regarded as a type [18].

There is no inheritance mechanism as structural relationship among classes in CLIX. Instead, CLIX incorporates the 'inheritance by delegation' mechanism[16] by means of programmer-controllable communication primitive - *forward*. It works as follows: When an object, O, issues an *ask* request to an object,

---

[3] We here ignore the finite message transmission time from S to R unlike Actor model[2]. Relying on the assumption of 'guarantee of message delivery' and 'preservation of message ordering,' the state where the message is queued at the destination is considered to be the next state in the transition of the system state. It has a drawback that the potential unbounded nondeterminism due to finite, but not bounded, message delay[10] may not be stated, but simplifies the execution model.

C_1, and C_1 cannot satisfy the request by itself, C_1 delegates the request to another object C_2 by the *forward* primitive. C_2 may also delegate the request to C_3, and so on, until an object, C_n, may be able to process the request and reply to O. Each object C_i may be regarded as the prototype object [16] of the object C_{i-1}. The *forward* primitive keeps the thread of request in the sequence $O \rightarrow_{ask} C_1 \rightarrow_{forward} C_2 \rightarrow_{forward} \cdots \rightarrow_{forward} C_n \rightarrow_{reply} O$ with the aid of mail headers *reply-to* and *message-id*.

4.3. Parallelism

The execution mode inside an object in CLIX is sequential in nature, and there is no explicit constructs for parallel composition of commands except for the simultaneous evaluation of expressions in select-command and let-command. Owing to the asynchronous communication and the inherent multitude of processes in the communicating process model, CLIX provides for the coarse grain parallelism.

There are a number of objects running simultaneously.

Some parallel object oriented languages like POOL[3] provides for the object body in an object. It renders a possibility of more parallelism since each object has something to do even without communications. In CLIX, an object acts only as the handler of request messages; Objects in a system is more closely coupled with communications. Asynchronous communications allow two or more objects to run in parallel, and the delegation mechanism frees objects as soon as they have done all they can do, hence being ready for another job.

The following example is a non-recursive factorial object exemplified in [19]. One can evaluate n! by

    (ask (new Factorial) eval: 3)

for example. The **Factorial** object then creates **IntMult** objects, and sends request messages to them. The number of **IntMult** object executing in parallel increases as the depth of the method invocation increases. The multitude of objects running in parallel like this is the major source of the parallelism in CLIX.

```
(define Factorial
  (method
    ([ eval: ?n ] do
      (if [n = 0]
      then (reply 1)
      else  (let ((mid [[n / 2] ceil:]))
              (let ((t1 [(new IntMult) low: 1 high: mid])
                    (t2 [(new IntMult) low: [mid + 1] high: n]))
                (reply [t1 * t2]))))))))

(define IntMult
  (method
    ([ low: ?low high: ?high] do
      (select
        ([low > high] (reply 1))
        ([low = high] (reply low))
        ([low < high] (let ((mid [[[low + high] / 2] ceil:]))
                        (let ((t1 [(new IntMult) low: low high: mid])
                              (t2 [(new IntMult) low: [mid + 1] high: high]))
                          (reply [t1 * t2]))))))))
```

Active data structure composed of several objects can be accessed concurrently.

Conventional data structures are represented as passive data that are operated by an imaginary control in a sequential manner. Data structures in CLIX are represented as a set of objects that operate on themselves cooperating through message passing. The following class definition shows a part of the implementation of the **Collection** class similar to that of Smalltalk.

```
(define Collection
 (state  value next)
 (method
  [tally: sum] (if [next = NIL]
                   then (reply sum)
                   else (forward next tally: [sum + value]))
  [add: aVal]  (if [next = NIL]
                   then (setq value aVal)
                        (setq next (new Collection))
                   else (send next add: aVal))))
```

One may create a new empty collection by

(setq aList (new Collection))

and add a new value to the collection by

(send aList add: 3)

When one issues a request,

(ask aList tally: 0)

each element examines whether it is the last element in the list. If so, it replies the accumulated sum thus far to the requester. If not, it forwards the request to the *next* element, and gets ready to process another message. When the collection is shared by a number of users and is accessed concurrently by the users, it can process several requests while processing a request. Thus, it increases the degree of parallelism.

Rather extensive examples on tree and graph data structure are provided in [11] in his Concurrent Smalltalk.

5. Conclusion

CLIX is a parallel object oriented language targeted for message passing architecture. Based on a communication system modeled by a mail system, it can support for object oriented programming with fair degree of parallelism. We have reviewed CLIX in terms of relevant issues in parallel object oriented programming.

We develop CLIX as an experiment on the object oriented programming environment in the Bee machine project [8]. Bee machine project embodies experiments on various programming environments including the conventional message passing operating system kernel. CLIX is designed as a way to study feasibility of the object oriented programming in the context.

In its own model, CLIX may be regarded as a descendent of the Actor model of the computation. CLIX however includes some features like versatile communication primitives and sequential execution of a method. We selected to design our own language for our experiment after surveying a number of parallel object oriented languages. Notable of them are POOL-T[5], ABCL/1[21], XCPL[6], and Orient84/K[15].

We are now developing a prototype implementation on a single CPU machine. In parallel, we are designing the object placement scheme including optimal object dispatch and object migration. The basic principle of the object placement scheme is to place objects in runtime without managing the state information based on the novel Client-Solicitor interaction model [9]. We will play a part of the build-up in our own learning on the development of programming environments in the multiprocessor systems as the experiment proceeds.

Acknowledgement

The authors would like to thank D. Lee, C. Chung, and H.J. Park in System Architecture Laboratory for the discussion which has made the idea in the paper what it is. Great thanks also are to P. America in Philips Research Laboratories, Eindhoven, The Netherlands whose comments pointed out what might have been missed otherwise in the design of the language.

Appendix

The semantics of four communication primitives is explained in terms of the manipulation of the mail header. Let's assume primitives *primitive-send* and *wait* available for asynchronous message sending and waiting for a reply, respectively.

(**primitive-send** to: R from: SELF reply-to: SELF message-id: τ <pattern>)
(**wait** τ)

The mail header is expressed as a sequence of 'name: value' pairs. SELF is the mail address of the object issuing the command, and τ is a new system-wide unique tag. The object can also access in the form '@name' the value of mail header of the message it is currently processing. Then, each communication primitive is translated as follows:

(**send** o <pattern>)
→ (**primitive-send** to: o from: SELF reply-to: *nil* message-id: τ <pattern>)

(**ask** o <pattern>)
→ (**primitive-send** to: o from: SELF reply-to: SELF message-id: τ <pattern>)
  (**wait** τ)

(**forward** o <pattern>)
→ (**primitive-send** to: o from: SELF reply-to: @reply-to message-id: @message-id <pattern>)

(**reply** e)
→ (**primitive-send** to: @reply-to from: SELF reply-to: *nil* message-id: @message-id e)

References

1. G. Agha, "An Overview of Actor Languages," *SIGPLAN Notices* 21(10) pp. 58-67 (Oct. 1986). Special Issue on Object Oriented Programming Workshop at IBM Yorktown Height, Jun. 1986

2. G.A. Agha, "Actors: A Model for Concurrent Computation in Distributed Systems," AI TR-844, MIT AI Laboratory (Jun. 1985).

3. P. America, "Definition of the Programming Language POOL-T," ESPRIT Doc.Nr. 0091, Philips Research Laboratories (Sep. 1985).

4. P. America, "Object-Oriented Programming: A Theoretician's Introduction," ESPRIT Doc.Nr. 0159, Philips Research Laboratories (May 1986).

5. P. America, "POOL-T -- A Parallel Object-Oriented Language," in *Object Oriented Concurrent Systems*, ed. A. Yonezawa, M. Tokoro,MIT Press (Sept. 1986).

6. W.C. Athas, "XCPL: An Experimental Concurrent Programming Language," TR:5196:85, California Institute of Technology (Dec. 1985).

7. H. Baker, "Actor Systems for Real-Time Computation," LCS TR-197, MIT Lab. for Computer Science (Mar. 1978).

8. K. Chon, "Bee Machine - Initial Assessment," Technical Memorandum SA-TM-01, KAIST (Feb. 1987).

9. C. Chung, K. Chon, J.H. Hur, and D. Lee, "A New Distributed Computing Paradigm Based on Asynchronous Communications: Client-Solicitor Model," *Submitted to IEEE Tr. on Software Engineering*, (Feb. 1987).

10. W.D. Clinger, "Foundations of Actor Semantics," AI TR-633, MIT AI Laboratory (May 1981).

11. W.J. Dally, "A VLSI Architecture for Concurrent Data Structures," 5209:TR:86, California Institute of Technology (1986).

12. A. Goldberg and D. Robson, *Smalltalk-80: The Language Definition and Its Implementation*, Addison-Wesley (1983).

13. C. Hewitt, "Viewing Control Structures as Patterns of Passing Messages," *Artificial Intelligence* **8** pp. 323-363 (1977).

14. J.H. Hur, "Definition of Programming Language CLIX," Technical Memorandum SA-TM-02, KAIST (Feb. 1987).

15. Y. Ishikawa and M. Tokoro, "A Concurrent Object-Oriented Knowledge Representation Language Orient84/K: Its Features and Implementation," *Proc. of ACM Conf. on OOPSLA '86*, pp. 232-241 (Oct. 1986). Also available as ACM SIGPLAN 21(11), Nov. 1986

16. H. Liberman, "Using Prototypical Objects to Implement Shared Behavior in Object-Oriented Systems," *Proc. ACM Conf. on OOSPLA '86*, pp. 214-223 (Sep. 1986).

17. V. Nguyen and B. Hailpern, "A Generalized Object Model," *SIGPLAN Notices* **21**(10) pp. 78-87 (Oct. 1986). Special Issue on Object Oriented Programming Workshop at IBM Yorktown Height, Jun. 1986

18. A. Snyder, "Encapsulation and Inheritance in Object-Oriented Programming Languages," *Proc. ACM Conf. on OOSPLA '86*, pp. 38-45 (Sep. 1986).

19. D.G. Theriault, "Issues in the Design and Implementation of Act2," AI TR-723, MIT AI Laboratory (Jun. 1983).

20. P. Wegner, "Classification in Object-Oriented Systems," *SIGPLAN Notices* **21**(10) pp. 78-87 (Oct. 1986). Special Issue on Object Oriented Programming Workshop at IBM Yorktown Height, Jun. 1986

21. A. Yonezawa, E. Shibayama, T. Takada, and Y. Honda, "Modeling and Programming in an Object Oriented Concurrent Language ABCL/1," TR C-75, Tokyo Institute of Technology, Tokyo, Japan (Mar. 1986).

22. A. Yonezawa, J-P. Briot, and E. Shibayama, "Object-Oriented Concurrent Programming in ABCL/1," *Proc. ACM Conf. on OOSPLA '86*, pp. 258-268 (Sep. 1986).